Jean Stafford
The Savage Heart

Jean Stafford
The Savage Heart

Charlotte Margolis Goodman

UNIVERSITY OF TEXAS PRESS
Austin

First edition, 1990

Requests for permission to reproduce material from this work should be sent
to Permissions, University of Texas Press, Box 7819, Austin, TX 78713-7819.

♾ The paper used in this publication meets the minimum requirements of
American National Standard for Information Sciences—Permanence of
Paper for Printed Library Materials, ANSI Z39.48-1984.

*See page 393 for acknowledgments of permission to use archival and previously
published materials.*

Library of Congress Cataloging-in-Publication Data

Goodman, Charlotte M. [date]
    Jean Stafford : the savage heart / Charlotte Margolis Goodman. —
1st ed.
        p.   cm.
    Includes bibliographical references.
    ISBN 0-292-74022-0 (alk. paper)
    1. Stafford, Jean, 1915–   .   2. Authors, American—20th century—
Biography.   I. Title.
PS3569.T2Z67   1990
813'.54—dc20
    [B]   89-37293
                                                                          CIP
                                                                          Rev.

Writing is agony but it also is life itself.

JEAN STAFFORD, IN AN INTERVIEW BY ALICE DIXON BOND,
BOSTON HERALD, JANUARY 27, 1952

Contents

Preface

I have read many moving lives of women, but they are painful, the price is high, the anxiety is intense, because there is no script to follow, no story portraying how one is to act, let alone any alternative stories.

—CAROLYN HEILBRUN, *WRITING A WOMAN'S LIFE*

A DECADE AGO, when I first became acquainted with the fiction of the American writer Jean Stafford, I was surprised to discover that very few people had read her work. Why, I wondered, was her fiction far less renowned than that of some other women writers of her generation, despite the fact that she had been awarded the Pulitzer Prize for fiction in 1970? Why had she published no novels and almost no short stories since the fifties, though she did not die until 1979? In the forties, when her first two novels, *Boston Adventure* (1944) and *The Mountain Lion* (1947), were published, she was considered one of this country's most promising fiction writers. In the fifties she published a well-received third novel, *The Catherine Wheel* (1952), and she regularly contributed short stories to the *New Yorker*. Yet only recently has Jean Stafford's work begun to receive the sustained critical attention it merits. Today her writing is still less well known than that of Katherine Anne Porter, Mary McCarthy, Carson McCullers, Flannery O'Connor, and Eudora Welty. Despite her impressive achievements as a writer, what most people probably think of first in connection with Jean Stafford is that she was the first wife of the celebrated and volatile American poet Robert Lowell.

"Why are so many more women silenced than men?" Tillie Olsen asks in *Silences,* a book describing the insurmountable difficulties that numerous writers have encountered. Although Jean Stafford was never "silenced," as were many women writers of her generation whom Olsen mentions, she might have been more productive had she not been compelled to contend with poverty, a difficult family situation, role conflicts she was never able to resolve, emotional instability, and poor health. Moreover, she too, for the most part, lacked the support of individuals Olsen calls "enablers": people who cook the meals, pay the bills, and put one's needs above their own.[1] In some ways more fortunate than many women writers of her generation, Stafford benefited from her association with several women who helped to promote her work. A number of influential men, moreover, also helped her to launch her literary career. Nevertheless, as did other women of her generation, she discovered how difficult it was for women to succeed in the public sphere, no matter how gifted or hardworking or ambitious they were. In fact, taking into consideration the trying private and public circumstances of her life, I find her literary achievement remarkable.

In 1944, critics hailed as a major literary event the publication of Jean Stafford's first novel, *Boston Adventure;* in the fifties, when her wonderful short stories were published in the *New Yorker,* her fiction reached a wider audience; and in 1970, after her *Collected Stories* was awarded the Pulitzer Prize, many people who had never read her work before discovered what a splendid writer she was. Yet until recently much of her fiction was out of print. Furthermore, over time the ardor of some of her early admirers cooled. Alfred Kazin, for example, who had praised *Boston Adventure* when it first appeared, devotes only one sentence to Stafford's work in his study of twentieth-century American writers, *Bright Book of Life.*[2] Today it is largely due to the efforts of feminist scholars that Stafford's fiction is being rediscovered by a new generation of readers.

One reason that Stafford's work was neglected may be that her fiction is set in a variety of locations. Consequently, critics could not define her as a "local color" writer or identify her with a particular geographical region, as has been true of so many other American women writers. Stafford's literary reputation might also have been adversely affected by her lack of productivity during the last two decades of her life. Between 1959 and 1979 she published only five short stories. Moreover, she never succeeded in completing *The Parliament of Women,* a novel on which she had been working for many years. Although she regularly contributed book reviews and essays to a variety of newspapers and periodicals to support herself, her reputation as a fiction writer declined.

Whatever the reasons for the neglect of Jean Stafford's work, her novels, short stories, and essays certainly deserve to be better known. Adept at writing in both the elegant manner of a Wharton or a James and in the colloquial style of a Twain or a Welty, she sensitively and poignantly portrays the entrapment, alienation, and despair of her characters in beautifully crafted works notable for their subtlety, their wit, and their irony.

As Maureen Ryan has observed in her recently published study, *Innocence and Estrangement in the Fiction of Jean Stafford,* Stafford's fiction focuses primarily on the experience of alienated and isolated young girls and women.[3] Her female protagonists not only serve as exemplars of human estrangement in the modern world but also illustrate the difficulties encountered by women in particular. Jean Stafford's best novel, *The Mountain Lion,* is a truly original double *Bildungsroman* whose disturbed young female protagonist, Molly Fawcett, is as memorable a creation as J. D. Salinger's Holden Caulfield or Carson McCullers's Frankie Addams. Equally skillful as a short story writer, Stafford depicts in her short fiction the frustrations of precocious ten-year-old girls in small western towns, defiant young women, unhappy wives, and feisty octogenarians. Her best stories—"In the Zoo," "A Country Love Story," "The Echo and the Nemesis," "The Interior Castle," "Children Are Bored on Sunday," "The End of a Career," and "An Influx of Poets"—are accounts of female experience as accomplished and as moving as the stories of Sarah Orne Jewett, Mary Wilkins Freeman, Willa Cather, Katherine Anne Porter, Flannery O'Connor, and Eudora Welty.

When I first became interested in the work of Jean Stafford, I planned to write a critical study of her fiction. However, once I realized how closely intertwined her life and art were, I decided instead to write a literary biography that would both trace the evolution of her career and shed light on the vital connections between her life and her art.

My investigation of Stafford's life has taken me to Boulder, Colorado, where she lived in her youth and where her papers are now located; to Boston, New York, Connecticut, and Maine; and, finally, to the eastern tip of Long Island, where she resided during the last years of her life. In the course of my research, I have encountered a fascinating though not always likable woman. An embittered alcoholic and neurotic, Stafford was quick to attack the stupidity, bad taste, and hypocrisy of others. However, though some considered her to be heartless and self-centered, many had not only great respect for her work but great affection for her. They respected her intellect, were amused by her caustic wit, and recognized how vulnerable and insecure she really was. I too have come to admire her formidable intelligence, her perceptiveness, her wit, her candor, her tenacity, and her unwillingness to compromise her high artistic standards. If I have not always approved of her actions, I have nonetheless tried to understand what motivated her behavior. Moreover, I have empathized with the conflicts she experienced as she tried to reconcile the often contradictory imperatives of her personal life and her career.

The name of the protagonist of Jean Stafford's uncompleted novel, *The Parliament of Women,* is Cora Savage. I have based the title of this biography on Cora's name, as *The Savage Heart* seemed to me an apt title for a study of this gifted but tormented and frequently angry writer who felt that she had been betrayed by her family, her lovers, her friends—and by life itself. And following Stafford's occasional practice of using the titles of other writers' works for her own short stories and essays, I have appropriated some of her titles for my chapter headings.

Knowing how much Stafford disapproved of people who misused the English language, Elaine K. G. Benson wrote after her death, "It is hard to write about Jean Stafford because you feel she may be looking over your shoulder, shaking her head at your choice of words."[4] Since I am fully aware of how much Stafford demanded of herself as well as others, it has been a formidable task indeed for me to write this biography. Frequently feeling overwhelmed, I imagined her calling me what a character in Henry James's "The Aspern Papers" calls the scholar who has intruded on her life: "you publishing scoundrel!" Once, in fact, I awoke with my heart pounding after a dreadful nightmare. In my dream I had written to Stafford requesting permission to interview her. Without waiting for her response or calling her first to make an appointment, I simply walked into her house. Having heard how meticulous she was, I was astonished to see that her living room was in disarray, its floor strewn with empty whiskey bottles. As I began to look around, the door slowly opened and Stafford walked in. With ghostly chalk-white face and crimson lips, she confronted me, asking me irately, "What are you doing in my house?" When I explained that I had written to her several weeks before to request an interview, she replied angrily, "I never gave you permission to enter my house." Then she walked quickly through the room to an open window. Horrified, I watched her body sink into the black waters of the lake below. This nightmare was so powerful, so paralyzing, that for several weeks I thought about it every time I sat down to work on the biography. I sometimes imagined Stafford peering over my shoulder and muttering one of her favorite colloquial expressions—"In a pig's valise!"—as she read what I had written about her.

I wish to thank the many individuals who helped me in this venture by speaking to me or writing to me about Jean Stafford, especially James Robert Hightower, William Mock, Eleanor Gibney, Marjorie Stafford Pinkham, Cecile Starr, Helen Rattray, Mary Elizabeth O'Rourke, Howard Higman, and Thomas Roberts, all of whom provided invaluable material. Ian Hamilton's biography of Robert Lowell, James Atlas's biography of Delmore Schwartz, Raymond Sokolov's biography of A. J. Liebling, and Eileen Simpson's memoir of the literary circle of John Berryman, *Poets in Their Youth,* were enormously helpful, as were Ellsworth Mason's catalogue of Stafford's papers at the Norlin Library and Wanda Avila's bibliography of works by and about Jean Stafford.[5]

I also wish to thank the many libraries that made relevant material available to me, including the Rare Books Room, University of Colorado at Boulder; Beineke Library, Yale University; Henry W. and Albert A. Berg Collection, New York Public Library; Butler Library, Columbia University; John M. Olin Library, Cornell University; Firestone Library, Princeton University; Harry Ransom Humanities Research Library, University of Texas at Austin; Houghton Library, Harvard University; Lilly Rare Book Library, University of Indiana; Special Collections, University of Maryland, College Park; Manuscript Division, University of Minnesota Libraries; and McFarlin Library, University of Tulsa. The following archives also supplied valuable material: the Atlantic Monthly Press, the John Simon Guggenheim Foundation, Kenyon College, the American Academy and Institute of Arts and Letters, Pennsylvania State University, the Rockefeller Foundation, the Rockefeller University, the University of Michigan, the University of North Carolina, the Wesleyan University Center for Advanced Studies, and Yaddo. I am especially grateful for the help of Nora Quinlan, Director of Special Collections at the Norlin Library of the University of Colorado, and to Sonia Jacobs and other members of the Norlin Library staff. I also wish to thank the reference librarians at Skidmore College for helping me to obtain quickly the many books and articles I needed for my work.

My work was facilitated by the generous assistance of Margaret Pearson at Skidmore College and of Laurence Rosenberg. They patiently explained to me the mysteries of my computer and were always willing to show me how to undo the mistakes I had made.

I am indebted, too, to the National Endowment for the Humanities, which awarded me a Fellowship for College Teachers that funded a year's leave to work on this project; and to Skidmore College, which awarded me a number of grants for travel and other expenses.

I also wish to express thanks to many colleagues and friends who helped me in this endeavor, especially to Susan Kress, Ralph Ciancio, and Jackson Bryer, who wrote letters on my behalf to the National Endowment for the Humanities; and to the community of feminist scholars both at Skidmore College and at large whose insights about women's lives and work have helped to shape my biography of Jean Stafford. Finally, I want to thank my own "enablers": my husband, David; my children, Andrea, Matthew, and Jeffrey; my mother, Margaret Margolis; and my sisters, Aniuta Blanc and

Vivian Rosenberg. Without their support and encouragement, I could not have completed this book.

Every biographer must necessarily perform an audacious act of interpretation, and any given biography may tell us as much about the biographer as her subject. I hope my biography has succeeded in conveying some essential truths both about Jean Stafford's difficult life and about the enduring art that she created.

Jean Stafford
The Savage Heart

One

The Shorn Lamb
1915–1922

Childhood is that fiery furnace in which we are melted down to essentials and that essential shaped for good.
>—KATHERINE ANNE PORTER, "REFLECTIONS ON WILLA CATHER"

This is a Paradise down here.
>—SAM SHEPARD, *TRUE WEST*

"THE CHILD SHOULD never have been born." These are the chilling words Sonia Marburg, the protagonist of Jean Stafford's first published novel, *Boston Adventure,* overhears her father telling her mother.[1] Although there is no evidence to suggest that Stafford ever overheard such a conversation between her own parents, she always thought of herself as an unwanted child. The last of the four Stafford children, Jean Wilson Stafford was born in Covina, California, on July 1, 1915. Her father, John Richard Stafford, a writer of Western tales who slept with a six-shooter under his pillow, would have preferred a second boy to round out his family of two daughters and one son. Also disappointed when they first saw their baby sister were seven-year-old Mary Lee, five-year-old Marjorie, and four-year-old Dick. Promised a "surprise" when they returned from their grandmother's house in nearby Los Angeles, Mary Lee had hoped for a pen to record her poems, Marjorie for a bicycle or a Shetland pony, and Dick for a dog to replace their big yellow hound that had been run over by a car almost immediately after they had acquired it. "Don't you like your new baby sister?" their father had asked the scowling little boy. "She's alright, I guess, but I wish she'd been a dog," Dick candidly replied. In later years, whenever Dick quarreled with his youngest sister, who was given to following him around and imitating everything he said and did, he would tease her by asserting, "I *still* wish it!"[2]

As the children crowded around the practical nurse who held the one-week-old infant, their father told them that their sister Jean, unlike the rest of them, was a "native daughter" of California. The other three Stafford children had been born in Tarkio, Missouri, where John Stafford had been employed by the telephone company. Three years earlier he had uprooted his wife Ethel and his small children when he decided to move to California and grow walnuts. Ethel McKillop Stafford and John Stafford had both been born in Missouri, and Ethel's mother and two of her sisters were still living in Rockport, a short distance from Tarkio. The move to California separated Ethel from her family, on whom she was extremely dependent. However, the Staffords would now be living near John Stafford's mother and sister, who had moved to Los Angeles several years earlier. A moody, misanthropic, restless man, John was bored with the work he was doing for the telephone company in Missouri; furthermore, both he and his wife had grown tired of Missouri's icy winters and blistering summers.

Cheered by the prospect of raising English walnuts in the more hospitable climate of southern California, John Stafford purchased ten acres of fertile land situated between the small town of Covina and rural West Covina in the San Gabriel Valley, set out seedling walnut trees, and had a comfortable eight-room house built for his family with money he had inherited from his father, who had been a prosperous cattle rancher. Facing east and set well back from S. Lark Ellen Avenue, the two-story brown wooden bungalow boasted a bay window with a window seat, a built-in buffet in which Ethel Stafford displayed her hand-painted china and cut-glass bowls, and a huge fireplace with a mantel displaying an Indian tomahawk, John Stafford's spurs, and a pair of sabers. In the den, decorated with Northwest Indian baskets and a colorful Mexican serape that the honeymooning Ethel Stafford had allegedly smuggled across the Tijuana border in her bustle, the Staffords had installed their big Victrola with its fluted horn, their *Encyclopaedia Britannica,* and their sets of books by Shakespeare, Dickens, Balzac, and a writer whose works Jean Stafford would grow to admire: Mark Twain. Also included among the family's assorted treasures were Ethel McKillop's scrapbook containing invitations to the slumber parties and taffy-pulls she had attended in her youth in Rockport; a Western novel, *When Cattle Kingdom Fell,* written by Jean Stafford's father and published in 1910 by Dodge and Company; and *A Stepdaughter of the Prairie,* a memoir of life in Kansas written by Jean Stafford's cousin, Margaret Lynn, who was a member of the English Department at the University of Kansas. Although Jean Stafford later claimed that she had never read either the novel by her father or the memoir by her cousin,[3] the very fact that there were two published writers in her immediate family might have played a role in her own decision to become a writer.

"It was a narrow, winding country road they walked along. On either side ran clear small ditches, making a mouth-like sound. On their right was an orange grove from which, at all seasons of the year, came a heavy fragrance and where they sometimes saw flocks of such bright, unusual birds that they thought they must have flown up from the South Seas or Westward from Japan. Some of the little pyramidal trees were always in bloom and some were always bearing fruit."[4] This passage from Jean Stafford's second novel, *The Mountain Lion,* recreates the Edenic terrain that she recalled as she thought about her earliest years in California. The ten-acre ranch, its boundaries marked by the small palm trees John Stafford had planted, was a wonderful place for the Stafford children to explore. Though Jean Stafford lived on the ranch only until she was five, she remembered it and the surrounding area clearly enough to describe in her fiction treasured places such as "the Wash," a dried-up creek bed filled with multicolored stones that had been hollowed out by a spring flood several years before she was born. She also recalled her father's solar water heater, down whose glass panes the children used to slide when no adults were around, and the dairy of the German farmer from whom they used to buy cream cheese. Among the botanical riches of the ranch were the lilies that grew in profusion in the pond, and a lippia lawn, a dense ground cover she later described fancifully as looking "like a head of cropped and decorated hair."[5] Each day she would sit under the umbrella tree to await the return of her sisters and her brother from school. In this fertile California soil many varieties of flowers flourished, including hollyhocks, calla lilies, dainty pink roses, and a three-foot-high geranium border in which the Stafford children hollowed out a cave. The children used to suck the sour juice from the stems of the oxalis plant that grew on their property, a pastime to which Stafford refers in her short story "The Lippia Lawn."[6] They also liked to observe the activities of great colonies of hibernating ladybugs on the undersides of the palm fronds that thatched the roof of the playhouse their father had built for them. Associating ladybugs with her early childhood, Stafford later mentioned that her protagonist in *The Mountain Lion,* a fictional incarnation of herself as a child, collects specimen ladybugs and sends them to the agricultural college, hoping "that in time her name would be mentioned in a monograph in an agricultural journal."[7]

A photograph taken of Jean Stafford when she was about two years old shows a pretty, very blonde, barefoot little girl affectionately petting the Staffords' cat Budge. A tomcat rather than the female cat by the same name that appears in *The Mountain Lion,* Budge once decapitated an entire litter of kittens delivered by a female stray who took up residence on the ranch. In *The Catherine Wheel,* a similar heinous act is committed by a cat who chews off the head of one of its kittens. An ailurophile from the time she was a child, Jean Stafford always had a resident cat or cats, the most celebrated of which appeared in a book she wrote for children, *Elephi: The Cat with the High I.Q.* Other animals on the Stafford ranch included a plow horse, a cow, and a black and white shepherd collie named Rover, who usually chose to sleep in the room Jean shared with her brother Dick. Sometimes a pack of coyotes could be seen walking single-file along the edge of the orange grove to the north of their property, and the coyotes' doleful cries were often audible during the still country nights.

As do most children who are the youngest in their family, Jean felt abandoned when her siblings went off each day to attend school. Remembering those days, she later observed that Mary Lee, Marjorie, and Dick were usually too busy with their own activities to pay much attention to her, though they used to bring her presents such as a jawbreaker or a necklace made of paper clips when they returned from school. "I spent most of my time waiting, in awful boredom, for my brother and sisters to come home," she later wrote.[8] In their absence, she would follow her mother and the hired help as they performed their daily chores. For a time the Staffords employed a morose teenaged Mexican girl who frequently cried because she was homesick for her family. On weekends they would drive her back to her family's small house. Another employee was a short, energetic Japanese woman named Honna, who always came to work accompanied by her small son and daughter, the "Jap kids" to whom Stafford refers in *The Mountain Lion.*[9] She recalled that she had once kidnapped Honna's daughter and had hidden her in a rattan chest in which Ethel Stafford stored linens, but her sisters pointed out to her that at the time the incident allegedly occurred, Jean could not have been more than two years old.

Indoor family activities frequently took place in the den, where the Stafford children would congregate to listen to their father's treasured recordings of Caruso and Melba singing selections from his favorite operas or to recordings of the marches of John Philip Sousa and the folk songs of Stephen Foster. Both John and Ethel Stafford often read aloud to the children. Having taken elocution lessons in her youth, Ethel Stafford would recite to them poems by Tennyson, Whittier, Poe, Longfellow, or Wordsworth; and John Stafford, a war buff, liked to describe the battles fought during the Punic Wars, the Civil War, and the Franco-Prussian War. "Until I was five I believed that he had personally been at Runnymede," Jean Stafford said of her father, and she observed that the only relative of her mother for whom he had had any respect was a man who had roomed with General Pershing at the University of Nebraska.[10]

The stories that most impressed the future novelist, however, were not the ones that originated in books but the tales about her forebears and her parents' frequently recited anecdotes about their early years. Her father's father, Richard Stafford, had emigrated from Ireland to the United States at the age of eighteen. He settled first in Illinois, then in Kansas, and finally in Missouri, acquiring cattle land in Texas and Arizona in addition to the fourteen hundred acres he purchased in Missouri. "My Grandfather Stafford, an Irishman from County Clare, died long before my birth," Jean Stafford would later write, "but I had a deep romantic attachment to him because he had had a Texas ranch in the Texas Panhandle besides extensive holdings in Missouri and he had a rapscallion brother, Great Uncle Tom, who jumped the bounty seventy-two times during the Civil War and had had his name on the honor roles from Maine to Oregon and then decamped for Australia."[11] The Stafford homestead in Atchison County, Missouri, became widely known as one of the most attractive homesteads in that part of the country. Richard Stafford married twice. His first wife was Elizabeth Wilson, and after she died, he married her younger sister, Phoebe Anne Wilson, Jean Stafford's grandmother. Jean Stafford was given as a middle name the maiden name of this grandmother. Like the fictional Captain Forrester in Willa Cather's *A Lost Lady,* a novel about which Jean Stafford would later write a sympathetic review, Colonel Thomas Wilson, the father of Phoebe Anne, had been one of the pioneer railroad men in the West.

Jean Stafford's maternal grandfather, Malcolm McKillop, was also a prominent citizen of Atchison County. He was born in Canada, to which his parents had emigrated from the Scottish Arran Islands about 1830. More ambitious than his father, a farmer, Malcolm McKillop aspired to become a lawyer. He attended the University of Vermont and served first as a principal of a private school in Vermont, then as principal of a school in Canada, where he prepared to enter the legal profession. In 1865 he served a law clerkship in Illinois, and following his marriage to Carrie Lee Thurber, he settled in Rockport, where Jean Stafford's mother, the second of four daughters, was born. The McKillops built a large Victorian house they called Maple Lawn near the center of town, and a small brick building on one corner of their property housed Malcolm McKillop's law office. A bald, portly, self-important man, Malcolm McKillop once served as mayor of Rockport and also was elected to the Missouri legislature.[12] Yet despite these achievements of her maternal grandfather, achievements which were frequently mentioned by her mother, Jean Stafford thought him uninteresting, especially when compared with her more flamboyant paternal grandfather. Influenced by her father's negative feelings about her mother's family, she said that she looked on them as "creeps," and although Ethel Stafford reminded her children that Malcolm McKillop had been a "scholar and a gentleman" and "bragged about the number of starched shirts he had dirtied in a week," her daughter Jean was far more intrigued by stories of her cowboy grandfather than accounts of the genteel Malcolm McKillop.[13]

Both of Stafford's grandfathers died in 1899, sixteen years before she was born. They have been immortalized in their granddaughter's novel, *The Mountain Lion,* as the bearded Grandpa Kenyon, a rugged cattleman, and Grandfather Bonney, the bald and plump "scholar and . . . gentleman" whose ashes are contained in a Florentine urn on the Fawcetts' mantel.[14] The schism in Stafford's family between the red-blooded Staffords and the blue-blooded McKillops is reflected in the very different fictional portraits she paints of her paternal and maternal grandfathers. Grandpa Kenyon wears a suit of scratchy gray material and enormous black boots with rawhide laces bearing his cattle brand, while Grandfather Bonney's attire is an elegant morning coat with a pink carnation in its lapel. As Stafford's own father claimed to have done, Grandpa Kenyon says that he saw Jesse James and his boys one night in Missouri when they rode into his yard and asked for a place to sleep. "If you haven't got a bed, you can hang me on a nail," Jesse James allegedly said on that occasion.[15] Whereas the disheveled, cursing Grandpa Kenyon would have been at home in the fictive world of Mark Twain, the genteel Grandfather Bonney, with his silk hat and gold-headed walking stick, might have stepped out of the pages of Stafford's other favorite American author, Henry James.

Stafford got to know both of her grandmothers. Phoebe Anne Wilson Stafford, a small, slender woman with dark, penetrating eyes, an aquiline nose, and a rather severe mouth, lived in the Highland Park section of Los Angeles, eighteen miles from West Covina. Bearing some resemblance to Miss Pride in Jean Stafford's *Boston Adventure,* she usually dressed in tailored suits and wore her hair in a tight bun, used no makeup, and carried a large leather handbag in which she stored peppermint lozenges for her dyspepsia. Well-informed and shrewd, she had been a member of the Women's Christian Temperance Union, had worked diligently for women's suffrage, and for a time had written a column for a local newspaper under the name of P. A. Stafford. Jean Stafford remembered her grandmother as "an austere, political woman, always hatted." Dressed in "clerical black," she came for Christmas dinner one year and gave her youngest grandchild a pink tatted bag for her handkerchief and her Sunday school nickel. Jean was surprised by the gift, for her grandmother had never demonstrated any particular affection for her until that moment, and her grandmother's "intellectual Scottish eyes, burning with dialectic," had never appeared to be conscious of her youngest grandchild. The pink silk bag with the full-blown carved wooden roses on the end of its drawstrings seemed to Jean an extraordinarily feminine and gay gift to have come from someone so "mind-minded." Thirty-six years later she could still recall how devastated she had been because, on the very same day she had been given this wonderful gift, she lost it when they drove her grandmother to the Covina train depot.[16]

During the first five years of Jean Stafford's life, she often visited Grandmother Stafford in Los Angeles. Organizing Sunday outings with his family, John Stafford would set out in their Model T Ford with his wife and children for a day at Redondo Beach or a visit with his mother. Once, en route, Ethel Stafford fell out of their car in the heart of Los Angeles. She was not hurt but "in rather a temper," Stafford recalled. Her father blamed the accident on the fact that his wife was wearing a narrow hobble skirt and insisted that, if she had not had on such a ridiculously tight dress, she might have been able to maintain her balance in the car.[17] Grandmother Stafford lived with her daughter Ida. An accomplished horsewoman in her youth, Aunt Ida had helped her brothers and father on their ranch, but after bruising her leg on a rusty nail when she was thrown from a horse, she began to suffer from constant severe pain in the injured leg and was no longer able to ride. Several years later she was found to have tuberculosis of the bone and had to have her leg amputated. Married to a minister and subsequently divorced, she lived with her children, Lois and Bud, in her mother's house in Los Angeles. Aunt Ida was an accomplished painter of pottery who did all her own glazing and firing. She got around on crutches and was one of the first women in Los Angeles to drive a car.

The Staffords, bearing gifts of produce and walnuts and homemade jam, would arrive hot and tired after a long trip down the two-lane country road that connected Covina to Los Angeles. The children always looked forward to playing with their cousins, and they were intrigued by their grandmother's live parrot and her big bearskin rug with head and fangs intact. Before they departed, their grandmother's German maid would serve them tea and arrowroot biscuits on a large screened porch that overlooked a deep canyon.

Jean Stafford saw her mother's mother much less frequently than she did her paternal grandmother. However, her mother frequently spoke about her childhood, about her mother, and about Jean's aunts in Rockport. Grandmother McKillop and "the girls," Jean's two unmarried aunts Ella and Bess, visited Covina several times and always sent homemade cookies and candy for Christmas. When Jean was five, her mother took her to Rockport to visit her Grandmother McKillop and her three aunts, Ella, Evangeline, and Bess. Evangeline was married, but her two unmarried aunts still lived with their mother in Maple Lawn. Jean Stafford recalled that the large white house on the hill had "an accumulation of bow-windows and turrets and columns and filagree." After her husband's death, Carrie Lee McKillop had taken in boarders to support herself, something that her daughter Ethel would soon have to do as well when her own family's financial status suddenly deteriorated. Stafford described Grandmother McKillop as "a plump teacosy of a woman who smelled of orrisroot and wore a crocheted cap on her thinning hair." Twenty-one years after her grandfather had died, her grandmother still kept his law office exactly as it had been when he was alive.[18] Though her fortunes had declined with his death, she continued to go out to make afternoon calls wearing the long bombazine dress, gloves, fur-trimmed cape, and bonnet of a genteel lady. Jean Stafford's mother exchanged frequent voluminous letters with her family in Rockport, visited there about once a year, and continued to subscribe to the *Atchison County Mail* as long as members of her family still lived in Rockport.[19]

Resembling in appearance and temperament their respective mothers, Jean Stafford's parents were very different from one another. Her father was a rather short, thin man with a large head, deep-set blue eyes, bushy eyebrows, and an aquiline nose like his mother's. He limped slightly as a result of a boyhood accident and sometimes carried a blackthorn walking stick. The second son of Richard and Phœbe Anne Stafford, John Stafford was born in London, Missouri, on December 6, 1874. He graduated from Amity College in College Springs, Iowa, majoring in classics and earning his bachelor's degree cum laude. He had a keen mind and a prodigious memory; in his nineties he could still quote Ovid and Virgil. Among his favorite books were Mommsen's *History of Rome,* Shakespeare's historical plays, and the works of Mark Twain. After college he worked for several years as a cowpuncher on a ranch his father owned in the Texas Panhandle, an experience that is reflected in his Western novel *When Cattle Kingdom Fell* and in the Western tales he published under the nom de plume Jack Wonder or occasionally Ben Delight. Jean Stafford later recalled that one of his works bore the improbable title "The Transmogrified Calf."[20]

In "Woden's Day," a posthumously published chapter of her unfinished novel *The Parliament of Women,* Jean Stafford relates the history of the Savage family, a family like her own. Describing an actual photograph of her father that shows him sitting at his writing desk, a large dictionary on a stand to his right, she says of Dan Savage, "The table is strewn with papers on one of which Dan is writing with a long-stemmed pen; his other hand is relaxed, the fingers (how filled with ease they seem!) touching another sheet. He is in profile and because his sharp aquiline nose is in shadow, his face looks delicate and young. How young, unlined, how cleanly his high forehead reaches up to meet the dense curls of his dark hair. . . ." She calls this photograph, taken to commemorate the publication of his first short story, "a portrait of youth in the youth of a year." However, realizing by the time she wrote this chapter of her novel how transitory his success as a writer had been, she concludes this passage with a reference to his vulnerability: "You read his mortal vulnerability in his lowered eyes (he does not yet wear thick glasses) and in his bent clean-shaven neck."[21]

John Stafford met his future wife, Ethel McKillop, in Tarkio, Missouri, the town in which his sister and brother had attended college. After a brief career as a news reporter in New York City, he had returned to Tarkio when his father died, and he lived with his mother in a rented house there. Ethel McKillop had briefly taught school in her hometown of Rockport as well as in Salida, Colorado, after graduating from high school. She was taking summer courses in Tarkio when she made the acquaintance of her future husband. A pretty, popular, blue-eyed woman somewhat inclined to plumpness, she was drawn to the intense young man who could quote verbatim long passages from the classics and who told colorful tales about his days on his father's cattle ranch. Ethel McKillop and John Richard Stafford were married at Ethel's home, Maple Lawn, on June 26, 1907, and continued to live in Tarkio until 1912, when they moved to California with Mary Lee, Marjorie, and Dick.

In the early years of her marriage Ethel Stafford was a cheerful, affectionate, sociable housewife who enjoyed setting the table with her own best china and linen when she entertained visiting relatives and friends. As Mrs. Fawcett does in *The Mountain Lion,* she took pleasure in domestic rituals and insisted that her children speak properly and mind their manners. Rather unintellectual, especially when compared with her fiercely intellectual husband, she was loquacious and sentimental. Her youngest daughter would later make fun of her tendency to spout clichés and aphorisms. Ethel Stafford's role in the family was that of peacemaker, which frequently involved trying to placate her irascible husband, a man Jean Stafford once described as "embattled from his bassinette."[22] In a letter to Jean, written just before he died, John Stafford admitted that his own mother had once told him, "John, you are too ornery to live and too ornery to die a natural death. You will have to be shot or hanged . . . either is too good for you."[23] His habitual pessimistic pronouncements and his irritability caused his wife to exaggerate her own cheerfulness for the sake of their children and to play Pollyanna to his Scrooge.

In a memoir of Jean Stafford, her sister Marjorie describes their life in West Covina as "idyllic" and "golden,"[24] and Jean Stafford herself used the words "pastoral serenity" to describe the early years of her life.[25] However, Stafford's portrait in *The Mountain Lion* of the troubled youngest member of the

Fawcett family, Molly, a portrait that is based on her own memories of herself, suggests that no matter how idyllic her physical surroundings were on the ranch, childhood was a time of pain and loneliness. One of the sources of that early pain, no doubt, was the troubled relationship of her parents. Beneath her father's bantering and teasing, the highly sensitive little girl could sense how much hostility and disdain he felt for her mother, whose bourgeois values he abhorred. While the friction between her parents was not as intense during the early years of her life as it would later become, Jean Stafford must have recognized even then how dissimilar her parents were in temperament and outlook. Her father, a Darwinian freethinker, sneered when her mother invited a visiting Presbyterian minister from Scotland to tea and asked Jean, in whose hair she had tied a taffeta Mackenzie plaid ribbon, to sing "Comin' thro' the Rye."[26] Her mother, in turn, was mortally offended when John Stafford made disparaging remarks about the McKillops or railed against women, who he claimed had dogged and persecuted him all of his life. The marital conflicts of the Staffords were depicted in their daughter's portrayal of the Marburgs' bitter quarrels in *Boston Adventure*, in her description of the battles of Dan and Maud Savage in *The Parliament of Women*, and in other fictional works as well. "Why Dan and Mama did not run away from each other and quit their endless insults, they could not imagine," Stafford writes, commenting on the reaction of the Savage children to their parents' endless squabbles.[27]

If there was friction in the Stafford family between the adults, there was also friction among the four children. Jean was happiest when her sisters and her brother would include her in their games of Run, Sheep, Run and mumblety-peg, or their favorite pastime, playing school. Drawn to books because their parents were both avid readers, the children taught Jean how to read before she began to go to school, and soon she was able to chant the alphabetical titles "A to And," "And to Aus," and "Aus to Bis" printed on the spines of their father's *Encyclopaedia Britannica*, just as Ralph and Molly do in *The Mountain Lion*. Occasionally, Marjorie and Dick took her with them to the two-room West Covina school, where their favorite teacher, Miss Melodile Seamons, would make a fuss over the little girl, admiring her big blue eyes and her even teeth, which she compared to "tiny grains of rice."[28] Often, however, Stafford's siblings either teased her or ignored her entirely, and whenever their friends, Bruce and Ethel Pratt, came over to play, they all were annoyed because Jean insisted on following them about. Her sisters used to tell her that she had been bought at a second-hand shop in Tijuana, she said, and they insisted that as a newborn she had been no larger than a can of talcum powder, with a head the size of an orange. Mary Lee frequently made dis-

paraging remarks about her somewhat chubby little sister's plumpness, offering to send for rubber underwear or a reducing balm or exercise records to
help her overcome her tendency to what Mary Lee described as Jean's "avoir-
dupois" or "adiposity." [29] Stafford later recalled that her sisters would fight
over who owned her and would ask her, "Whose little girl are you?" In response to their interminable teasing, she would attack them, pulling their hair
and hollering, "I'm my own little girl, you big fat nitwits!" [30] As an adult she
often lamented that during their childhood she and her three siblings usually
were at odds with one another.

Like Molly in *The Mountain Lion,* Jean was happiest when her favorite
sibling, her brother Dick, would include her in his games, but all too quickly
he would become irritated at something she did or he would make a disparaging comment about the fact that she was a mere girl. One of the episodes from
her childhood that she recounted in *The Mountain Lion* was the time Dick
reprimanded her for wearing his outgrown Boy Scout shirt with the motto
"Be Prepared" embroidered on the pocket. "Having that on a girl is like drag-
ging the American flag in the dirt," he had remarked icily. [31] What she did not
note in her novel, however, was the fact that after he had chastised her for
wearing his shirt, she had hastened to remove the motto with a razor blade,
cutting herself a good deal in the process. [32]

In a letter written when she was an adult, Jean Stafford mentioned that she
had mutilated herself repeatedly as a child to gain pity and love from her
elders. [33] She refers to this in *The Mountain Lion* when she shows Molly deliberately pouring acid on her hand and then sobbing to her mother, "I have hurt
myself!" [34] Another manifestation of Stafford's troubled state of mind during
her early years was the fact that she was prone to nightmares and sleepwalk-
ing. She was also a poor eater, a characteristic that would persist during the
remainder of her life. In *The Parliament of Women* she reveals her own negative feelings about food when she has her protagonist Cora Savage observe, "I
looked at food as a punishment; early I learned to cheat, slyly storing dreadful
slabs of bitter liver in the pocket of my dress to feed undiscriminating dogs, or
in the middle of the meal, being seized by hiccups." [35] Recalling what she had
been like when she was a young child, Stafford later wrote, "I was unhappy
and afraid." [36]

Included in *The Mountain Lion* is a poem the precocious Jean composed
when she was five or six:

> Gravel, gravel on the ground
> Lying there so safe and sound,
> Why is it you look so dead?
> Is it because you have no head? [37]

Perhaps one should not overinterpret a poem written so early in childhood, but these lines do suggest that for the young Jean Stafford, having a "head" was at once what made one human and what caused one to be vulnerable. After she had recited the poem to her family, her dad pronounced this budding writer to be "a chip off the old block." [38]

Whenever the Stafford children left the Covina ranch for more than a day, they would chant, "Good-bye, house, good-bye garage, good-bye tankhouse, good-bye water-box." [39] Little did they realize that soon they would be forced to say good-bye to this magical place forever. In 1920 John Stafford decided to put his property up for sale and move his family to San Diego. He planned to invest money from the sale of the ranch as well as some of his mother's savings in the stock market there, hoping to double or triple his investment. On March 7, 1920, the Staffords had dinner with their neighbors, the Pratts, allowed Dick to spend one last night with his friends Ethel and Bruce Pratt,[40] and then departed for San Diego. "I began my education in San Diego," Jean Stafford said, recalling this period of her life. "My father, a mercurial man, decided that his fortune lay in the stockmarket rather than in English walnuts and we moved to be near an exchange. We lived so near Balboa Park that I could hear the lions roaring at night, and I dwelt in perpetual terror except when I was distracted by measles or mumps or whooping cough, blood blisters or pink-eye." [41] In *The Mountain Lion,* remembering her fear of the lions in Balboa Park, she mentions that "Molly often had a dream that she was being chased mile after mile through the streets of San Diego by the lioness who almost overtook her at every mailbox." [42]

Life was very different for the Stafford children in San Diego than it had been in Covina. They lived in a rented white stucco house on a city street and played softball in the paved roadway. Their father no longer puttered around the house or sat in an upstairs bedroom writing stories during the week as he had done at the ranch. Instead, dressed in a respectable suit and fedora, he would set off for the stock exchange each day. On weekends, John Stafford took his children to the waterfront to fish or to the San Diego zoo. Sometimes they drove to Coronado, across the bay from the city, where they had a picnic lunch on the beach and then went to the park to listen to the performance of a uniformed brass band. Once, when their Grandmother Stafford paid them a visit, she treated her grandchildren to a ride in a glass-bottomed boat in the waters off Coronado. The water was rough that day and everybody succumbed to seasickness except for their grandmother, who maintained her usual erect stance and stern composure. She was fortified by her belief in the doctrines of Mary Baker Eddy, having recently become an avid convert to Christian Science. It is probable that Stafford was depicting her own father's response to his mother's adoption of Christian Science when Dan Savage exclaims in "Woden's Day": "I mourned to see my ma go daft. I lamented the degeneration of that fine intellect. It riddled her like ergot through a stand of oats. You see there yonder that fair crop shimmering? Now close your eyes and what do you see? Black blight."[43] Recalling later their ride in the glass-bottomed boat, Jean Stafford emphasized not her joy but her terror at the spectacle of eels and monstrous gargoyle-headed fish. She said her brother made fun of her for acting like a big baby, threatening he would make her walk the plank so that she would end up in Davy Jones's locker with the octopuses and jellyfish.[44]

Visits to and from their Los Angeles relatives occurred less frequently when they lived in San Diego, but the Staffords now made the acquaintance of two brothers and a sister of their mother's father. Great-uncles Duncan and John and great-aunt Annie had never married. Born in Quebec, they had all settled in San Diego. Marjorie Stafford Pinkham has described these McKillop relatives as "very Scottish, very God-fearing and full of dry humor."[45] On Sunday evenings the Stafford children regularly attended a prayer meeting held in the rose-covered bungalow of these relatives, who were staunch Presbyterians. Uncle Duncan would deliver a brief sermon and quiz the children on the sermon they had heard at the Presbyterian church that morning. Mary Lee and Marjorie would then read a Bible verse and Uncle John would recite a blessing. The refreshments, invariably consisting of donuts and peppermint sticks, were the only part of the weekly ritual the children remembered with pleasure. Since Jean Stafford's Grandfather McKillop had died before her birth, it is probably these Sunday prayer meetings in San Diego that gave rise to her description in "Woden's Day" of Grandfather McKinnon's interminable Sunday service, during which the little Cora Savage feels "demented with discipline, distempered with swallowed screams and swallowed yawns."[46]

In San Diego, Jean entered kindergarten. As an adult she recalled that a brawny girl in the second grade had tricked her into giving her the nickel she had been saving for a small blue bathtub she had admired in the ten-cent store; that she made herself a dress out of paper, a feat which was applauded by her teachers but laughed at by her "beastly" sisters; and that she learned braille. Later her sisters informed her that she had not learned braille, as she had remembered, but instead had probably been introduced to the rudiments of counting by being given an abacus.[47]

Judged sufficiently mature that year to be included in such an activity, Jean was given a part to play in a melodrama written and directed by her sister Mary Lee and performed for their neighbors, the Caseys. Jean played the part of a child of a wealthy couple who was kidnapped by gypsies. When "the law," played by her brother Dick, rescued the child, the villainous gypsy king, played by Mary Lee, stabbed himself with John Stafford's still-sheathed hunting knife as the rest of the cast chanted, "Good riddance to bad rubbish, good riddance to bad rubbish!"[48] In San Diego Jean also acquired a friend of her own named Earlene and consequently did not have to depend completely on her brother and sisters for companionship.

No sooner had the Stafford children begun to adjust to their new surroundings than the cataclysm befell them that would dramatically alter the shape of their lives: within the year, John Stafford's investments in the stock exchange were wiped out. Recalling that fateful event in "Woden's Day," Jean Stafford observes succinctly about the Savages when they experience a similar cataclysm in their lives, "Afterward, they began to be poor."[49] Looking through her father's papers when she was an adult, she was chagrined to discover how much money he had squandered on the stock exchange in 1920. His property in stocks and bonds, most of it left to him by his father, had been worth almost two hundred thousand dollars, and in addition he had owned property in California, Texas, and Missouri worth another seventy thousand dollars. "I knew he had money, but I did not know he was actually rich!" she commented with dismay when she discovered how much money he had once had.[50]

After learning the news of her husband's financial disaster, Ethel Stafford was so depressed that she took to her bed; however, soon she had no choice but to accept the dire fact that their style of living would be drastically altered. She did her best to console her husband, who sat overwhelmed with despair in his study. An austerity program was put into effect immediately that involved home haircuts and home shoe repairs. "His lumpy leather half-soles hurt our feet, and his strange haircuts caused us embarrassment at school," Marjorie Stafford Pinkham recalled. A most unhappy recipient of one of John Stafford's home haircuts was his youngest daughter, who bolted after he had cut the flaxen locks on one side of her head, using a bathing cap as a guide. She remained hidden behind a clump of hydrangea bushes until mealtime, and nothing would induce her to let him complete the job he had begun. For months she went about with one side of her hair cut short and the other side hanging to her shoulders.[51] Years later, Jean Stafford might have had this traumatic experience in mind when she wrote a story she originally called "The Shorn Lamb" and subsequently retitled "Cops and Robbers," a tale about a little girl whose father takes her to a barbershop and has her beautiful hair cut like a boy's. After the haircut, when the father tells his sulking daughter, "You look as cute as a button, young fellow," she replies angrily, "I do not. I'm not a young fellow," and she moves as far from him on the car seat as she can get, "hating him bitterly and hating her nakedness."[52]

Always a moody man, John Stafford became more morose than ever after his financial debacle. He blamed his mother for driving him from the house initially so that he did not become the successful writer he had hoped to be; he blamed his wife for not understanding him; he blamed his children for making so much noise that he was forced to leave the house and seek refuge in the stock exchange; but, most of all, he blamed a world run by "thieves and skalawags" who had seduced him into squandering his patrimony.[53] For the remainder of his life he would devote much of his energy to writing a treatise on economics designed to prove that the corrupt American economic system was responsible for his financial ruin.

Jean Stafford's later insecurity and bitterness can be traced in part to her early childhood experience in California. Her position in the Stafford family, the troubled relationship of her parents, the fact that she had been uprooted from the beloved ranch in Covina, and the upheaval that her father's fiscal irresponsibility had caused—all these factors had played a part in shaping her subsequent vision of herself as a hapless victim of circumstance. If, in her fiction, she recreates the Edenic physical world in which her life began, she also reveals how painful these early years were for a highly sensitive, intelligent, lonely little girl who often felt unwanted, unloved, and unprotected by her elders.

Two

Cowboys and Indians and Magic Mountains

1922–1936

. . . my roots remain in the semi-fictitious town of Adams, Colorado, although the rest of me may abide in the South or the Midwest or New England or New York.

—JEAN STAFFORD, "AUTHOR'S NOTE," *THE COLLECTED STORIES OF JEAN STAFFORD*

JOHN STAFFORD OFTEN amused his children with tales of the West, a territory that oddly enough was located east of California. The characters who inhabited their father's West were scurrilous villains and dashing heroines, intrepid cowpunchers and beautiful damsels in distress. When he suddenly announced his decision to move the family to Colorado, his two youngest children, Dick and Jean, were pleased, for they looked forward to having the kinds of adventures that befell the characters in their father's Western yarns.

Anxious to make a new start after his financial disaster in San Diego, John Stafford chose Colorado Springs as their next destination. In her unpublished autobiographical novel *In the Snowfall,* Jean Stafford describes a man resembling her own father who decides to settle in Colorado because he has some anachronistic idea of panning for gold there, but it is not clear whether this was John Stafford's motive for moving to Colorado. A more likely reason for the Staffords' move to Colorado was that Ethel Stafford had once spent a year as a teacher in Salida, Colorado, which might have made her more kindly disposed to resettling in that state than elsewhere once she realized that her husband was determined to uproot the family again.

How traumatic this move was, particularly for the youngest member of the family, is revealed in "Going West," an unpublished story in which Stafford describes the departure of a family like her own for Colorado. The narrator recalls how her mother tried to allay the apprehensions of the children about the impending move by referring to their forthcoming trip as "a lark in a machine" and by assuring them that they were going to have jolly times en route living in a tent in tourist camps as gypsies did, sleeping on army cots, and cooking out under the stars on a portable kerosine stove. As Stafford's own mother did, the mother in her story buys olive drab clothing, cavalry hats, and khaki canteens for the children and promises them that they will see buffaloes and Indians and squaws with papooses. Yet even though the children are momentarily distracted by the elaborate preparations and the fanciful descriptions of their forthcoming journey, leaving California is traumatic for their mother, who hates to abandon her rose gardens, and for the children as well. "We brooded, crying, and protested, yelling, in our morbid sense of loss," the narrator says. "I would wander from room to room, staring morosely at emptied out bookcases and cupboards and rolled up rugs and undressed windows and be as grief-stricken as if the house had died."[1]

The actual departure of the Stafford family from San Diego became even more stressful when the children, one by one, were stricken with measles just when they all were scheduled to set out for Colorado. Dick was the first one to get sick. Having been invited to spend their last night in San Diego at the home of their Uncle Duncan, the children awoke to discover that Dick was too ill to travel. John Stafford took his three daughters to Los Angeles for the day, while Ethel Stafford remained to tend to the sick boy. By the time they returned from Los Angeles, Uncle Duncan's household had been placed under quarantine by the San Diego Health Department. Then, one by one, the girls became ill, and the family had to spend almost a month in the overcrowded house of their uncle until everyone was well enough to travel.

Before leaving California, they paid one last visit to their Aunt Ida and their cousin Bud in Los Angeles, but were unable to bid good-bye to their grandmother or their cousin Lois, for Grandmother Stafford had taken Lois abroad with her. The final traumatic event that occurred on the eve of their departure for Colorado was the "loss" of their dog Rover. Their aunt tried to persuade them that he had either run away or had been stolen, but they insisted that they would probably find Rover on the road to Colorado. They did not discover for many years that their father had taken their beloved dog to the pound so that he would not have to deal with a dog as well as his four children when they set out in their Reo, already overcrowded with people, clothing, bedding, and groceries. All of their furniture had been sold; however, John Stafford did manage to bring his *Encyclopaedia Britannica* with him in a case that he strapped to the running board.

The journey to Colorado took almost a month. At night they stayed in tourist camps or at old Indian campsites, where they searched for arrowheads and shards of Indian pottery. En route they visited the Painted Desert and the Grand Canyon. They later recalled impoverished Navajo women who were living in miserable dwellings and herds of wild burros that galloped ahead of their car. They also vividly remembered how their father had repeatedly made nasty remarks to the motorists he would overtake on the road and how they themselves, hot and cranky and bored, had quarrelled endlessly with one another in the back seat. But the most distressing thing of all, Jean Stafford later recalled, was their bitterly disappointing discovery that they had been duped about the West by their mother, whose notions of that terrain were principally derived from postcards sent by friends, and by their father, who had filled their heads with pictures of a mythical West that no longer existed. The dusty, rubbish-littered tourist camps near town dumps reeking of smoldering inner tubes and infested with flies were a far cry from the romantic places their parents had described to them. In an essay called "Disenchantment," which was awarded a prize in a statewide high school essay contest, Jean Stafford would later describe their sense of betrayal when they saw for themselves what the West was actually like: "There were no savages. There wasn't anything the least bit extraordinary. Colorado was just as uninteresting as California and more spread out. It was monstrous that we had been tricked by Tom Mix and Zane Grey and all the others whose bloated fancies have produced such glamorous exaggerations about dashing cowpunchers on big roans defying death on landslides in order to do justice to the black-mustached villains." [2] Though Stafford does not mention her own parents in this passage, it was their "bloated fancies" as well as Zane Grey's that had caused their children to conjure up a West bearing no resemblance to the colorless places and people they actually saw en route.

The first house the Staffords rented in Colorado was located in the Ivywild section of Colorado Springs. Mrs. Benson, the owner, was a spiritualist who wore multitudes of bracelets. Resembling the nervous postmistress Miss Runyon in *The Mountain Lion,* the hysterical Mrs. Benson maintained that she had heard someone swallowing outside her window. Ethel Stafford promptly volunteered the services of Dick, who for a time agreed to sleep on a daybed in Mrs. Benson's dining room, until he finally insisted that he could no longer tolerate listening to Mrs. Benson's repeated accounts of how she communicated with her dead husband during the seances she regularly held.

Jean began first grade when the Staffords were living in Ivywild, attending the same school as Marjorie and Dick. During their first winter there, however, their studies were interrupted after the children and Ethel Stafford came down with influenza. To care for his ailing wife and children, John Stafford hired a practical nurse, a stern woman who scolded the children for wasting toilet paper and succeeded in terrorizing them. She was soon replaced by a small, wiry black woman who wore a gray-streaked black wig. According to Marjorie Stafford Pinkham,[3] it was this woman who served as the inspiration in *The Mountain Lion* for the "wonderfully wise" black woman called Magdalene,[4] whom Molly and Ralph Fawcett meet at their Uncle Claude's ranch.

As they had done in California, the Staffords regularly set out on Sunday expeditions to explore the surrounding area. Mary Lee, who was attending high school at this time, refused to accompany the rest of the family on their Sunday outings, but the other three children would drive with their parents to visit the state penitentiary in Canyon City or the Garden of the Gods, a local geological spectacle they proudly showed off to their former Covina neighbors, the Pratts, when they paid the Staffords a visit in Colorado. During one of their Sunday trips the Staffords acquired a collie named Laddy to replace the dog they had been forced to leave behind in California.

A more extended trip was one they took to Rockport, Missouri, to visit their mother's youngest sister, bedridden with terminal cancer. When the rear axle of their car broke en route, they rented rooms in the small town in Missouri where their car was being repaired. To amuse the restless children, the elderly woman who owned the house showed them a box that held what looked like a large chocolate drop surrounded by a dozen or so small, tan, diamond-shaped candies. As Marjorie greedily reached out to sample one of the succulent morsels, the woman informed them that the box contained her gallstones and not candy. It was probably this experience that Stafford was recalling in *Boston Adventure* when she described a white-haired woman in a mental hospital who holds up a pink candy box that rattles and then proceeds to show Sonia Marburg the treasures it contains: fifteen gallstones of various sizes and shapes.[5]

John Stafford did not get a regular job in Colorado. Instead, he spent his days exploring the outdoors or working on his stories and on his economic treatise, activities that generated little capital. Ethel Stafford received a small legacy when her Uncle Duncan died, but money was scarce. To supplement their meager income she made loaves of brown bread and baked beans in her kitchen to sell to her neighbors. It was the Stafford children's job to take the orders and to deliver the food in their wagon.

In a short story Stafford wrote when she was a child, she described a family she called the Smiths. As would be true of much of her fiction, the characters were thinly disguised versions of herself and her family: a mother who is too busy to pay attention to the needs of her children; a father who states that there is no God; two older sisters; and a brother who claims, as a boy, "the most outrageous privileges." Ursula, a character who resembles Jean Stafford herself, is attached to her brother, and the first word she utters is his name. Ursula's father is described as an "unassuming and struggling author," about whose rare successes she writes, "At various intervals checks for stories came

in long and fascinating envelopes, and on occasions like this the family celebrated with beef steak and bananas and considered the advisability of paying
the light bill."[6]

Just as Jean was getting accustomed to her new school, she was uprooted
once again when her family moved to Stratton Park, a neighborhood that was
closer to the mountains surrounding Colorado Springs. Many tuberculosis patients lived in this area, and whenever the children walked through the neighborhood streets, they would hear the frightening sounds of incessant cough-
ing coming from the screened-in sleeping porches of the cottages. Stafford
might have had Stratton Park in mind when she later wrote "The Healthiest
Girl in Town." The narrator of this story recalls that as an eight-year-old she
was at once terrified and fascinated when she encountered pink-cheeked tuberculosis patients in the town, people whose "death was an interior integu-
ment that seemed to lie just under their sun-tanned skin."[7]

Although they always found it difficult to have to resettle in a new area, the
Stafford children appear to have been more pleased with Stratton Park than
Ivywild, for the progressive Cheyenne Mountain School that they attended
there emphasized dramatics and folk dancing as well as traditional academic
subjects, and it supplemented regular classes with frequent hikes to a mountain cabin, followed by a steak fry or chili dinner and communal singing
around the fireplace. After school, Jean liked to roller-skate at the pavilion in
the nearby park, and on Sundays she would listen with fascination to the
preaching of traveling evangelists there. Dick, in particular, loved this more
rural neighborhood. He was able to climb Pike's Peak several times and also
spent many pleasurable hours trapping skunks, much to the dismay of his
three sisters. "He stank. He used to be sent home from school every now and
then because of the closeness of the fifth grade schoolroom. People would
come up to me at recess and say, 'Your brother smells bad!' . . . It was with
vengeful joy that I learned he had flunked out of fifth grade because of being
out of school so much on account of stinking," Jean Stafford later recalled.[8]
She herself preferred to spend her free time reading or writing about lives
very different from her own. The heroes in the stories she wrote, like those in
her father's stories, were "daring, dashing, tall in the saddle and easy on the
eye," men whose "steely-blue eyes" matched the barrels of their Colt .45s.
When she was eight, she wrote a story called "The Unsuccessful Amateur."
She later observed that in all of her stories, which she carefully used to type on
an old Smith Premier typewriter that had eight banks and looked like an
organ, she adopted the persona of a thirty-year-old man. An avid reader of the
dictionary, she had, by her own account, an "incredible" vocabulary at an

early age, and she remembered writing a mystery story about a man with "oleaginous black hair."[9]

Her retreat into an imaginary world was in large measure prompted by her desire to escape her father's curses and her mother's tears, an everyday occurrence during these years. In *The Parliament of Women* she would recapture the effect that her father's unpredictable outbursts and sullen periods of withdrawal had on his wife and children in her descriptions of the irascible Dan Savage. Fearing her husband's temper, as Maud Savage does that of Dan, Ethel Stafford was perpetually on her guard to avoid any circumstance that might provoke his displeasure, but despite her own unhappiness and her contempt for him because of his failure to provide for his family, she nevertheless frequently used to remind her children that their brilliant father was a highly unusual man. Thus their own feelings about him were compounded of fear and awe.

Until she was much older, Jean Stafford tended to side with her father in family squabbles. She saw him as a misunderstood genius and believed, because he mentioned it repeatedly, that his literary career had suffered from the burden of too many family responsibilities. Revealing her identification with her father is a photograph of her that was taken during this period: in it she is dressed in her father's suit and felt hat, and she is carrying his blackthorn walking stick. John Stafford was eager to foster an alliance between himself and his youngest child. Sometimes he would invite her to accompany him on hunting or fishing expeditions, and quickly perceiving how bright she was, he introduced her to the treasures to be found in the pages of the encyclopedia and the unabridged dictionary. When she was eight, he began to teach her Latin, and two years later he taught her Greek as well. Although Jean Stafford was pleased by his attention, she nevertheless had mixed emotions about having him instruct her because he frequently would lose his temper and swear at her when she made errors in her declensions. For the future writer, however, his early encouragement of her literary efforts was invaluable. Whereas her harassed mother was usually too busy with household chores to pay much attention to her, he was always eager to read her stories.

The prospectus that Jean Stafford later wrote for the novel *In the Snowfall* suggests that increasingly, as she grew older, she began to fathom what a deleterious effect her close relationship with her father had had on her own emotional development. Joyce, the protagonist of this unpublished novel, laments the fact that she had acquired many of her father's "useless and ill-natured attitudes, including the habit of taking the other side of any argument for the keen pleasure of indulging her anger at an imagined injustice." Joyce is impelled to reject the feminine side of her nature because her father openly expresses his disdain for women and his disappointment that Joyce was not a son. Trying to please her misogynistic father, Joyce has her hair cut short like a boy's and, instead of wearing dresses as her sisters do, prefers blue jeans and boys' shirts. It never occurs to Joyce, Stafford writes, "that she will not be a writer, and only occasionally does it occur to her, depressingly, that she is going to grow into a woman and not a man."[10] As Stafford herself had done in her youth, Joyce identifies with her misanthropic and misogynistic father rather than her hardworking but more conventional mother.

Thinking back to her early years in Colorado, Stafford remembered twenty years later what a "wounded, angry child" she had been then. She observed that despite his interest in fostering the growth of her intellect, her father had been too awkward and cold to show her any real affection; her mother had been too busy to express much interest in her; her brother resented her for tagging along after him; and her sisters found her too young to be of any real interest to them. "Is it any wonder that I wanted to marry Laddy?" she lamented.[11]

When Jean's eldest sister, Mary Lee, was a senior in high school, the Staffords decided to move once again, this time to Boulder, where the University of Colorado was located. Since their funds were so limited, they realized they could not afford to send Mary Lee even to the relatively inexpensive state university unless she could live at home. Thus the idea of moving to Boulder was born, and along with it, Ethel Stafford's plan to open a tea room in order to support her family. Like many of her other money-making schemes, this one too was doomed to fail. When the first house they rented in Boulder proved unsuitable for such a venture, she decided instead to operate a boardinghouse for women students, who were not then provided with housing on campus. Before long, the Staffords moved once more, this time to a modest four-bedroom house on University Hill near the campus.

Boulder was no longer the very small town consisting of "a hideous collection of frame houses on a burning plain" that the Englishwoman Isabella Bird had described in 1874 in *A Lady's Life in the Rocky Mountains* after she had visited there.[12] Nevertheless, the town was still rather provincial. It owed its existence, as did many of the towns in this part of the West, to the discovery of gold in the surrounding area. Thirty-two miles northwest of Denver, Boulder was established on November 3, 1871; the railroad connection between Boulder and Denver was completed in 1873; and the university, consisting initially of one building and having an enrollment of twelve students, was founded in 1877. In addition to the university, Boulder boasted a Chautauqua Society and a large tuberculosis sanitarium. The salubrious mountain air attracted many tuberculosis victims to Boulder, including some members of the faculty and a number of students at the university. Situated at the juncture of the Rocky Mountains and the Great Plains, Boulder was dominated by massive purple rock formations resembling the flatirons after which they were named. Very much impressed by the scenic vistas that the town afforded, Stafford would later describe the Front Range, to which the Flatirons belong, as "a splendid mountain range which stretches, peak and chasm and hummock of rock, miles beyond vision," with vast glaciers visible above its timberline.[13]

By the time the Staffords moved there, Boulder had approximately eleven thousand inhabitants, including some Mexicans and a small number of black people. The university had expanded enormously and now had almost four thousand students, several graduate programs, and quite a few impressive buildings on its spacious campus. Its handsome newer buildings, constructed in a style known as Rural Italian Renaissance, had facades made of un-trimmed pink native sandstone and steep tiled roofs. The university domi-nated the town, but in addition to the university buildings, Boulder contained numerous churches, a few rows of banks and small shops, several movie thea-ters, the rather impressive Victorian Boulderado Hotel, and an assortment of undistinguished-looking brick or wooden houses situated on wide, tree-lined streets.

By no means a partisan of the Western town in which she had spent her youth, Stafford later said of Boulder, the Adams of her fiction, "Surrounded by the violent and primitive landscape, Adams is in no way affected by it, for it is a plain little town without a single ambitious dwelling nor any 'local color'."[14] Her brother Dick, overjoyed to discover that the mesa and the foot-hills of the Front Range were but a short walk from their house, spent many happy hours hunting for arrowheads and collecting interesting specimens. Once he discovered the skulls of two deer whose antlers were so tightly inter-locked that he could not get them apart, just as Ralph Fawcett does in *The Mountain Lion*.[15] Jean, however, found the surrounding mountain terrain rather forbidding. She used to accompany her brother on his rambles and oc-casionally went along with her father on hunting expeditions. In a secluded spot on the mesa she liked to recite poetry out loud when there was no one around to overhear her, or to work on her stories without interruption. But she said that she found the Rocky Mountains "too big to take in, too high to understand, too domineering to love," and she felt that the very spaciousness of the range and the endless prairies intimidated her. "They baffled my eye, humiliated me in my picayune stature, and out of self-respect I had to make them vanish and to reduce the world to a rational arena where I knew, at all times, what was going on," she wrote.[16] She later remarked that she had never liked "Mother Nature" very well.[17]

A feeling of apprehension engendered by the natural world is evident in a number of Jean Stafford's fictional works. In "The Darkening Moon," for example, a young girl remembers how fearful she had felt as a five-year-old when she accompanied her father on a fishing trip: "The fish were so thick that they swarmed slimily over her and she had nearly gagged at the smell," she says. In contrast to a character like Hemingway's Nick Adams, who sees fishing as a sacramental rite, Stafford's female protagonist hates the very feel of the fish, which she describes as "fat slithering blobs in her bare hands." Her memory of the "horror of the reptilian odor" of the water makes the girl conclude that if her father, who had died soon after the fishing trip, were alive, she would refuse to accompany him on another fishing expedition.[18]

If Jean Stafford was not completely at home in the outdoor world that was one of Boulder's principal attractions, she was also not at ease in Boulder's social environment. Despite the presence of the university, Boulder in the twenties and thirties was politically conservative and socially provincial. *The Rocky Mountain American,* a newsletter of the Ku Klux Klan, was published in Boulder for a brief period in the twenties, and discrimination against blacks and other minorities was evident. When a young black woman named Ruth Cave graduated from the public school, for example, the headmaster denied her a diploma because of her race, and when she subsequently enrolled in the university, she was not permitted to participate in athletics or other recreational activities, nor could she live near the campus. Although Boulder was situated only a short distance from Denver, few people ever traveled to Denver to participate in its cultural activities, and in Boulder itself attendance at plays, concerts, and lectures sponsored by the university or the Chautauqua Society was poor. The daily newspaper noted how sparse the audience had been at a performance by the Los Angeles Philharmonic in the auditorium of the college.[19] "We want to retain our boys and girls here. We lose too many because they say the place is dull," an editorial stated in the newspaper in 1923.[20] Jean Stafford would have agreed with those young people who said they considered Boulder a "dull" place.

Growing up in Boulder during this time must have been particularly difficult for a gifted young girl who aspired to be a writer. Although Colorado was the second state in the Union to grant suffrage to women, the "cult of true womanhood" prevailed there, as it did in most western towns during that era. Women were expected to cultivate the virtues of purity, piety, domesticity, and submissiveness, finding their fulfillment in satisfying the needs of their husbands and children.[21] In 1910 the dean of women at the University of Colorado described the "perfect lady" in this way: "a perfect lady has a gentle voice and a gentle air; she is deferential to everyone, but especially to older people; she is modest and retiring, gracious to men but always dignified when near them; . . . she does not occupy all the sidewalk when meeting anyone."[22] Two decades later, the same attitudes were still in evidence. When asked whether women came to college for a major in matrimony or a minor in education, the majority of students who were interviewed by the university paper said that women came to college to seek a career behind a broom.[23] It is true that the university had a number of women teachers on its faculty and that several women held important administrative positions in the town, but more women students aspired to be homecoming queens than professors, and according to the *Colorado Clubwoman,* most women still believed in the old adage "The hand that rocks the cradle rules the world."[24]

Jean Stafford was ten years old when her family moved to Boulder. In a talk she gave at the Boulder Writer's Conference in 1952, she recalled that at age ten she "wore a hideous haircut, was tearfully inept in Palmer Method at the University Hill School and still believed in the spanking machine."[25] Spurred on by her own interest in books and fearful of incurring her father's displeasure if she did not excel, she was a good student. However, she thought of herself as a social outcast because of her poverty and the eccentricity of her father. Sometimes she would take a perverse pleasure in behaving in an eccentric fashion herself. Once she wore a Civil War saber belonging to her father to school,[26] and she invented a private language consisting of "cross and Latin words" that, she said, made her "the most disliked child in Boulder, Colorado."[27] In her short story "Bad Characters," she would later describe a volatile young girl who resembles what she herself was like at that age:

> Up until I learned my lesson in a very bitter way, I never had more than
> one friend at a time, and my friendships, though ardent, were short. When
> they ended and I was sent packing in unforgetting indignation, it was always
> my fault; I would swear vilely in front of a girl I knew to be pious and prim
> (by the time I was eight, the most grandiloquent gangster could have added
> nothing to my vocabulary—I had an awful tongue), or I would call a Ten-
> derfoot Scout a sissy or make fun of athletics to the daughter of the high-
> school coach.[28]

She claimed that as a child what she really wanted to be was an acrobatic dancer, but she could not afford toe-dancing slippers and instead had to dance in her brother's basketball shoes with socks stuffed in the toes.[29] Recalling her unhappiness during her childhood, she would portray in her short stories a series of cross, irritable, dissatisfied young girls. Although the tone of her stories about Adams, Colorado, is usually humorous, beneath the surface one can detect the frustration and anger of a self-conscious young girl who believed she was different from most of her peers and felt isolated both at school and at home.

When Jean Stafford wasn't practicing cartwheels, or playing one of the many varieties of solitaire she had learned, or working on a crossword puzzle, her favorite pastime was writing. In seventh grade she began her first novel, a thriller set in the British Museum, and after typing its twelve pages and filling in the punctuation by hand with colored pencils, she bound the manuscript with cardboard and tied it with white rick-rack. "For a long time," she said, "I read it over at least once a day with undiminishing reverence. I am under the impression that someone else—beside the dog—read it and said at the time that I had talent, but I am not sure that I was not my own discoverer." [30]

One memorable summer Jean Stafford and her father spent several weeks together in a cabin in the mountains that a friend allowed them to use. There, on separate typewriters, they worked side by side on their stories. In a fragment entitled "Fame Is Sweet to the Foolish Man" she depicts a similar episode, describing a father and a daughter who spend more time playing chess and talking than writing. While they are away from home, they receive letters from the rest of the family full of disparaging remarks about their foolish plans to become famous by means of their pens. The young girl who narrates the story remarks at its conclusion, "So I gave up, abandoning all hopes of ever becoming a second George Eliot." [31]

The bitter conflicts between John and Ethel Stafford intensified after the family moved to Boulder. Remembering the strife-ridden atmosphere in her home, Jean was later to write to her sister Marjorie that the "Stafford-McKillop predilection for complaint, for perpetually blaming others for their misfortunes" was one of the many reasons that for all practical purposes she had left home when she was seven. [32]

According to Jean Stafford, after the stock exchange disaster her mother soon became a real-life version of Thomas Wolfe's parsimonious Eliza Gant. Always anxious about money, she tried her best to keep the bedrooms filled with student boarders for whom she cooked meals and did the laundry. Describing in *Boston Adventure* the reddened and peeling hands of Mrs. Marburg, a woman who helps to support her family by working as a chambermaid in a hotel, Stafford was no doubt recalling the chapped hands of her own mother. While Ethel Stafford bore most of the burdens of managing the household, the rest of the family had to accommodate their lives to the needs of the boarders. When all of the available rooms were rented, the family members occupied very cramped quarters, at least until 1931, when everyone but Jean had left home. There were always tedious household chores for the children to do, from setting the table for the boarders' breakfast to dusting their furniture, and since the Staffords frequently owed money to the butcher or the coal man, all the children had to get odd jobs baby-sitting or washing dishes to earn their own spending money. The summer Jean was twelve, she worked as a maid in a small lodge in Boulder Canyon. There she had her first glimpse of a famous writer, the poet Robert Frost. Recalling this event in 1952, she wrote:

> He ordered a glass of milk to drink with his lunch and I was so light-headed that when I was cutting a lemon for his companion's iced tea, I nicked my finger nastily and a drop of my blood fell into the poet's glass. I gave it to him just as it was—it didn't show much and this romantic transfusion gave me something to think about when I was kept awake at night by pack-rats gallivanting through the attic over my head.[33]

During these years John Stafford's behavior grew increasingly more eccentric, his black moods more frequent. In her fiction Jean Stafford has created a number of characters who resemble her father, including the learned but always unkempt Mr. Marburg in *Boston Adventure* and the misanthropic Fulke Bartholomew in *The Catherine Wheel.* John Stafford rarely shaved or got a haircut, dressed in old clothes, and to taunt his wife and daughters, whose bourgeois values he liked to criticize, he would chew tobacco in public. A loner, he had no close friends, and since he was unemployed, it was rumored that he had weak lungs, as did many people in the town. When he chose to do so, he could be courteous, even charming, but such occasions were rare. Most of the time, when he was not out hunting or roaming the streets, he sat in the filthy basement furnace room on an old leather seat salvaged from an abandoned car. There he typed his manuscripts on an archaic typewriter, and the sounds of his muttering and cursing would go up the hot-air registers, much to the embarrassment of his wife and children.[34]

During adolescence Jean Stafford's feelings of isolation increased when her siblings left home. Her eldest sister, Mary Lee, had graduated from the University of Colorado, and after obtaining a position as a high school English teacher in Hayden, Colorado, she had married a rancher named Harry Frichtel from Hayden and settled there; her sister Marjorie was attending the university; and her brother Dick was studying botany in nearby Fort Collins. When she created her portrait of the morose Molly Fawcett in *The Mountain Lion,* who thinks of herself as "a long wooden box with a mind inside,"[35] Stafford drew upon memories of what she herself had been like as a lonely adolescent. Photographs of Jean Stafford as a high school student show a pretty young woman with regular features and straight blond hair gathered into a bun. Except for her tall stature and her large hands and feet, she bears little resemblance physically to the ungainly, bespectacled, black-haired Molly. However, despite the fact that Jean Stafford once entered a look-alike contest at a local movie theater, pretending to be the beautiful blond actress Ann Harding,[36] she hated the hand-me-down or homemade clothes she usually wore and did not consider herself attractive.

Still a poor eater when she was a teenager, Jean Stafford seems to have had an obsessive desire to be thin. In her copy of the 1930 high school yearbook, she scissored out a picture of herself taken during her sophomore year in which she appears somewhat plump. However, by the time she posed for her college graduation picture in 1936, she was very much thinner. It is interesting to note that in Stafford's "Beatrice Trueblood's Story" a young girl finds herself unable to swallow her food because there is so much friction at the family dinner table. "Dinner, nightly, was a hideous experience for a child, since the parents were not inhibited by the children or the maid and went on heaping atrocious abuse upon each other, using sarcasm, threats, lies—every imaginable expression of loathing and contempt," Stafford writes of Beatrice Trueblood, observing that, as she listened to her parents' nightly quarrels, Beatrice "miserably pushed her food about on her plate, never hungry . . ."[37]

Several of Stafford's other characters may reflect her own anorectic tendencies. In *The Mountain Lion,* for example, Molly Fawcett is morbidly obsessed with her weight. Associating obesity with people she dislikes, she resolves that "if she ever got fat . . . or ever said anything fat, she would lock herself in a bathroom and stay there until she died."[38] As many adolescents with anorexia nervosa are now said to do, she fears the changes that are beginning to occur in her maturing body, and she thinks of procreation as the "tommy rot with which people were constantly trying to ruin her life." To keep her abdomen as flat as possible, she wraps her stomach with a piece of flannel and pins it tightly.[39] Another of Stafford's female characters who is preoccupied with her weight and rejects sexuality is Ramona Dunn, a compulsive eater in "The Echo and the Nemesis." Stafford suggests that Ramona has become obese to discourage males from making advances to her. Perhaps Stafford associated obesity with her own plump mother, for whose intellect she had great contempt, and thinness with her slight father, whose mind she admired.

Jean Stafford excelled in her studies at Boulder Prep, the public high school she attended, and was both feature editor of the school newspaper, the *Prep Owl,* and editor of the yearbook. However, she was not very popular with her classmates. Her peers were offended by her preference for polysyllabic words and her tendency to show off her intelligence. Robert Berueffy, a former class-mate, recalled that at age fourteen she had once said disdainfully in English class, "I am not well acquainted with that work because I am not sufficiently gregarious to be interested in that type of literature."[40] She told him that she wanted to be a writer and said that she had sent a letter to Henry Ford asking him either to give her a typewriter or the money to purchase one. Another of her classmates reminded her when they were adults that she had astonished their English teacher, a lover of Tennyson's poetry, by remarking that she her-self disliked Tennyson, finding his poetry "far too melodramatic."[41] Her good grades often made her vulnerable to hostile remarks. Reporting in the school newspaper what various students had done during their spring vacation, one of Stafford's fellow students observed snidely that Jean Stafford had "beamed on her report card most of the time, letting up to sleep, lunch, and dine."[42]

According to one male student who was interviewed for the *Prep Owl*, the ideal girl was a "personally charming and always sweet-tempered" person who didn't drink or smoke and was "a perfect hostess at formal and informal affairs."[43] Stafford realized all too well that she did not approximate this ideal—nor did she choose to conform to these standards. Nevertheless, she was depressed by the thought that most boys were probably more interested in her Virgil translation than in asking her out on a date.

Two boys who befriended her in high school were Goodrich Walton, the editor-in-chief of the *Prep Owl*, and Howard Higman, an art illustrator for the yearbook who later was to become a professor of sociology at the Univer-sity of Colorado. Admiring her intellect, they enjoyed discussing literature or religion with her,[44] something they ordinarily did not do with girls. She was not usually invited to the parties of the most popular students in her class, nor did she feel comfortable about inviting her classmates to her house because she feared that they might encounter her mother's boarders or be confronted by the embarrassing spectacle of her unshaven, disheveled, acrimonious father. Once, however, Howard Higman did invite her to a party he hosted in the dimly lit basement apartment he occupied in his parents' house. A classmate later reminded her that she had worn a bottle-green velvet dress to this "deli-ciously Bohemian" party.[45]

Whereas Goodrich Walton and Howard Higman both enjoyed Stafford's biting wit and were impressed by her intellect, most of her peers, put off by her sarcasm and offended by her air of superiority, were not astute enough to perceive the vulnerability and insecurity that she masked with her aloofness and cynicism. She had a deep voice she once described as being that of an undertaker,[46] and her tendency to make cutting remarks about the many people and things she disliked alienated other students. Like Molly Fawcett in

The Mountain Lion, she demonstrated "a talent for writing themes of a savagely satiric nature."[47] As feature editor for the *Prep Owl,* for example, she wrote an article she called "Vox Populi" that antagonized most of her schoolmates. In it she attacked those students who chose to belong to a "gang." Calling girls who tried their best to be charming "a race of social climbing sniggering hypocrites" and the "grand boys" who attended the university "brainless," she observed that these "inferior" people ought to be "serving apprenticeships in onion-stinking kitchens and blacksmith shops, in order to knock some of the nonsense out of them."[48] The vitriolic tone of this article, which resembled one of her father's diatribes, was hardly one that would endear her to most of the student body. Anyone who is familiar with Stafford's later satiric pronouncements about such matters as the student protests of the sixties, the misuse of the English language, or the excesses of the women's movement will recognize in this article the acerbic tone that would be evident in her later essays and articles.

On July 2, 1932, two years after the stock market crash ushered in the Depression and two weeks after Amelia Earhart became the first woman to make a solo flight across the Atlantic, Jean Stafford was graduated from the State Preparatory School in Boulder. Although another young woman in her class was designated as valedictorian, Stafford, too, had excelled in high school and had won both a school and a statewide award for her writing. In her senior year she was secretary-treasurer of her high school honor society, feature editor of the school newspaper, and an assistant editor of the yearbook. However, in retrospect she thought of her high school years as far from happy ones. Ashamed of her family and contemptuous of many of her fellow students, who in turn disliked her, she had not formed many close ties and had felt herself to be an outsider. While she was openly critical of those who heartily participated in the football rallies, beefsteak fries, and dances that played such a big part in the social life of her contemporaries in Boulder, she would nevertheless have liked to have been invited to such events.

The summer before she began college, Stafford worked as a chambermaid and waitress at a dude ranch called Lodge of Pines in the nearby town of Ward. Her experience at this dude ranch served as the basis for her short story "The Tea Time of the Stouthearted Ladies," a story she might have intended to incorporate into her unpublished autobiographical novel, *The Parliament of Women.* The protagonist of this story, Kitty Winstanley, has the same background and outlook as two other fictional alter egos of Jean Stafford, Joyce Bartholomew in *In the Snowfall* and Cora Savage in *The Parliament of Women.* Kitty's mother, having grown up in Missouri as Jean Stafford's own mother had done, now runs a boardinghouse. Burying her "woe and bile" during the day, Mrs. Winstanley invents genteel fictions to cover up the fact that her husband is unemployed and that as a result she must support the family herself. At night, however, in loud whispers that her daughter Kitty cannot help but overhear, she reproaches Kitty's father for having failed to earn a living. Mrs. Winstanley tries to persuade herself, the other landladies in the neighborhood, and—most of all—her daughter Kitty that the ranch where Kitty is employed for the summer, with its swimming pool, its square dances, and its clientele of affluent people from the East, is a wonderful place to work. Kitty, however, is aware that the hired help live not in the lodge but in what had once been a filthy chicken coop; perform exhausting, tedious chores; are patronized by the rich "dudes" from the East who are the guests; and are ordered about by the two hard-drinking women who operate the ranch. She thinks of her summer there as "friendless, silent, long, and exasperating"; nevertheless, being away from home allows her to avoid the spectacle of her defeated father and to escape her mother's "palliative fibs" about their sorry circumstances. Furthermore, in the mountains she enjoys the nonhuman world of nature, watching with pleasure the eagles as they soar and bank across the cloudless sky and the saddle horses grazing in the meadow at dusk.[49]

When Stafford began her freshman year at the University of Colorado in Boulder the following autumn, the Great Depression had already caused widespread unemployment in the town. For her the national cataclysm had a more positive side. She later observed that during this period her father's conspicuous lack of employment was no longer a source of embarrassment to her: now he was but one of the many unemployed men who sat on benches before the courthouse or in the municipal park and inveighed against the government.[50] As she reveals in the prospectus for *In the Snowfall,* her autobiographical novel about her college years, she was not certain how she felt about either of her parents during this period of her life. Describing the divided loyalties of her literary persona, Joyce Bartholomew, she writes: "She is half her aristocratic and Olympian father and half her bourgeois mother so that she is constantly at war with herself. She is persuaded that only with wealth can there be peace of mind and that it is only among the poor there are to be found quarelling [sic] and violence, and yet she believes—because her father taught her this in her basinette—that only this very turbulence and misery can produce things of value, that the great intellectual thrives only in hardship."[51] Stafford would never completely be able to resolve the conflict between her bourgeois and artistic inclinations, one part of her craving material comforts and social acceptance, the other, the abstemiousness and solitude she believed were essential for the artist to flourish.

By the time she enrolled in the university, she was the only one of the

Stafford children still living at home. Her sister Marjorie was now teaching at an Indian reservation in Tahlequah, Oklahoma, a school very much like the one Stafford describes in her short story "A Summer Day." One summer when she was a college student she visited Marjorie in Tahlequah, and the two of them set off on a trip to Carlsbad Caverns in New Mexico and to Juarez, across the border, where Stafford purchased a pair of huaraches that she later said smelled "incurably like some strong cheese long gone by." But they were delighted by Juarez itself, finding its churches "gaudy and beautiful and their bells sweet and loud." [52]

Marjorie had majored in art at the University of Colorado, and it was she who gave her younger sister the idea of modeling in the nude for art classes there to earn some money, as Marjorie herself had done. An unpublished short story Stafford wrote suggests that she never forgot how humiliating she had found posing in the nude for the art students. The story's protagonist remembers "the most dismal years of her life, lived out in the tribulations of the Depression." Years later she is visited by a woman from her hometown who upbraids her for having modeled in the nude in college and discloses the fact that some engineering students had circulated a pamphlet with nude pictures of her and "dirty wise-cracks." [53] One draft of this story suggests that Stafford had kept the fact that she was modeling in the nude from her parents, who believed she was posing in a "prim frock" for a portrait and were pleased that someone thought she was pretty enough to be painted.

The experience of modeling before a college art class is also recounted in Stafford's short story "The Philosophy Lesson," another episode about Cora Savage that Stafford undoubtedly had intended to include in *The Parliament of Women*. In the chilly tower room of Macky, an "exorbitantly Gothic building" where Professor Trucksess's drawing classes met three mornings a week, Jean Stafford would pose in the nude, as did her protagonist, Cora Savage. Remembering her own ordeal as a model, she writes of Cora that during these tedious modeling sessions she would "faint or cry out against the pain that began midway through the first hour, began as an itching and a stinging in the part of her body that bore the most weight and then gradually overran her like a disease until the whole configuration of bone and muscle dilated and all her pulses throbbed." [54] Though Stafford was pleased to have a regular job that provided her with spending money and enabled her to contribute some money to the indigent Stafford household as well, the fact that she had to expose her nude body to the scrutiny of her classmates was a great source of embarrassment. She also thought it humiliating to find herself sitting in a lecture hall next to one of the boarders whose blouse she had ironed the evening before. In the rigidly stratified society of the university, fraternity members dated only young women belonging to sororities. Too poor to join a sorority, so poor in fact that she had to pose in the nude to earn money, Stafford felt she was as much of a social outcast at the university as she had been in high school.

But if she could not compete socially with the affluent sorority girls who won the hearts and wore the fraternity pins of the campus heroes, she could win the approval of her professors and at least some of her classmates by excelling in her studies. Dorothy Thompson, a graduate student who subsequently would serve as a surrogate mother for her during Stafford's junior and senior years at the University of Colorado, recalled how impressed she had been by a paper Stafford had submitted on James Joyce. "She was way beyond any other student," Dorothy Thompson observed.[55] Much more challenged intellectually by the university curriculum than she had been by her high school courses, Stafford began to explore new areas of study, and a number of her professors soon recognized her superior academic abilities. One course she found particularly stimulating was Professor Joseph Cohen's course on the interrelationships between philosophy and literature. Years later he would include her novels, along with those of Jane Austen and George Eliot, in the reading list he compiled for the college honors program. Another of her favorite professors, an urbane young assistant professor of English named Dixon Wecter, confirmed her worst fears about her social position when he gave her top grades on her papers but dated and subsequently married a rich, beautiful member of one of the most prestigious sororities on campus.

Stafford's most influential female mentor during her college years was Professor Irene P. McKeehan. "Her tailleurs and her hats and her shoes were accurately cut, sewn without error, and impregnable to blemish or to disarray," she would later write about McKeehan in an essay entitled "Miss McKeehan's Pocketbook."[56] Stafford said that during the first week of a course McKeehan taught on the Victorian Age she was too terrified of this formidable professor to look directly at her; instead, she feverishly wrote down every single word of the lecture. Impressed by the brilliance of this scholarly woman, she elected a second course taught by her that dealt with the Middle Ages, studied Anglo-Saxon under her tutelage, and in her senior year asked McKeehan to direct her master's thesis, "Profane and Divine Love in English Literature of the Thirteenth Century." Well written and carefully researched, though lacking some of the brilliance and vitality of her non-academic prose, the thesis enabled her to earn a master's degree along with her bachelor's degree. In view of the fact that Stafford would be twice divorced, it is interesting to note that in discussing an early homily about marriage in her thesis, she observes that its author "warns against the anxieties and vexations of love on earth and especially the trials of married life," pointing out that if one marries an earthly lover rather than Christ, "the child screams, the cake burns, the surly husband scolds." Only the bride of God leads "a most blissful and beautiful life."[57]

Although she did not participate in many of the social activities on campus, Stafford did become a member of a group of intellectuals known as the "barbarians" because they did not belong to sororities or fraternities. Occasionally they attended a meeting of the Young Communist League on campus, and several evenings each week they would meet in an overheated sandwich and beer restaurant to drink the watered-down beer that was legal during Prohibition and to discuss the writers they had just discovered: Plutarch, Joyce, Pound, Eliot, Veblen, Dostoevsky, Kafka, Whitehead, Plato, and Donne. One member of this group, a former Marine named Joe Chay who was somewhat older than the rest, had acquired an unexpurgated copy of *Lady Chatterley's Lover* that he rented out for a dollar and a half per day to fellow students. "How we in the Mermaid Tavern excoriated those poor plebeian boobs who paid our friend only to read the dirty words and never took in the genius of D. H. Lawrence!" Stafford recalled.[58] Fifty years later, in a letter she sent to a relative of Joe Chay's, she lamented that although she had been infatuated with Joe, he had largely chosen to ignore her. "How could Joe Chay have been so cold-hearted?" she wrote. "All I wanted in the world was to cook his meals and wash his clothes and speak only when he spoke to me!"[59]

Whereas Stafford's association with the group of campus intellectuals had a positive influence on her own intellectual development, her friendship with another group of students proved to have disastrous consequences for her. During her sophomore year she befriended a student from Iowa named Lucy McKee, who had transferred to the University of Colorado from Northwestern. Affluent, sophisticated, well dressed, and popular, Lucy appeared to Jean Stafford to have everything she herself lacked. Lucy owned a car, and she had recently spent a summer traveling in Europe. In the diary Lucy kept during her trip, she described visits to museums, rendezvous with members of the Yale Glee Club, dinner dates with dashing Europeans, and shipboard romances. "Rubens can curl up and die!" she exclaimed about the Rubens paintings she had seen in an Amsterdam museum.[60] Although Stafford might have disapproved of Lucy's inelegant prose or her philistine remarks about a European master, she nevertheless was drawn to this clever and rather unconventional young woman. It is not clear how much Stafford knew of Lucy's somewhat sordid past when she first met her. Before Lucy left Iowa to attend Northwestern, her fifteen-year-old brother had died of what was described as an "accidental" gunshot wound. At Northwestern, Lucy quickly acquired the reputation of being sexually available and was finally expelled during her sophomore year after she contracted a venereal disease.[61] With such a history, it is surprising that she was admitted to the University of Colorado, but in Boulder she proved to be an extremely able student, though she spent a good deal of time going to or giving parties where a large quantity of alcohol was consumed.

Soon after Stafford met Lucy McKee, Lucy entered the law school and married a fellow student named Andrew Cooke. The young couple rented a house on the edge of town and frequently invited their many friends to parties there. During her junior year, Stafford moved into a room in the Cookes' house and attended many of their raucous parties in the house as well as in an abandoned cabin in the mountains. Soon rumors began to circulate about these wild gatherings. It was alleged that at parties the guests administered whiskey enemas to one another and that they regularly hypnotized willing subjects.[62] Jean Stafford herself was one of their willing subjects; often, in the presence of her guests, Lucy would "hypnotize" Jean and then run a needle through the fleshy part of Jean's hand between the index finger and the thumb, during which procedure Jean did not dare to wince or show any signs of discomfort. She later admitted, however, that she had felt acute pain during these sessions. Alcohol was always available at the Cookes'—and the consumption of alcohol was something Stafford had begun to enjoy. On occasion, she had arrived home drunk in the past; now, while living with the Cookes, she neither had to purchase liquor with her own hard-earned money nor did she have to risk incurring the wrath of her father if she overindulged.

During the summer of 1935 Lucy developed ovarian cysts and underwent surgery to remove them. For several months prior to the operation, she had been very moody and, feeling confined by her marriage, had suggested to her husband that they both should have extramarital affairs. According to Andrew Cooke, his wife had also hinted that she was interested in the possibility of having a lesbian relationship with Jean, and she told him that she wanted to travel in Europe with Jean after she herself graduated from law school. However, even though both Andrew and Jean perceived that Lucy appeared troubled, neither was terribly alarmed by her behavior.[63] Then, in November 1935, the tragic event occurred that would have a lasting effect on Jean Stafford. Returning from Denver, where she had gone for a medical checkup, Lucy began to argue with her husband as Jean looked on. When Andrew suggested that both he and Lucy ought to be a bit more conventional in their behavior, Lucy threw the contents of the glass she was holding in his face, ran to their bedroom, and grabbed a small pistol she used to shoot at empty beer bottles. Running out of the bedroom, she then shot herself in the left temple as both Andrew and Jean looked on in horror and disbelief. Lucy did not die immediately. Jean was able to control her own emotions sufficiently to call a local physician, and, according to a newspaper account, two physicians arrived at the Cookes' house a few minutes after the shooting just as the distraught Andrew, compounding the horror, grabbed Lucy's gun and threatened to kill himself. As a precautionary measure, he was taken into custody.[64] An ambulance soon arrived, but the situation was hopeless. Jean Stafford was later notified that her friend had died on the operating table.

The stuff of melodrama or soap opera, this horrifying incident was one that haunted her for the rest of her life. When she attempted to write about it later in *In the Snowfall,* she discovered that she was too emotionally bound up with those events to write about them directly.[65] It is clear, however, that Lucy McKee served as the model for both Maisie Perrine in the unpublished *In the Snowfall* and for the troubled Hopestill Mather in Stafford's first novel, *Boston Adventure.* Hopestill Mather, a spoiled, rich, unconventional young woman, does not commit suicide, as Lucy McKee did, but when she becomes pregnant, she recklessly continues to ride horses and as a consequence has a miscarriage that results in her death. The funeral of Hopestill Mather takes place in a cemetery very much like Green Mountain Cemetery in Boulder, where Stafford numbly witnessed her friend's funeral on November 12, 1935.

It is amazing that Jean Stafford did not break down completely after these harrowing events not only had deprived her of a close friend but also had caused her to achieve the kind of notoriety that would have been difficult for the most stable and secure individual to tolerate. Several people hinted that Lucy committed suicide because she was jealous of Jean's close relationship with Andrew Cooke, while others speculated that she had been worried about her health or that she had been working too hard. Stafford continued to feel so guilty about Lucy's death that she wrote to a friend several years later, "I killed Lucy McKee."[66] In the prospectus for *In the Snowfall,* however, she writes that Maisie Perrine, Lucy's fictional counterpart, killed herself because she feared she had been born "without the talent to love and to lose herself." Maintaining that Maisie's motives could never be understood completely, Stafford described her suicide as symptomatic of the malaise of a whole generation. She concluded that rather than seeming like a shocking tragedy, Maisie's death was "only a dismal petering out, a final, trifling impudence."[67]

Unable to face the gossip about their daughter's involvement in this scandalous event, Ethel and John Stafford left Boulder soon after the suicide and moved to Oregon, where Dick Stafford was then employed. Jean Stafford, however, was fortunate to find surrogate parents in an English professor named Paul Thompson and his wife Dorothy. Hearing that Stafford had fainted while posing for an art class because she had not eaten any breakfast, Dorothy Thompson extended an invitation to the lonely young woman, who was then living in a rented room. Breakfast with the Thompsons became a daily routine for her, and on Sundays she would come for breakfast and stay all day. The Thompsons admired her talent for mimicry and her way of telling amusing anecdotes about her own mishaps or the foibles of others. "She was one of the funniest people I ever knew," Paul Thompson observed.[68] Even after she left Boulder, Stafford remained close to "Mama Dorothy" and "Daddy Paul." She visited them whenever she came to Boulder, saw them when they came east, and telephoned them when she was troubled or lonely. During the last years of Stafford's life, it was the Thompsons who were instrumental in making arrangements for Stafford's papers to be housed in the Norlin Library at the University of Colorado in Boulder.

After Lucy McKee's death, Jean Stafford also sought the help of a Catholic priest named Father Agatho. Very soon after they had settled in Boulder, Stafford's parents had stopped attending church. For a while the children continued to go to Sunday school at the United Presbyterian Church, but religious observance was a matter of habit rather than conviction. Later, through her study of medieval literature in college, Stafford became interested in mysticism; but it was Lucy McKee's suicide that finally led her to Father Agatho at the Sacred Heart Church for instruction in Catholicism. She subsequently wrote to her friend Joe Chay about these sessions with Father Agatho: "They did not, I'm sorry to say, have the result they should have, not through any fault of Father Agatho's but through my own indolence, and it was seven years later that I was confirmed."[69] Her observations about a priest named Father Agatho in *In the Snowfall,* however, are far from charitable. Although Stafford's protagonist does get baptized by the Catholic priest, she discovers that despite her great need she is incapable of believing in the Blessed Sacrament or the Real Presence of Christ. After she is baptized, she thinks, "Thank God, now I am a Catholic and I no longer have to put up with Father Agatho's banalities."[70]

One additional relationship that was important to Stafford during her senior year in college was a short-lived love affair with a pre-med student named Lawrence McCarty Fairchild. She was engaged to be married to him for a brief time, but they soon parted company. She later told her friend Robert Berueffy that Fairchild broke the engagement because he felt that a wife who had graduated from a prestigious school in the East, such as Vassar or Bryn Mawr, would be better able to help him further his career as a physician than a poor young woman from Boulder could.[71] Stafford's comments about Fairchild suggest that she soon realized he was hardly the soulmate she was seeking; nevertheless, she was distressed that her lack of the "proper" credentials had caused him to terminate their engagement.

Despite all her personal turmoil during her college years, Stafford not only succeeded in completing the requirements for her bachelor's degree but for her master's during the four years she attended the University of Colorado. In addition, she wrote a one-act play that was awarded first prize in a campus contest. The play, *Tomorrow in Vienna,* was performed at the university on April 16 and 17 of 1936. In it she depicted the dying composer Ludwig Van Beethoven; his nephew Carl, a sullen youth of nineteen or twenty; and a motherly, well-fed housekeeper named Frau Weber. Unmistakable echoes of Jean Stafford's own family drama are evident in this play, which is seemingly based on a historical incident, for Stafford uses very similar words to describe Beethoven that she used in her fiction to describe her own father. Beethoven, a brilliant man with "no clothes, no money, no friends," is described by his nephew as having a tongue with "a wicked sting to it." Frau Weber, who resembles Ethel Stafford in appearance and temperament, dreams pleasantly of cups of coffee and apple strudel as the greatest musician of all time lies dying. It is she, however, who defends the "wicked" genius, reminding her sullen nephew that his uncle loved him dearly and that he ought to appreciate what a really great thing it was to be loved by such a man. The nephew articulates Stafford's own feelings of guilt for failing to love her father sufficiently. "Priests, doctors, women, fools, do you know what music means? Have you ever heard it?" the nephew says at the end of the play, exonerating the dying genius from committing sins to humanity because, despite his human shortcomings, he has created in his music something divine.[72] What is suggested by this play is how preoccupied Stafford still was with thoughts of her parents and the divided legacy they were handing down to her. In the prospectus for *In the Snowfall,* Stafford later wrote about her persona Joyce that in college she hated her father and was embarrassed by his assumption that the same close relationship existed between them as it had when Joyce was a little girl. However, the play Jean Stafford wrote during her senior year suggests that she still found it easier to forgive her irresponsible, intellectual father than her bourgeois mother, who was unavoidably concerned with more mundane matters.

On June 17, 1936, an article about Jean Stafford appeared in the *Boulder Daily Camera* announcing the fact that she had graduated cum laude and that she was the only member of her class to obtain both a bachelor of arts and a master of arts at the same commencement.[73] Stafford's parents and her sisters attended the commencement exercises, but her favorite sibling, Dick, who was then an assistant forest ranger in Republic, Washington, did not come to the graduation. No doubt Stafford was disappointed by her brother's absence. She was probably also disappointed that, despite her high grades, she had failed to be elected to Phi Beta Kappa. According to Robert Berueffy, whose mother was then a member of the History Department at the university, though Stafford's high grade point average qualified her for Phi Beta Kappa, she was not elected because of her alleged "immoral" conduct, a term that was then used to describe women who were sexually active or who drank and smoked. Her connection with Lucy McKee might have also been held against her. A real irony was the fact that it was her mentor, Irene P. McKeehan, who had opposed her election to Phi Beta Kappa.[74] If Stafford had known this, she might not have chosen to pay tribute to her former professor in an essay entitled "Miss McKeehan's Pocketbook," published several years before her own death.

Twelve years after her graduation from the University of Colorado, Stafford wrote to Joe Chay about Lucy McKee: "I should rather suffer a mortal illness than ever go back to Boulder again. I daresay I have been unhappy all my life, and I was never so wretched before I knew that awful girl and her terrifying modus vivendi and her limp entourage."[75] Thanks to a fellowship she had won to study in Heidelberg, she was finally able to leave Boulder, where she had been humiliated by her poverty, isolated from most of her peers, and nearly destroyed emotionally by the tragic death of a friend. Many years later Mary Elizabeth O'Rourke, a Boulder acquaintance, sent Stafford a portrait she had drawn of Jean when Jean had posed in Mr. Trucksess's art class. "It recalls to me my severity and solemnity," Stafford wrote in reply.[76] The years in Boulder had often been painful ones for her. However, it was in Boulder that her identity as an intellectual had been established, and there she had also begun to think seriously about becoming a writer. Perhaps most important of all, she had stored up impressions and memories of life in this small town in the West that would serve as the raw material for some of her finest writing.

Three

Old Flaming Youth
1936–1938

. . . I could not wait to quit my tamed-down native grounds. As soon as I could, I hotfooted it across the Rocky Mountains and across the Atlantic Ocean.

—JEAN STAFFORD, "AUTHOR'S NOTE," *THE COLLECTED STORIES OF JEAN STAFFORD*

AS THEY DRANK watered-down beer in a shabby, overheated establishment on the edge of campus, Jean Stafford and her friends would speak enviously of expatriate writers like Hemingway and Pound who had fled their own Main Streets to the broad boulevards and quaint cafés of Paris. "Landlocked, penniless, ragtag and bobtail, we planned splendid odysseys. Europe was to us the land of opportunity, and more than that, it was the world, not this halfway house in which we dawdled, where the only glory and the only grandeur were what we read about," she later wrote.[1]

One day a notice appeared on a bulletin board at the University of Colorado announcing that the famed University of Heidelberg was offering fellowships to American students. Jean Stafford and a friend of hers named James Robert Hightower, a pre-med student with literary interests, decided to apply. Her intention was to study *Beowulf* under the University of Heidelberg's renowned Anglo-Saxon scholar, Professor Johannes Hoops, in preparation for enrolling in a graduate program in philology when she returned to the United States.

By 1936 American educators already had begun to denounce the Nazification of German universities, and even a small-town newspaper like the *Boulder Daily Camera* was featuring accounts of the ways in which the civil rights of Jews and other minorities were being stripped by the German government. However, as Stafford later admitted, she was so uninformed politically at the age of twenty-one that she didn't "rightly know who Hitler was or what he had in mind." Much to her delight, the German government offered her a fellowship to study at the University of Heidelberg. During the remainder of her senior year she earned as much money as she could by doing housework for the woman from whom she was renting a room, by typing theses for graduate students, and by ghostwriting term papers. She also borrowed some money from the parents of Lucy McKee to finance her trip to Europe.[2]

After graduation Stafford spent several weeks at the ranch of her sister Mary Lee and her brother-in-law Harry in Hayden, Colorado, but returned to Boulder in time for its annual Writer's Conference. Established in 1930 as a modest regional undertaking, the Boulder Writer's Conference had begun to attract participants from all over the country, in part because Professor Edward Davison, a poet who was in charge of organizing the two-week conference each August, was successful in recruiting such luminaries as Robert Frost, Thomas Wolfe, and Sherwood Anderson to give lectures and conduct writing workshops. That summer, eager to impress the visiting lecturers with the talent of one of the university's best students, Davison suggested to Stafford that she show her poetry and fiction to Martha Foley, an editor of Story Press, who was one of the conference leaders. Before the conference ended, Stafford gave Foley several chapters of the autobiographical novel on which she had been working, *Which No Vicissitude,* a fictional account of the suicide of Lucy McKee, and she sent the remainder of the manuscript to Foley when she was about to sail to Europe. "I am leaving Friday for New York and shall be eager to see you again and hear your criticism of my work. I hope you will not be revolted at the sloppiness of each and every page," she wrote.[3]

Early in September Stafford boarded a ship bound for Europe, where she expected to be met by her friend Hightower and another friend, Robert Berueffy, who had preceded her. "The boat was pretty nice but I got mighty sick of seeing nothing but ocean day after day," she wrote to Andrew Cooke.[4] She said she had enjoyed the novelty of being on a ship and the plentiful beer on board, but nevertheless she was relieved when the ship docked. Much to her chagrin, however, Hightower and Berueffy were nowhere in sight. Instead, a letter from Hightower awaited her with detailed instructions about how she was to proceed to Heidelberg on her own. Still in Schweidnitz, Hightower told her that he was planning to meet her in Heidelberg and would leave his address at the university. In addition, he said,

I plan to get a room where we both can stay for a week or so until we find a permanent dwelling. But we hafta have headquarters for the immediate future. By the way, you are my 1/2 Schwester. Berueffy is still in Bruxelles. He will probably come later. I will explain everything in detail when you arrive; that includes bitching about leaving this place where I eat 4x a day and sleep free and hear Bach in the evening and read German lit and sit on my ass all I want, but I'll be there. Don't get panicky; this is just the prelude to bigger and better things. We have made an awkward beginning, but at least we are all here.[5]

In writing this letter, Hightower probably wanted to allay the fears of his easily agitated friend Jean, who knew no German and would have to travel to Heidelberg alone.

Hightower's assumption that Stafford would not be pleased about having to make her way to Heidelberg on her own proved to be correct. "When I got to Hamburg I was really the most wretched of human beings," she wrote to Andrew Cooke. "I had packed my dictionary and couldn't make them understand that all I wanted to know was when the next train left for Heidelberg."[6] She reported to her sister Mary Lee that she had traveled all night in a third-class compartment crowded with people who ate garlic sandwiches and looked as though they wanted to stab her. After a night of sitting bolt upright on a wooden seat in the train, she arrived in Heidelberg early in the morning during a downpour.[7]

Heidelberg, situated on both sides of the Neckar River and full of old-world charm, appeared very beautiful and picturesque to Stafford. In a *New Yorker* article she wrote after she paid a second visit to Heidelberg in 1949, she described her first impressions of its Gothic buildings and winding streets. Though Heidelberg, like Boulder, was a university town, it was very different from the small town in the Rockies. She admired the houses and gardens and the vineyards on the tree-covered hills that rose from the wide banks of the Neckar River, and was enchanted by the "well-groomed paths through fairy-tale woods" that were traveled by "stalwart boys in 'Lederhosen,' by companies of healthy, ugly little pigtailed girls, with their ears pierced and their front teeth gone, eating green pears and bedevilling everyone they met, and by solitary gentlemen of academic mien." Barges and sightseeing steamers floated by on the Neckar River, beyond whose banks were squares of golden wheat fields and lavender cabbage patches tended by the Benedictine monks from the abbey of Stift Neuberg. Most picturesque of all was an enormous decaying castle built early in the thirteenth century as the residence for the electors of the Palatinate.[8]

For the first month of her stay in Heidelberg, Stafford rented a room from an elementary school teacher named Fraulein Ströck, who did not speak English. Since there was no bathtub in the house and no hot water, she bathed at a hotel about a mile away, and in the absence of central heating or a fireplace in her room, she shivered during the cold and damp month of October. "I am at the moment slowly congealing in beautiful Heidelberg," she wrote to Andrew

Cooke in a letter that reveals her characteristic use of irony and hyperbole. "It rains here 24 hrs. a day and they say this will keep up till April when it becomes quite pleasant. It will be nice to have warm spring winds blowing over my grave. Alas I have developed a monstrous cold which I will never get rid of in this monstrous climate where the air is thick as dough."[9]

In addition to complaining about the weather and the lack of conveniences, she also spoke critically of the academic life at the University of Heidelberg, where students apparently attended only two or three lectures and then spent the rest of the year drinking beer, until the summer vacation, during which they studied for their exams. She observed that among the many foreign students at the university there were more "incipient student princes than sages," and she said that nothing was done to humanize the large lecture classes where there was absolutely no give-and-take between the professor and the students.[10] But if she was critical of her fellow students, she soon followed their example: during her stay in Heidelberg she learned only a smattering of German in the language course required for foreign students. Moreover, she herself spent little time attending other classes while she was in Heidelberg. Even the famous Professor Hoops proved to be a disappointment. At first he seemed to be delighted to have her in his class in Anglo-Saxon, but after she failed to show up at a gathering he had arranged at his house for his students, he took little notice of her.[11]

In November she moved to a cheaper but more comfortable room with running water and central heating at the Hotel Haarlass. Located in a little village about a mile and a half up the Neckar River, the hotel got its name from the fact that long before it had become a hotel, it had been the place where postulants from the nearby abbey were tonsured.[12] Her friend Hightower also rented a room at the Haarlass, and for a brief time in February their friend Robert Berueffy, who had been living in Brussels and composing music, joined them there as well.

At the time that Stafford had become acquainted with Hightower in Boulder, she had been engaged to Lawrence Fairchild and Hightower had been in love with a Japanese student. In Heidelberg, too, though Stafford and Hightower were together much of the time, they did not become romantically involved with one another. The following year she confessed to Hightower that she had "scorned the Dante-Beatrice asexualism" but had not encouraged him to make love to her for reasons she herself could not fully fathom.[13] Nevertheless, during the time they were in Heidelberg together, they very much enjoyed one another's company. They spent hours each day reading one another's fiction and poetry or taking turns reading portions of *Ulysses* aloud, smoking many thin German cigarettes, and drinking large quantities of cheap red wine. After she returned to America Stafford fondly reminisced about the evenings she had sat in Hightower's room at the Hotel Haarlass beneath portraits of Joyce, Hemingway, and Lawrence that he had tacked above his desk. On his bedside table were a copy of Pound's cantos, dictionaries and grammars, and a volume of Blake's poems, she recalled. One day, as she and Hightower were "moseying through Woolworth's on the Haupstrasse," they saw a Japanese student fruitlessly trying to explain to a clerk what he wanted. Hightower, who knew some Japanese, introduced himself to the young man, and subsequently Herr Hai, Hightower, and Stafford arranged to meet once or twice a week to read *Ulysses* together, comparing texts in English, German, and Japanese. "Somehow the snap went all out of Joyce's puns when we tried them on in German and Japanese," she later observed.[14]

Stafford would have preferred to ignore the ominous political situation in Germany during her stay there, but she was increasingly aware of the new regulations the Nazi regime was introducing. Most of the professors at the University of Heidelberg were Brownshirts, and before and after each lecture students were required to give the full Nazi salute and to proclaim "Heil Hitler!"[15] One of her professors, a youthful "*Sturmabteilungsmann,*" asserted that all Shakespeare's history plays had supported the kind of nationalism that the Nazis in Germany were advocating.[16] In accordance with the recently declared policy of "cannons instead of butter," butter and margarine were rationed, as were potatoes, and fruit was virtually impossible to find or so expensive they could not afford it.[17] Jews were no longer permitted to teach in the university, and everywhere huge signs were posted that said, "Die Juden sind unsere Unglück!"[18] Encouraged by the official Nazi policies, the citizens of Heidelberg openly expressed their hostility to the Jews in the town. Once, when she, Hightower, and Berueffy were in a bakery, the proprietor refused to wait on a Jewish customer. The brutality of the Nazi regime was dramatically demonstrated to them when they witnessed a young Frenchman who was also staying at the Hotel Haarlass being arrested by Nazi storm troopers and being led away. Soon the guests at the hotel learned that he had been shot as a spy.[19]

According to her friend Robert Berueffy, wherever Stafford went in Heidelberg, she attracted a good deal of attention. The Nazi regime advocated that German women dress plainly, wear sensible oxfords, and avoid the use of makeup. Women using makeup were thought to be prostitutes, and Stafford, who liberally applied rouge and lipstick and wore high-heeled shoes, was often stared at by the hausfraus leaning out of their windows as she walked into town and by the Brownshirts drinking beer in the pubs. Once a group of boisterous Brownshirts in a beer hall began to pull at her clothing, and only with considerable difficulty were she, Hightower, and Berueffy able to leave the tavern without being physically assaulted.[20] In 1960, recalling her sojourn in Heidelberg, Stafford admitted ruefully that, even though she soon began to be critical of the Nazis, she had found their antics rather amusing at first.[21] When a group of storm troopers in the Roter Ochsen pub asked her to join them, she insisted drunkenly, much to Hightower's disgust, that she wanted to link arms with them and sing "Gaudeamus Igitur."[22]

Stafford would later think back with nostalgia to the months she had spent in Heidelberg. However, Robert Berueffy recalled that during this period she was often depressed. As she had done in Boulder, she continued to smoke constantly and to consume excessive quantities of alcohol, on one occasion imbibing so much red wine that she became acutely ill. Alarmed by her continuous retching, Hightower and Berueffy first gave her a sedative, and when that failed to help, called an ambulance, which took her to a local hospital. After a handsome blond German physician had given her an injection to stop her retching, she looked up at him and said, "God, what a beautiful man. He must be Woden or Thor himself. I never want to leave here. I just want to look at that man." On another occasion she tried to talk Berueffy into making a joint suicide pact with her, and though he suspected that she might have done this to see what his reaction would be so that she could then write about it, he was somewhat alarmed by her logical explanation of why suicide was "the best way out" for both of them.[23]

On the whole, however, Stafford's experience in Germany was a positive one for her. She enjoyed exploring the quaint town and surrounding countryside as well as several other cities in Germany and elsewhere. Sixteen years later she would write about the Christmas Eve she had spent in Freiburg: ". . . entirely unacquainted with the town, I went out for a walk in a warm and rapid snowfall; the shops were shuttered and the curtains in all the houses were drawn; I was alone in the streets except for a policeman and his . . . dog; abruptly, as I took a turning, I came upon the small and exquisite cathedral within which someone was playing the organ, practicing for midnight mass."[24]

One of her many adventures that year was a trip to Rome that she managed to take without having to spend any money for her train fare. When an Italian businessman offered to take her to Rome with him, she agreed to accompany him but insisted that he buy her a round-trip ticket. After she returned from Rome, she told Berueffy and Hightower that she had not permitted her would-be Italian suitor to make any advances toward her during the trip to Rome, and she maintained that as soon as the train had reached the station, she had jumped off and disappeared into the crowd.[25]

Although Stafford never succeeded in perfecting her German in Heidelberg or in completing any course work, she did spend several hours each day diligently working at her writing. One day Berueffy found her sitting in her room, pencil and paper in hand, staring at the door. She explained that she had set herself the task that day of writing one thousand words describing the door knob.[26] Each day in her journal she would record her reactions to Germany, and though her journal was never published, as she hoped it would be, several people, including the influential scholar Howard Mumford Jones, were very favorably impressed by her vivid descriptions of Germany during this historically significant period. She would later allude to her *Wanderjahr* in several articles, and she would also use Heidelberg as the setting for a number of short stories, including "The Cavalier," "The Echo and the Nemesis," and "My Blithe, Sad Bird," as well as for her novella *A Winter's Tale*.

At the end of January, as Stafford was beginning to consider leaving Heidelberg for good, she received a letter from Martha Foley about *Which No Vicissitude*. Having read the manuscript and having also shown it to the other editor of Story Press, Whit Burnett, Foley wrote:

> It is with reluctance that we . . . let it go back to you but it is a little inchoate in places and Whit and I feel that it would be better for you to put this aside and go on with other books. We feel too that parts of it parallel a little closely Joyce and Boyle but that there is enough of your own splendid writing in it to show that you will be doing very important work. And we look forward with definite interest to seeing what you write next.[27]

Stafford must have been disappointed that her manuscript had been rejected but elated that Foley had praised the "splendid writing" in it. Her reply reveals that she tried to follow Foley's suggestions. Mentioning that she had begun a new novel and hoped to have the first draft completed by July, she said, "I'm trying to purge my writing as much as possible of Joyce. Strangely enough, I have never read Kay Boyle, but I'm trying to get something at once to see what the similarity is. For the time being I'm not reading anything but Shakespeare, the newspapers, and the dictionary. It's not safe—I'm too much a chameleon." Thanking Foley for the encouragement she had given her, she said that had it not been for the Boulder Writer's Conference, she would probably never have typed out the manuscript, nor written anything else except perhaps a doctoral dissertation. Writing, she added, "is about five hundred times harder work than studying what's already been written." She mentioned that she was keeping very full notes of her experiences abroad but concluded somewhat melodramatically, "In fact, I probably won't get out of this country alive."[28]

The new novel to which Stafford referred was one she later called *Autumn Festival*. In it she describes the experiences of a somewhat naive young American named Gretchen Marburg, who goes to Germany to study at a time when Nazism is on the rise. Her protagonist at first is very much stirred by the nationalistic fervor of the Germans and is indifferent to the plight of the Jews. However, by the end of the novel, following the disappearance of a Jewish friend and the death in Spain of a German pilot to whom she has become engaged, Gretchen Marburg begins to comprehend some of the more sinister implications of the Nazi regime. Although this novel was never published, Stafford later incorporated some of its subject matter into *A Winter's Tale,* and Gretchen Marburg became Sonia Marburg, the protagonist of Stafford's first published novel, *Boston Adventure*.

Before leaving Heidelberg, Jean Stafford wrote to her thesis advisor at the University of Colorado, Irene P. McKeehan, asking McKeehan to recommend her for a graduate fellowship at Radcliffe College. Since she had worked so closely with McKeehan and was one of her most able students, she was abashed when McKeehan refused to sponsor her because she believed she did not have the makings of a scholar. "Why don't you get married?" McKeehan replied. "Or, better, why don't you write?" Stafford later described how disheartened she had been to learn that McKeehan did not think she had what it took to publish learned articles in *PMLA* or *Speculum*. Furthermore, she observed, "Nobody had ever asked my hand in marriage and I doubted that anybody ever would. And I didn't know how to write—not 'really' write and thereby earn my living."[29] Nevertheless, despite McKeehan's lack of support, she did send an application to Radcliffe; even though graduate school seemed somewhat unappealing, it appeared to be a more prudent alternative than trying to earn her living as a writer.

Early in the spring of 1937, Hightower and Berueffy decided to leave Heidelberg and find a place to live in Paris. Very soon after her two closest friends in Heidelberg departed, Stafford too made the decision to leave Heidelberg. She informed them that she planned to return to America before the academic year was over to begin looking for a way to support herself so that she could pay back the money she had borrowed from the McKees. "Mrs. McKee says I'd jolly well better get a job for next year and I've gotta go back to Am.," she wrote.[30] Although subsequently, in her application for a Guggenheim Fellowship, she stated that she had studied medieval literature and philology at the University of Heidelberg from September 1936 until June 1937, in actuality she had attended few classes during her stay in Heidelberg. By April 5, 1937, she had left Heidelberg to join Hightower and Berueffy in Paris before returning to America.

After making brief stops en route in Munich and Rome, she appeared late one night at her friends' apartment. Hearing a knock at the door, Robert Berueffy looked out the window and saw his friend Jean standing there with six or eight French soldiers. She explained that when she had shown the soldiers a slip of paper with her friends' address, the soldiers had insisted on delivering her there in person. "She seemed to have a way of gathering up men, even though she spoke not a word of French," Berueffy observed.[31]

A year after she returned to the United States, Stafford would reminisce fondly about the days she had spent with her friends in Paris. Writing in a style that imitated Hemingway's, she told them: "When I think of Paris I go soft in the stomach and want to cry and I think how lonely all three of us are. We aren't geniuses, we used to say. But for a while for a few days in Paris we were happy. Oh, very happy in Paris, and full of literature and music, and sometimes laughing hard, getting very drunk and reeling in the rain at midnight. We were very happy. We were like a family in a way, loving each other and laughing very hard and sometimes drunk."[32]

Jean Stafford's *Wanderjahr* enabled her to flee temporarily from her real family and her unhappy past, to fill her notebooks with interesting material, and to experience a sense of kinship with those expatriate American writers whose work she admired. Perhaps most important of all, she now imagined herself to be very different indeed from the many young women in Boulder who had never succeeded in escaping from that provincial university town.

On April 9, after bidding a reluctant farewell to Hightower and Berueffy at the Gare du Nord, she took a ferry across the channel to London. Once again, as she had done earlier, she succeeded in finding a male to pay some of her expenses. She explained to her friends in Paris afterwards that she had had no qualms about taking advantage of a Hungarian "gent" who had treated her to two meals because he had an income of thirty dollars a week while she was virtually penniless. Before she left London for Southampton, where she was to board a ship bound for New York, she went to see the changing of the guards at Buckingham Palace, a sight she said she much preferred to watching the Nazi troops parade. By April 11 she was on her way home. In a letter she wrote to Hightower and Berueffy when she was aboard the Hamburg-American ocean liner, she said, "The jolting is partly due to the Atlantic Ocean and partly to me being very unhappy about being one day closer to New York." Even though many of her memories of Heidelberg were pleasant ones, the great number of German Jews on board were a vivid reminder of the Brownshirts, the Hitler Jugend, and the anti-Semitic acts that she had witnessed during her sojourn there.[33]

When she arrived in New York, Stafford stayed with Donald and Dorothy Hays, friends of hers from Boulder who were then living in Brooklyn Heights. She intended first to try to get a job in New York, and if that plan failed, to retreat to her sister and brother-in-law's ranch to write. Distraught about her lack of funds, she immediately contacted Edward Davison in Boulder and asked him if he could suggest how she might find a job in New York. Evidently she described her plight in such dramatic terms in her letter that he promptly sent the following telegram to his wife Natalie, who was visiting relatives in Manhattan:

> Jean Stafford penniless and probably starving at nine Willow Street Brooklyn Feed and finance her and interest Collins Wittenbergs Martha and as many others as possible.[34]

Natalie Davison immediately came to Jean Stafford's aid. She gave her husband's protégé the name of an influential person at *Harper's* to contact, and she tried through someone she knew to get Jean Stafford a job at the Museum of Modern Art.

In the letters Jean Stafford sent to Hightower and Berueffy from the Hays's Brooklyn apartment, she complained about her hosts, to whom she referred as "the Babbitts." Comparing them to her two friends in Paris, she said she missed Hightower and Berueffy dreadfully. Nevertheless, she was enjoying New York City, finding it exciting and glamorous. She reported that soon after her arrival, she had had lunch with Martha Foley and Whit Burnett, who praised her writing; had attended a performance of *Candida,* starring Katherine Cornell; and had been present at a rally at which Thomas Mann, one of her favorite writers, had tried to persuade people in the audience to go and fight the fascists in Spain.[35]

Although Stafford's lack of funds was a constant source of worry to her, she found with each passing day that she was more and more convinced she wanted to be a writer. She reported to Hightower and Berueffy that Edward Davison had invited her to come to the Boulder Writer's Conference in August and had offered to give her a scholarship to pay for her living expenses; that Radcliffe had turned down her application for a graduate fellowship, saying "*frightfully* sorry, Miss S., we just have such a lot of trouble making both ends meet in our poverty stricken little billion dollar university"; that her sister Mary Lee was urging her to come and live on the ranch in Hayden; and that her parents were living "on optimism" in Portland with her brother, who was almost penniless himself. As was usually the case when she referred to her parents, she dwelled on their shortcomings, deriding her mother for sewing unwearable garments and her father for ranting about Roosevelt, her mother, and "all the ape-stage men, sonsofbitches, scoundrel-minded defeatists, intellectuals, blatherskites, piss-ants, and the brain trust." Remembering her unhappy past in Boulder and contemplating her uncertain future, she wrote: "I at last can imagine myself as nothing but a writer, and I consider with stark horror how I might have married Larry, how Harvard might have given me a fellowship, how I might have had an assistantship at C.U., how Hoops might have read my thesis—what might have happened if I had never known you." She said that her future success as a writer was dependent, at least in part, on being reunited with Hightower and Berueffy. "All we needed were two worn out tables, half a dozen Berliners, and we turned out masterpieces," she wrote.[36]

Just as Stafford was beginning to come to terms with being back in the United States, a new crisis arose: she developed acute abdominal pain and a fever. Alarmed, she consulted with Natalie Davison, who tried to lend her some money, and then she "crawled back to Brooklyn." When her temperature reached 103 degrees, Don and Dorothy Hays insisted on calling in a physician, and after he had examined her, he arranged to have her admitted to a nearby hospital. During a hospital stay of close to three weeks, she was subjected to all sorts of unpleasant diagnostic procedures to determine whether she had kidney disease, a malfunctioning gallbladder, tuberculosis, dysentery, ulcers, malnutrition, or a toxic reaction to alcohol. Unwilling to summon her family and without any other intimates to turn to, she resorted to writing detailed descriptions of her symptoms and the procedures she had undergone to Hightower and Berueffy. For a brief time she was transferred to a hospital in Manhattan, but she soon returned to the ward in the first hospital, which was located in Brooklyn. In her letters to her friends in Paris, she complained about interns who called her by her first name and leered when they said the word *vagina;* about the inedible food; and above all, about the failure of her doctors to find out what was wrong with her.[37] Worried and depressed but still able to maintain her sense of humor, she quipped to Natalie Davison, "Ten years from now the tabloids will issue an extra with a full length photograph of me emerging from The Brooklyn Hospital. Plucky little Jean Stafford after 10 yrs. of constipation."[38] She was relieved that her stay in a hospital charity ward wasn't costing her any money, but she was distressed by the constant wails and moans of the two other patients in her room, ancient women who were "mere skeletons." Even more distressing was witnessing a patient being treated with leeches and watching the steady procession of corpses being wheeled by from another ward. One night, after a priest had administered extreme unction to another patient in her room, a ceremony that Stafford found gruesome, the woman died "in a pool of blood and her breathing sounded like a saw." Much to her disgust, a Catholic priest also came to her own bedside one day. "They had a priest in here yesterday to confess me and I was so revolted by his sordid Brooklyn accent and his filthy cheap-piety that I swore I shd. never set foot inside a chapel again," she reported to Hightower and Berueffy.[39]

Ill, lonely, and often too depressed by her experience in the hospital ward to so much as reread the unfinished manuscripts she had brought with her, she resolved to take better care of herself if and when she was ever released. "I just decided that the reason it's bad to have a body like mine is that your brain goes to pot," she wrote to her friends. "The artist simply can't have gut complaints, though Dante did. I wonder if Vaughan was constipated. I bet Raleigh was as regular as Leopold Bloom." She was envious of Hightower and Berueffy when a letter arrived from them describing a visit they had paid to James Joyce in Paris. Hightower confessed they had been "scared to death" when they simply showed up unannounced at Joyce's Paris apartment, and though he admitted that Joyce had not invited them back, he said triumphantly that Joyce had spent two hours talking to them. Remembering how happy she herself had been in Paris, she wrote:

> Having had to be conscious of my body for so long, during the rare intervals when I don't hurt, I have become savagely spiritual and I swear, having realized that the only time your brain can work is when it is not bothered with a malfunctioning body, that I am going to get healthy and I want to get on the earth somewhere with some books, paper, pianos, typewriters, and you boys. Now I know we've been talking of this for a year now, but never before did I realize that it was the only salvation, and never before I got on that train at the Gare du Nord did I realize how essential you are to me.[40]

Gradually, Stafford's symptoms began to abate, but she now began mentioning a new symptom in her letters, trench mouth, and despite the improvement in her health, her depression continued. Although she was furious because she had received no letters from her family,[41] she was nevertheless annoyed when her mother, worried because she had gotten no mail from her youngest daughter, sent a telegram to Jean saying, "Mother's Day greetings. Wire whereabouts immediately." Writing to Hightower and Berueffy about the telegram, Stafford referred to her parents as "those simpletons" and said, "Anyone that uses the word 'whereabouts' with me is unwise and anybody who mentions Mother's Day gets mightily snarled at."[42] As she lay in her hospital bed day after day, she also obsessively ruminated about her past life in Boulder. Faulting herself for having been so blind about people like Lawrence Fairchild and Lucy McKee, she confessed to Hightower and Berueffy that her grief for Lucy was "as hypocritical as most grief is." It was only the horror and strangeness of the night Lucy died that appealed to her so that she "returned, fascinated, to the subject over and over."[43] The only activity that she found pleasurable during her hospitalization was reading, but she was critical of everything she read except for Joyce's "The Dead" and *Portrait of the Artist as a Young Man*. She found George Santayana's *The Last Puritan* tedious and called *Gone with the Wind* "bilge more embarrassing than the 19th c. novels of Ethel M. Dell" that her "lamebrained ma used to read." Much to her delight, however, in rereading her own manuscripts she discovered that the writing pleased her, though she felt sure once she started writing again, she would probably be as critical of her own writing as she had usually been in the past.[44]

By the time Stafford was released from the hospital, the physicians in charge of her case had decided that her symptoms were caused by an inverted uterus and ovarian cysts. "It's *female trouble* which heretofore has always been good for a laugh," she wrote to Hightower and Berueffy. "It will be months before I have recovered and until then I've got to be a bloody invalid of the E. B. Browning variety, so, whipped and in the bleakest state of despair I am crawling back to Colorado." Still running a fever of 103 degrees several times a week and experiencing severe pain, she was terrified that she might have to undergo surgery if her health did not improve. However, when mentioning this possibility to her friends, she adopted a jocular tone that would characterize many of her future discussions of her frequent health problems: "Eventually I will probably have to have an operation & then they will remove my ovaries & I will become a man," she wrote. Contributing to her distress was the knowledge that Lucy McKee had apparently suffered from a similar condition during the months preceding her suicide, but Stafford assured Hightower and Berueffy that she herself was not thinking of suicide because she had seen "too much horrible dying in the hospital ward."[45]

Stafford's state of mind as she boarded a bus for the long trip back to Colorado is reflected in a poem called "Bessie's Debacle," whose style shows unmistakable traces of both Carl Sandburg and T. S. Eliot. The "Bessie" in the title is a reference to Stafford herself, who used to call herself Bessie in the letters she sent to Hightower and Berueffy, addressing Hightower as "Ma" and Berueffy as "Brother." The only poem written by the mature Stafford to survive, it is worth quoting in its entirety:

Bessie's Debacle

With a voice like a Baptist minister
he called Scranton, Erie, Cleveland, Chicago, and points west,
the cesura coming before the and.
Here are some cigarettes and crysto-mints, dear,
a little something to munch on:
                So that you don't think
                My God Paris is far away.

Cities first and then the country with bright trees
and the dustdimmed horizon of the plains
and then the mountains.
Well, goodbye, give Homer my love, I hope your hayfever isn't bad this year.
                When the train pulled out of the
                Gare du Nord I knew.

They thought I was a German and the officer said Fraulein caressingly.
And all the way to London I kept thinking:
                Paris is farther away every minute.

And the little street, the dirty door, the treacherous stair and the rough
        sheets—
Well, hell, boys, I said, I gotta eat next year.
And everytime I think about those music scores and those dictionaries
and the pictures of
                James Joyce
                Ernest Hemingway
                Ezra Pound
                and
                D. H. Lawrence
Well, I just want to sit down and have a good cry.

Paris, Texas; Hamburg, Iowa; London, Missouri,
And a glass of old Heidelberg beer for ten cents.

The hills of Pennsylvania were bright in the green light
And darkness came at last and the manifold mysteries
                of mind
                of soul
                of sickness of despair
                O lawd!

And each second of Eastern Daylight Savings Time I was farther away from
        the Gardens of the Tuilleries
Where the three of us walked saying to each other, we are geniuses.

I live in Cleveland she said. I've been married twice.
She crossed her dawngrey legs and gleamed at the busdriver's neck.
Think of it! And her so young.
Well, I always say the joy of travelling is you meet up with such interesting
     people.
Ain't it a sin for a minister of the gospel to join up a pair of half-wits?

N.Y., Penna., O., Ind., Ill.
The spirit of Carl Sandburg rose from the hot pavement to greet me.
               Gott sei dank wir haben Freunde da.
               Don't say Heil Hitler to the communists, Bessie, they might
                    not understand.

I was in Italy five weeks and I didn't say a word.
               Entrata
               uscita
               no capisco
               o, hell, i said, ich verstehe nicht,
               o, hell, you fool, i said in english
               this was hell what are you going to
               do i thought for a minute i'd go
               with him the way he kept following me along
               the Santa Lucia but what are you going
               to do if you can't speak a guy's language even if he is a good
                    looking wop.
There was a storehouse for bathtubs across the alley:
naked body basins, quite obscene in shape with little Chippendale legs so
     sweet.

Pottesville, Pa.

I came to america in the sprintime [sic], o with the lilacs blooming and the
     new summer batch of signs in subways:
The laxative of beautiful women.
I walked down fifth avenue and turned at a hundred and third street.
It looked like Naples lots of niggers and orange peelings in the gutter
               I should have known from those dreams i had what it would
                    be like.
               well, boys, i guess i'm done for
               the Gare du Nord and then the Greyhound
               bus station across from Pennsylvania,
               Paris and then New York and now Pottesville, Pa.

my country tis of thee: N.Y.
Penna
Ind
Ill

The laxative of beautiful women
Kozy Kleen Kamping Kabins
james joyce lives in paris and ezra pound lives in rapallo, but e a guest does
    not evade the income tax give me america any time hell those europeans
    must smell awful if they never take a bath.

Think of the harbor, the boat, the stars, the water, the days, the train and the
    station
And two young men to meet me there embarrassed all three
Now encompasses my mind and my soul and the sickness of my despair
    o, helpless in america

The "e a guest" to whom Jean Stafford referred in her poem was an American poet who wrote popular verse. His folksy poems with their saccharine morality epitomized for her the literary provincialism of the America from which she had fled and to which she had now perforce returned.[46]

During the early part of the summer of 1937, Stafford recuperated at her sister's ranch after paying a brief visit to Boulder. She reported to Hightower and Berueffy that she had seen her former fiancé Lawrence Fairchild in Boulder and had found him so revolting that she could not imagine why she had once considered marrying him. Although she complained to them about her trench mouth, which she could not afford to have treated unless Mrs. McKee loaned her some more money, she said she felt much better than she had when she left New York. Describing the ranch in Hayden as "swell," she said:

> Last night my mouth bled about a pint, and it is full of pus all the time. Pretty picture, isn't it? I just sit around all day long typing, as my mother always spoke of my pa's writing, and I have a good room the only trouble with which is that the gun cabinet is here and my brother-in-law frequently pokes me in the head with a shotgun. We have good food and go to bed at nine and get up at six. I am so used to not bathing that I just think it will be a real chore when I get back to civilization.[47]

In this letter she also quoted a brief fable called "The Snake and the File," which a friend of Mary Lee's had written when they were in grade school in Covina. Stafford would later include this fable in *The Mountain Lion* as an example of the strange stories her protagonist, Molly Fawcett, writes when she is a child.

One of the things Stafford enjoyed most about the ranch was that it gave her the opportunity to spend many hours dissecting her family with Mary Lee. She said she was storing up lots of interesting material for the novel she was planning to write about their father. Mary Lee told her, for example, that he had complained bitterly about how heartless his wife had been after he lost his money in the stock market. Hearing this, Stafford wrote to Hightower and Berueffy, made her madder than ever at her mother. Her father, she said, had never harped on the fact that her mother's father, who was such a "fine man" that he "wore a clean starched shirt every day" was "a drunken sot and lecher." In addition, she said, he had rarely talked about his own father, who was "regarded by the McKillops as a philistine because he made two million dollars on cattle and didn't fall down in his law office in a drunken stupor and break his ankle." She added that she was having a fine time recording her mother's clichés in a notebook so that she could quote them in the autobiographical novel she was planning to write. When she wasn't writing or talking to Mary Lee, she spent her time reading; she had just reread *Huckleberry Finn,* a favorite of her father's that she herself considered "the best book that ever came out of America." [48]

The ranch offered Stafford a temporary haven, but she was still determined to find a job for the coming year. Although she had applied for a number of teaching positions, all she had gotten thus far were letters of rejection. Perhaps she was only half in jest when she wrote to Hightower, "I think we may as well get married and see if yr pa will support us for a while," for her letters to Hightower reveal how much she had come to count on his friendship, his emotional support, and his opinions about literary matters. [49]

By the end of July, Stafford had returned to Boulder to attend the Writer's Conference. Her decision to participate in the conference that summer proved to be one of the most fateful decisions of her life. Not only did she meet several individuals who would be instrumental in helping her to launch her literary career, but she also befriended a handsome, lanky, untidy, somewhat ungainly, tempestuous undergraduate. This young man, an aspiring poet dubbed "Cal" by his prep school classmates at St. Mark's—after Caliban in *The Tempest* as well as the depraved Roman emperor Caligula—was Robert Lowell, a Boston Brahmin from the prominent Lowell family. His mother was descended from Edward Winslow, who came to America on the *Mayflower,* and his father was a member of the same family that produced the poets James Russell Lowell and Amy Lowell as well as A. Lawrence Lowell, president of Harvard University from 1909 to 1933. During his sophomore year at Harvard, Cal Lowell had become engaged to a woman several years his senior named Anne Dick, and after a violent quarrel with his parents over his engagement, he had knocked his father to the ground. Finally, he had reluctantly agreed to part from Anne Dick for a while. In April of 1937 Robert Lowell had been introduced to British novelist Ford Madox Ford by a Boston psychiatrist named Dr. Merrill Moore. Once a member of the Fugitives, a group of Southern poets who included in their ranks Allen Tate, John Crowe Ransom, and Robert Penn Warren, Moore had become a close friend of Lowell's mother. When Ford Madox Ford made the acquaintance of Robert Lowell, he was so impressed by Lowell's brilliance that he offered to introduce him to Allen Tate and to Tate's wife, novelist Caroline Gordon, with whom Ford was then residing. As a result, Moore accompanied Lowell to Tennessee, where Tate and Gordon were living, and Lowell subsequently spent three months living in a tent on the grounds of the Tates' home, Benfolly. In July, Lowell accompanied the Tates, Ford Madox Ford, and Ford's wife, the painter Janice Biala, first to a writers' conference at Olivet College in Michigan and then to the Boulder conference. By this time Lowell had decided to transfer from Harvard to Kenyon College in Ohio, where John Crowe Ransom would be teaching that fall. Lowell might have been recalling the occasion on which he first met Stafford in 1937 in this later poem entitled "Jean Stafford, a Letter":

> "Towmahss Mahnn: that's how you said it . . .
> That's how Mann must say it," I thought
> I can go on imagining you
> in your Heidelberry braids and Bavarian
> peasant aprons you wore three or four years
> after your master's at twenty-one.[50]

Frances Lindley, a participant in the Boulder Writer's Conference that summer, remembered Stafford as a pale, rather unkempt-looking young woman who seemed defensive, resentful, and embittered.[51] Anxious to help Stafford earn some money, Edward Davison had hired her to work as his general factotum at the conference. He had also given her novel to Ford Madox Ford, her poetry to John Crowe Ransom and Howard Mumford Jones, and both a short story and excerpts from her Heidelberg journals to Whit Burnett. However, Stafford was somewhat disappointed that she did not establish any contact with Sherwood Anderson, who was also at the conference that summer. "I am pretty well satisfied," she wrote to Hightower and Berueffy, "although I had several other things in mind—such as Sherwood Anderson."[52]

Initially Stafford had intended to avoid the one woman novelist on the staff, a Southern novelist named Evelyn Scott, who wrote, she said, "the most ponderous stuff" she had ever read.[53] Soon, however, she was mentioning Evelyn Scott with enthusiasm in her letters to Hightower and Berueffy, for it

was Scott, more than any of the other participants, who offered encouragement and advice to her, both at the conference and afterward. In a typewritten
letter to her friends describing the conference, a jubilant Jean Stafford added
the following handwritten note after meeting the second day with John Peale
Bishop and Evelyn Scott:

> Saw Bishop. Said I was best. Not surprised after spending morning idly con-
> templating 60 fat female rumps in the W. C. Said I had an eminent nerve
> writing s. of c. [stream of consciousness] and thereby putting myself up to
> compete with the biggest boys meaning Joyce. Said I cd. however make the
> grade. Was *v* encouraging. Evelyn Scott who read journal & short story said
> hell, gal, you ain't serving apprenticeship, you're graduate professional. Said if
> I can get away from the academic will become great writer. Wrote enthusi-
> astically to Scribners & said I've found something in Boulder city beautiful,
> said she wanted to send them the novel. Said I was the most unusual for age
> had ever seen. Have not embellished. Am not embarrassed. Know for sure
> I'm good—like hell. Will doubtless spend life writing novels. Have almost
> definitely decided on the ranch for the winter. Scott said it was wisest. Said I
> wd. be a success pretty soon if I keep on. Will not be able to write a coherent
> sentence now, however, until I have been properly discouraged again.[54]

Three other people who were favorably impressed by Jean Stafford were
Howard Mumford Jones, John Crowe Ransom, and Ransom's young protégé,
Robert Lowell. Howard Mumford Jones took her Heidelberg journal with
him when he left Boulder, intending to show it to the editors of the *Atlantic
Monthly,* and Ransom also said encouraging things about her writing. One
evening she was invited to a party at the home of Edward and Natalie
Davison. Describing this event to Hightower, she wrote, "That was the night
Evelyn Scott said let's ask the poet in our midst, we will be hearing from Jean
Stafford in ten years and we will be talking about her on occasions like this,
and Ransom said, yes, she is unique, and Davison sat there pleased as punch,
not saying anything, just pleased because he thought of me first."[55] Ransom, in
fact, was so taken with her that he subsequently tried to help her get a teaching position. Writing to Allen Tate about her, he described her as "the sanest
and most charming and at the same time most promising girl at the Boulder
Writer's Conference."[56]

It is not clear whether Robert Lowell was also present at the Davisons'
house on the evening when Ransom publicly praised Stafford, but Lowell was
undoubtedly told by Ransom and Ford how highly she was regarded by the
leaders of the conference. When he had arrived in Boulder, Lowell had
pitched a tent in the Davisons' backyard, just as he had done earlier at the

Tates'. However, sometime before the conference ended, he was asked by the Davisons to stay somewhere else since he was making a mess of their property. Robert Berueffy said Stafford had told him that Lowell was reprimanded for "shitting" in the Davisons' yard. The fact that she uttered this vulgar word somewhat surprised Berueffy since the young women he knew did not use such language.[57]

At the close of the conference both Lowell and Stafford were awarded honorable mention for the work they had submitted. Although they had not had a chance to get to know each other very intimately, Lowell was very much taken with her, and before he left for Kenyon College he asked her to write to him there.

The many literati Stafford met during the conference made her feel that she might soon be successful in finding a publisher for one of her manuscripts. The decision to become a writer has never been an easy one to make, however, especially for young women without any financial resources. Stafford could hardly have been unaware of the fact that women writers were barely visible at the Boulder Writer's Conference. While most of the male conference leaders delivered lectures there, none of the women did so. Even Evelyn Scott, who had published a number of novels by that date, including the very popular Civil War novel *The Wave,* did not play a prominent role at the conference. Moreover, misogynistic views of women were widely held and frequently expressed by the male writers whom Stafford admired. In view of the prevailing male attitudes toward women, it is not surprising that Stafford herself tended to identify with males and to make disparaging remarks about other women. She must have felt disconcerted during the conference, however, when Howard Mumford Jones read aloud a satirical account of his students at Radcliffe, condescendingly describing "thirty-seven virgins" who answer the professor's literary questions "with mouths intended for kisses" but in their talk carefully avoid the word *kiss.*[58]

Although Stafford was determined to find a job to support herself for the next few years, she was still uncertain as to whether she wanted to marry and have children, or whether she wanted to pursue a career. In her unpublished novel *Autumn Festival* Gretchen Marburg wrestles with a similar dilemma:

> Which is better, a career woman or a homebody? Gretchen Marburg, Ph.D.
> or Gretchen somebody else settled into a mesmerizing routine of cooking
> potatoes and using a vacuum cleaner and opening cans of Gerber's baby foods
> and making morning telephone calls to the grocer, chummy with him over
> her pork chops and peanut butter sold in bulk. Would it be better to be
> Gretchen hurrying lonely to an early morning lecture or Gretchen picking up

the milk and the newspaper from the front porch and reading the headlines while squeezing the oranges . . ."[59]

Like Gretchen Marburg, Stafford had toyed with the idea of obtaining a Ph.D. However, she had not succeeded in obtaining a fellowship to Radcliffe. Moreover, when she had discussed the possibility of pursuing a doctorate with the chairman of the English Department at the University of Colorado, George Fulmer Reynolds, he had said that he would not advise her to get a Ph.D. She was not certain what he meant by that, she said, but she suspected that he meant she did not have "the footnote mind." She later told Hightower that no one—not George Fulmer Reynolds, nor Irene P. McKeehan, nor Dixon Wecter, nor Howard Mumford Jones, nor John Crowe Ransom, nor Edward Davison—seemed to think she would advance very far in teaching, even if she did secure a doctorate, because there was "too much prejudice against women."[60]

The question of how she was going to support herself during the following year was finally resolved when she was hired at the end of the summer to teach composition at Stephens College in Columbia, Missouri. From her meager salary of one hundred dollars a month plus room and board she did not expect to save much money, but she hoped she would be able to repay her debt to the McKees; more important, she anticipated that she would have a good deal of time to spend on her own writing during the course of the coming academic year. In accepting the position at Stephens College, however, she realized that she would be unable to rejoin Hightower and Berueffy in Europe, something about which she had daydreamed since she had had to part with them in Paris. "For God's sake write to me, boys. Not all this can alleviate the agony of not being with you," she wrote to them, and she added, "If I should sell anything for a reasonable sum I will teach till Christmas and come then."[61]

By the end of August Stafford learned that Hightower and Berueffy were both returning to America. War was imminent, and remaining in Europe or going to China, two possibilities they had been considering, no longer seemed feasible. Hightower informed her that his father had offered to pay his tuition to Harvard, where he planned to study Chinese, and that Berueffy, too, would be coming back to the States. Although Hightower was not at all certain that studying Chinese was what he really wanted to do, he had definitely decided he did not want to go to medical school, and he also had serious doubts about whether he had the makings of a writer. Enrolling in graduate school seemed a more attractive alternative to him than returning to Salida, Colorado, the dreary town where his parents lived.

Delighted to learn that her two friends would soon be back home, Jean Stafford replied to Hightower's letter immediately:

> I had yr. l. this morning & I am weak with joy . . . I will try like hell to come to N.Y. for Xmas. At Harvard, look up Howard Mumford Jones in the Eng. dept. He was at the W.C. and was the one who took my journal back to the Atlantic.
>   Thank God, yr. back son . . .
>   Lovingly,
>   Fraulein S.[62]

Hightower might have been a bit chagrined by the rapid shift of focus in this letter from *his* plans to *her* interest in having him contact Howard Mumford Jones; nevertheless, the letter clearly expressed her joy at the prospect of seeing Hightower again.

Early in September, Stafford packed up her manuscripts, her typewriter, and her favorite books and boarded the train for Missouri. Stephens College was a two-year college attended largely by the daughters of affluent Arkansas cotton growers, Texas cattle ranchers, and Oklahoma oil magnates. Recollecting the year she spent at Stephens College in an article she wrote in 1972 about a former Stephens student named Martha Mitchell, wife of the attorney general during the Nixon administration, Jean Stafford wrote:

> Two days a week the students were taught composition, and on the third day they were taught conversation, the recommended textbook for which was *The Reader's Digest.* . . . I was frequently summoned to the office of the head of the department, or more terrifyingly, to the dean's office for hurting students' feelings by asking them to come to class in something other than their sleeping pajamas and to refrain from knitting while I was demonstrating sub junctives on the blackboard. By and large, though, I was so intimidated by these pretty, breezy hoydens that after a few protests, I retired into a sullen acceptance of the college creed, which was that we were "turning out wives and mothers of tomorrow . . ."[63]

As was her wont when discussing difficult or unpleasant situations she had encountered, Jean Stafford used irony, hyperbole, and parody to describe events that were undoubtedly more painful than humorous to her at the time they occurred. She ridiculed her students, calling them "loathsome little bitches who are homesick and have rumps like a kitchen stove."[64] Yet despite her contempt for her students, she was painfully insecure about how she came across to them in the classroom. "I just had my first class and you just can't imagine how aful [*sic*] it is. They didn't laugh at one of my pearls and they all hate me and I was so damned scared that I didn't say anything I intended to say," she wrote to Hightower.[65] Although she made fun of the "Grooming Clinic" at Stephens in her article about Martha Mitchell, she did not mention how humiliated she had been when a member of the faculty, observing Stafford's straggly hair, ragged fingernails, and unfashionable clothes, had suggested to her that she herself might "pick up a few pointers" at the Grooming Clinic.[66] She hated having to dress each night for dinner and to wear formal clothes once a week instead of her customary attire: huaraches or German oxfords and an unfashionable dirndl skirt like the ones women had worn in Heidelberg. "They're all so damned well groomed," she said of the students at Stephens, "that the only place I feel at home is in the local pool hall."[67] Some of the younger members of the faculty who were also critical of the college were amused when she began to refer to Stephens as "a training school for concubines."[68]

No more charitable about most of her fellow teachers than she was about her students, she complained about them as well. One teacher with whom she did spend a great deal of her free time, however, was a member of the English Department named Bill Mock, who was a friend of her friend from Boulder, Paul Thompson. Initially she found Bill amusing, and since he owned a car, she was able to escape from the cloistered atmosphere of the campus, going with him to movies and to picturesque, seedy waterfront bars in nearby St. Louis. Once, dressed in evening clothes, they drove to St. Louis to hear Kirsten Flagstad sing in *Tristan and Isolde,*[69] and on another occasion, much to her delight, he presented her with a paperbound 1927 French edition of *Ulysses.*[70] She related to Bill Mock tales about her family, describing her mother's insensitivity and her father's frustrated ambitions to be a writer. She was convinced, she said, that her talented but misanthropic father had failed to have any of his writing published ever since he began including the sentence "Roosevelt is a piss-ant" in everything he wrote. She even discussed the suicide of Lucy McKee with her new friend, who had attended Northwestern several years after Lucy had been enrolled there. According to Bill Mock, Lucy McKee had achieved notoriety at Northwestern, having allegedly tried to seduce as many faculty members as possible. Stafford usually enjoyed Mock's company, but she did not find him physically attractive. Wishing, perhaps, to fend off his amorous advances, she told him that any physical contact "made her flesh crawl." She explained that after Lucy McKee's suicide she was traumatized when the police interrogated her about her relationship to Lucy's husband and hinted that Lucy had committed suicide because she was jealous of Jean.[71]

In a short story called "Caveat Emptor," which deals in part with her experience at Stephens College, Stafford describes a young teacher at the Alma Hettrick College for Girls who falls in love with a fellow teacher. On Sundays, she accompanies him to a quaint town where they dine on crème brûlée at the Hotel Dauphin. The same town in Missouri that she and Bill Mock discovered one Sunday in April and the Hotel Dauphine where they were served dinner by two elderly French ladies who were sisters are also described in an article Jean Stafford wrote for *Mademoiselle* in 1952.[72] In contrast to the protagonist of "Caveat Emptor," however, Stafford did not fall in love with her fellow teacher, though Mock did fall in love with her and insisted that he wanted to marry her after the school year was over. Although she continued to spend a great deal of her free time with Mock, in her letters to Hightower she repeatedly made disparaging remarks about the short stature and plumpness of her would-be suitor.

It is clear that, though she was not in love with Mock, she did not mind having him treat her to expensive dinners and free drinks. Anxious to flee from Stephens during the Christmas vacation, she gladly accepted his invitation to stay with him at his parents' elegant home in an affluent Chicago suburb that December. After she returned to Stephens College, she described her holiday activities to Hightower: "I met some Chi. debutantes and of all the ornery looking bodies I ever see they was the wust. For a while I sorta liked having all I wanted to eat and drink and nothing to do and a bathroom to myself and a lot of cocktail parties at ritzy clubs and going to see plays in formal clothes. . . ." She maintained, however, that Mock's parents and their friends made her feel uncomfortable. ". . . all the time they were thinking I looked like hell," she said. "I made one concession. I didn't wear German shoes but twice."[73]

What pleased her most about her trip to Chicago was the fact that at the meeting there of the Modern Language Association she had spent time with a number of her former professors from Boulder, including Paul Thompson and George Fulmer Reynolds, and had also seen some of the people whom she had met the previous summer at the Boulder Writer's Conference. After hearing her complaints about Stephens College, Howard Mumford Jones suggested that she write a novel about her experiences there,[74] and John Crowe Ransom, with whom she drank three highballs at the Drake Hotel, mentioned that she might be able to get a job teaching the following year at the Women's College of the University of North Carolina, where his friend Allen Tate would be teaching.[75] She made the most of these contacts. When she sent Whit Burnett, editor of Story Press, a revised version of her novel, she mentioned the names of several of the scholars she had seen in Chicago, including John Crowe Ransom and Howard Mumford Jones, and she spoke of Bernard De Voto's "intelligent tirade against the scholarly approach to the psychological novel," a topic about which she herself would lecture several years later.[76]

In January, faced with the tedious prospect of grading the final exams and papers of her students, she realized how much she loathed teaching at Stephens. "I have been here five months now and still it is with the most paralyzing dread that I enter my classroom," she wrote to Hightower. "I have for my students such complete and unreasonable contempt that I can teach them nothing I am so bored. I dismiss them early and I don't assign many papers because I am too busy writing to grade them."[77] She had sent off two of her stories, she said—one to *American Prefaces,* the other to Whit Burnett at Story Press. Taking Howard Mumford Jones's advice, during this period she also began a satirical novel about Stephens College that she called *Neville.*

More and more convinced that she did not want to earn her living by teaching, Stafford decided to apply for a Houghton Mifflin Fellowship. Since she was in need of people who would be willing to write letters of recommendation for the fellowship, she contacted Ford Madox Ford and Evelyn Scott. To Ford Madox Ford, who had been known to be supportive of fledgling writers in the past, she wrote: "It has been some time since you read the first third of my novel in Boulder, and by this time you have perhaps forgotten it. I am hoping that you have not, and that my sending you these excerpts will not be too presumptious [*sic*]. And, too, I hope that the request I am going to make most humbly will not be too impertinent."[78] Complaining that at Stephens the curriculum demanded that she spend time teaching students how to write "letters of condolence, diary-writing, and . . . what to say on a dance floor," she said that instead of teaching she wanted to have the opportunity to find out whether she was "a writer or a non-writer." She explained that at the age of twenty-two, she would hate to "chain" herself to teaching before she had tested herself fully as a writer. The book on which she wanted to work was one about Stephens College, she said, "about the falsehoods upon which America's rotten educational system is built, and . . . the way in which the minds of young Americans are turned by myopic professors into channels of sweet-smelling muck." She included the last chapter of her novel *Which No Vicissitude,* explaining that the title was derived from a poem by Wordsworth which contained the line "The tomb / Which no vicissitude can find."[79]

Recuperating in Paris from a long illness and preoccupied with thoughts of his own unfinished work, the sixty-five-year-old Ford must have groaned when he received this lengthy missive, but he responded promptly to her letter, offering to write a strong recommendation to Houghton Mifflin about her "admirable work."[80] Ford's letter and one from Evelyn Scott that praised the distinction of her mind and the "very knowing quality of her prose" temporarily made her spirits soar, but she became despondent again when Whit Burnett returned the revised manuscript of *Which No Vicissitude* to her. He informed her that the editors of Story Press did not feel the book would sell, nor would it do her much good as a writer if it were published. What he reacted to most negatively, he said, was her use of stream of consciousness and her tendency to meander around in the minds of characters whom he found "extremely boring." Apologizing for his harsh comments, he observed, ". . . I think this whole book is a miasma that should have been gotten out of your system and now that it is out of your system, I say, the hell with it."[81] His words must have seemed harsh indeed to Stafford, who had devoted four years to writing and painstakingly revising this manuscript, but if the surviving fragments of *Which No Vicissitude* are any indication of what the rest of the manuscript was like, it is not difficult to comprehend Burnett's reaction. As the following example from the "Prologue" suggests, much of the writing was overwrought:

> Which of the three of us has died? what ghost, followed only by the night, seen only by it, has gone into the valley of the shadow of death? I, Ishtar, gathered a handful of white flowers and cast them on the unmarked grave. Like a great wind she moved among the tombs, she locked the gates behind her and she lost the keys. . . .
>
> One of the three of us has died. The branches of the elm tree beside the west wall of the house waver, quiver, tremble. Everyone knows death. Yes, we have all seen the bodies as they lay covered with roses. And we think, how beautiful. We wonder which of us is lying there? There were three of us in the same room, and time ended suddenly with the cracking of an explosion from a small caliber pistol. The rhythm of time was pressed down, down, so deeply that we could not say nor conjecture which of the three of us lay there with a bullet in the head. One of us called a doctor. And the doctor said, it's too late.[82]

If Stafford was dismayed by Burnett's letter of rejection, she did not disclose to him how distressing she had found it. Instead, she agreed with him that stream of consciousness was "dying a probably justifiable death," and she announced to him that, even though she was not sorry she had experimented with this style for four years, she had put this style behind her now. She assured him that her new novel had only a few traces of the "mutation style" left and those would be eliminated when she revised the manuscript.[83]

Depressed by this letter of rejection and by the daily irritations at Stephens

College, she decided to go to confession one Saturday evening. "All that happened was that my knees got sore," she wrote to Hightower afterwards:

> I was just dead. Nothing happened at all. I looked at the vigil lights and I listened to the murmuring in the confessional and I tried to tell myself that it was all mysterious and beautiful, but it didn't work. I left without being confessed. When I went out it was raining and as I walked home I wanted to die more than I have ever wanted anything before. I haven't got a feeling in my whole being, and it's not very comfortable. The next day I went to mass. I think that's the last time I will ever go. It's foolish. I expect so much and I get so little.[84]

Obsessed with thoughts of how swiftly time was passing, lonely and often unable to sleep, she imagined a very different kind of life than the one she was leading:

> I would like a farm with dumb animals on it. I would like to live in a big house and not just one room. I would like to eat and sleep in the same place. I would like to have everything clean and have the windows open and the sun shining. I would like to have bookcases and no suitcases and no trunks. I would like to do some physical labor and some mental labor but at my own ease.[85]

She disliked teaching so much that she even daydreamed about going out to Hollywood and getting a job as an actress. "My face photographs well because I have big bones," she wrote to Hightower. "My voice is good and low. It might work. It would be better than teaching school and more profitable. . . . Sometimes I turn pure Philistine and think of money and no bills."[86]

As the end of the school year approached, Stafford debated endlessly whether or not she would consider teaching the following year at Stephens if she were rehired. However, she was mortified and furious when the head of her department told her that her contract would not be renewed. He said that many people realized she was discontented. Furthermore, he had heard that she talked over the heads of her students and that she spent too much time discussing literature in her composition classes and not enough time discussing writing. What was mortifying, however, was that he insisted she go to a physician to undergo a "test" since some members of the department had heard she had a contagious disease. She concluded that he was hinting at syphilis and recommending that she take a Wasserman test. Hating the people at Stephens more than ever as a result of this humiliating episode, she would have liked to quit on the spot, but she knew she had to have a job. "Otherwise," she wrote to Hightower, "my family will starve and Mrs. McKee will die of apoplexy." Signing her letter "Maria Magdalena," she confessed, "I am scared about next year because I have been comfortable this year and I have got soft."[87]

Another person to whom she wrote about her latest trauma was Evelyn Scott. Angered by the way Stafford had been treated, Scott sent a letter to the president of Stephens College protesting "the particular brand of calumny" Stephens College seemed to favor and threatening that she would feel it her duty "to give this remarkable incident all the publicity it deserves" unless the allegations about Stafford were retracted.[88]

Some of Stafford's colleagues suspected that the real reason the administration wanted to fire her was that they had heard she was writing a novel about the school.[89] In time, the head of the English Department backed down and suggested that Stafford should not only be rehired but encouraged to introduce some new literature courses the following year. But she had already decided that she did not want to teach at Stephens or anywhere else. As she explained to Hightower, "There would always be someone that didn't like me, I would always be rebellious, I would always hate students, I would always be impatient of stupidity, I would always get fired. I would always be criticized for the way I dress, for smoking where students can see, for saying 'guts' in class, for saying unamerican things, for hating all these bitches represent . . ."[90]

The issue of whether or not she would return to Stephens the following September was finally resolved once and for all when she received a letter notifying her that her contract had been terminated. She was probably relieved that she would not have to return, but she resolved that she was going to get revenge for the humiliation she had suffered by writing "dozens of articles on the teaching of English in American colleges."[91] Her pain at her ignominious exit from Stephens was somewhat mitigated by her contempt for the college and everything it represented.

As she packed her belongings, she had one consoling thought: *American Prefaces* had accepted a short story she had written called "Meridian." Jubilantly, she wrote to Hightower, "I am in print at last."[92] She still hoped that she would succeed in getting the Houghton Mifflin Fellowship for which she had applied, and she knew that if all else failed, she could always enroll in a doctoral program in creative writing at the University of Iowa, for Wilbur Schramm, editor of *American Prefaces,* had been so impressed by her writing that he had urged her to apply to Iowa, where he was teaching, and he had told her that he could probably arrange to secure a modest fellowship for her.

When she left Stephens College at the end of the school year, Stafford was still unsure of what course she would follow. Her immediate plans were to drive to New York City with Bill Mock. She intended to see several publishers whom Evelyn Scott had suggested she should contact, as well as Martha Foley and Whit Burnett. Once she concluded her business in New York, she was looking forward to meeting Hightower. She planned to travel west with him to visit his parents in Salida, Colorado. Then she would proceed by train to Oregon to visit her own parents and her brother, whom she had not seen for two years. Nothing had been resolved about her future, but she was relieved to be leaving Stephens College and was cheered by the prospect of being re-united with her friend Hightower, whose amusing and encouraging letters had meant so much to her during the dismal year she had spent teaching in Missouri.

I Love Someone
Summer and Fall 1938

Yesterday I began my novel over again with an idea that has been working in my mind for a long time: the question: why is it that a woman cannot write a book like A Portrait of the Artist. I mean, why is it that her experiences cannot be those of a man.

—JEAN STAFFORD, IN A LETTER TO JAMES ROBERT HIGHTOWER,
OCTOBER 28, 1938

WHEN JEAN STAFFORD departed from Stephens College early in June of 1938, she still was not certain where or when she would be meeting Hightower. "I am good and sore at you. Am I supposed to meet you in New York or Boston? And when? . . . And god damn your capricious ways," she wrote angrily to him just before she and Bill Mock set out for New York.[1] Having received no word from him about their meeting, perhaps she was reminded of Hightower's earlier failure to meet her when she had first arrived in Europe. A note from him finally reached her at the Brooklyn Heights apartment of Donald and Dorothy Hays. He suggested that she meet him at the train station in Albany on June 10; from there they would take a train to Michigan, proceed to Flint to pick up a new Buick his father had ordered, and drive it to his parents' house in Salida, Colorado.

Somewhat annoyed that she had so little time to spend in New York City before setting out for the West, she nevertheless left New York on June 10. "I met Hightower in Albany. He had his shoes done up in a paper bag. We looked like imigrants [*sic*]," she wrote to Bill Mock. She complained to Mock about the sooty train they had traveled on, whose seedy bathrooms appeared to "have been bought up cheap in the Latin Quarter of Paris and broken in in the Bowery"; about some "dreadful" people from Hightower's hometown with whom they spent one night in Battle Creek; about Hightower, who would knock loudly at her door at four in the morning and then would not stop to have breakfast until seven o'clock, by which time both of them "were good and cross and had headaches and constipation." The eastern part of

Colorado, she said, was "really and truly the wasteland," and admitting to being a "great snob," she confessed that the simple people of America bored her "to lassitude."[2]

What she did not reveal to Mock, however, was that en route to Salida, Hightower had announced he was in love with her and had tried to persuade her to marry him, nor did she inform Mock that by the time she left Salida for Oregon, she, in turn, had decided that she was in love with Hightower. Remembering the night in Salida when she had first realized she was in love, she later wrote to Hightower, "I started loving you just after we got on the wrong road or thought we got on the wrong road up to Salida and it was a nice night. One of the things was the way your right wrist looks when it's driving a car. Another was that I began thinking and realizing that you are the only person who *always* laughs at the right things."[3]

After she parted from Hightower, she stopped briefly in Boulder to visit her friends, the Thompsons, and their new baby, whom she described as being "hideous as all babies are." She quickly discovered that her year-long absence from Boulder did not make her feel any more kindly disposed to the town than she had before. During her brief stay there she had a discouraging conversation with Edward Davison, who pointed out to her that she really hadn't written anything of note yet and suggested that she ought to think of getting married so that she would "have an income." When she demurred, insisting that she didn't approve of marrying for mercenary reasons, he accused her of being young and naive.[4]

Depressed by her visit to Boulder and dreading her coming reunion with her family, she boarded the train for Oregon. Her two-day train trip did nothing to improve her spirits. As usual, she enumerated to her friends all the annoying things that had occurred during the journey: being delayed four or five hours as a result of a train wreck somewhere in Idaho; sitting near a woman with three constantly squealing and howling babies; being asked repeatedly by four teachers from Oklahoma to join them in a game of bridge; meeting a tobacco-chewing old woman in the ladies room and being told an endless lewd story. "I am a great snob," she observed once again. "I hated being in that train where there were people in superior sections. I hated being mixed up with babies and lewd old women." When she arrived in Portland, she was greeted by her mother, her seventy-two-year-old maiden aunt, Ella, who had come to live with the Staffords after Jean Stafford's Grandmother McKillop had died in Rockport, and her "old dwarfish father," who whispered crazily as they got into his car to drive home to Oswego, "I will have you wearing diamonds pretty soon."[5]

Stafford would later refer to the summer of 1938 as the worst summer of her life.[6] Although she found the house in which her parents were living to be more comfortable than she had expected, all of her former feelings of being a supernumerary member of the Stafford household were revived. "I came with a heart full of charity and kindliness, and I would have kept it up if they had been interested in me at all," she said. She was hurt that neither of her parents asked her about her experiences in Germany, about teaching at Stephens College, or about her friends. "For months I have been idealizing this and telling people that I am going home, but this is no more home than Donald and Dorothy's apartment is. These people are like strangers that I got tired of and have never had much interest in. There is no one to talk to," she lamented.[7]

Once again she felt the familiar hostility toward her parsimonious mother "with her horrible Eliza Gant complex" as she watched her, accompanied by Aunt Ella, scouting for bargains or "canning 57 varieties of free fruit" while "figuring up how much it didn't cost them."[8] She was irritated when her mother gossiped about unfamiliar people or reminisced about the days when she was a charter member of the Sorosis Club in Rockport, or described in detail John Stafford's shortcomings as a husband and father. But most painful of all was the fact that her mother completely failed to sympathize with her desire to be a writer. Stafford complained bitterly to Hightower:

> Mother said she did not understand how I could write, having witnessed Dad's thirty-year miscarriage. I pointed out that writing was not, as she persisted in thinking, a manual art which was to be cast aside or picked up at will and that once having got the notion that you could write you were henceforth, to yourself at least, a writer. I went on in that fatuous vein for some time, hinting that I thought literature was important, etc. until I realized that she was miles away canning imaginary cherries and "scouting" in Portland.[9]

Even more difficult for Stafford than spending time with her mother and her aunt, to whom she mockingly referred as "the McKillop girls," was being in the company of her father. She was amused that he insisted on wearing his hat to the breakfast table, and she was intrigued by the admixture in him of the intellectual and the workman. Nevertheless, she found his frustrations and his misery almost unbearable to observe. In one of her letters to Bill Mock, she wrote about her father:

> Pa writes from five in the morning until eight at night not stopping for lunch. He asked me the other day how many words I wrote per day. I said about fifteen hundred. He gasped. He said he thought he wrote at least 5,000 which

is his minimum. After eight o'clock he reads Swift and snorts all through it with delight. He goes out on the porch, smoking his pipe and looks up at the sky and snorts and says by God, there was a man. And then he comes back in and reviews the section of plumbing in the Montgomery Ward catalogue. I have not, after all these years, accustomed myself to these contrasts. He will say . . . that he shore thinks Hamlet is a "flossy play with a ripsnorting yarn combined with the perfection of understanding of human emotion as it manifests itself in times of tension."[10]

On one occasion she accompanied her father to the public library, where he took out a "forbidding array" of books, including three volumes of Mommsen's *History of Rome,* Mann's *Joseph in Egypt,* Veblen's *The Theory of the Leisure Class,* and a treatise by Einstein. After they left the library, they ate corned beef sandwiches and drank beer at a restaurant, as he drew pictures on the paper napkin to illustrate to her how Archimedes squared the circle. During this outing she thought about what a "nice gent" he really was and felt very fond of him. However, as of old, his frustrated ambitions were almost unbearable to watch. "I don't want to look upon the spectacle of my father's defeat and yet it seems to me it must be easier for him when I am here," she said sadly.[11]

John Stafford not only discussed intellectual matters with his youngest daughter: whenever his wife was away from home, he would seize the opportunity to complain bitterly about Ethel Stafford's shortcomings. He told Jean, for example, that when she had sent money to them during the preceding year, Ethel had taken charge of it and had "raised hell" if he bought paper, typewriter ribbons, stamps, or tobacco. Hearing about the "torment of his life among the Scotch," Stafford observed acrimoniously about her mother, "She does not understand those necessities. Toilet paper is something she can get her mind to work on."[12] The fact that her father could not afford to buy the new eyeglasses that he desperately needed made her feel terribly guilty that she had squandered her salary from Stephens College on a velvet cape instead of sending additional money to him.[13]

Most troubling of all to Stafford during this period—when she was beginning to think of her own writing as a vocation rather than a hobby—was contemplating her father's failure as a writer. He continued to send his stories and articles to editors, only to have them rejected. She said it pained her to watch her father shining his shoes because he hoped to receive from an editor a check that he would have to go to Portland to cash, only to witness his dejection when the article was returned.[14] Not certain herself whether her father had any talent as a writer, she sent one of his recent efforts, an article on the consequences of overproduction, to Hightower and was relieved when Hightower told her that he had liked it and thought her father's style was "definitely professional."[15] She too had begun to send her articles and stories to various periodicals, but the thought that she might succeed as a writer while her father had to face one humiliating defeat after another made her feel terribly uneasy. Describing her conflicting feelings to Hightower, she said, "Look, what consoles me is this: I am unpublished, and I hope to Christ that when I am published, he will be dead. What else consoles me (and this still makes me laugh) is that the same thing that has happened to him will happen to me." Unable to come to terms with her father's misery and defeat, she hoped he would soon die. "I cannot convey to you how desperately I wish for his gentle death," she wrote, "and the wish is, I suppose, really selfish because I cannot stand this needing to cry and not being able to. But if I could bury his ashes, I could forget his misery."[16]

All that summer Stafford thought constantly about her parents' poverty and her own lack of funds. Having managed to save only twenty dollars from the salary she had been paid at Stephens College and with no prospects of a job for the coming year, she was terrified she would not be able to sustain herself or give her parents any money. "I cannot and will not let them starve," she told Hightower, pointing out that in the past her siblings, Mary Lee, Margie, and Dick, had all assisted in supporting their parents, but Mary Lee now had a husband and two children of her own, Margie was also married, and Dick was employed only three months out of twelve.[17] During her visit to Salida, she had learned that she had not been awarded the Houghton Mifflin Fellowship. Instead, it had been given to a woman named Inez Whipple, whom she had met at the Boulder Writer's Conference the preceding summer. She nastily observed that Whipple had worn "rump-sprung sleeveless purple bouclé outfits with enormous dirty hats," and remarking that she "loathed" her, she recalled bitterly that John Peale Bishop and the other conference leaders had observed that, even though she herself had more brain power, Whipple told a story better.[18]

Desperate to find a job, Stafford registered with a teacher's agency in Portland, although she had vowed after her experience at Stephens College never to teach again. She also applied for a job as a model.[19] Her anxiety about her finances was exacerbated by the letters Mrs. McKee kept sending her, which reminded her of her unpaid debt. She said that she hated being called an "impractical dreamer" by Lucy's mother. "If *only* I could think of this as an adventure! If only I could deeply convince myself that adversity is what makes one a big brave artist! If only I could believe that I don't want velvet capes,

champagne, fine editions, Coty's eau de cologne, a dubonnet candlewick bed-
spread! If only, in short, I could be more than a beer-hall communist!" she
wrote plaintively to Mock.[20]

Despite her worries about her family and her own future, Stafford nevertheless managed to get a good deal of writing done during the summer of
1938. On June 27 she sent to the Atlantic Monthly Press an article she called
"Manicure with Your Diploma," which she had written to express her out-
rage at the educational policies of Stephens College. Much to her chagrin, the
article was returned several weeks later with a covering note from the managing editor explaining that it was too much like some other "acid" things the
magazine had printed during the preceding eighteen months.[21] In addition to
writing the article about Stephens College, she began a short story, called
"January and Fresshe May," that painted an unflattering portrait of a college
president, and she also continued to work on *Neville,* a satiric novel based on
her experience at Stephens. Originally, she had intended to make the protagonist of her novel a Jew, but Edward Davison and another friend with
whom she had discussed the novel had pointed out that she did not know
enough about Jews to make the character convincing.[22] Somewhat dismayed
to discover that she kept reverting to the stream-of-consciousness mode that
Whit Burnett had criticized in her first novel, she was pleased nevertheless by
the comic possibilities of the situation she was describing. However, she had
difficulty in inventing suitable actions for her characters. "The characters are
there, but what in hell shall I have them do?" she said. "I can't have just chapter after chapter of staff meetings. I don't know why I style myself a novelist
when I can't write novels."[23]

Another writing project she undertook that summer was an autobiography she tentatively called *If This Be Quenched.* "I have decided that I am better
at that sort of thing and I can work at it along with this other novel," she told
Hightower, but she hastily added that she knew it "wasn't art." Evelyn Scott's
autobiography, published when Scott was only twenty-two, had inspired her
to try her own hand at autobiography, she said.[24] She was also considering the
possibility of writing a novel about her father, a project she believed would be
her "most serious attempt," but she feared she was still too immature to tackle
this difficult subject and, furthermore, that she could not actually bear to write
about him while he was still alive.[25]

The one work of fiction Stafford completed during the summer of 1938
and later published was a short story entitled "And Lots of Solid Color." It has
the distinction of being the first of her short stories to appear in print, for the
editors of *American Prefaces,* who previously had also accepted a story by her
called "Meridian," chose to publish "And Lots of Solid Color" instead. Auto-

biographical, as were many of her short stories, "And Lots of Solid Color" accurately reflects her situation during the summer of 1938. It portrays the desperation of an unemployed young woman who anxiously waits for the mail each day, hoping for a letter informing her that she has secured a teaching position. Though their names have been changed, all of the members of the Stafford family appear in the story: a father who makes idle promises to his daughter that she will be riding in a Packard if he succeeds in selling the article he is writing; a mother who loves to recount how she smuggled a serape out of Mexico in her bustle; a pathetic old maiden aunt; a brother who used to work in a seed laboratory; a sister who lives on a ranch; and another sister who works on an Indian reservation. Even Mrs. McKee plays a part in the story. Stafford's protagonist mentions that she had received the following letter: ". . . it is not that we are asking for the money you borrowed, but we feel that you ought to be financially independent. Can't you get a job, just any kind. You are such an impractical dreamer." [26] This story does not exhibit the brilliant use of language that would later become Jean Stafford's signature as a writer. Nevertheless, it is of interest not only because it is her first published story but because it reveals how she transformed the daily events of her life into the stuff of her fiction. Her protagonist, impatient and guilt-ridden, longs for a lovely house like the one she remembers living in as a child; for the kind of potatoes, "as firm as Japanese ivory buttons," that are mentioned in Proust; for "solid color pottery dishes"; for "beautiful friends, happy and rich, not worried." [27] It is obvious that the story's protagonist is a self-portrait of Jean Stafford during the summer of 1938.

Although Stafford was quite productive that summer, she still had little confidence in her abilities as a writer. On her twenty-third birthday she wrote to Mock, "Today is my birthday and I do not feel very good about it. A summing up, which I am afraid to do, would reveal so little of importance that I should be pathologically ashamed." [28] With only two apprentice novels completed, *Which No Vicissitude* and *Autumn Festival,* she confessed to being "scared to death" that she had already written herself out. She was gratified that her new friend and mentor, Evelyn Scott, continued to send her supportive letters, but she feared that Scott had overestimated her talent. [29] Moreover, the career of Evelyn Scott herself was hardly encouraging to a young would-be woman writer, for at the age of forty-five Scott had reluctantly accepted a teaching position at Skidmore College because her publisher was putting intolerable pressure on her to repay some of her debts. [30] Encouraged by Scott to submit the manuscripts of her two completed novels to a publisher Scott recommended, Stafford was depressed when, several months later, the novels were rejected. [31] That summer she was also discouraged because Edward

Davison seemed much less enthralled by her work than he had been earlier. Although he had urged her to reapply for a Houghton Mifflin Fellowship and had suggested that she attend the Boulder Writer's Conference once again that August to seek new sponsors, she was distressed by the somewhat less than enthusiastic letter she received from his secretary, who wrote, "It is possible that we can find someone to read the 20,000 words of your new novel." After receiving this letter, Stafford said she felt "unwanted" or at least "unsolicited" and consequently decided not to return to the conference that year.[32]

During this trying summer, one of the few events that Stafford awaited with pleasure was the almost daily arrival of a letter from Hightower. Several months earlier, while she was still at Stephens College, she had written the following journal entry about Hightower, whom she sometimes called "Ruprecht":

> Sometimes the hardest thing is that I do not love a man. In such a town as this you are constantly aware of youth, and you remember how it was in former years when the snow had melted from the foothills and the spring was gentle. You recall the darkness and the coolness and young men beside you and wonder if it will ever happen again and you know damned well it won't because you ask of a man a brain as well as a body and when you get the brain you want to twist it and you ignore the body and give them nothing. I am uneasy thinking about my life and the way it has no relationship to anyone else. Always I will be thinking where shall I go to get away from the uneasiness . . . and sick inside, queer, afraid, unrelated, I won't ever marry anyone now and my desire to love someone is desperately futile because I have destroyed everything in my soul. I will not because of Ruprecht and I cannot marry him because he would be unhappier with me than he is without me.[33]

Now, certain of "Ruprecht's" love for her and loving him in return, she felt affirmed by their relationship. "What really amazes me is that this is the first time in my life that I have not made a compromise, the first time that everything has been complete—the understanding, the admiration, the laughter, the scorn, the physical," she wrote to him.[34]

Their correspondence early that summer reflected the happiness they both felt. Yet at the same time each had troubling doubts about whether their relationship could endure. Hightower kept on thinking about the night they had spent in Geneseo on their way to Michigan. It was then that he had first told Stafford that he loved her and wanted to go to bed with her. She had refused, however, explaining subsequently that she had not yet been in love with him at that time. She had also been upset when he said that if they got married, the stipend for his fellowship at Harvard might be increased; she inferred from this comment that his interest in marrying her had more to do with his financial difficulties than with being in love with her. "When I was waiting for you in Albany, I was excited. I was excited all the time until you said—I think I could get more money if we got married. You over-estimate me, Comrade. I couldn't take it that way," she wrote to him soon after she had parted from him in Colorado.[35]

Although Hightower wanted to believe that Stafford was now in love with him, feeling that he was lacking in charm and was also much less talented than she was, he could not fully convince himself that she really loved him. He made little attempt to conceal his self-doubts from her. Enclosing two snap-shots of himself in a letter to her, for example, he said that they would remind her that he was not very handsome. "I had the 1 I got of you developed and it reminded me you are beautiful and that worried me somewhat," he said. "I do not want you to leave me for some more likely prospect as I am aware of my limitations and right now I feel especially diffident."[36] In another letter he described himself to her as "incompetent" in everything he did,[37] and though he jokingly accused her of stealing some of his best material for her novel, he admitted that because he was far less talented a writer than she was, he could never have used the material as well as she did.[38] He soon regretted his candor, however, fearing that once he had disclosed his own inadequacies, she would no longer find him desirable.[39]

Unhappy when he was apart from her, Hightower tried to persuade Stafford to come back to Salida for the remainder of the summer, but though she too said she was miserable when they were apart and would be "the glad-dest soul on earth" when everything was settled and they were together,[40] she observed that she had no money to travel, nor did she want to spend the rest of the summer at his parents' house. She explained, moreover, that she was pleased to be back with her family, for whom, despite what she sometimes said to the contrary, she felt "a sort of instinctive love," making her miserable when she reflected on her own selfishness. What he undoubtedly found some-what threatening in this letter was her comment that she felt she could also get more writing done in Oregon than she would be able to do in Salida. Realiz-ing that he might interpret what she had said to mean that her writing was more important to her than he was, she had added, ". . . it is not that I do not love you. It is that I love both you and my novel and for the time being any marriage of the two of you is out of the question."[41] In the meantime, she said, she was trying to arrange a temporary job for him as hayman and for her as assistant cook at her sister and brother-in-law's ranch in Hayden so that they would be able to spend the end of the summer together before he had to re-sume his studies at Harvard.

When Stafford informed Hightower that she was applying for a teaching

job in Oregon, he told her that he was concerned about the effect being separated from her during the coming year would have on their relationship and
insisted that he did not want to return to Harvard if she were to remain in
Oregon. Admitting that she was terrified by the thought that he was willing to
sacrifice his own future prospects for her sake, she replied:

> I think your fellowship is the best thing that has happened to either of us. It is
> certainly the most *tangible* thing, if you get what I mean. And I think you will
> be imbecilic if you don't take it and keep it. I am trying not to sound harsh,
> but listen, we aren't children any longer, we aren't going to Heidelberg after
> leaving Boulder. That was something temporary, it was a sort of *grand tour,* a
> sort of purge, but this is different, it is important, and I will say now that if I
> think that what has happened to my mother and my father is going to happen
> to you and me, I will never marry you because my love for you isn't a colle-
> giate infatuation that sees nothing but the immediate future in the presence of
> the beloved.[42]

What frightened her most was the thought that, if either her own ambitions or Hightower's were sacrificed for the sake of their relationship, the relationship itself would ultimately be destroyed and they would become "bitter,
acrid, miserable misanthropes," like her own parents. Insisting that she did
not want to harm either his chances or her own to gain recognition in the
future, she stated that the hardest job now facing her was breeding out of her
mind all of the resentments that had accumulated there. She said she firmly
believed that literature "has only two functions and those are the functions of
Sidney: to teach and delight." That conviction had prompted her to resolve, "I
will not write any more books that are discouraging; I will not be a writer
of defeat."[43]

In her letters Stafford assured Hightower that she was certain they would
be able to resolve all their present difficulties; however, she was so troubled
about their relationship that she decided to turn to Evelyn Scott for advice. In
response to her description of the diffident Hightower, Evelyn Scott cau-
tioned her: "One can make mistakes by accidents of blindness and survive
their effects; but to make mistakes as it were, 'on purpose' really is suicidal.
And the comparative ambition . . . isn't that the most dangerous? If two artists married they avoid the risks of such a combination only if each has the
urge with an equal fanaticism. Otherwise, surely, the superior talent is half
wasted by the need to pour into the possessor of inferior talents the conviction
that comes with nature's gifts." Scott expressed the opinion, moreover, that
Hightower's bitterness about everything and everybody, a trait Stafford had
mentioned to her, might turn out in the end to corrode his spirit completely,
and she concluded, "Oh, don't marry your man if it is as you describe, for

heaven's sake. The enslavement of someone (you) by pity (what it amounts to) represents such a lurid mutually degrading bond . . . You do have to *begin* by *presuming* equality, even if you are proved wrong later."[44] It is obvious that neither Scott nor Stafford nor Hightower himself would have predicted in 1938 that he would later have a distinguished career as a sinologist and professor in the Department of East Asian Languages and Civilization at Harvard University.

As the summer wore on, Stafford began to sink into one of her "foulest sloughs of despond."[45] When she found herself unable to write, she spent hours playing solitaire, or reading Proust, or picking fruit and beans for her mother to can. "I have never liked Mother nature and at present, covered with big welts and scratches, dirty, having an apple headache, I am feeling no kindlier," she remarked after working in her parents' garden.[46] Each evening her father would measure out a meager ration of port for all of them, making her long for the days when she and Mock had spent the evenings drinking in the waterfront bars of St. Louis.[47] Moreover, her routine was completely disrupted at the beginning of August when her parents moved to another house. The tension caused by the move resulted in tirades by her mother and "sullen mutterings" by her father, reminding her of the moves from Covina to San Diego and San Diego to Colorado. "We are moving and everything is in disorder and Mother and Dad are cross at each other and that makes me very unhappy and I wish I were dead," she wrote to Mock. She went on to explain,

> Simply being away from here won't solve the problem because I will always know what is going on even though I am not witnessing it. Lately I have been sort of sleepless nights and I lie there thinking and thinking and trying to find a solution or an assuagement of their unhappiness and there isn't any. If it were not that I would be leaving worse misery behind me, really I think I would resort to Lucy's remedy because I can think of nothing that I want except that which is impossible to gain—the happiness of my unfortunate family. Money, of course, would do part of the trick and I desperately want money now, tons of it, but I will never have any and it is useless to dream of impossible mansions for them or even impossible comfort.[48]

In the process of moving her trunk full of books, she sprained her ankle and hurt her shoulder.[49] Feeling that she was in the way and upset by the confusion, she also found that she could no longer concentrate on her writing. "I have quit writing for the summer because I can't settle down and if I did I couldn't work very well in the dining room which is the only available place," she complained to Mock.[50]

Although Stafford kept on postponing her departure from Oregon because she still hoped to find a teaching job for the coming year, she had pretty well decided to accept an assistantship that she had been offered at the University of Iowa. The prospect of enrolling in a doctoral program at Iowa that fall, however, was not an appealing one to her. As she cynically explained to Mock about Iowa, "And then I will get a big lovely juiceless PHD for my very *Own*. And then I will start reading old newspapers again and by that time I will have discovered my métier is not literature but millinery & I will come to the Change of You Know What and Hightower will still be writing me those letters saying hell, Bessie, we gotta make plans quick."[51] To Hightower she confided that she was terrified of the courses she would be obliged to teach at Iowa, of the poverty she would have to endure, of the language exams she would have to take, and of the preliminary exams, which would include questions on Hebrew, Greek, English, and American cultures, political philosophy, aesthetics, and criticism. "Not only am I terrified," she said. "I am also vastly uninterested."[52]

A visit from her brother Dick, home from his job as a forest ranger, provided a pleasant if temporary distraction late that summer. She described him to Hightower as "a rather nice gent" who did not "believe in working except with his hands" and who was "the original critic of colleges."[53] It is obvious from her remarks about her brother that, though she was still fond of him, they no longer had much in common. After her brother left, however, she felt lonely and bored, and she was increasingly alarmed by her father's "psychopathic" behavior. For days he did not say a word to anyone, but she frequently would hear him sardonically laughing to himself.[54] Much of the time she just sat and daydreamed about talking to "bright, clever, beautiful people who read the *New Yorker* and drink rum."[55] An inveterate list-maker, she sat down one day and enumerated fifty-three of her recent activities and some of the things she desired most. The last five items she listed were:

> 49. I want to be a rich lady.
> 50. And have a lot of velvet dresses
> 51. " " " " " " gardenias
> 52. " " 24 lb. typewriting paper
> 53. Or better yet, I want to be dead.[56]

As the weeks passed, Stafford began to feel uneasy because fewer and fewer letters from Hightower were appearing in her mailbox. "If you have stopped being in love with me, why dontcha tell me instead of sulking?" she wrote to him on July 14.[57] By August 16 she was complaining to Mock that no one wrote to her anymore, not even Hightower. And though she had earlier assured Hightower that she was not at all romantically interested in Mock, now, feeling rejected by Hightower, she adopted a somewhat flirtatious tone in her letters to Mock. "I want to laugh again and play our absurd games and talk about Paris in the Outside Inn. I didn't realize last year, of course, that you are a saint made of gold from Ophir," she said, describing herself as being "as wistful and lip-quivering" as she had been "that day 100 years ago" when she had parted from him at Union Station.[58]

It wasn't until early September, when she and Hightower met again at her sister's ranch, that she learned why she had received so few letters from him during the preceding month and a half. After she questioned him repeatedly about why he had written so infrequently, Hightower very reluctantly confessed that in recent weeks he had become romantically involved with a music teacher in Salida. Although he tried to defend his unfaithfulness by pointing out how problematic their own relationship seemed to him, she was too wounded by his defection at first to think of forgiving him. Writing to him soon after he had left the ranch to return to Cambridge, she said:

> . . . after you told me about the music teacher I wanted to die and that was the reason I said I should never see you again—because I loved you so desperately I could not endure it to think of your saying "and by the end of the summer I was in love with her and I was miserable at leaving" and that I was desiccated. That day we sat on the hay rack and you said she was the sort of woman you needed because she would darn your socks I wanted to tell you how all summer long in Oregon I had daydreamed about that . . . But I didn't tell you and anyway you would have laughed.[59]

Hightower's comment to her about wanting to marry the kind of woman who would darn his socks must have been particularly painful to Stafford, as such a comment would be to many a woman who believes that she must choose either to have a career or to be a dutiful housewife. But if she was conflicted about whether she wanted to devote her future life to darning Hightower's socks or to writing, she nevertheless insisted, "I have wanted domesticity. I have wanted to be your wife and not much more. I have wanted to bear a child for you. I have wanted you to be sick so I could nurse you . . ."[60]

One of the issues Stafford would grapple with for virtually the rest of her life was how a woman artist can possibly reconcile her need to create works of art with her desire to have a home and a family. So preoccupied was she with this dilemma that she decided to make this question the focal point of her next novel. That fall she wrote to Hightower from the University of Iowa:

> Yesterday I began my novel over again with an idea that has been working in my mind for a long time: the question: why is it that a woman cannot write a book like A Portrait of the Artist. I mean, why is it that her experiences cannot be those of a man. The main character, Gretchen Marburg, will make

an attempt to live such a life, that is with a male mind in which there is such
and such a compartment for literature and such a one for love, but in the end
she will be faced with the realization that a woman's mind can never be neatly
ordered and every experience is tinged by every other one.[61]

Unable to resolve this conflict between her "mind," which she considered
male, and her emotional needs, which she considered female, she nevertheless
tried to convince Hightower that she was passionately in love with him and
wanted to marry him. Now, when she felt his interest in her was flagging, she
desperately wanted to prove to him that she was not "desiccated," as he had
accused her of being. Attempting to woo him with words in place of deeds,
she wrote, "I am aching for you, Robert, I am aching to touch you, to kiss you
. . . I want to look at you over coffee cups and feel pride that you belong to me
and I want to tell you how much I admire you . . . I want to live with you
because I love you and I shall make you love me again."[62] Since he had blamed
his love affair with the music teacher on the fact that she herself had never
been willing to sleep with him, what she now dwelled on was not their friendship but the physical side of their relationship. Even though she feared that
her words might sound like the gushing confessions of a schoolgirl, she nevertheless resorted to penning torrid phrases that might have made her blush had
she reread them several years later. In the purplest of prose, she wrote:

> I have wanted to be consumed in your body. I have wanted to bend over your
> desk with my clean hair brushing your back. I have wanted you to look at the
> line my hips make on the counterpane. *I have wanted* is wrong. It is what I
> want now as I write this and I shall always want it. I know I am a woman.
> Never so much before have I been one. I look at myself, undressed, in the
> mirror and I desire your eyes to be on me. . . . I would like to promise you
> physical delight greater than any you have ever known, tenderness and
> understanding and the preservation of all that was good in Heidelberg. . . .
> One thing I can promise you is this: I am a woman romantically in love with
> you, vibrant at the memory of touching you, aching to touch you again, to
> know at last . . . the full articulation of passionate love.[63]

After reading this letter, Hightower felt more abject than ever about
having made "such a hideous mess of things." But though he was now sure
that it was Stafford he wanted to marry, he told her that by writing such a
letter, full of erotic phrases that were designed to arouse his passion for her,
she had taken "unfair advantage" of him in a situation that involved not only
him and her but the "ubiquitous" music teacher, to whom he felt he had also
incurred certain obligations.[64] In response to his letter, Stafford said that she
suspected he would react as he did, but she defended having tried with words

to rekindle his love. "Robert, what do you want of me?" she wrote. "I am, as I have told you, one thing: I am a writer, as a writer I love you, as a writer I read books, as a writer I live." She acknowledged that she was jealous of the music teacher, but said she would try to forget this whole painful episode because of her own love for him. Reverting then to the purple prose of her previous letter, she concluded, "I am asking you to receive a gift which I have: secret laughter, secret memory, thighs and lips and breasts and hands, friendship come to such a perfect consummation."[65]

In addition to worrying about her personal problems that fall, Stafford also had to deal with the stresses of being in an academic environment once more. Almost as soon as she arrived at the University of Iowa, she realized she had made a big mistake in going there. Feeling intellectually inadequate, she exclaimed to Hightower, "I hate all this. I hate it like hell and I shan't like it any better as time goes on. I am not smart enough for this place." She described her male colleagues as "intense, erudite young men with PHD's" who made jokes about Gothic verbs.[66] Finding them aloof, she complained that they were not impressed at all by her.[67] Her "de-ovarized, desiccated" female colleagues were also not to her liking.[68] "I have examined the other women in the eng. department (darling, you can't let that happen to me!) and I have found that I am superior to them only in one way—physically. I am built for bed, not for a classroom," she insisted.[69] Furthermore, she disliked having to live in a small, drab room without a real desk or adequate lighting;[70] and she did not enjoy teaching composition to "apathetic football material and militant women."[71] Though she was pleased with the seminar she was taking on Carlyle and Newman, she was distraught because she was scheduled to give a seminar paper on Newman's *Apologia* the following month and had not yet read even one page of the book. A visit from Mr. and Mrs. McKee only added to her woes: they insisted on speaking about the events that had led up to Lucy's suicide, and reminding Jean of the money she still owed them, they berated her once again for being a "dreamer."[72]

Intensely unhappy in Iowa, Stafford lay awake night after night, trying to figure out how she could possibly leave there. Almost immediately, she began to implore Hightower to let her join him in Cambridge. Although she said her primary reason for wanting to come to live in Cambridge was that she could not bear being separated from him, she also admitted that her other compelling reason for wanting to leave Iowa was that she disliked teaching, hated the people there, and was terrified that she would flunk her exams since she was "out of the habit of studying."[73] At first Hightower tried to point out to her how impractical she was being since neither of them had enough money to support themselves, but just as she had finally persuaded him to try and make arrangements for her to join him in Cambridge, she informed him that the director of the program at Iowa had let her drop her course work so that all she had to deal with was teaching and working on her novel. "I am somewhat over my desperation," she said, "and while I shall never be quite integrated until I start living with you, I shall be able to survive a little longer now that my work is coming on." Perhaps she realized that Hightower might be reminded of the preceding summer when she had chosen to work on her novel instead of joining him in Salida, for she added: "I know this sounds frightfully matter-of-fact. It is something I do not understand. Sometimes I feel that I *do* have a masculine mind. I cannot otherwise explain how it is that loving you as I do I can separate myself from you for the sake of my novel."[74]

Exactly two days after Stafford wrote this letter, however, she changed her mind once again and began to make plans to leave Iowa immediately, without informing anyone at the university of her decision. It is not clear whether she reached this decision primarily because, as she claimed to Hightower, she could not bear to be apart from him or whether her unhappiness about being a graduate student in large measure prompted her departure. On November 3 she wrote to Hightower: "I am leaving here Friday night in a wonderfully dramatic fashion, so dramatic that I'm sure I'll get caught up. I have been terrified today thinking of what I am doing. I have packed, graded my papers, and now I am going to class." She said she intended to leave no forwarding address. She would tell her family only that she was going to Boston and that Howard Mumford Jones would help her get a job. She had to make stops in Chicago, in Cleveland, and in New York, where she hoped to see Robert Berueffy. Then she would proceed to Boston. "I am full of joy and fear and I love you and I am so glad that we are going to be together at last . . . ," she told Hightower.[75] Neither Hightower nor Stafford could have predicted that her brief stop in Cleveland would forever alter the course of their lives.

Five

Boston Adventure
Winter 1938–Spring 1940

Boston Society, founded on the basis of nineteenth-century wealth and First Familyhood, was never designed to be a fluid one. . . . The ordinary Bostonian has been taught by the Proper Bostonian to give the West a wide berth.

CLEVELAND AMORY, *THE PROPER BOSTONIAN*

DURING JUNE OF 1932, the month Jean Stafford graduated from Boulder Prep, installments of a serial called *Kitty Frew* appeared each day in the *Boulder Daily Camera*. "WIFE OR MOTHER," its caption read, following which the author went on to say: "Who has the stronger claim? Garfield Frew disappointed his snobbish family by marrying a 'commoner' and his mother tried to create a rift between the young couple. Wealth, social position and autocratic power were on the mother's side, and Kitty Frew soon realized she was struggling against uneven odds."[1]

Five years later, Jean Stafford's own Garfield Frew, Robert Traill Spence Lowell IV, had begun to pay court to her via the mails after meeting her at the Boulder Writer's Conference during the summer of 1937. Whenever she received a letter from Cal Lowell during the year she was teaching at Stephens College, she would read passages from it aloud to her friend Bill Mock, who later observed, "The intensity of his adoration was obvious and amused us both."[2] She also used to relate to Hightower choice bits of literary gossip gleaned from Lowell's letters to her, but she never revealed their source, fearing perhaps that Hightower would be jealous if he knew she had been corresponding with this young man. Another person who knew that Lowell had been writing to Stafford from Kenyon College was Evelyn Scott. Remembering vividly the clumsy, disheveled, rather arrogant young poet who had been a member of the Tate-Ransom entourage during the summer of 1937, Scott commented to her, "Yes, that Lowell struck me as a proper ass." Scott made disparaging remarks not only about Lowell but also about the group of

Fugitive poets with whom Lowell had chosen to affiliate himself, observing: "But all that Tate-Ransom crowd has to revive the 'mysteries,' in their worst meaning, in order that Tate-Ransom may be sure of dictatorial officiation at the altar. . . . The reality in a measure—of art produced by people who are humanly false is one of those paradoxes my own stomach or conscience is always refusing to digest."[3]

Stafford herself made negative comments about Robert Lowell, but she was more interested in him than she admitted to her friends. When she left Iowa and found she had to change buses in Cleveland, she impulsively decided to wire Cal Lowell at Kenyon College in nearby Gambier and ask him to meet her at the Cleveland bus station. Describing her encounter with Lowell to Mock several weeks later, she said:

> But now cast back in your memory until you find the name of Cal Lowell and recall that he is a Boston poet of the Boston Lowells whom I knew in Boulder at the writer's conference. He is the one who pursued the Fords and pitched a pup tent in Allen Tate's backyard. . . . Well, anyway, he had written me this summer and said he wanted me to come up to Kenyon sometime and he wd. pay the fare, etc. so when I left, I figured he was probably good for a couple of drinks in that town you may recall, namely Cleveland O. so I wrote him and said meet me and he did and we drank a good deal of beer and he said he was in love with me and wd. I marry him and to avoid argument I said sure, honey, drink your beer and get me another one.[4]

Perhaps this was not the only time that Lowell had asked Stafford to marry him. According to Lowell's biographer, Ian Hamilton, Stafford might well have been the young woman to whom Lowell was alluding in his early poem "Walking in a Cornfield, After Her Refusing Letter." In this poem Lowell describes the despair of an unkempt young man in a dirty coat and "chafed shoes" who has received a "last dismissive" from a young woman with whom he is in love.[5]

After her rendezvous with Lowell in Ohio, Stafford boarded another bus and headed east. As she left the West to begin her life anew, her feelings might have been similar to those of the protagonist of her short story "The Liberation." A college teacher in a small western town, Polly Bay becomes engaged to a Bostonian named Robert Fair, who owns a handsome house at the foot of Beacon Hill. Announcing to her aunt and uncle, with whom she has been living, her intentions of leaving the West forever, Polly proclaims, "I hate, I despise, I abominate the West!"[6] She is convinced that the "dogmatic monotony of the town's provincialism" has almost succeeded in destroying her, and she shudders "to think of her narrow escape from wasting away in these arid foothills . . ."[7]

In a letter Stafford sent to Mock after she arrived in Cambridge, she described her own decision to leave Iowa and "stake her whole life on books [she] hadn't written yet" as one about which she had no regrets: "I was *piddling* with study, piddling with teaching, piddling with writing and doing nothing seriously," she said, "and now, although I'm starving, I'm working furiously."[8] After she settled into Hightower's apartment in Cambridge, she contacted Howard Mumford Jones at Harvard and soon joyfully reported: "I just took down the first 200 pages of my novel to the Atlantic with a letter from Mr. H. M. Jones who calls me his darling and says I have guts and entertained me twice in his study in Harvard College with wit and wisdom and Phillip Morris cigarettes, letters to everyone, a substantial loan of money . . ."[9]

The novel in question was the one entitled *Neville*, which dealt with her experiences at Stephens College. In his editorial report, A. O. Ogden, editor of the Atlantic Monthly Press, praised Stafford's ability to "handle the English language as a skilled carpenter handles a chisel—with ease, deftness, accuracy, and rhythm. A situation is summed up in a line of conversation; a character delineated by one fatuous remark that tells the whole story," he wrote. Much to Stafford's disappointment, however, he voted against publication of the novel because he thought it would be difficult to market a novel about college faculty life in a small town, and because he felt that if the Atlantic Monthly Press were to publish her thinly disguised portrait of Stephens College, the press might be subject to a libel suit.[10]

Despite the fact that *Neville* had been rejected, making contact with Archie Ogden proved to be very beneficial for Stafford: he was so favorably impressed by what she had written to date that he decided to offer her an advance on her next novel. On December 9, 1938, after meeting with Ogden and two other editors, Stafford received a check for two hundred and fifty dollars and an option on her next novel. Entitled *Autumn Festival,* it would include some of the material from *Neville* but would primarily be based on material in her Heidelberg journals, which Howard Mumford Jones had taken back to Boston with him after the 1937 Boulder Writer's Conference.

If, after her arrival in Cambridge, Stafford was jubilant about the encouragement and financial support she had finally begun to receive for her writing, during the same period she was distraught about her relationship with Hightower. During the month of November, she shared an apartment with Hightower that he had rented for them in Cambridge, but almost immediately both she and Hightower began to realize that they were far less compatible as lovers than as friends. Later, remembering the agonizing quarrels that had erupted during their nights together, she wrote to him:

I knew as I lay there beside you every night that what you wished was my
death so that you could grieve but no longer desire me. I knew that you did
not believe in my frigidity—you have so rarely believed me at all. . . . I was
afraid of you those nights, sometime frantic when you touched me. . . .
Robert, no aphrodisiac has yet been devised to make me desire, to make me
submit, yes, but not to revel in it. I want children, I want a house, I want to be
a faithful woman. I want those things more than I want my present life of a
writer, but I shall have none because my fear will make me unfaithful and
desire cannot be hoped for, it is too late and I have been too much revolted.[11]

It is not clear whether Stafford had any understanding of why she was "revolted" or why she was sexually unresponsive. Perhaps her "frigidity" was
one of the problems she dealt with in therapy later on when she became a
patient of Dr. Mary Jane Sherfey, a psychiatrist interested in female sexual
dysfunction who would write about this issue in *The Nature and Evolution of
Female Sexuality.*

No doubt Jean Stafford's growing infatuation with Robert Lowell, an infatuation that she did not at first admit to others or even herself, exacerbated
the tension between her and Hightower during these difficult weeks. On November 20, soon after her arrival in Cambridge, she received a telegram from
Lowell announcing that he would arrive in Cambridge the next day.[12] The
sender, who had been given Robert Berueffy's address by Stafford and Hightower's address by Berueffy, had also sent a friend in New York City to ask
Whit Burnett and Ford Madox Ford whether they knew where she was staying. Once Lowell was informed about Hightower's address and phone number, he telephoned Hightower several times and asked him to give Stafford
the telephone number of a place in Cambridge where he would await her call.
Describing to Bill Mock a traumatic meeting with Lowell that occurred the
following day, Stafford still portrayed herself as the very unwilling object of
Lowell's ardent pursuit: "So I called him the next day and he came over and I
had to go up to Bedford with him for lunch and he kept saying if I didn't
marry him he wd. just run the car off the road, etc. so I said he cd. go to hell
and don't bother me any more and he got savage and I got scared, so I said well
I will see you once more but only in the company of other people." She also
described a meeting she had had afterward with an unnamed friend of
Lowell's from Harvard who had told her that Lowell had said he wanted her
"more than anything else in his life" and had proclaimed that she would never
be free of him. "It makes me perfectly sick," she said about Lowell's pursuit of
her, "because he is an uncouth, neurotic, psychopathic murderer-poet . . ."[13]

After Lowell had appeared at Hightower's apartment, Stafford was forced
to admit to Hightower that she had been corresponding with Lowell and had

seen him in Ohio. Although she adamantly insisted that she was not in love with Lowell and that in fact she was frightened by his persistence, Hightower could not have been pleased to learn that the young woman he hoped to marry was being pursued by a handsome, wealthy, aspiring poet who was a member of the Boston Lowell clan. Several months later, discussing with Hightower why she had betrayed him, she admitted that she had begun to wonder whether she was capable of being faithful to any man. "I make myself attractive to men because I am afraid not to," she said, "because I still want what I wanted in Boulder and did not get, but the men are damn fools because I'm evil and I know it."[14]

After the Thanksgiving holidays were over and Lowell had returned to Kenyon College, Stafford and Hightower sadly acknowledged that it would be foolish for them to continue to live together, so strained had their relationship become. Hightower helped her find a room in Concord where she hoped she would be out of Lowell's reach and could settle down to work on her novel. Concord, she thought, was "a wonderful place for a lady writer." She was pleased that her room, located in a "monstrously Victorian" house at 2 Monument Street,[15] had a window seat as well as a fireplace, and she was charmed by the typical New England town, with its neat, well-kept, colonial wooden houses, its imposing old trees, and its unobtrusive shops. When the weather permitted, she enjoyed walking through the quaint streets or reading the Sunday papers in the Sleepy Hollow Cemetery, where Emerson, Hawthorne, and the Alcotts were buried. In Concord, too, was the Alcott house containing Louisa May Alcott's desk and diary. This desk was to serve an important symbolic function in *Boston Adventure:* it is one of the significant pieces of furniture in the "red room" that Stafford's protagonist, Sonia Marburg, conjures up as a private sanctuary for her troubled spirit.[16]

One of Stafford's short stories, "The Bleeding Heart," describes the experiences of a newcomer to Concord. Recalling her own feelings of alienation during the brief period that she had lived alone in a rented room in Concord, Stafford wrote movingly of the loneliness of Rose Fabrizio, a Mexican girl from the West. Envying the people who were lucky enough to have been born and raised in this tranquil and quaint New England town, Rose longs to be adopted by a New Englander. As John Stafford liked to do, Rose's father wears "miner's shoes studded with cleats that tore up the lineoleum and made a harsh racket."[17] As Ethel Stafford had done, Rose's mother feels like a social outcast and broods about "the impertinence of a salesgirl in the five and ten."[18] And Rose, a college graduate, regrets, as Stafford did, that she had not gone to Radcliffe and considers her own education to have been a "shabby, uninteresting affair."[19] What Stafford reveals as well, however, is Rose's gradual realization that even in this New England town everything is not as idyllic as she had first imagined it to be. Nevertheless, Rose cannot help comparing Concord to the dreary town in the West where she grew up:

> Her own town, out West, had next to no trees and those were puny and half bald. The main street there was a row of dirty doorways which led into the dirty interiors of pool halls, drugstores where even the soda fountain bar had a flaccid look, and small restaurants and beer parlors and hotels whose windows were decorated sometimes with sweet-potato vines growing out of jam cans painted red, and sometimes with a prospector's pick-ax and some spurious gold ore . . .[20]

Although Stafford found the town of Concord to her liking, as the following note to Hightower suggests, she was very lonely there and looked forward to her visits to the apartment of Hightower, to whom she remained emotionally attached even after they stopped living together: "I am very lonely & I wish I were sick so that I could come home. I love you the most and I think I can work better with you . . . I love you So Much and will be home Frd. afternoon if you want me to."[21] Seeking additional congenial companionship, she was also planning to meet Mock in New York City after Christmas and to attend the annual Modern Language Association meeting there. She told him, however, that she feared Lowell might follow her to New York City: "I will probably be again hounded by Cal (Caliban) Lowell who is the worst monster I know. He is laboring under the delusion that I am leading him a Romantic Chase and that in the end he will carry me home as his bride. He is twenty one. It's too bad."[22]

On December 14 Stafford wrote again to Mock, telling him she was "working like a dog" but expected to be in New York City by December 27 and would call him at his hotel.[23] The next communication he received about her was a telegram from Hightower dated December 22, which read: "JEAN IN ACCIDENT   NOT COMING NEW YORK   SKULL FRACTURE   NOT SERIOUS."[24] This "not serious" accident, however, was to have the most serious consequences, both physical and emotional, for Jean Stafford.

The accident had occurred a day earlier, when Robert Lowell, in Boston for the Christmas holidays, had borrowed his parents' car to take Stafford to a Boston nightclub. Despite her frequent protestations to the contrary, she seems to have been interested enough in him—or worn down enough by his pursuit—to consent to go out with him. Lowell was known to be a very careless driver and had very bad eyesight; furthermore, he had been drinking before they set out in the car together for that fateful ride. Stafford claimed subsequently that the car crash into a wall at the end of a dead-end street in Cambridge had not been an "accident" at all: when she had told Lowell once more that she would not marry him, he had become so angry that he threatened to kill them both and headed for an embankment.[25] Though the car was damaged, Lowell was unharmed. He was later fined seventy-five dollars in the Cambridge District Court for driving dangerously while intoxicated.[26] Stafford, however, was seriously injured in the accident: her nose was smashed, and her skull and jaw were fractured. She was taken by ambulance to a Cambridge hospital, where she would remain for almost a month before she was well enough to be released. The immediate physical effects of the accident were bad enough: she would need two operations on her nose and many visits to physicians to repair it; her face was lacerated, and the nerves of two of her upper teeth were so badly damaged that she had to have the teeth replaced; and she also sustained some skeletal injuries. Three weeks after the accident she told Mock that she looked "hideous," and though photographs of her taken several years later show that she was still attractive albeit somewhat battered-looking, after her nose was surgically repaired following the accident, she lamented, ". . . it isn't *my* nose."[27] When she first met Jean Stafford, Eileen Simpson, who was then married to the poet John Berryman, was less impressed by the appearance of Stafford's nose than she was by her tear-filled eyes, another aftermath of the accident. "They seemed to be bathed in an excess of fluid, so that they looked permanently welled-up, giving the impression that she had been crying or might do so at any moment," she said. "It may have been this, as well as her expression in repose that made her look sad."[28] Lowell's good friend, Blair Clark, observed that as a result of the accident "there was about a 25 percent reduction in the aesthetic value of her face."[29] As for the other long-lasting effects of the accident, during the rest of her life Stafford would have back pain and breathing difficulties that might well have resulted from the car crash. She also never could bring herself to learn how to drive a car, a skill that would have been very valuable to her during the many years when she lived alone.

During her lengthy hospital stay, Stafford was visited by Mock, who arrived at the hospital with new nightgowns for her. Realizing how insolvent she was, he also sent her small sums of money from time to time. Another person who visited her was Lowell's former English teacher at St. Mark's, the poet Richard Eberhart. In addition to visiting her at the hospital, after she was released Eberhart treated her to dinner at an elegant Boston restaurant and introduced her there to W. H. Auden, whom she described as "the ugliest pansy you ever clapped eyes on."[30] Following her release from the hospital,

Archie Ogden, her editor at the Atlantic Monthly Press, also offered to help her, insisting that she stay with him and his wife Betty until she felt well enough to manage on her own.

Despite all this attention, Stafford was both worried and depressed, for in addition to having to deal with the pain and the physical problems the accident had caused, she was frantic about how she would pay her doctor bills. Furthermore, the small advance she had received for her novel was almost exhausted, and although her editor told her to rest and give no further thought to her novel until she had fully recuperated, she felt guilty because she was much too upset to write.[31]

Perhaps what upset Stafford most of all was Hightower's reaction to her accident. Early in January he sent her a long letter in which he told her he did not want her to write to him again or to see him because she had lied to him repeatedly and had hurt him too badly for him to forgive her. After reading his bitter accusations and his negative assessment of her character, her first reaction was to attempt to mollify him by accepting the full blame for what had occurred. She did not try to defend herself but admitted that her selfishness had destroyed both of them. Wishing to dramatize how unhappy she now was and how filled with self-loathing, she said: "After a while maybe I will not be able to stand it and then in a burst of tears that are inside of me and cannot come out, I will kill myself. . . . I love you and I have killed us both and now as I end the letter the tears are starting, warm against my eyelids."[32]

After several weeks had elapsed without any response from Hightower, she wrote another letter to him. This time she was less contrite and also less maudlin. Though she still conceded that she was "self-centered," "disintegrate," and "weak," she told him that after thinking about some very basic issues on which they disagreed, she had concluded reluctantly: "What has happened, ugly though it is, we must both grant is probably for the best. The things we disagree on (money, frivolity, urbanity) are not as trifling as they seem when you merely write them down on paper. In the matter of money we tend to exaggerate each other's feelings so that you regard me as prodigal and I think of you as parsimonious." She also reminded him that though she too had been hurt in the past, she had forgiven him for his indiscretions. Insisting that, contrary to what he seemed to believe, she herself had not been drunk when the accident occurred, she said that she was not as irresponsible as he made her out to be. She offered to contribute ten dollars a month for the apartment he was living in—the one that he had expected to share with her—and choosing her words very carefully, she finally implored him, "For the love of God, Robert, think one decent thing of me sometime."[33]

Moved by her letter, Hightower responded immediately. He conceded that

she had done nothing to him for which he had not set an unfortunate prece-
dent, and sadly agreeing that "no two people were ever less suited to each
other," he tried to reassure her that his thoughts about her were "mostly decent thoughts," that he still admired her, and that he regarded her as his "one
friend."[34] Only the frightening realization of how close they had come to permanently severing the connection between them allowed both Hightower
and Stafford to admit that each had failed the other.

After Stafford left the hospital, a friend from Boulder named Ruth Stauffer also offered to help her. The older sister of one of Jean Stafford's childhood
playmates, Ruth Stauffer had known her as a "friendly, freckled little girl"
who had often visited Ruth's sister Martha when Jean and Martha were in
fifth grade together. The friendship between Jean and Martha had ended
abruptly, however, when the Stauffers moved to Denver. Although Martha
Stauffer later returned to Boulder to attend the university, she and Jean had
not resumed their friendship. Martha, Stafford said, had "lived happy as a
happy and beautiful young girl should live amongst friends and in the midst
of campus merriments—tea dances, junior proms, formals at the Beta house,"
whereas she herself, conscious of her own poverty, her plainness, and her
awful clothes, had resented "the glorious blooming" of her childhood friend.[35]
Soon after Stafford had arrived in Cambridge, she contacted Martha's sister,
Ruth, who was then working on her doctoral dissertation at Harvard after
matriculating at Radcliffe, and the two women met for dinner. "She looked
regal, with her blonde hair braided in a coronet," Ruth Stauffer recalled.[36]
When Stafford was discharged from the hospital, she called Ruth and told her
that she was at the Ogdens' overcrowded apartment and was sleeping on their
sofa. Ruth mentioned her friend Jean's plight to Mr. and Mrs. Malcolm Donald, a wealthy couple for whom Ruth was then working as a governess, and
her employers generously invited Jean to stay in the guest room of their spacious home in Milton until she was feeling well enough to return to her own
room in Concord. Although Stafford would later make nasty remarks about
the female Ph.D. candidates from Radcliffe who were Ruth's friends, as she
often did when she referred to women she considered to be better educated
than she was, she was fond of Ruth. Furthermore, she found that living in the
luxurious Donald home and being waited on by the Donalds' maid was a
pleasant change from living alone in one room in Concord.

While Stafford was staying in Milton, Robert Lowell's mother invited her
to lunch. Stafford later confided to Mock that since the accident she had developed "a hideous complex" about her head and was afraid of falling on icy
pavements or riding in automobiles. As a result, she was terrified when
Charlotte Lowell, on an icy day in January, drove her back to Milton in her

blue Packard, the very car in which the accident had occurred. Describing her encounter with Charlotte Lowell, she said:

> . . . the most ghastly experience I have ever had in my life was driving home to Milton with Mrs. Lowell (who is a Lowell driver) in that same car on icy streets. I went to lunch there and we had spinach, pork, cornbread and emetic steam pudding with a blob of whipped cream on top. . . . She is a woman of very little brain and I had great difficulty in talking to her. She is a match-maker, very embarrassing in a neurotic woman, and an advocate of psycho-analysis and I suspect that she herself is being psychoanalyzed—it's quite the Boston fashion.[37]

It is difficult to imagine that Charlotte Lowell, descendant of the plutocratic Winslows and very much aware of her own elevated position in Boston society, would have chosen to play the role of "matchmaker" between her son and Jean Stafford. She probably did not want her only son to marry anyone while he was still an undergraduate, and, moreover, she would not have approved of having him marry a "nobody" from Colorado who was older than he was and who had been involved with him in an accident that she considered scandalous. Recalling how Charlotte Lowell had later snubbed her, Jean Stafford told Eileen Simpson: "Charlotte Lowell, introducing me to her Beacon Hill friends, would say, 'Tell us, Jean dear, where is it you come from?' Rolling the word around in my throat, and using my undertaker voice, I'd say, 'Colorado,' at which the assembled guests would turn to each other and murmur—as if I'd said I was from the upper reaches of the Orinoco!"[38] It was more likely her curiosity rather than her interest in matchmaking that led Charlotte Lowell to make the acquaintance of the young woman who had captured the fancy of her son "Bobby." Perhaps she also wanted to see for herself whether or not reports of the serious injuries Stafford had sustained in the accident were accurate.

In February and again in April Stafford had to have a surgical procedure performed on her nose. The first, for which local rather than general anesthesia was used, caused her to experience such excruciating pain that she "nearly leapt from the operating table";[39] and following the second operation, she began to suffer from debilitating headaches, projectile vomiting, and faintness. According to Eileen Simpson, Stafford later loved to talk about the medical details of her case, relating her symptoms with "clinical detachment," but she refrained from discussing the emotional trauma the accident had caused her.[40]

Eight years after the accident occurred, however, she published a fictional work that anatomized both the physical pain and the mental anguish she had endured. Its title, "The Interior Castle," was derived from the confessional work by the sixteenth-century mystic, St. Teresa of Avila, who had described the soul as both an "Orient pearl"[41] and a "castle made of a single diamond of very clear crystal, in which there are many rooms. . . ."[42] Using similar words to describe her brain, Stafford's protagonist, Pansy Vanneman, pictures it as a "jewel," a "flower," a "light glass," an "envelope of rosy vellum containing other envelopes, one within the other,"[43] a "pink pearl,"[44] a treasure "always fragile, always deeply interior and invaluable."[45] As Pansy lies immobilized in a hospital bed six weeks after an automobile accident, the surgeon who is in charge of her case wonders whether she had been a beauty before the crash; now he cannot tell "what the face had been, for it was so bruised and swollen, so hacked-up and lopsided. The black stitches the length of the nose, across the saddle, across the cheekbone, showed there would be unsightly scars."[46] Slowly, methodically, Stafford dissects her protagonist's pain, just as the surgeon in the story dissects the minute nerves in his patient's nose with his scalpel, penetrating regions that are not completely anesthetized. In its terrifying evocation of the icy atmosphere of the operating room, "The Interior Castle" resembles a short story by Conrad Aiken called "Mr. Arcularis," which Hightower had recommended to Stafford in 1937. It is also reminiscent of William Carlos Williams's short story "The Use of Force," for both Williams and Stafford depict the examination a doctor performs on his female patient as a kind of violation, almost a rape. As the surgeon probes the nostrils of Pansy Vanneman, Stafford writes, "beyond the screen as thin as gossamer, the brain trembled for its life, hearing the knives hunting like wolves outside, the sniffing and snapping."[47] Stafford's remarkable short story suggests how traumatic her own accident and subsequent medical treatment had been to her. Although her protagonist physically survives the harrowing ordeal of the operation, she bitterly calculates nevertheless what she has lost as a result of her accident and the surgical procedure she is forced to undergo as a result. "The Interior Castle," one of Stafford's most impressive short stories, concludes as Pansy, back in her own hospital room, reflects bitterly on what her experience has cost her: "There was great pain, but since it could not serve her, she rejected it and lay as if in a hammock in a pause of bitterness. She closed her eyes, shutting herself up within her treasureless head."[48] Although she never specifies what "treasure" her protagonist has lost, the story is a meditation on the loss of innocence and the violation of selfhood.

During much of the winter and spring following the accident, Stafford regularly experienced severe headaches that greatly hampered her ability to concentrate on her writing. Although she realized that her lack of productivity was due at least in part to her physical condition, she nevertheless felt guilty about how little progress she was making on her novel. Depressed and anxious and lonely, she spent many evenings consuming more alcohol than was good for her, on one evening drinking half a bottle of sherry alone when Lowell's friend Blair Clark failed to visit her as he had promised to do.[49] Not the least of her worries was the sorry state of her finances. After squandering some of her remaining funds on having a local dressmaker sew a fur cape and hat for her, she confessed that she feared she would never be able to pay her outstanding medical bills. She admitted, however, that she was looking forward to having Lowell's insurance company "pay through the nose" when her case against Lowell was settled.[50] Yet despite her own interest in the money she eventually expected to receive from Lowell to compensate her for her suffering and to help pay her medical bills, she criticized her family for eagerly inquiring how much money she hoped to receive when the case came to trial. The Staffords, she complained, were "wild" when they heard she might be awarded a substantial sum of money for damages and had written her letters filled with "the yapping of bloodthirsty wolves."[51] She wanted to keep her life as separate as possible from that of her family and, consequently, was also very much perturbed when she received the "hideously embarrassing" news that her father was sending his own articles to her editors at the Atlantic Monthly Press.[52]

Although she constantly feared that she would be destitute and would, as a result, be forced to give up her hopes of becoming a writer and take a mundane job to sustain herself, she nevertheless managed to feed herself and to pay her rent that winter. Helping to sustain her was the money that Mock continued to send her; moreover, thanks to the fact that Howard Mumford Jones had interceded on her behalf, she was able to earn a bit of money by reviewing books for the *Boston Evening Transcript*.[53]

Somehow, despite her very real poverty, Stafford managed to scrape together enough money to finance several trips to New York City between March and June of 1939 so that she could meet with Evelyn Scott, Martha Foley, Whit Burnett, the Davisons, and Ford Madox Ford. After a visit to Ford and his artist wife at their New York apartment, "dimlit, cluttered with teacups and easels," she reported to Mock that she had gotten a little drunk but was pleased that they seemed to find her amusing. Troubled to hear that Stafford had become the victim of "the Back Bay Grizzly," Ford's wife told her grimly that she was convinced Cal Lowell "was capable of murder," and she declared that she pitied "any girl that he should fall in love with."[54] After Stafford returned to Concord, she wrote to Archie Ogden that the Fords had convinced her Cal Lowell was really "pathological and capable of murder." She said they had told her such horrible things about him that she was thinking of securing the services of a lawyer and taking out an injunction against Lowell.[55]

During one of her visits to New York City that spring, Stafford stayed at the apartment of Robert Berueffy, who was working as an accompanist for a ballet company and was also employed part time as an arranger for the Irving Berlin Music Company. When she showed up unexpectedly at Berueffy's apartment, she explained that she was running away from Lowell and needed a hiding place. Always amused by her hilarious recitations of her endless misfortunes, Berueffy was treated during the days that followed to tales about his friend Hightower, about the Lowells, and about the Lowells' fractious son. She told Berueffy that Hightower, furious at Lowell for hounding her, had said he was going to sell his typewriter, buy a gun, and shoot Lowell. Stafford also delighted in speaking about her meeting with Lowell's parents. According to Stafford, when she had been introduced by Charlotte Lowell to Cal's father, who was confined to a wheelchair, Charlotte had said, "Yes, the Commander hasn't been the same since Bobby hit him." The altercation to which she was referring was one that had taken place several years earlier: outraged when he had learned that his father had written a letter to the father of his girlfriend suggesting that Anne not be allowed to go to his rooms at Harvard without proper chaperonage, Cal had knocked his father to the ground.[56]

Stafford remained at Berueffy's apartment for several days. Then, at five o'clock one morning, Berueffy was awakened by the sound of someone loudly knocking on his door. There stood Robert Lowell, "looking very large and unkempt." The half-asleep Berueffy heard the strange young man on his doorstep mumble, "I see you do indeed have the mark of genius on your brow," after which Lowell asked whether "Miss Jean Stafford" was in the apartment. Having heard her stories about Lowell's volatile temperament, Berueffy decided not to allow Lowell to awaken her, and he somewhat reluctantly showed Lowell to an empty bedroom after Lowell asked whether he could possibly sleep on the floor since he had been up the whole night. Stafford did not awaken Lowell until late the following afternoon. Much to Berueffy's surprise, for she had insisted that she had no interest in her would-be suitor, she spent the next few days in Lowell's company. Berueffy himself found Lowell amusing. He recalled that Lowell remarked one evening, "A man thinks better in dirty drawers," and Lowell also commented that he had no familiarity with the common people. Berueffy, who had heard about Lowell's erratic behavior from Stafford, felt that he was dealing with a person who might become violent without too much provocation; however, Lowell was on his best behavior during this visit.[57]

Shortly after Stafford returned from New York City, Lowell came back to Boston from Kenyon College for his spring vacation and resumed his courtship. He seemed "completely metamorphosized," she later reported to Mock. She said that Lowell had taken her "politely to tea" at his Grandmother Winslow's and to the opening of Evans's uncut *Hamlet*. Both she and Lowell wore formal attire for the latter event and sat in the fourth row "among Old Boston," making her feel as decadent as if she had lived all her life on Beacon Street.[58] She delighted in accompanying Lowell to five o'clock tea at his grandmother's house, an elegant brownstone on Beacon Hill where servants were summoned by ringing a bell and visitors left engraved calling cards. Originally something of an outsider herself in Boston society, Lowell's Grandmother Winslow, who had grown up in North Carolina, was probably looking forward to meeting her unpredictable grandson's girlfriend from Colorado since Lowell's Grandfather Winslow had made his fortune in Colorado as a mining engineer. In *Boston Adventure* Stafford would soon describe the elegant and intimidating world of Beacon Hill society through the eyes of her poor, provincial protagonist. At first Sonia Marburg, dazzled by Boston society, refuses to believe that it is "decadent" though it has been described as such by one of its members. "Decay," she muses, "must come from within and I could imagine nothing but an external calamity, a social revolution that could eradicate this solid society."[59] As Stafford described Sonia Marburg's initiation into this world of affluence and elegance, she might well have been recalling her own visit to Lowell's grandmother's elegant house on Beacon Hill, or the evening when, dressed in a hand-me-down evening dress that had once belonged to her sister Margie, she had sat in the fourth row of a theatre with Lowell and the cream of Boston society.

Observing Cal Lowell in his own elegant world no doubt helped to change Stafford's attitude toward him. By the end of Lowell's spring vacation, she had agreed to marry him. It is curious that she did not tell many of her friends about her engagement and that she still continued to make snide remarks about Lowell to people like Hightower and Mock. Perhaps, as David Roberts has suggested, she did not want word to get out that she and Lowell were engaged since she feared that might jeopardize her chances to win her lawsuit against him.[60] Nevertheless, she might have wanted to hint that she was becoming more intimate with Lowell than she had been earlier when, on May 3, she sent Mock a letter written on stationery with the Lowells' address on the letterhead.[61] That spring, however, she did not actually admit to him or to Hightower that the persistent "Back Bay Grizzly" had prevailed.

After Lowell returned to Kenyon College at the end of his spring vacation,

Stafford resumed her "lady-writer life." Her solitude was interrupted only when Lowell's former teacher, Richard Eberhart, took her to Marblehead for a lobster dinner and gave her a book of his poetry. In *The Mad Musician,* a verse play that Eberhart published in 1951, he wrote about his former student, Robert Lowell, and about Jean Stafford as well. It is obvious that Son, Father, and Mother, and an intellectual young woman from the West whom Eberhart calls "Miss Savage" are portraits of Lowell, Lowell's parents, and Stafford. Insisting to Son that "he must not see Miss Savage any more at all," Mother and Father in Eberhart's play within a play urge him to "become more practical." As Father threatens to cut off Son's income, Mother exclaims about Miss Savage:

> Give up that wretched girl. You must!
> She is beneath you, not even in the register,
> From the West, and her family is unthinkable.[62]

The Schoolmaster, who is obviously a character based on Eberhart himself, urges his brilliant pupil to keep his feet on the ground. The college psychiatrist says that Son "eats his toenails," and he pronounces his patient, who "talks with bitter, cryptic wit," to be not only "rude, vain, cruel, gloomy," but "mad."[63] Despite his parents' objections, Son continues to see Miss Savage; he cracks up the car in which she is a passenger, causing her jaw to be badly broken and her face lacerated; subsequently, he marries her; and as the play ends, he is incarcerated in a federal penitentiary after he has proclaimed himself a conscientious objector, an event that was to mark Lowell's life as well. Although Eberhart's play has little literary value, it is an interesting portrayal of the Lowell-Stafford relationship. Moreover, the name Savage, which Eberhart gave to the character who represents Jean Stafford, is the same surname she would later give her own female protagonist from the West, Cora Savage, in her autobiographical novel *The Parliament of Women.*

That spring Stafford had to pay many visits to the doctor to have her nose repaired. Attempting to be humorous, but at the same time graphically describing her ordeal, she wrote to Mock:

> I hear the needle going in and it sounds very much like the various noises a person might hear in a butcher shop. . . . The result is that I feel very bad and am rarther [sic] gloomy and sometimes feel as if I were going to have a fainting fit going upstairs and I have let my housework go something fierce and can hardly stir my stumps to put up the children's lunches and pore Joe hasn't had a square meal since I don't know when. The score seems to be sawbones sawbones sawbones ad infinitum ad nauseam . . .[64]

In addition to her physical pain, she also had to endure the disappointment of being given a negative response to a draft of *Autumn Festival* that she had submitted to the Atlantic Monthly Press. "The Atlantic Monthly says, 'Miss Stafford has read too much Joyce.' To hell and be damned," she complained to Mock. Something she did not mention to him, however, was that she was not the only one whose manuscript had recently been turned down by the editors of the Atlantic Monthly Press. A poem Lowell had asked her to send to her friends at the Atlantic along with her own work had also been rejected. In view of Lowell's later successful career as a poet, it is interesting to note how the poetry editor had responded to his early work. Archie Ogden noted that even though the poetry editor had found the poem "interesting for its play on sounds and for the infusion of the contemporary with the past," the poem ultimately had been judged "too artificial" to be of interest to their readers.[65]

Stafford paid her final visit to her doctor on June 4. Though she was relieved to be finished with the unpleasant treatments she had been receiving, she continued to be restless and found it difficult to complete the revision of *Autumn Festival.* "If I had passage and money for candy en route, dear Cousin, I wd be sailing with you on the Ile de France, having had quite enough of Emerson's tombstone and Thoreau's eternal pond as well as of Bostonian inanities," she wrote to Mock on the eve of his departure for Europe. But, she explained, her bank balance was zero, her case against Lowell's insurance company was pending, and the revision of her novel was still not completed.[66] Despite the sorry state of her finances, she nevertheless managed to make yet another trip to New York that month. On her return, she wrote a humorous letter to Hightower. She described to him all the mishaps she had encountered, including missing a train, taking a night boat to Boston, discovering that its destination was not Boston but Providence, and being pursued by a Health Scientist who presented her with a pamphlet entitled "The Christian Way to Diet. How to get rid of constipation forever." Having consumed nothing but coffee, beer, and whiskey for twenty-four hours, she said she felt terrible as she wended her way by bus and commuter train back to Concord.[67]

As the weeks of June and July dragged on with no dramatic change in her mood or circumstances, Stafford began to be concerned about her tendency to drink too much to ease both her psychological and physical pain. "I have taken the veil and at the moment do not think I will become alchoholic [*sic*]," she wrote to Hightower. She also told him in the same letter that she was distressed because Robert Lowell's parents had departed for Europe "under peculiar circumstances," taking "enough clothes to last three years," withdrawing all their valuables from the bank vault, and making the "sinister remark that they might be gone indefinitely."[68] Several days after her twenty-fourth birthday, she enumerated her current woes to Hightower: "I do not have piles. But there is the nose. I am very tired. I have not done anything on the novel for two weeks. I have not done anything for two weeks. I don't have anything to write. That was a good dream. . . . Well, brother, the summer is sure going quick. I was 24 yrs. old the other day and I felt right bad about it as I figured up that the next time I wd be 25 which is what a person might call advanced."[69]

Although she had been discharged by her doctors in Boston, Stafford continued to have headaches and problems with her breathing. Feeling guilty about her condition, Lowell finally insisted that she come to Johns Hopkins in Baltimore to be seen by a specialist that his classics professor at Kenyon had recommended. Lowell's friend Blair Clark accompanied Stafford to Baltimore, but when she got there and was told by the specialist that she ought to have another operation, she adamantly refused. According to Clark, there was "a scene" at the railroad station in Baltimore as he and Stafford were about to board the train for Boston; however, Lowell had no choice but to respect her wishes. After this fiasco Lowell returned to Kenyon for the summer. Merrill Moore, who was acting as Lowell's guardian during his parents' absence, assured Lowell's father that John Crowe Ransom, Lowell's mentor at Kenyon, had told him Lowell intended to spend the summer diligently studying at Kenyon, where Stafford would "not be welcome."[70] Lowell was sorely tempted to defy his parents by marrying a young woman of whom, as he well knew, they did not approve. Nevertheless, he followed a more prudent course and remained in Gambier for the entire summer.

At last, at the end of July, preliminary hearings were held to settle the lawsuit. The cast of characters, as outlined by Stafford in a letter to Hightower, included the attorney for the defense, a Jewish lawyer named Mr. Wein, whom she described as "fat and excessively greasy," "not quite a shyster," and a "social climber"; Mr. Blatt, the auditor, "a pleasant, droll and softspoken Jew"; her own attorney, Mr. Evarts, a "shrewd, logical, quiet" Boston Brahmin; the general physician Dr. Stevens, a kindly "doctor of the old school"; the nose doctor, Dr. Butler, also a "social climber," who said that she had received daily treatments from him from January through May, though in fact she had not, and presented a bill for $950; the young, honest intern; and her editor Archie Ogden, who was dressed in an immaculate white linen suit and appeared "rather fatuous." Revolted by the Bronx accent of the Jewish defense attorney and by his repeated references to her as a "lady writer," she expressed the hostility that this man aroused in her, remarking to Hightower, "How do

I feel about the pogrom in America now, Mr. Hitler, well, I say tomorrow isn't soon enough. I have been dealing with Jews in the legal profession. I have been badly abused by them."[71]

Early in September, after submitting the revised manuscript of *Autumn Festival* to the Atlantic, Stafford left Concord to visit her sister and brother-in-law at their ranch in Hayden. She remained there for almost two months. As she gleefully reported to Hightower, she felt relaxed and happy on the ranch, whether she was helping her brother-in-law Harry skin a heifer, churning butter, reading Jane Austen, or riding on a horse. Although she had never expressed much enthusiasm before for horseback riding, she boasted that she could now stand up in her stirrups and didn't have to hold on to the saddle horn. Delighted about her newly acquired equestrian skills, she asked Hightower to mail her his camera so that she could be photographed in the saddle.[72] The only activity that she professed not to enjoy was a party given in her honor by a Mrs. Carpenter, "a dude interested in uplift and Present Day Germany" who suggested to Jean's sister Mary Lee that a picture of Jean be used on the place cards. Describing disdainfully the afternoon gathering of "sixteen ladies past thirty," she wrote to Hightower: "I got a bivalve spell in the middle of it and couldn't make a murmur. This was when some of the ladies were talking about Shirley Temple. During this period I saw one of the cowpunchers look in the window and though I could not hear him I could tell by his face that he was snorting obscenely."[73] Enjoying both the peacefulness of the ranch and being surrounded by people again, she fantasized about staying on the ranch forever, though she feared that if she did, her parents might show up there. So painful had her visit with her mother and aunt been during the preceding summer that she said to Hightower, "I don't think I could put up with the McKillops."[74]

When Stafford returned to Boston at the beginning of November, she decided that she had had enough of Concord. Instead of renting a room there again, she made arrangements to share an apartment in Cambridge with two recent Vassar graduates, Anne Cleveland, who was studying art history at Harvard, and Bunny Cole, the daughter of her former Concord landlady. This move was to have important consequences both for Stafford and for Hightower, for soon after she married Robert Lowell, Hightower married her roommate Bunny, a young woman Stafford did not feel was a suitable mate at all for her dearest friend. Not only was she critical of Bunny but of Anne Cleveland and of Anne Cleveland's dog, who completed their ménage. "The dog deposits excrement. Anne is being reduced at Elizabeth Arden. We are still eating shrimps, caviar, olives, and other disagreeable delicacies designed to be included in the diet only of incurable dyspeptics," Stafford complained to Hightower.[75] A twin, Anne Cleveland was to serve as the model for the obese, compulsive eater Ramona Dunn in Stafford's short story "The Echo and the Nemesis," a tale in which a young woman invents a dead twin to represent a thin alter ego. Perhaps Stafford's antipathy to her roommates stemmed more from her own insecurities than from simple meanspiritedness. Well-to-do graduates of a prestigious Ivy League women's college, they had been fortunate to have had the kind of upbringing and education for which Stafford herself had always yearned.

Until her pending lawsuit was settled, Stafford's lawyer suggested that she refrain from being seen with Robert Lowell. "The prohibition gave a certain piquancy to our clandestine rendezvous; we saw each other more than ever," she later observed to Eileen Simpson.[76] Even while she was making plans to see Lowell, however, she would sit in the smoking room of Radcliffe's Longfellow Hall with her friends Ruth Stauffer and Sylvia Berkman and speak of him "with the greatest loathing." When she announced in the spring of 1940 that she was leaving Cambridge to marry Lowell, they were "thunderstruck."[77]

The short story "1939," written by Lowell's Kenyon College roommate, Peter Taylor, suggests that one of the "clandestine rendezvous" between Jean Stafford and Robert Lowell may have taken place that year in New York City during Lowell's Thanksgiving vacation. In this story about the trials of early love, two roommates from Kenyon College drive to New York City for their Thanksgiving holiday. The narrator is a young man very much like Peter Taylor himself, and his roommate, Jim Prewitt, bears an unmistakable resemblance to Robert Lowell. A Bostonian, Jim Prewitt has transferred to Kenyon from Harvard. "At Kenyon," the narrator says, "he was usually the most slovenly and ragged-looking of us all. He really went about in tatters, sometimes even with the soles hanging loose from his shoes. But in the closet, off our room, there were always to be found his 'good' shoes, his 'good' suit, his 'good' coat, his 'good' hat, all of which had been purchased at Brooks Brothers by his mother."[78] The narrator of "1939" and Jim Prewitt, who both aspire to be writers, share a room in Kenyon's quaint Douglass House, just as Peter Taylor and Robert Lowell actually did. There they spend hours reading Henry James's *The Wings of the Dove* aloud or discussing the works of W. H. Auden, Yvor Winters, Wyndham Lewis, James Joyce, and the newly discovered "enfant terrible," Delmore Schwartz.

Like Stafford, Jim Prewitt's girlfriend, Carol Crawford, wears her hair in a bun, and she carries her four-hundred-page manuscript in her suitcase. After attending a writer's conference, she has come to New York to seek a publisher for her novel. Jim Prewitt boasts about his girlfriend to his roommate, assuring him that he will quickly discover the "originality" of Carol's mind and "the absence of anything commonplace or banal in her intellectual makeup."[79] When the narrator finally meets his roommate's girlfriend, she is dressed in huaraches, a peasant blouse and skirt, and a long green cape—exactly the kind of "arty" clothes Stafford favored during that period in her life. After spending the evening surrounded by Carol's New York friends, who include a "musicologist and composer," probably modeled after Robert Berueffy, Jim is annoyed that he never has the opportunity to be alone with her. Yet to publish his own literary works, he is also threatened when she announces that she has sold her novel and that two sections from it are scheduled to appear in the *Partisan Review.* "Poor Carol Crawford!" the narrator exclaims, offering this comment:

> How unfair it is to describe her as she was that Thanksgiving weekend in 1939. Ever since she was a little girl on a dairy farm in Wisconsin she had dreamed of becoming a writer and going to live in New York City. She had not merely dreamed of it. She had worked toward it every waking hour of her life, taking jobs after school in wintertime, and full-time jobs in the sum-mer, always saving the money to put herself through the state university. She had made herself the best student—the prize pupil in every grade of gram-mar school and high school. . . . Through all those years she had had but one ambition, and yet I could not have met her at a worse moment in her life. Poor girl, she had just learned that she was a writer.[80]

Peter Taylor's short story provides a realistic portrait of the young woman who not only had been his roommate's girlfriend but who would continue to be one of his own best friends during the course of her lifetime. Although some of the details of Stafford's life have been altered in this work of fiction, the story enables us to see an intimate portrait of Stafford and Lowell as they appeared in 1939.

Peter Taylor's story was published well after Stafford's career as a writer had been launched. In 1939, however, with the exception of one short story that had appeared in *American Prefaces,* her fiction was still unpublished. That fall, although her editor Archie Ogden recommended publication of *Autumn Festival,* calling it "an interesting story with a freshness and strength that au-gurs well for her literary future," his colleagues at the Atlantic overruled him and the book was rejected.[81] If Stafford had not been awarded a cash settle-ment by Lowell's insurance company, she might have been forced to leave Cambridge that winter unless Lowell had been willing to contribute to her upkeep. As it turned out, however, though the "measly" four thousand dollars she received from the lawsuit was far less than the twenty-five thousand dol-lars she had requested, she nevertheless had more money in her bank account after the case was settled and her debts were paid than she had ever had before.[82]

When Lowell returned to Boston for Christmas vacation, Stafford felt that she could no longer hide the fact that she was planning to marry him. She dreaded informing Hightower of her plans. On December 19 she wrote to him:

> I am going to write this instead of say it because it will be much less painful for both of us and if, when you have read it, you don't want to see me again, all you have to do is reply by mail. I am going to say it very simply like this: I am engaged to marry Cal Lowell. I will marry him next summer. You said it would happen, you said it in your letter and I did not believe it. Then I hated him but he does what I have always needed to have done to me and that is that he dominates me. He is here now and will be until January fourth. If you want to meet him, as I wish you would, I would like to have you come to dinner on Wednesday night about six-thirty—and when you come, Robert, try to bring good-will. I will explain nothing to you. Our trouble has always been that it has made us heartless even when we have been much touched. I know you are not in love with me now but there may be a scar still. For God's sake let's leave the scars healed. I have no fewer scars than you.[83]

As subsequent letters from Stafford to Hightower reveal, whatever Hightower's personal feelings about Lowell were, he was cordial to Lowell and he continued to act as his friend's confidant. She would soon regret that she had chosen to fall in love with a man who dominated her, but for the time being, she felt that she much preferred the forceful, single-minded Lowell to Hightower. No doubt Lowell's wealth and social position also played a part in her decision to marry him, though she would not have readily admitted this to others or even to herself.

For a brief period that year, Stafford worked at the Basic English Institute, writing shortwave transcriptions of books. However, in the course of transcribing "The Cricket on the Hearth" into Basic English, she was forced to describe a huntsman as "a man who goes into the woods with instruments to find animals" since there was no Basic English word for "hunter." She was so exasperated that she quit immediately.[84]

In the spring of 1940 Jean Stafford left Boston for New York to marry Robert Lowell. By this time she was fully aware of how difficult Lowell could be. Just before her departure she wrote to Hightower about an argument she and Lowell had had the preceding evening, though she blamed herself for having said something that was sure to provoke Lowell. "Today," she went on to say, "I feel purged, weary, and in love. . . . I am really and truly in love now." The letter suggests that Lowell satisfied some deeply neurotic masochistic need of hers for punishment. It is of interest to note that she concluded this letter with the somewhat cryptic observation, "I feel as trivial as a mouse," suggesting that she was beginning to recognize, however dimly, that she was also somehow diminished by her relationship with Lowell.[85]

Before they were married in New York City in April of 1940, Jean Stafford and Robert Lowell spent three days in Manhattan, during which time she sent two letters to Hightower reflecting her troubled state of mind. In her first communiqué from the Biltmore Hotel, which she described as a "gold brocade undertaker's parlor," she said that her train trip to New York with Lowell and his friend Blair Clark had made her "so nostalgic for Boston" that she could not speak to either Cal or Blair and instead had read Walpole, "who seemed tediously unaware of the pain of things." The high point of the day following their arrival was a visit they paid to Robert Frost, who talked about farms with her. She and Lowell were waiting for their Wasserman reports, she said, and she was filled with "general panic" as she contemplated the "very frightening business" of getting married.[86] In her next letter, written in the Hotel Albert in Greenwich Village, she sounded even more depressed. She said that she and Cal had spent the day apart, he with the writer Harry Brown, she with an old friend from Boulder who introduced her to "a pretentious bk. agent, a seedy actor and 2 writers & 1 dancer and 1 musician all 10th rate and unwashed." When she returned to the hotel, Cal was awaiting her and was furious. "He should not have left me tonight," she wrote, "and yet at this moment we are so irritated we hate each other. Say a novena for me— you've got to." She mentioned that she had confessed to Cal that although she had spent many months in Heidelberg, she had learned virtually no German; Cal had been "absolutely stopped in his tracks and revolted." As she sat in her room drinking rum and writing to Hightower, Cal came in and ordered her to stop drinking. ". . . I shall perhaps not marry him & if I do not I shall be invisible for the rest of my natural days," she concluded, lamenting, "What wd. he do if he knew me?"[87]

On April 2, 1940, Jean Stafford and Robert Lowell were married in St. Mark's Episcopal Church in the Bowery. The fact that they were married in a church bearing the same name as Robert Lowell's prep school probably did not escape the notice of either of them. Present at the wedding were Blair Clark, Allen Tate, and Caroline Gordon. ". . . we hope for luck tomorrow at 5 with a famous American poet living in Princeton as our chief support," Stafford wrote to Hightower on April 1, April Fool's Day; on April 2, the day the wedding ceremony was performed, she added a postscript: "At 5 it will be over. *Terrified*. Happy."[88]

Entering the church on the arm of her persistent suitor, the future author of *Boston Adventure* might be likened to the red-haired protagonist of an earlier novel about Boston, Verena Tarrant in Henry James's *The Bostonians*. Describing the union of Verena Tarrant and Basil Ransome, the intense young man who relentlessly pursues her, James had written of Verena, "But though she was glad, he presently discovered that, beneath her hood, she was in tears. It is to be feared that with the union, so far from brilliant into which she was about to enter, these were not the last she was destined to shed."[89] Most onlookers would have said that in contrast to James's Verena Tarrant, Jean Stafford, a poor young woman from the West, had made a "brilliant" match indeed. Nevertheless, those who knew both Jean Stafford and Robert Lowell might well have predicted that the future relationship of these two fledging writers would be fraught with difficulties. Just as James's Verena Tarrant was destined to shed many tears during her marriage to Basil Ransome, so was Jean Stafford destined to shed many tears during the eight years she would be married to the brilliant, attractive, but unstable young poet who had finally accomplished what he had been determined to do ever since he had met her in the summer of 1937.

Six

Sensations Sweet and Sour
Summer 1940–Fall 1943

Oh, love, why do we argue like this
I am tired of all your pious talk
—ANNE SEXTON, "A CURSE AGAINST ELEGIES"

Them lady poets must not marry, pal . . .
—JOHN BERRYMAN, "DREAM SONG 187"

IT IS NOT clear why Jean Stafford and Robert Lowell decided to get married in April rather than waiting until after Lowell's graduation that June, for they parted almost immediately after the wedding, he to return to Kenyon College and she to visit friends in Boulder and then to spend some time with her sister Mary Lee in Hayden. Lowell was still uncertain about his plans, having been dissuaded from applying for one of the Harvard Fellowships by his cousin, A. Lawrence Lowell, president of Harvard. Stafford reported to Hightower, "Cousin Lawrence wrote abominably to Cal," and she said bitterly, "I have been stirred up continually by the evil predictions for Cal's destruction through me . . ."[1] Perhaps Lowell hoped that once his marriage to her was a fait accompli, his parents would finally begin to treat him as an independent adult and would also begin to show more consideration for her feelings than they had heretofore. Soon after the wedding he wrote to his parents, making no attempt to disguise his anger. He berated them for disapproving of the path he had chosen to follow, and instead of signing the letter "Bobby," as he was in the habit of doing, he signed it "Cal."[2]

If Charlotte Lowell was offended by the scolding tone of this letter from her only child, she must certainly have been even more offended by a letter she received from Caroline Gordon ten days after the wedding, for it was one thing to be chastized by her recalcitrant son and another to be criticized by a woman she had never met. Caroline Gordon informed Charlotte Lowell that several days before Cal and Jean were married, he had brought his bride to Princeton to introduce her to his friends, Caroline Gordon and Allen Tate, and had confessed "quite frankly" that his parents were opposed to this marriage. Maintaining that she had expressed no opinion about the marriage itself, Gordon addressed herself not to that issue but to the question of the young poet's career. Instead of the "badly adjusted boy" she and her husband had first encountered when Cal spent the summer with them in Tennessee at Benfolly, she said, she now found him to be quite "sane," though like other artists and poets, he was "typical in his singlemindedness, his powers of concentration, and his clear vision" of the vocation he wished to pursue. Appealing to Charlotte Lowell to be supportive of his literary ambitions, she concluded, "What Robert needs is cooperation. . . . A literary career is impossible without it, and Robert cannot exist without a literary career." [3]

After he returned to Kenyon, Lowell studied for his final exams and prepared a valedictory address he had been selected to deliver at his graduation. Stafford told Hightower that following a "bizarre" weekend in New York and the "utter dreariness" of their leave-taking in Cleveland, Cal had departed by bus for Gambier and she by train for Chicago, thinking numbly that they were married and "the worst was over." [4] In a second letter that she sent to Hightower as she traveled west, she mused, "How typical that I should have had a honeymoon on a train and in Cleveland. And while I may lay it all to external circumstances in my soul I know it is only my peculiar genius for the uncomfortable. Poor Cal! What a life he will have with me!" [5]

When Stafford arrived in Boulder, newly married but unaccompanied by her husband, she realized how "perilous" it was to have begun her married life that way. Furthermore, she was "chilled to the bone" when she learned that John Crowe Ransom had suggested that she and Cal ought to spend the coming year at Kenyon, where Cal would be able to teach several courses. The job Ransom had suggested for her, however, was that of typist for the *Kenyon Review*, despite the fact that it was she and not Cal who had taught before. Although she was comforted by the thought that she would probably be kept very busy and therefore would be excused from "Faculty Wives' Amateur Charades," [6] she nevertheless could not bear to contemplate the way she was beginning to dwindle into "Mrs. Lowell" or "Mr. Lowell's wife." [7]

Returning to the town where she had been so unhappy in the past aroused familiar feelings of anxiety and depression in Stafford. Denver looked to her "like what easterners are thinking of when they say they don't like the West," [8] and Boulder was no better. Describing to Hightower the "gloomy" week she had spent in Boulder, she enumerated all the things that had depressed her there: the cool reception she had received from Irene McKeehan; the fact that no one in the English Department had ever heard "even vaguely" of William Empson, a critic very much admired by John Crowe Ransom, Allen Tate, and

Caroline Gordon; the boasting of Edward Davison, who claimed that I. A. Richards was his oldest friend, though Richards had informed her that he had never heard of Davison; a disappointing reunion with Robert Berueffy, who had returned to Boulder to write music but was doing no writing. Trying once again to come to terms with Lucy McKee's suicide, to sort out her feelings of grief and guilt about Lucy's fate, she also paid a visit to the cemetery, but she found, much to her horror, that at first she could not even remember where Lucy was buried, and when she finally located Lucy's grave, she saw that it was covered with weeds. "She is forgotten as a story so automatic that it has neither horror nor tragedy in it," she said.[9]

Stafford felt no more cheerful at the ranch in Hayden. Although she quickly settled into a comfortable routine, she found her sister Mary Lee's possessiveness annoying. Inspired by her visit to the cemetery in Boulder, she began a long story about the suicide, expressing how guilty she had felt at the time of Lucy's death because secretly she had wished for Lucy to die. She explained to Hightower: "As a murderer I wish to hide and with a novice's naïveté, think they will not find me in the dark though I know the only person who looks for me and accuses me is in the room, in my body and in my brain and that throughout my life, though every year I will be less afraid, I will never again be whole . . ."[10] In addition to the story about the suicide, she was reworking her novel about Stephens College, which Caroline Gordon had promised to promote with her own publishers, Scribners, once the novel was completed; and she was planning to reapply for a Houghton Mifflin Fellowship with a proposal for a new novel about one of her brother-in-law's ranching partners who had absconded with some funds.[11]

Yet despite the fact that Stafford was relieved to be free of responsibilities on the ranch and happy that she was able to spend many hours a day on her writing without interruptions, a number of things were bothering her. Angry that she had not heard from her former roommate, Anne Cleveland, and irritated by a "disastrously affectionate" letter from her other roommate, Bunny Cole, she wrote to Hightower, "I nurse my grievances in solitude and plan sweeping condemnations of humanity in a series of pointed short stories."[12] She was furious when she learned from Ruth Stauffer that Cal's mother had announced "all over town" that the hasty steps taken by Cal and Jean had made their marriage look like a "forced marriage," and had also blamed his failure to secure a Harvard Fellowship on the fact that he had married Jean. Another thing that was troubling Stafford was the realization that if she and Cal were to spend the coming year at Kenyon, they would be paid next to nothing, and whereas he would only have to teach one section of freshman English and would not begin work until October, she would have to work five hours each day on the *Kenyon Review* to get the summer issue out. When she complained in a letter to Evelyn Scott about her "dismal" marriage and mentioned her frequent fights with Cal about his family, her own career prospects, and other issues, Scott replied, "We don't have to marry our mothers-in-law, really." Scott also advised her to seek John Crowe Ransom's assistance in promoting her own writing career as well as that of his protégé, Cal. Recalling, however, that Ransom had recently attacked the poetry of Edna St. Vincent Millay for being "too feminine," Scott observed, ". . . you may persuade him [Ransom] that 'feminine' art is not, after all, any more femine [*sic*] in his meaning than 'masculine' art is masculine in the same sense—in short, that not all women writing exploit their sex in ways external to art [as he suggested of Edna Millay]."[13]

Unenthusiastic about the prospects at Kenyon College, Stafford hoped to convince Cal that instead they should accompany Hightower to China. Going to China with Hightower, who had recently been awarded a traveling fellowship from the Harvard-Yenching Institute, would be more exciting, she thought, than working at Kenyon and would also put an ocean between her and her meddlesome mother-in-law. Referring to Charlotte Lowell and Charlotte's confidant, Merrill Moore, she exclaimed to Hightower, "China is none too far away from Harpy Charlotte and Nutsucker Moore and I hope we will be on that boat with you early in July, oh, Christ, I hope it. We have enough money for passage and everything right now and the trust fund will fall due again in July, I think."[14]

The frequency of Stafford's letters to Hightower during this period suggests that she was still extremely dependent on him and wished to maintain her close ties with him even though she was now a married woman. At first this didn't seem impossible since, even though Lowell knew about her earlier sexual relationship with Hightower, he did not seem jealous of Jean's friend. However, just as she was busily hatching schemes for a Stafford-Lowell-Hightower jaunt to China, she began to infer from Hightower's letters that he was becoming more than casually interested in her former roommate, Bunny Cole. After learning that he had visited Bunny's family in Concord, Stafford chided him playfully: "If, in the end, you get so involved that you marry her or take her to China, I'll not give you my blessing. I will, further, give you my curse not only orally in the presence of many people but I will also harry you with abusive letters and write a novel about you in which I will give you the surname Hightower."[15] Before long, learning that Hightower was thinking seriously about asking Bunny Cole to marry him, she implored him not to make the mistake of marrying her former roommate. She said that she disliked Bunny's social snobbery; had contempt for her intellect; disapproved of her "protestant conformity"; and found her lacking in a sense of humor. She concluded that Bunny lacked "any merit but the ornamental one,"[16] and also questioned whether her own intimacy with Hightower would still be possible if he married Bunny. "I, being married, can tell you what marriage is," she said. "Even with respect, with awe of a superior mind and a shining talent— there is claustrophobia." And she added sadly, "I would like to say *you must not,* you *cannot,* I will not let you. If it is love, I will henceforth hold my tongue, but if it is not love, I must beg you to escape."[17]

Once Stafford realized that, despite her warnings, pleas, and imprecations, Hightower was still intent on marrying Bunny Cole, she was determined to see him alone one last time before he left for China. Comparing her own marriage with his, she wrote: "I am sure you will be very happy. You are starting off very well, much better than Cal and I have started . . . have, in theory, started since we have not yet had the peculiar and gratifying experience of living together. You will have China and enough money, a beautiful and healthy wife and your life will become to use Cal's phrase, 'as single as your skeleton,' as, through your marriage, mine must necessarily become."[18] Initially she proposed that they meet in Denver at the beginning of June, when he and Bunny would be traveling to the West Coast to embark for China. She emphasized her "great need" to see him alone and dramatically told him she had a great secret, "a lie told out of bewilderment, which was the truth," that she wanted to reveal to him in person. Her genuine despair about his forthcoming marriage, which she believed would create a rift between them, is evident in the letters she wrote to him that month. Expressing her hatred of anyone who would come between them and destroy a friendship that preserved "the tenderness of romantic love," she said: "At times last night when I could not sleep, I could see the abusive humor of this last joke we have played upon ourselves to God's delight, and none of ours. Oh, no, you are happy and confident and I play you false in seeing humor. But it is repulsively absurd to find myself, a new bride, called upon to wish happiness to a new bride who has come to me inquiring like a thief and has carried off my amulet." As she had done in the past when difficulties between them had arisen, she alternated between blaming herself and blaming him for what had transpired. She also alluded to "an aged wound" that had not been healed by marriage, suggesting that her marriage to Lowell had failed to resolve her sexual problems.[19] Viewing her own life as an appropriate subject for melodrama, she said, "In myself, I am not a bad woman, but my appearance in people's lives is usually a disastrous accident. I have written no novel so bizarre as my own life and have fashioned no characters so improbable as you and I, and have developed no emotional relationship so unrealistically geometrical as ours."[20]

Delaying her departure for Kenyon College as long as possible, she suggested various cities where she might be able to meet with him one last time. After fruitless negotiations about a feasible time and place, they finally settled on Omaha, a city that would allow them some time to be alone since Bunny planned to visit a friend there.[21]

On May 25 Hightower married Bunny Cole. Six days later he and Stafford met briefly in Omaha. According to Hightower, she was "angry, bitter, desperate." She insisted that she didn't love Lowell and didn't want to return to him. She also confessed to Hightower that she had believed she was lying when she had said in Cambridge that she was sexually frigid, but, in fact, this had proved to be true. Finally, as the hour of their separation approached, she suggested in desperation that they run away together, abandoning both Cal and Bunny. "Since I had nothing to run away from, I was not receptive," Hightower later observed.[22]

As she traveled from Omaha to Gambier, Stafford mulled over her long, complicated relationship with Hightower, who had meant so much to her during the last five years. Writing to him about their past, she said sadly,

> When I left there was a fog over that valley beyond Omaha and though I knew it was like Heidelberg, I had, for the first time, no nostalgia. It may have been fatigue, but I think not. That past is gone and Berueffy's is not a greater desolation than mine. My feeling is one of disappointment, very bitter disappointment. I felt about you last night the way you felt about me when you saw I had brought no books to Heidelberg . . . I have the feeling that you will be happy and I don't curse you for that. I feel exiled and it breaks my heart to think I am now extraneous to your life as you say I am to those you're now allied to . . . I was of course envious that you had married without sordidness, with, on the contrary, public approval.[23]

She regretted that she had given Hightower reason to pity her, and instead of being elated at the prospect of being reunited with her husband after a separation of two months, she was overwhelmed with despair that her relationship with Hightower would probably never be as close as it had been in the past. Desperately anxious to maintain some communication with him nevertheless, she suggested: "All our lives, in health and in anything but serious sickness we must write to each other once a week and write at our very best. We must, in writing, preserve our shared experience of Boulder, Heidelberg, Paris, Cambridge, Salida, the ranch, just as we have preserved it in our conversations. It is the way our friendship . . . o hell, our love . . . will be kept alive and, thereby we, or anyway I, will be kept alive . . ."[24] Her wish that they would be able to sustain their close friendship proved to be illusory, however. Although they did continue to correspond with one another occasionally during the rest of her life and even managed to meet from time to time, their intimate friendship ended on the day that Stafford boarded the train in Omaha to meet her husband in Ohio.

"Lowell brought Jean Stafford to Kenyon, shining she was, wearing a hat and gloves, tucked under her arm a mint copy from England of something mysterious to us, *Goodbye to Berlin*"—so wrote John Thompson, one of Lowell's friends at Kenyon College who was to remain a lifelong friend of Stafford's.[25] However, at the graduation, it was not she but Lowell who was the center of attention, for he was the most outstanding senior, graduating summa cum laude, Phi Beta Kappa, and first in his class, with honors in classics. As she listened to her husband's valedictory address in which he attacked the irresponsibility and ignorance of the majority of students at Kenyon College, she might well have been reminded of the article she herself had once written for her high school newspaper in which she too had attacked the complacency and materialism of her fellow students.

During her brief stay in Gambier, Stafford had an opportunity to socialize with a number of the writers and would-be writers in Lowell's circle of mentors and friends at Kenyon: John Crowe Ransom, Randall Jarrell, and Peter Taylor. In the gabled upstairs room of Douglass House that he shared with Peter Taylor, Lowell had spent most of his days lying abed and reading, surrounded by heaps of books, letters, drafts of poems he was working on, and unwashed socks. Taylor recalled that even among the bohemian students who were members of their coterie at Kenyon, Lowell had stood out as "the most slovenly and ragged looking."[26] Although Stafford herself was rather careless about her appearance during this period of her life, she could not bear to be in untidy surroundings. As soon as she and Lowell would begin to live together, his untidiness would cause endless friction between them, causing her to complain about "a certain person's blue socks and poem manuscripts all over the floor as well as covering all elevated surfaces."[27] Like the poet Theron Maybank, a character in Stafford's autobiographical story "An Influx of Poets," Lowell was disdainful of his wife's "nesting and neatening compulsions,"[28] and she, in turn, could not tolerate his messiness.

By the time Lowell graduated from Kenyon College, he was no longer being considered for a position there. Although he had been highly recommended by John Crowe Ransom, the president of the college insisted that Lowell was not mature enough to qualify even as a part-time instructor. Annoyed that his recommendation had been overridden by President Chalmers and anxious to assist his brilliant if erratic student, Ransom arranged a fellowship in English for Lowell at Louisiana State University in Baton Rouge, where two of the Southern Fugitive poets, Robert Penn Warren and Cleanth

Brooks, would assume the role of mentor to Cal. Instead of serving as secretary for the *Kenyon Review,* Stafford was hired to be the business manager of the *Southern Review,* which Warren and Brooks edited. In a letter to Allen Tate, Ransom said that he had recommended both Cal and Jean to Charles Pipkin, another editor of the *Southern Review:* "I told him I would have only envy of him if he got that team (Cal and Jean) as it was precisely the team that we had wanted here. Jean's qualifications for the summer thing are superlative, I should think. So I hope for the best. Am delighted that Cal is not sulking, is eager for the job, and it may prove better for him than our job would . . ."[29] But if Cal was not "sulking," Stafford was certainly less than jubilant that she would have only a lowly secretarial job, whereas Lowell would be a coddled graduate student. She realized that her salary would help pay the rent, supplementing the small sum of money Lowell received regularly from his trust fund. Nevertheless, she was no happier about the prospect of working as a secretary for the *Southern Review* than she had been about the thought of working in a similar capacity at the *Kenyon Review,* and she was terrified moreover that with a full-time job and domestic responsibilities, she would have little time or energy left for her writing.

Before facing the task of getting settled in Baton Rouge, Stafford and Lowell spent several pleasant weeks visiting Peter Taylor's family in Memphis. Taylor later recalled: "My parents loved Cal and Jean, and my sister did. And we had parties. And Cal—he looked so awful, his long hair, his shoes— worse in those days than later—but he was still an attractive person and I remember a girl in Memphis saying: 'That marriage won't last long. He's such an attractive man.'"[30] Even casual onlookers could sense how filled with tension the relationship of these argumentative and high-strung newlyweds already was.

Having to set up an apartment in the debilitating heat and humidity of a Baton Rouge summer was hardly an auspicious beginning for the wedded life of Jean Stafford and Robert Lowell. Although Lowell reported to his Kenyon College classmate Robie Macauley that he and Jean found themselves "unexpectedly normal and happy in their Chimes Street three room apartment,"[31] Stafford's later recollection of the "moist, verminous, vile" summer she had spent in "wretched" Baton Rouge was much less positive.[32] "The traveler should go to Louisiana in the winter: it is certain death to venture there any time between April and October," she would write in 1973.[33] And in her novel *The Catherine Wheel,* she would describe Louisiana as resembling "something drawn by Doré, every inch of it covered with tendrils and naked roots and vines and that hairy moss hanging from the oak trees."[34]

In his biography of Robert Lowell, Ian Hamilton mentions that Lowell enjoyed watching Jean arrange the furniture that had been sent to them by his parents and his Aunt Harriet Winslow.[35] Stafford, however, was exhausted from unpacking in the heat and humidity and from performing various chores as well in the sweltering offices of the *Southern Review*. She complained later that in those days before people routinely installed air-conditioners, the mildew and damp macerated book bindings and made the *Encyclopaedia Britannica* she had sent to Baton Rouge so "edematous" that all the volumes would no longer fit into the wooden case in which they were stored; that the humidity warped phonograph records and gave salt "the consistency of gritty sherbet"; and that every surface was covered with "a mysterious fungoid slime." She also loathed the numerous cockroaches "the size of hummingbirds" that abounded in their apartment and "ravenously devoured the glue in the spines of books, particularly the collected works of Cardinal Newman."[36]

Stafford's workday at the offices of the *Southern Review* began at half past seven. The offices consisted of two small rooms, one for the editors and one for her, with a rusty black fan on the floor. Though she told Taylor that the job wasn't bad and that her superiors, Cleanth Brooks and Albert Erskine, were pleasant to her, she complained that the offices looked "like a hogsty with an accumulation of years of manuscripts . . . and magazines and review books and third class matter for Mr. Warren . . ."[37] At half past four she would crawl home and lie in the bathtub for an hour, soaking her weary bones and munching frozen cubes of Coca-Cola and mint.[38] Since a black woman named Loyola arrived at half past six every other morning to give the apartment "a grand house-cleaning,"[39] Stafford did not have to do very much of the housework herself. Nevertheless, there were daily meals to prepare and, occasionally, more elaborate dinners to cook for guests. Thirty-six years later Lowell would fondly recall how he and Peter Taylor would sit in their pajamas and wait for her to return from the office to make lunch for them.[40] Stafford's own memories of those days when she had to return home to fix lunch for two grown men who were still in their pajamas at noon were probably far less pleasant than Lowell's.

By the end of August Stafford realized that her job and her housekeeping kept her so busy that she had little time or energy to write. Many years later Cleanth Brooks would boast that the *Southern Review* was "lucky" in its secretaries: "One of them was no less a literary figure than Jean Stafford."[41] During the time that she served as secretary for the journal, however, Stafford was not a "literary figure" at all, though she dreamed of becoming one. In fact, she was extremely discouraged about her writing. While her husband attended class or read Dante with Robert Penn Warren during a two-hour lunch period, she was usually engaged in performing more mundane tasks at home or in the office.[42] She had asked Edward Davison if he would be willing to read the manuscript on which she was then working and if he would write a letter of recommendation on her behalf for a fellowship, but she subsequently informed him:

> . . . now I'm writing to cancel the request for I'm so up to my ears with working in the Review office, with housekeeping, the heat, etc. that I can't find the time to type up and revise my manuscript . . . I feel frustrated and angry that the years are going so quickly and I'm still totally unpublished and my desperation has reached the state where I feel publication in anything is better than nothing, but I know that's not true and I'll probably wait on in the same old way and eventually arrive though god knows how far off that is.[43]

In addition to communicating with Edward Davison about her frustrations concerning her writing, she also sent a draft of a long short story to Caroline Gordon. By 1941 Gordon already had published five novels, including *Penhally; Alec Maury, Sportsman; None Shall Look Back; The Garden of Adonis;* and *Green Centuries.* A Southerner like her husband, Allen Tate, she had been taught Latin and Greek by her father, the director of a boys' academy in Clarksville, Tennessee, and had later attended college, something that relatively few Southern women of her generation did. Twenty years older than Stafford, Gordon liked to play the role of mentor to younger writers. She would soon promote the writing career of one of Stafford's contemporaries, the extraordinary writer from Milledgeville, Georgia, Flannery O'Connor. In a lengthy letter to Stafford, Gordon first praised the story Stafford had sent her: "I read your story carefully and was impressed by it. It is evident that you are already an accomplished writer and can do the thing you set out to do. You will probably have a hard time getting this story published, because of its length, but I think any editor who read it would be impressed by your talent and it ought to be helpful in getting you a publisher." Gordon then went on to discuss specific matters of diction and form. Critical of Stafford's predilection for using long words when shorter ones would suffice, she said, "I balk at 'dulcified.' I think I have reason for balking. A high-falutin word like that ought to be *forced* from you. It isn't here, it's rather poured on from the top." In view of the fact that Stafford's use of "high-falutin" words would become a noteworthy characteristic of her writing style, it is obvious that this bit of advice was later discounted by her. Another of Gordon's suggestions was that the dialogue should sound less artificial and more "like talk—a sentence can ring in the memory."[44] Such a letter from an established writer might be construed to be either glowingly positive or discouraging, depending on the mood of its recipient; it was hardly the kind of letter, however, that would have given Stafford sufficient courage to abandon all her other obligations so that she could devote her time exclusively to her writing.

Usually too tired during the weekend to sit down at her typewriter, Stafford accompanied Lowell instead on trips to inspect the decaying antebellum mansions in the vicinity. "Sometimes, when I lived in Baton Rouge, we would struggle out of our torpor on Sundays and take the ferry back and forth across the Mississippi, playing the slot machines while boogie came from the jukebox," she later recalled.[45] She vividly remembered the Louisiana landscape, observing, "To my western eyes, accustomed to a frugal vegetation, the gorgeousness of the landscape with its exuberance of trees and shrubs and marvelous flowers was breathtaking and bewildering."[46]

One weekend she and Lowell traveled to New Orleans to meet Lowell's friends from Boston, Frank Parker and Blair Clark, who were on their way to Mexico. The trip to New Orleans turned out to be far more upsetting than remaining in Baton Rouge would have been. According to Frank Parker, one night Jean came to his hotel room and told him and Blair Clark that she had left her own room because Cal was in an ugly mood. When she finally returned to her room sometime later, Lowell was furious, so furious that he tried to strangle her and hit her hard enough to break her nose again. Clark was summoned to take her to the hospital.[47] That Lowell's anger could result in an act of violence was not news to Parker and Clark, who had witnessed their friend Cal's abusive behavior in the past, but others who had not seen this side of Lowell before soon began to hear accounts of his violent outbursts. Sometime in 1941 Robert Berueffy was told by his mother that people in Boulder were saying Jean Stafford's husband "beat her up for breakfast every morning."[48]

A major source of conflict between Stafford and Lowell that year was his increasing obsession with the doctrines and practices of Roman Catholicism. Lowell spent more and more of his time reading such Catholic writers as Newman, Maritain, the Jesuit poet Gerard Manley Hopkins, and Pascal. "Except for meals and two games of chess after dinner he does nothing but read. I think he'll die soon and die blind," Stafford wrote to Robie Macauley.[49] In the spring of 1941 Lowell, a Protestant, was baptized into the Roman Catholic Church. While Jean Stafford, Peter Taylor, and another friend named Patrick Quinn stood outside, he went to confession, remaining there for half an hour. One week later, having decided that their marriage ceremony, performed in a Protestant church, was not valid, Lowell insisted on being remarried in a Catholic church in Baton Rouge.[50]

Although Stafford herself had taken instruction in Catholicism after Lucy McKee's suicide, she was not a practicing Catholic at the time of her marriage to Lowell. Suddenly she found herself married to a man for whom the rituals of the Catholic church had become an obsession. Lowell zealously instituted a daily regimen of rituals not only for himself but for his wife. He insisted that they attend mass each morning and that they recite two rosaries a day. Furthermore, he prohibited the reading of newspapers, permitting only serious works of fiction and religious works like *The Confessions of St. Augustine* and her own favorite, St. Teresa of Avila's *The Interior Castle.* He carefully scrutinized as well all the food she prepared, making sure that no meat was served on Fridays or during Lent. One Friday, Stafford said, he thought he tasted meat in the soup she served him and angrily dumped the contents of his bowl into the kitchen sink.[51] If a later remark she made to one of her friends was true, Lowell's obsession with purity and piety after his conversion also resulted in his decision not to have sexual relations with her.[52] Stafford once told another friend that she became so distressed by his religious fanaticism that she actually considered leaving him that year. As she began to pack her bags one day when she felt she could not stand his preoccupation with Catholic ritual one moment longer, Lowell rushed into their bedroom and exclaimed, "Don't go, Jean, don't leave. I'll stop it now. I've got the vocabulary."[53]

In her short story "An Influx of Poets," Stafford would later make reference to the traumatic events that occurred during the first year of her marriage. Some of the details have been fictionalized, but the story appears to be an accurate portrayal of her own reaction to Lowell's conversion and to his tyrannical behavior after he became a devout Catholic. "What had become of the joking lad I'd married?" her protagonist, Cora Savage, muses about Theron Maybank, a poet and zealous convert: "He'd run hellbent for election into that blind alley—that's what had become of him—and yanked me along with him, and there we snarled like hungry, scurvy cats. If I had stubbornly withstood him from the beginning, or if I had left him when he left me for the seraphim and saints—but I had tried to withstand and had got for myself only wrath and disdain."[54] Cora Savage stoutly maintains that she herself does not "believe in any of it—not in the real Presence, not in the Immaculate Conception, not in God," but nevertheless she continues to receive the Host each Sunday without confessing her disbelief. An inveterate list maker, as was Stafford herself, Cora endures the tedium of daily mass by making lists of cities she has visited or buildings on her college campus or all the people she knows whose given name is John.[55]

In "An Influx of Poets" Cora Savage observes about her husband, "Leaving him had not really occurred to me, for I had married within my tribe, and we were sternly monogamous to death."[56] However, in contrast to her protagonist, Stafford often fantasized about leaving Lowell during these difficult months in Baton Rouge, for no matter how brilliant, handsome, and socially well connected the real-life counterpart of Theron Maybank was, he was also a bully. As Stafford quickly learned, if one chose to contradict him, one might be subjected to verbal or even physical abuse. Yet the alternative to being married to Lowell was even more frightening to her than remaining with him, for she knew she did not want to join her parents in Portland or remain at her sister's ranch indefinitely, nor did she want to teach or work at some menial job to support herself. So remaining with him, she continued to quarrel with him, and as she had done in the past and would do in the future, especially during periods of stress, she drank and smoked much more than was good for her. Consequently, in addition to fighting with Lowell about Catholicism, she also fought with him about her excessive drinking and smoking.

That winter she began to develop various lingering maladies: flu, a kidney infection, a cough, and a fever. In April, when a physician thought that he detected a spot on her lung, she decided to take a trip to Colorado, where the climate would be more conducive to her recovery than the miasma of Baton Rouge. Her illness also provided her with a convenient excuse to escape temporarily from Lowell's harangues.

After Lowell had completed his courses at Louisiana State University that spring, he and Stafford packed up their belongings and moved to New York City, where he had been hired to work as a copy editor at Sheed and Ward, the distinguished avant-garde Catholic publishing house. They rented an apartment in Greenwich Village at 63 West 11th Street, in the same neighborhood Henry James had immortalized in his novel *Washington Square*. The quaint, rather elegant brick or brownstone houses in Greenwich Village, replete with shutters, iron railings, and window boxes, were very different indeed from the squat, architecturally undistinguished houses of Boulder. And right at her doorstep Stafford discovered the wonderful Dauber & Pine Bookstore, where one could purchase a first edition of Henry James's *The Spoils of Poynton* for one dollar. Stafford reported to Peter Taylor that she was "very proud" to have chosen this particular apartment to rent since Cal heartily approved of their superintendent and his wife, both of whom were "perfectly charming" Catholic refugees from the Rhineland. Pleased to be back in this cosmopolitan city, she added, ". . . I like New York tremendously, little as I have seen of it, and I really believe I will get some work done here."[57]

Still in poor health when she arrived in New York, Stafford was relieved to be told by a physician she consulted there that she had pneumonia rather than tuberculosis, as her physician in Louisiana had led her to believe. Although she felt very fatigued as a result of her illness, she managed to set up their new apartment, hanging the religious pictures they had recently acquired: Fra Angelico's *Annunciation* and lithographs of St. Francis, St. Thomas More, and St. Jerome. She also planted their window boxes with pansies. For one day they were the proud owners of a boxer puppy, but decided to give it up when she realized she would have to devote "an 8 hour day for two years to rear the thing."[58]

Soon Stafford, too, was hired to work part time at Sheed and Ward, where Lowell's new boss, Frank Sheed, dictated to her a definitive translation of Saint Augustine's *Confessions.* "My father remembers Jean as a cheerful, un-cynical country girl," Frank Sheed's son Wilfrid said.[59] Among the anecdotes about her association with Frank Sheed and Maisie Ward that Stafford de-lighted in relating to friends was a description of a weekend she and Cal had spent at the Sheeds' home in Torresdale, Pennsylvania. She told Eileen Simpson:

> I packed a typewriter case, the only thing we had which could pass for lug-gage, with two pairs of pajamas, unironed, and two toothbrushes. As our taxi pulled into the driveway, the butler came down the stairs, opened the door and before I could stop him, whisked away the typewriter case. After being greeted by the Sheeds, we were shown to our room. There was the type-writer case, open on the luggage rack. The toothbrushes were in a glass in the bathroom. Two pairs of unironed pajamas were neatly arranged, one on ei-ther side of the bed. Cal thought it was a scream. You can imagine . . . how I felt—*un*ironed."[60]

In addition to visiting the Sheeds, Stafford and Lowell also made several trips to Princeton to visit Caroline Gordon and Allen Tate. There they were introduced to such luminaries of New York intellectual life as the gruff, out-spoken editor of the *Partisan Review,* Philip Rahv, and his wife Nathalie. Stafford and Lowell entertained other writers who were passing through New York, including Randall Jarrell and Robert Penn Warren. They also met some interesting couples their own age, including the photographers Diane and Allan Arbus, who were friends of Lowell's former girlfriend Anne Dick and her husband Alex Eliot. Eliot recalls an elegant dinner party at Cal and Jean's apartment that he and Anne attended. After dinner Jean said, "Come into the bedroom and see the crucifix we just bought!" Over the head of the bed an antique Christ was hanging. "Isn't it great!" Jean exclaimed. "The real agony!"[61]

During the twenties, when Caroline Gordon and Allen Tate were living in New York City, she had blamed her slender literary output, in part, on the fact that all too frequently she was called upon to entertain friends and her husband's students. "It is these young poets from the South. They call us up as

soon as they hit Pennsylvania Station and they stay anywhere from a week to a
month. I have gotten a bit bitter about it," she wrote to her friend Sally
Wood.[62] Now it was Stafford's turn to entertain the "influx of poets" who
came to New York. "Randall was a rather exhausting joy to see," she told
Peter Taylor. "He stayed with us off and on for about a week between light-
ning-paced trips to Princeton and to the Cape to see Edmund Wilson."[63]

In addition to her part-time job and the time she had to devote to entertaining their friends, Lowell also insisted she spend some time doing "Catholic
work." Describing her visit to the offices of the *Catholic Worker* after she went
there, prodded by Lowell, to volunteer her services, she wrote to Peter Taylor:

> The first time I went down, I was terrified just by the approach to the place. It
> is a block from Pell Str. and two blocks from the Bowery, just off Canal. I had
> to walk seven blocks through the kind of slums you do not believe exist when
> you see them in the movies, in an atmosphere that was nearly asphyxiating.
> The Worker office was full of the kind of camaraderie which frightens me to
> death and I was immediately put at a long table between a Negro and a
> Chinese to fold papers, a tiring, filthy job. The second time, it was the same
> except that Mott St. seemed even more depressing and that time I typed.[64]

As they had done in Baton Rouge, Stafford and Lowell fought continually
about his involvement in Catholicism. After she had told him about the quarters of the *Catholic Worker,* which also provided rooms for homeless indigent
people, he said he wanted to go down there to live. "I vainly argued against it,"
she wrote to Peter Taylor. A reprieve came only when a priest whom Cal
admired convinced him that the work he could do best was intellectual work.
"And now," Stafford said, "we are quite happy here in a respectable neighborhood and henceforth I do not have to go to the Worker but instead I have to go
to work in a friendship house in Harlem under a Baroness de something."[65]

Despite her other obligations, Stafford managed nevertheless to get a good
deal of writing done that year. Seeking John Crowe Ransom's support for a
Houghton Mifflin fellowship, she sent him a pile of her manuscripts and was
subsequently invited by him to review Kenneth Patchen's *The Journal of Al-
bion Moonlight.* The review, signed "Jean Stafford Lowell," appeared in the
winter issue of the *Kenyon Review* that year. Attacking Patchen's bleak outlook, she wrote, "If Mr. Patchen really believes the world to be as rotten as he
intimates, then he is operating on carrion and the performance is neither dex-
trous nor fragrant."[66]

Even more exciting than seeing her review appear in the same prestigious
journal as the one in which her husband's poems had first appeared was the
response of Robert Giroux to her novel. Early in 1942 Giroux, a young editor

at Harcourt, Brace, was handed the manuscript of Stafford's novel, which then bore the title *The Outskirts*. Although he later claimed that he had not met Stafford until after he had been given the manuscript in 1942, he had actually met her in October of 1941, when he had been a dinner guest at the apartment of Stafford and Lowell. According to Stafford, on that occasion Giroux said that he had not realized she had worked at the *Southern Review* or knew John Crowe Ransom or, indeed, that she "was anything but a quiet talented mole working year after year on a novel down on 11th St."[67] When Giroux was given Stafford's manuscript to read, he took it with him on a trip to Connecticut. "I was so enthralled with Sonie [Jean Stafford's protagonist] and so oblivious to everything else," Giroux recalled, "that I rode past my stop and returned to reality only when the conductor yelled, 'New Haven!'" On the strength of Giroux's strong recommendation, Stafford was offered a contract and a modest advance from Harcourt, Brace. On April 30, 1942, she signed a contract for her novel *Boston Adventure*. The actual signing took place at the home of Allen Tate and Caroline Gordon in Princeton. Stafford and Lowell had accompanied Giroux to Princeton to attend a lecture given by Randall Jarrell; when Gordon learned that Giroux had brought Stafford's contract with him, she turned the signing of the contract into a ceremony by lighting candles on either side of the desk.[68]

Ian Hamilton has observed that Stafford's success in securing a book contract coincided with a dry period for Lowell. Instead of easing the tensions between them, the official endorsement of his wife's talents increased Lowell's anxiety about his own work.[69] But no matter how Lowell felt about her book contract, Stafford could not help but be elated. The preceding summer Evelyn Scott, asked to write a letter on her behalf to Houghton Mifflin, had assured her, "I do think you have every qualification for writing great books except, apparently, cash and leisure."[70] While finding the time to write without interruption would still remain a problem for Stafford, the advance from Harcourt, Brace improved her finances and, more important, made her feel, after years of struggle, that she was really a writer after all.

By the summer of 1942 war had been declared, and Lowell was facing the possibility that he might soon be drafted. Nevertheless, delighted when Allen Tate and Caroline Gordon invited them to spend the next year with them in their large house in Monteagle, Tennessee, Stafford and Lowell gladly seized the opportunity. Reminiscing to her friend from the University of Colorado, Joe Chay, about that year with the Tates, Stafford later wrote: ". . . quite fed up with being wage-slaves, we went off to the mountains of Tennessee with Allen Tate and Caroline Gordon where, in a monstrously hideous house (it was so Victorian that the fly swatter was embroidered) the four of us produced books."[71] The four books to which Stafford referred were Lowell's first volume of poems, *Land of Unlikeness,* Tate's *Winter Sea,* Gordon's *The Women on the Porch,* and Stafford's *Boston Adventure,* which she completed that year and sent off to Harcourt, Brace. In the past, Stafford had occasionally visited her hosts in Princeton and had corresponded with Caroline Gordon about her work. Having spent a summer with the Tates at Benfolly in 1937, Lowell, however, knew the formidable Tate and his equally formidable wife much better than Stafford did.

Six miles from the university at Sewanee, the Tates' house in Monteagle was situated on a mountaintop on the heavily wooded grounds of a large summer cottage colony resembling the Chautauqua colony Stafford remembered from Boulder. She and Lowell shared the third floor of the commodious house with the Tates' daughter Nancy, who was then a senior in high school. Two cats and two dogs completed the ménage, and a maid came in each day at nine to clean up and prepare lunch while the four authors devoted their time to their respective manuscripts. Describing their life at Monteagle, Caroline Gordon wrote to her friend Katherine Anne Porter, "Four of us here on this mountain-top, leading what would be an idyllic existence if it weren't for the news from the outside world and for the surges of creative energy which shake the house. I guess I'm identifying Jean's typewriter with her Muse. Sometimes it sounds like the sea breaking on rocks or a small explosion."[72] Jean and Caroline took turns preparing dinner, after which Jean and Allen and Cal played bridge, and on the not infrequent occasions when they had visitors, they all participated in a game of charades. Then, after everyone else had gone to bed, Cal would stay up until all hours working on his poems.

Lowell still insisted that his wife accompany him to mass each morning, as he had done in Baton Rouge and New York City. According to Eileen Simpson, it was during this year, when they waited for the two buses they had to take to reach the Catholic church, that Lowell introduced his wife to an imaginary world peopled by bear characters he called the Berts, dreaming up fantastic adventures for these characters who resembled friends and relatives.[73] Now Stafford became a part of this world in the guise of Bigless Bert, friend of Big Bert. Among Stafford's papers at the Norlin Library in Boulder are two drawings, one of Bigless Bert sitting on a toilet and reading, the other of Bigless smoking and typing. There is also a note addressed to "Deer Been" in which Big Bert, a weak speller like Lowell himself, says, "Thank yu for tiping my opoch."

Although Caroline Gordon referred to the year Stafford and Lowell spent at Monteagle as "idyllic," almost as soon as they had settled in, Stafford became ill again. Lowell took her to Nashville, where she was hospitalized for five days for an upper respiratory disorder that turned out to be bronchitis. "We expected to come home that night so Cal didn't take any clothes with him and he got frightfully dirty," Stafford wrote to Peter Taylor, explaining that Cal had spilled ice cream on his suit the second day. "Cal isn't very cross with me any more because the trouble seems to originate in my nose which you know who broke," she said.[74] Another cause for concern was the fact that even in Monteagle she felt her time was not her own. She was frequently obliged to clean up after the kittens and to type poems for Cal. The fact that despite these distractions she was more productive that year than Lowell probably made him uneasy. Later Lowell would remark about Monteagle that Stafford and Gordon were far more productive that year than he and Tate.[75] Unhappy about the way Lowell treated her, somewhat ill at ease with the Tates, and tense about her work, Stafford continued to drink and smoke too much that year. The Tates told their friends the Cheneys that "Cal beat Jean and made her sleep under the bed,"[76] but apparently the Tates did not choose to interfere in the private life of the younger couple. In addition to her troubles with Lowell, Stafford had to endure having her writing criticized by the three other writers in the house, though she herself solicited their opinions about her work. Caroline thought of Cal and Jean as her children, and she often behaved like a rather severe mother, particularly to Jean. The following year, Caroline expressed remorse about the way that she, Allen Tate, and Robert Lowell had all taken "wacks" at Jean's novel,[77] and Lowell blamed the depression Stafford suffered after she left Monteagle on Caroline's cruelty to her there.[78]

The tensions of that year were dramatized in Gordon's novel, *The Strange Children,* which she published in 1951. The novel is about a couple called the Reardons, who resemble Jean Stafford and Robert Lowell, and their hosts, the Lewises, characters based on Gordon, Tate, and their daughter Nancy. As Lowell had done, Kevin Reardon is said to have gone "into awful rages" when he was in prep school;[79] he had been treated by a psychiatrist; he had a car accident; and he is a staunch Catholic who threatens to "sell all his goods and give them to the poor."[80] Like Stafford, Isabel Reardon is a tall, blonde writer from a poor family who seems much younger than she really is and looks "as if she wanted you to like her and was half afraid that you wouldn't."[81] She formerly had been married to "a crazy fellow" who was overly attached to his mother, "a regular old Back Bay Bitch."[82] Now married to Kevin Reardon, she drinks too much and is terrified of her husband, who shuts her up for weeks on end and refuses to permit her to communicate with her friends. Like Allen Tate and Caroline Gordon, who were divorced by 1951, when *The Strange Children* was published, the Lewises, too, are frequently at odds with one another. Critical of all their friends, they engage in endless gossip, and they dislike the company of people who don't write well.[83]

If this fictional portrait of the Tates and the Lowells is an accurate reflection of what they were really like, and indeed it appears to be, one can understand how difficult that year in Monteagle must have been for Stafford. Although Gordon's Isabel Reardon is very sympathetically drawn, the novel was written a number of years after Stafford and Lowell had stayed at Monteagle. That year, however, Gordon apparently did not fully appreciate how vulnerable Stafford actually was. It is doubtful that these two women ever exchanged intimate details about their personal lives then, for Gordon was a good deal older than Stafford. The letters Gordon sent to her during the following year were cordial, but they hardly suggest that they confided in one another. Eileen Simpson conjectures, nevertheless, that Stafford must have learned a great deal from the older woman not only about writing but about performing domestic chores expeditiously so that there would be sufficient time to get one's writing done as well. According to Simpson, Caroline Gordon "had little patience with married feminist writers who 'whined' about having domestic chores to do."[84] Gordon chose to play the role of gracious lady and willing dispenser of Southern hospitality without complaining in public about her domestic burdens.

Yet even though Gordon liked to boast to others about all the meals she had cooked for the many guests who regularly came to stay with them at Benfolly and Monteagle, her correspondence with her friend Sally Wood suggests that she too was often distressed by the tug of domestic responsibilities when she would have preferred to be writing instead. When the Tates' daughter was born in New York City in 1925, Gordon had decided to let her mother take the baby back to Kentucky instead of attempting to juggle baby care, writing, and housekeeping in the cramped, badly heated apartment where she and Tate were living at the time. Although she discovered that she missed her daughter dreadfully, this seemed to her the only way to resolve the conflicts that being both a writer and a mother had created. Later, after she was reunited with her daughter and had moved to Benfolly, she complained, "I can't write when I'm doing scullery work because even when I get the time my mind won't take hold of any problems."[85] It was Gordon and not Tate who felt responsible for keeping the household running smoothly. Perhaps she was remembering her own situation during the year the Lowells were in residence when she had the daughter of the Lewises in *The Strange Children* remark: "Daddy never seemed to be doing much work himself, but he had strict ideas about other people. Mama's hands looked perfectly dreadful."[86]

In the fifties, when Gordon was analyzed by a Jungian psychiatrist, she began to record dreams that suggest how conflicted she actually was about her dual role as wife and writer. In February of 1954, for example, she recorded a dream in which she has a large study but finds it much too inaccessible: "I am in a large house, with a lot of other people . . . I discover that for the first time in my life I have a study of my own—a capacious, almost luxurious study. I am not pleased with its location. In order to reach it one has to go through the common living-room . . ."[87] The following October she recorded a dream that clearly suggests how much she resented her role as caretaker of others: "There are a lot of things I want to do but I have a burden that I must get rid of before I can set about them. It is a huge ball of human ordure (not mine). I have undertaken to carry it."[88] And the dream she recorded the next day also dealt with the burden of domestic chores. In this dream she was held captive in a house. Her captor loaned her his knife, and she busied herself "chopping the watercress into infinitesimally small dots to adorn the canapes."[89] If, as these dreams suggest, Gordon had indeed experienced conflicts between her role as a housewife and her role as a writer, it is unfortunate that she never discussed these conflicts with Stafford. Had such a discussion taken place, it might at the very least have forged a bond of sympathy between these two women writers, both married to domineering poets who relegated the quotidian details of domestic life to their wives.

In June of that year the union of another writing couple was celebrated when Lowell's roommate from Kenyon College, Peter Taylor, married Eleanor Ross at Monteagle. Eleanor Ross Taylor would later publish two distinguished volumes of poetry, *Wilderness of Ladies* in 1960 and *Welcome Eumenides* in 1972, as well as a number of short stories. Describing the use of domestic imagery in her poetry, Randall Jarrell, who wrote the introduction to *Wilderness of Ladies,* observed, "Many of these are what I think of as woman's-work-is-never-done images." He was thinking, no doubt, of a poem like Eleanor Ross Taylor's "The Bine Yadkin Rose," which begins:

> Move into a house that's not yet built,
> And there's scant time to prune a rose and spray.
> You dish potatoes up three times a day.
> And put your wedding dress into a quilt.[90]

Twenty-five years after her first volume of poetry was published, Eleanor Ross Taylor published a short story called "Early Death," which reveals how difficult it is for a woman artist to combine the imperatives of family life with the imperatives of an artistic career. The story describes the frustrations of a middle-aged would-be artist whose domestic obligations have caused her artistic career to flounder. When she is called upon to take care of her granddaughter, the protagonist of Taylor's story muses that even though she is willing to resume the role of nurturer for the sake of the baby, "there was no consolation for not being in Paris, for never seeing those Cassatts face to face." Taylor observes about her female protagonist, "In a gush of clarity she had seen it was over for her possibilities."[91]

Soon after her wedding, Eleanor Ross Taylor wrote to Stafford, "Mrs. Tate and I talked mostly about the difficulties of housework."[92] Subsequently, as Eleanor helped to support her husband Peter by taking a job in a library or at Sears Roebuck, he began to feel sorry that his wife was leading such a hard life. "I hope to make it easier for her by helping more," Peter Taylor wrote guiltily to Stafford, and he added, "But all summer, Jean, I have slaved over my little novella."[93] Peter Taylor's letters continued to refer to the domestic chores his wife was performing. In one letter to the Lowells, for example, he remarked: "Don't ever let Jean own a vacuum cleaner. There is one in this house, and Eleanor plays with it all morning long in the carpeted front rooms—Zoom-Zoom-Zoom. I know that Jean would run it at midnight and I can just imagine the fury with which she would go about it."[94] Aware that Peter's wife was probably experiencing the same conflict between work and domestic obligations that she was, Stafford wrote to them during the summer of 1943: "I want to know if Eleanor is writing too. I don't see how she can, poor thing. Did I tell you that the housework problem gets easier with time? It really does, but it takes about three years—at least it did with me . . . Ask Peter to tell you what it was like the first year I was married. It is an insoluble problem the first year."[95]

As they had done at the end of their year in Baton Rouge, Stafford and Lowell temporarily parted company that summer after they left Monteagle. Lowell returned to New York, and she happily retreated to the artists' community at Yaddo in Saratoga Springs to revise her novel. In a letter John Crowe Ransom had written on her behalf to Elizabeth Ames, director of Yaddo, he described Stafford as "a lovely girl who is just about to become an important writer."[96] Since three other distinguished men of letters—Lionel Trilling, Philip Rahv, and Allen Tate—also wrote letters of recommendation on her behalf, Stafford had little trouble being accepted for a two-month stay there.

At first, Stafford was favorably impressed by Yaddo. She was fascinated by the luxurious mansion, "full of Florentine thrones and three-cornered chairs and tremendous gold plush sofas," as well as Yaddo's vast and perfectly beautiful grounds "full of lakes and pools and gardens and woodland walks." She described a superb dinner of "squab and wild rice and red raspberries soaked in rum" that she and the other guest artists were served, and she did not appear to be at all dissatisfied with her "rather stark and ascetic" bedroom and studio.[97] All too quickly, however, the tone of her letters from Yaddo began to change. Soon she became so anxious that she feared she was on the verge of a nervous breakdown. Describing her depression, she wrote to Peter and Eleanor Taylor: "Imagine the Bean Bert having a nervous breakdown. It is too grotesque and I am real cross at myself. My humor has departed. Everything seems bitterly grave."[98] She blamed her depression, in part, on Yaddo itself, saying that it was haunted by the spirit of its founder, Katrina Trask, and she described the "incredibly monstrous" mansion house, filled with seraphim, Russian sleighs, ikons, statues, and "portraits unbelievably hideous."[99] After receiving a letter from Stafford full of complaints about Yaddo, Gordon admonished her that if Yaddo began to pall she should just recall the burden of cooking for many people at Monteagle and feel fortunate to be at Yaddo, where guests were served elegant dinners at the mansion and had lunch pails distributed to them each day.[100]

In part Stafford's problems at Yaddo appear to have been triggered by a recurrence of the fever and infection from which she suffered intermittently in Baton Rouge and Monteagle. She told the Taylors that she felt weak and had lost thirteen pounds in a month.[101] Soon, however, she began to fear that she was also "on the verge of some kind of nervous crack-up . . ."[102] Contributing to her malaise was the fact that each evening she was expected to socialize with the other artists who were guests at Yaddo, for she felt awkward in social situations like these and also disliked some of the people there. She reported that Carson McCullers, who in 1940 at the age of twenty-two had become a celebrity with publication of *The Heart Is a Lonely Hunter,* was "by no means the consumptive dipsomaniac" she was rumored to be, but nevertheless she thought McCullers was "strange." She also made disparaging remarks about Agnes Smedley, the author of *Daughter of Earth* (1929). One might have thought that Stafford would have found Agnes Smedley interesting to talk to, for Smedley had just returned from China, where Hightower was then living. Smedley had also grown up in the West and had written an autobiographical novel whose protagonist, like the protagonist of Stafford's *Boston Adventure,* was the daughter of a bitter mother and a ne'er-do-well father. Instead, Stafford said that she disliked Smedley's clothes and "masculine haircut" and found her too talkative.[103] She expressed admiration for Langston Hughes but was bored by another black poet, Margaret Walker, objecting to Walker's "cantankerous" comments about the South and Ransom and Tate and racial prejudice. After commenting snidely to others that

Walker used "her black skin as a weapon," Stafford then feared that she herself was "profusely gossiped about as having race prejudice." [104] As Lowell was
to do when he was a guest at Yaddo in 1949, Stafford believed that many of her
fellow guests were "half baked communists," [105] and when the group con-
vened for cocktails, meals, and social gatherings, she did not feel that she belonged in this happy throng of chattering intellectuals.

Two people at Yaddo whom she liked better than the rest were Kappo
Phelan, a "great (six feet tall) angry Irish girl with wit and charm and furious
morality," [106] and a forty-three-year-old German Jewish refugee named Alfred Kantorowicz, a close friend of Carson McCullers who was a literary critic
and foreign correspondent. Both Jean Stafford and Kappo Phelan preferred
drinking in the bars in Saratoga Springs to having cocktails in the gloomy
mansion of Yaddo, and Stafford reported to the Taylors that Kantorowicz, an
expert on Thomas Mann, had given her all the "lowdown on the Mann tribe."
Many years later Kantorowicz told Virginia Spencer Carr, the biographer of
Carson McCullers, that there had been "a temporary hectic love story" between Stafford and himself at Yaddo during the summer of 1943. [107] However,
Harold Shapero, a musician who was also at Yaddo during the summer of
1943, claims that the romance was one-sided and that Stafford found the at-
tentions of her suitor annoying. She described Kantorowicz to Peter and Eleanor Taylor as "the one refugee I have ever met whom I liked and could talk
with," [108] but it is unclear whether she ever felt any real affection for the tall
Jewish intellectual who found her so appealing. [109]

By the end of August Stafford was feeling sufficiently improved in health
to pay a visit to Katherine Anne Porter at Porter's country house ten miles
from Yaddo. Earlier that summer, when she had been feeling so unwell and
depressed, she had considered turning to Katherine Anne Porter for advice,
but she was discouraged from doing so by Caroline Gordon. Explaining that
the very thought of having anyone dependent on her made Katherine Anne
Porter "wild," Gordon observed, "This is just the way she is and she can't help
it. It goes along with her talent. Without it I doubt if she could have got as
much work done as she has." [110] In Baton Rouge Stafford had visited the home
Albert Erskine had shared with Katherine Anne Porter during the brief period when he and Porter had been husband and wife, but she had never met
Porter. "It is a perfectly beautiful house and she is utterly charming, and she
spoke very highly of your stories, Peter, which was, of course, endearing,"
Stafford wrote to the Taylors about her two-day visit with Porter. She described the late eighteenth-century facade, the green shutters, and the pedi-
mented windows of Porter's house as "perfect" and said that the silver
tumblers in which Porter had served mint juleps reminded her of the first day

she and Cal had spent in Baton Rouge, when Erskine had offered them drinks in the very same tumblers.[111]

As she prepared to leave Yaddo at the end of August, Stafford was still running a fever intermittently and wanted to make an appointment with an internist in New York City whom Caroline Gordon had recommended. Realizing that Stafford lacked the necessary funds to pay a specialist's fees, Gordon wrote to Charlotte Lowell about her daughter-in-law's health problems. Lowell, who was about to be inducted into the armed services, also tried to persuade his mother that the need to have his wife's recurring illness properly diagnosed was urgent.

With the completed manuscript of *Boston Adventure* in hand, Stafford left Yaddo at the beginning of September. Worn out and ill, she was dreading the fact that in New York she would have to deal with setting up an apartment once again. Furthermore, the pattern of her married life would necessarily be disrupted after Lowell left for the army. She was pleased, however, that after years of working on her novel, she had finally completed it to her own satisfaction. Although she was distraught about her marriage and her poor health, she looked forward to the day in the not too distant future when *Boston Adventure* would at last be published by Harcourt, Brace.

Back row, left to right: *Grandmother Phoebe Ann Wilson Stafford, Ethel Stafford (Jean's mother), Lois, Bud (cousins), John Stafford (Jean's father).* Second row, left to right: *Marjorie, Mary Lee, and Dick Stafford.* In front: *Jean Stafford. About 1917. Courtesy Marjorie Stafford Pinkham.*

Stafford car en route to Colorado. Left to right: *Dick, Ethel, Mary Lee. Courtesy Marjorie Stafford Pinkham.*

Malcolm McKillop, Jean's grandfather.
Courtesy Marjorie Stafford Pinkham.

Carrie Lee Thurber McKillop, Jean's grandmother.
Courtesy Marjorie Stafford Pinkham.

Jean Stafford, about two years old.
Courtesy Marjorie Stafford Pinkham.

Marjorie Stafford.
Courtesy Marjorie Stafford Pinkham.

Mary Lee Stafford.
Courtesy Marjorie Stafford Pinkham.

Dick Stafford. Graduation, 1933.
Courtesy Marjorie Stafford Pinkham.

Jean Stafford: a glamour shot (university days).
Courtesy Marjorie Stafford Pinkham.

New Orleans, 1941. Left to right: Peter Taylor, Jean Stafford, Robert Lowell. Courtesy Peter Taylor.

Yaddo, 1943. Jean Stafford is third from left in the bottom row; Carson McCullers is second from right. Courtesy George S. Bolster.

Jean Stafford and Robert Lowell, Damariscotta Mills, Maine, summer 1946. Courtesy Gertrude Buckman.

Oliver Jensen and Jean Stafford on honeymoon in Ocho Rios, Jamaica, 1950. Courtesy Oliver Jensen.

Jean Stafford and A. J. Liebling, The Springs, about 1962. Courtesy Joseph Mitchell.

Jean Stafford's loyal housekeeper and the executor of her estate,
Mrs. Josephine Monsell, 1983.

Seven

An Influx of Poets
Fall 1943–Fall 1946

*It is just as well my husband did not have a literary wife as there had to be
someone to do the washing and cooking . . .*
—NORA JOYCE, 1939, QUOTED IN BRENDA MADDOX, *NORA*

Some women marry houses . . .
—ANNE SEXTON, "HOUSEWIFE"

WHEN JEAN STAFFORD returned to New York from Yaddo at the beginning of September, she had expected that Lowell would be inducted into
the army on September 8. However, instead of showing up for his induction,
he sent a Declaration of Personal Responsibility on September 7 to President
Franklin Delano Roosevelt explaining why he refused to serve. In this letter
Lowell stated that even though he had volunteered to serve in the armed
forces in March and August of 1942, after the mining of the Ruhr Dams and
the razing of Hamburg, his conscience would not allow him to do so.[1] After
sending off the declaration of his refusal to serve in the armed forces, he also
wrote to his mother, asking her to offer her love not to him but to Jean, who
would have to deal with the consequences of his act.[2]

Stafford's ambivalence about this dramatic turn of events that would have
an impact not only on Lowell's life but her own is reflected in a letter she sent
to her sister Mary Lee. Describing how she and Cal had mailed 110 copies of
his letter to the president and to various other influential people, she observed,
"I should never have allowed it but most of it had been done by the time I got
there and I couldn't stop anything." She said she regretted that Allen Tate,
who was working that year at the Library of Congress and had gotten someone in the Department of Justice to grant Cal a week to reconsider, had not
persuaded him to change his mind. "Day after tomorrow we go before the
Grand Jury," she said, "after which we can bail him out for a week (if I can
raise the bail) and then it will be a federal pen. for from 3–5 years." Expressing the hope that Cal might get into noncombatant medical service, she said

that she found his decision to be a conscientious objector "frightening" but that she was "obliged to admire him."[3]

One of the recipients of Lowell's declaration was John Crowe Ransom. "Poor Cal!" Ransom wrote to Allen Tate. "But he's not a man whose prison term in itself ought to be mourned for; it's his degeneration inside."[4] On October 13 Lowell was sentenced to be imprisoned in the Federal Correctional Center in Danbury, Connecticut, for a year and a day. While waiting to be transported there, he was incarcerated in New York's West Street jail in a cell next to the infamous gangster, Lepke Buchalter. "I saw Cal Thursday under the most depressing circumstance. A great slab of plate glass was between us and we had to talk over the telephone," Stafford reported to Eleanor and Peter Taylor.[5]

After ten days in the West Street prison, Lowell, "handcuffed between two marijuana peddlers,"[6] was transferred to the facility in Danbury. Stafford had been allowed to visit her husband only once when he was imprisoned in New York, and during his prison term in Danbury from October to March, she was permitted to visit him only for one hour on Saturdays. In November, writing to the Taylors from the small apartment on East 17th Street in Manhattan that she had rented, she described her most recent visit to the prison: "I saw Cal yesterday for the first time in five weeks. He looks very well and has gained weight and is in pretty good spirits. He is the most attractive and lovable man I know . . . I cannot tell you how glad I am that I am married to him and how sick down to my bones it makes me that he isn't in this room and won't be for ages."[7] Since Stafford was allowed to visit Lowell once a week, it is not clear why she visited him only one time during a five-week period. What is evident from this letter, however, is that she felt more kindly disposed toward him when he was behind bars than when they were in the same room together.

That fall and winter Stafford worried even more than usual about finances. Although she had assured her mother-in-law that she could and was willing to support herself while Cal was in prison, she was infuriated when Charlotte Lowell wrote to her in November that if she availed herself of all the money in the trust fund, a course of action Lowell himself had urged Jean to pursue, he would be penniless when he was released.[8] Complaining about "Mrs. Hideous" to Caroline Gordon and Allen Tate, Stafford said that her mother-in-law had imagined she was about to get a job and learn "courage, self-development, and integrity the hard way in the OWI or the five and ten or a soap factory or whatever."[9] Concerned about how she would survive during the period when Cal was in prison, she said that she felt envious of "two flashy looking articles" in fur coats who had shared a taxi to the prison with her, for the opulent dress of these women suggested that their husbands, in contrast to

Cal, had "left them well provided for while they were off being castigated for their ideals."[10]

Initially Stafford had considered applying to be chief reviewer for *Time*, a job for which Allen Tate had recommended her. She was not very enthusiastic about doing so, however, because she had heard disturbing rumors that no one had been able to keep this position for more than six months. After her interview with the managing editor, she learned from Allen Tate that this editor had no intention of hiring a woman. Although she desperately needed money, she was somewhat relieved when she was turned down. "I was very glad," she told the Taylors.[11]

One stroke of good fortune that fall was that Mary Lou Aswell, an editor at *Harper's Bazaar*, purchased Stafford's short story "The Darkening Moon." One of a group of stories to appear later in Stafford's *Collected Stories* under the heading "Cowboys and Indians and Magic Mountains," it was published in *Harper's Bazaar* in January of 1944. As many of her short stories did, it relates the experiences of a young girl growing up in a western landscape she finds alienating and sometimes terrifying. Originally Stafford had submitted the story under the name Jean Lowell, but subsequently she decided she preferred to have the story published under her maiden name.[12] One can understand her rationale for doing so. However, it is harder to understand why that spring she chose to publish a second story, "The Lippia Lawn," in the *Kenyon Review* under the name Phoebe Lowell, a combination of her Grandmother Stafford's given name and Cal's surname. Perhaps she was afraid that this story, which alludes to her childhood in California and her sojourn in Heidelberg and which describes an angry old man like her father with "wiry old legs,"[13] was too self-revealing. A list of names she wrote on the inside back cover of a notebook from that period suggests that she was still undecided about what pen name to use. "Jean Stafford Lowell," "Jean Wilson Stafford," "Mrs. R T S Lowell," she wrote in her best Palmer-method script.[14] One might conclude that she was unsure which name best identified who she really was. It is odd that the pen name she finally chose—Jean Stafford—does not even appear on this list.

During the period when Lowell was in prison, Stafford was forced to construct an independent life for herself in New York City. She continued to see Kappo Phelan, whom she had met at Yaddo, and she befriended a young woman named Cecile Starr, who was a friend of Lowell's friend from Louisiana State University, Patrick Quinn, and a niece of two affluent minor figures in the Nashville Fugitive Poets group, Milton and Alfred Starr. She also spent time with Gertrude Buckman, who had just separated from Delmore Schwartz.

As associate editor of the *Partisan Review,* Delmore Schwartz was one of the youngest, most gifted, but most neurotic of the New York literati. William Phillips, an editor of the *Partisan Review,* has written of him: "Trained in philosophy, an accomplished critic as well as a writer of fiction and poetry, sensitive to political ideas, with the uncanny intelligence that only functioning paranoids seem to have, he possessed all the equipment for the modern sensibility and a miserable life."[15] The son of Jewish immigrants, Delmore Schwartz resembled those "first generation metropolitan boys" whose familiarity with "everything political and artistic and metaphysical and scientific" Stafford would write about in her short story "Children Are Bored on Sunday."[16] Although Schwartz's background was very different from her own, she began to spend a good deal of time with him that year. Both liked to drink, and since they enjoyed gossip about people in the literary world, Schwartz said they both belonged to the "black tongue circuit whose founding fathers are Juvenal, Horace, Dante, Swift, and Lear."[17] Stafford spent so much time in Schwartz's company that rumors began to circulate on "the black tongue circuit" about the two of them. When Schwartz's biographer, James Atlas, interviewed Robert Lowell years later, Lowell murmured, "People say Delmore slept with Jean . . . Someone said he could tell by the way he lit her cigarette."[18]

A measure of Stafford's acceptance into the charmed circle of the New York intellectuals was the fact that she was invited to a cocktail party by Philip Rahv that November. According to William Phillips, Rahv was very selective about whom he invited, making up his guest list for his parties "more carefully than the President chooses the Cabinet."[19] Broad-shouldered, argumentative, domineering, this self-educated intellectual from the Ukraine was committed to publishing the works of the best modern writers in the pages of the *Partisan Review.* He, too, loved literary gossip, and according to Stafford's friend Dorothea Straus, his heated monologues sounded like "violent rebuttals directed at an invisible, inaudible opposition."[20] In the fall of 1944, Stafford would make her debut in the eleventh volume of the *Partisan Review* with an excerpt from *Boston Adventure* as well as a short story called "A Reunion," which describes the painful reunion between a young woman and her aged dour father from whom she feels permanently estranged. After reading the story, Rahv wrote to Allen Tate, "Jean sent us a story which is quite good but terribly morbid. There is a great deal in that girl I hadn't realized was there."[21]

While Stafford might have been flattered to receive an invitation to the Rahvs' party, she was sorry afterward that she had been subjected to this "revolting experience." She later described it in detail to the Taylors: everyone had been drunk; Sidney Hook, known for his ability to demolish anyone who chose to disagree with him, had first accused Cal of being a heretic because by refusing to serve in the army he was going against the dictates of the Pope, and then had argued with her about the merits of St. Augustine; and Sidney Hook's wife, angry when Jean had murmured that she was sure there was something to be said for Franco, had screamed to her husband, who was on the other side of the room, "Sidney, there is no point talking to this girl." Sidney Hook remembered the occasion vividly: "She had this kittenish quality," he said of Jean Stafford, remarking that she wore no makeup and seemed very vulnerable. He described her as "a bright little girl who had been attracted to the aesthetics of Catholicism," and, though he acknowledged that people in the *Partisan Review* crowd believed she was a coming writer, he said that like "Tom-cats on the prowl" they were also drawn to her because she was young and good-looking. Already on edge after being told by various men at the party that "Cal was a fool or hysterical," when confronted by the formidable Sidney Hook, Stafford burst into tears and could not stop crying. According to Hook, it was she who had persisted in discussing Aquinas and St. Augustine with him, though he himself was reluctant to pursue the subject with her since he detected "a streak of religiosity in her" and also realized that she was quite drunk.[22] In her letter to the Taylors she observed snidely that "the greatest snobs in the world are bright New York literary Jews and the name of Lowell works like a love philtre." She was angry at herself, she said, for continuing to socialize with these "cut-throats," these "ambitious bourgeois frights."[23] Thirty years later she would mention the party at the Rahvs' house during which she had turned herself into "a great gawky knobby-kneed school girl from the Rockies." She admitted that she had been "very green and very western," while Hook "was very grown-up and dictatorial and very, very New York."[24] Just as she took pleasure in satirizing the Beacon Hill world of her socialite in-laws in *Boston Adventure,* so in her short story "Children Are Bored on Sundays" she would seek revenge for the way the New York intellectuals had treated her by describing with deadly wit and irony their drunken parties at which absent friends were "garrotted."[25]

More pleasurable than the evening with the Rahvs was one that she spent in December with Allen Tate. Confined to his hotel room when he became ill, Tate invited Stafford, Mary McCarthy, and his friend Joe Horrell to have dinner with him in his room. After they arrived, the house doctor, who had been summoned by Tate, appeared: "He obviously thought we were in for a gay evening and his lascivious eyes wandered from Mary to Joe to Allen to me," Stafford gleefully reported to the Taylors.[26] The two literary women who were present that evening, Jean Stafford and Mary McCarthy, had both been born on the West Coast within three years of one another and had endured economic and psychological hardships during their early years. Not too long before this meeting took place, McCarthy had been a patient at Payne Whitney Psychiatric Hospital, and in the near future Stafford would be admitted to the same hospital as well. However, McCarthy had emerged from the traumas of her youth encased in armor and equipped with a pen that she wielded like a rapier, while Stafford at that point in her life was still vulnerable, her laughter and satiric comments barely camouflaging the tears that might well up without warning. Educated at Vassar, McCarthy had been associated with the *Partisan Review* as a drama critic, had had an affair with Philip Rahv, and had been married to one of the central figures in New York intellectual life, Edmund Wilson. What Alfred Kazin has described as "her brilliance in putting down friends, enemies and various idols of the American tribe"[27] had served her well. During the next decade she would pillory her former lovers and literary acquaintances in her satiric novels, *The Oasis* and *The Groves of Academe,* the latter the kind of satire of academic life that Stafford herself had hoped to write when she began her novel *Neville.* In 1954 Randall Jarrell, a friend of both McCarthy's and Stafford's, would also publish a satire of academic life in *Pictures from an Institution.* In it appears an acerbic novelist named Gertrude Johnson who some people thought was supposed to represent Mary McCarthy and others identified as Jean Stafford.[28]

While Jean Stafford was making her way somewhat painfully through the thorny paths of the New York literary world, her husband was washing floors in a prison in Danbury. Although many people pitied him, he does not appear to have minded terribly his term in prison. No doubt he relished the scandal that the imprisonment of a Lowell had created in Boston, and since the work he was assigned to do was not arduous, he had plenty of leisure time to read Proust and to correct the galleys for his first volume of poems, *The Land of Unlikeness.* Dressed no longer in Brooks Brothers suits but in the ill-fitting shoes and uniform of a prisoner, he must have felt like a true Christian penitent. In a letter to Peter Taylor, Stafford described Lowell's incarceration as "the pleasurable monasticism of the penitentiary," and she expressed her dismay at Lowell's intention when he was released from prison to be "a sort of soapbox preacher with an organization called the Catholic Evidence Guilds." Admitting that she found frightening what she perceived to be a drastic change in his personality, she said: "And when I inquire of him how we will live, he points to the Gospels and says that we must not worry about that, that God will take care of us, that one cannot be a wage slave but must have leisure in which to serve the church . . ."[29]

A short story Stafford wrote that year, "Between the Porch and the Altar," reflects her own ambivalent feelings about Catholicism. It is of interest to note that Lowell wrote a poem with the same title in which he expressed a desperate need "To cry and ask God's pardon of our sin."[30] Stafford's story, however, describes a female protagonist who finds going to church on Ash Wednesday repugnant. She is repelled when she is asked for alms by a drunken beggar; she shudders when she feels the coldness of the church steps and the holy water; she is revolted by the sight of the stubble she detects under the coif of a nun; she finds the church, with its gaudy statues and sentimental crucifixes, "ugly and in bad taste"; and she is horrified when an old crone with "sour gray hair" will not leave her alone until she gives the old woman her last dime. As soon as she reaches home, Stafford's protagonist washes away the ashes with which the Jesuit priest has marked her forehead. Even her mission of lighting a candle for "the safe-keeping of two friends, captive in China by the Japanese," is thwarted. Obviously autobiographical, the story refers not only to Stafford but to Hightower, who had recently been detained in China by the Japanese.[31] As she awaited Lowell's release from prison in March, Stafford realized that the difference between his religious commitment and her own was no less an impenetrable barrier between them than the plate of glass that had separated them when she had visited him in the West Street jail.

During the spring of 1944 Stafford gave up her apartment in New York City and settled with Lowell in Bridgeport, Connecticut, for his parole board had assigned him to work as a janitor in the nurses' quarters of St. Vincent's Hospital there. Immediately after his release from prison Lowell had lived in a dingy rooming house similar to the one Stafford describes in her short story "The Home Front." Since all available apartments in Bridgeport were occupied by the munitions workers in the local factories, decent housing was hard to come by. Finally, Stafford located a two-room apartment for them in a large building called Harbor View on Ocean Avenue in Black Rock, Connecticut, an address immortalized in two of Lowell's poems, "Colloquy in Black Rock" and "Christmas in Black Rock." Formerly owned by a rumrunner during Prohibition, the building had been bought by a Roman Catholic priest, a fact that pleased Lowell. Harbor View, however, was a misnomer: all that was visible from their windows was a tiny patch of water. Stafford and Lowell both referred to the depressing location of their dwelling: Lowell described "the mud-flat detritus of death," "watermelons gutted to the crust," and the thud of "armored Diesel fishing tubs"[32] outside their door; and Stafford in "The Home Front" spoke of "the black and stinking mud-flat" that was evident at low tide and the nearby dump heaped with "all the frightful refuse of the city, the high-heeled shoes and the rotten carrots and the abused insides of automobiles."[33]

Stafford's "The Home Front," which appeared in the *Partisan Review* in the spring of 1945, is as bleak as its Black Rock setting. It is about an intellectual Jewish physician named Dr. Pankheiser who is a refugee from Germany. Dr. Pankheiser is overwhelmed with nostalgia as he thinks of his student years in Heidelberg, years that were "rich and full of importance."[34] Middle-aged and alone, an exile in industrial America, he is subjected to the anti-Semitic remarks of Mrs. Horvath, a Hungarian woman who manages his apartment building, and he has nothing to console him but his books, his prints, and his only "friend," an ugly tomcat that comes to his room each evening. At the story's end he is deprived even of that companion when the Horvaths' malevolent son, a boy whose hobby it is to capture birds, persuades his father to shoot the cat because it is scaring his birds away. Dr. Pankheiser, however, scores a Pyrrhic victory over the Horvaths when he provides a sea burial for a beautiful oriole that had gotten caught in his chimney. Making wonderful use of the wasteland landscape of Bridgeport, Stafford succeeded in creating a moving fable of human isolation. It is unfortunate that she did not include this excellent story in her *Collected Stories,* for it deserves to be better known than it is at present.

"I find Bridgeport more deadly and evil-smelling every day," Stafford wrote to her friend Cecile Starr. Describing the stench from the harbor that invaded her room at night when the tide went out as "an essentially organic odor," she said, "It lingers in our hair and clothing and coats the caramels and gets into the apples. It does not more closely resemble a stock-yard than a smell of a boy who traps skunks, nor is it more like a condemned privy than an ice-chest in need of attention."[35]

As she anxiously awaited the publication of *Boston Adventure* during the summer of 1944, she was always aware of her depressing surroundings, and when she managed to get down to New York City, she was annoyed that her time was taken up with running "a million errands" for Cal.[36] She was finding it impossible to write that summer, but Lowell, after doing no writing for almost a year, was suddenly working with the same kind of concentration he had demonstrated in Monteagle, and she found his productivity threatening: "Cal started writing poetry again and his intensity and industry make me feel completely worthless. I've done nothing at all this summer," she complained to Eleanor Taylor.[37] By September, however, all her anxiety was channeled into worrying how *Boston Adventure* would be received. She wondered not only about what the reviewers would say of the novel but how her in-laws would react to her mostly unflattering portrait of their hallowed society. As they examined the best-seller written by their daughter-in-law, Lowell's parents were probably chagrined to discover that this outsider from Colorado who had married their son had had the audacity to write about their world. On the other hand, they must have been relieved to discover that the name Jean Stafford rather than Jean Lowell appeared on the cover of *Boston Adventure* and that the novel was dedicated not to their son but to Cal's friend Frank Parker, who was then a military prisoner in Germany.

In an essay called "Truth and the Novelist," published in *Harper's Bazaar* in 1951, Stafford describes a conversation she once had with Ford Madox Ford about the writing of fiction. Ford, she said, warned her to avoid painting portraits of people in her fiction exactly as she had known them in life, calling such a practice "impolite" and maintaining that such portraiture was not "fiction." Reiterating Ford's dictum, Stafford advised the would-be writer of fiction to escape the pitfalls of autobiography by "the simplest expedients: by shifting the scene from the North to the South or the East to the West, by changing the occupation of a character or the color of his hair or the fit of his clothes." She also had this suggestion: ". . . take with a grain of salt the cliché that it is possible to rid oneself of a grief or a guilt or an ugly memory by writing of it; if you write of yourself, write with compassion and lay the blame for setting the house on fire on someone else." [38] Her discussion of the novelist's craft sheds light on the composition of *Boston Adventure:* even though the details of its plot and its characters are fictitious, the novel is in part transparently autobiographical. Not only does Stafford include characters resembling the Lowells and their Boston circle, but she also portrays her misanthropic father, her embittered mother, Hightower and his Japanese girlfriend, Lucy McKee, and even Lowell in barely disguised form in this female *Bildungsroman* that critics likened to the novels of Proust, the Brontës, and Dostoevsky. It is patently obvious, moreover, that Stafford's first-person narrator, Sonie Marburg, a blameless victim of poverty and of her parents' unfortunate marriage, as well as a person of intelligence and sensitivity who both longs for and loathes the privileged world of Boston society, is a character bearing a great similarity to Stafford herself. Incorporating in disguised form the "ugly memory" of Lucy's suicide but exonerating Sonie for the death of Lucy's fictional counterpart, Hopestill Mather, Stafford obeyed her own dictum, writing about Sonie "with compassion" and laying "the blame for setting the house on fire on someone else."

Boston Adventure traces the growth and development of Sonia Marburg, who at the novel's beginning lives with her parents and her younger brother in Chichester, a fishing village not too far from Boston. Her father is a well-educated but impoverished German artisan; and her mother, a Russian immigrant, helps to support the family by working as a chambermaid in Chichester's Hotel Barstow. It is here that Sonie meets Miss Lucy Pride, an elderly

member of the Boston aristocracy whose elegant, conservative dress and re-
strained demeanor contrast markedly with the slovenly clothes and frenzied
behavior of her own mother. She also meets Miss Pride's spoiled niece, Hopestill Mather, a character whose resemblance to Lucy McKee Stafford acknowledged.[39] By the end of Book One, Sonie's irresponsible father has abandoned his family, Sonie's younger brother Ivan, an epileptic, has died, and
Sonie's mother has been admitted to a mental hospital after suffering a nervous breakdown.

In Book Two, entitled "Pinckney Street," Sonie enters Miss Pride's upper-
class Boston world when she is employed as the older woman's secretary. Here
Sonie learns about various members of the Boston aristocracy, including a
young poet resembling Lowell who is the author of "some vicious lines on the
Granary Burying Ground" and who carries about with him the Holy Sonnets
of John Donne.[40] Sonie rejects one suitor, a Jewish intellectual from Denver
who gives up the "pipe dream" of becoming a writer, as Hightower had
done,[41] and she falls in love with Philip McAllister, a Boston Brahmin like
Lowell whose mother tells "damning anecdotes" about her son and relates
"instances of his devotion to herself."[42] But Philip McAllister marries Miss
Pride's niece, a wealthy, reckless, neurotic young woman who dies, as Lucy
McKee had done, soon after she is married. *Boston Adventure* concludes with
Sonie outwardly conforming to the role expectations dictated by her gender
and her position in society: female and outsider, she accepts the subordinate
role of secretary to the domineering Miss Pride, whom she admires but also
fears. Tormented by her desire to enter a world of elegance and civility that
seems beyond her reach, Sonie conjures up a sanctuary for her troubled spirit:
a "red room" filled with books and furnished with Louisa May Alcott's writing desk.

The editors of a recent volume of critical essays on the female *Bildungs-*
roman have observed that unlike the plot of the typical male *Bildungsroman,*
which culminates with the hero's accommodation to society, the female *Bil-*
dungsroman "typically substitute[s] inner concentration for active accommodation, rebellion or withdrawal."[43] Wishing to escape the fate of her embittered, demented mother, whose abandonment by her husband has resulted in
a mental breakdown, and rejecting as well the sterile if orderly life of the celi-
bate Miss Pride, Sonie is unable to conceive of an alternative way of life for
herself. As does the protagonist of the prototypical female *Bildungsroman,*
Sonie outwardly submits to her fate by returning to the house of the overbear-
ing Miss Pride, but her rebellion takes the form of maintaining inviolate the
hallucinatory vision of her place of refuge, the imaginary "red room" in which
her spirit resides: "It was a sanctuary and its tenant was my spirit, changing

my hot blood to cool ichor and my pain to ease. Under my own merciful auspices, I had made for myself a tamed-down sitting-room in a dead, a voiceless, city where no one could trespass, for I was the founder, the governor, the only citizen."[44]

The appearance in 1944 of *Boston Adventure* was a major literary event, for this first novel by an unknown writer was applauded by reviewers in newspapers and magazines and by critics in literary journals. A number of critics, including the anonymous reviewers in the *New Yorker* and in *Time,* Ruth Page in the *New York Times Book Review,* and Alfred Kazin in the *New Republic,* compared Stafford's style and vision to that of Proust, and other critics saw parallels between Stafford's novel and those of the Brontës, Dostoevsky, and J. P. Marquand, who had also written a novel about Boston's upper class. Diana Trilling, who said that she found Stafford's depiction of the mature Sonie in Book Two somewhat more convincing than her portrayal of the "Dostoevskian horror" of Sonie's childhood in Book One, nevertheless expressed the sentiments of the majority of critics when she wrote that it would be "hard to name a book of recent years which, page for page or even sentence for sentence, was so lively and clever."[45]

Today, when *Boston Adventure* has been all but forgotten not only by the casual reader but also by literary historians and even feminist critics who have done so much to revive forgotten novels by women writers, it is hard to believe that Stafford's first novel created such a stir when it was first published or, indeed, that it was subsequently reprinted almost a dozen times. When one compares *Boston Adventure* with a superior novel of manners such as Edith Wharton's *The House of Mirth,* it is evident that Stafford's portrait of Boston society lacks the kind of authenticating detail that Edith Wharton, herself a member of the upper class, was able to provide in characterizing the wealthy members of New York society. Only a person like Stafford, who had never actually stayed at a hotel frequented by the members of the Boston aristocracy, could describe a paperweight in the lobby of the Hotel Barstow as having a picture inside of "a burro whose mouth released a balloon to hold the words 'Hee-haw! Howdy, folks! You're looking at a Rocky Mountain Canary'"[46]; and only a stranger to Beacon Hill, as Theodore Spencer pointed out in his review of *Boston Adventure* in the *Sewanee Review,* would situate Miss Pride's house on Pinckney Street instead of a more elegant street on Beacon Hill, or call the Boston Public Garden the "Public Gardens."[47] When asked her opinion of "the admirable novel" *Boston Adventure,* Elizabeth Hardwick, who married Robert Lowell after he and Stafford were divorced, once observed, ". . . the answer invariably comes, 'Not Boston!'"[48]

A more serious weakness of *Boston Adventure* than its inclusion of several inauthentic details is Stafford's depiction of her protagonist, Sonia Marburg. In her recent study of Stafford's work, Mary Ellen Williams Walsh mentions Sonia's "cold objectivity," her failure to love anyone, and her hypocrisy.[49] These negative qualities are indeed evident in Sonia Marburg, but what Stafford fails to provide is any sense of how we are to view Sonie's shortcomings. That is to say, Stafford appears to lack sufficient distance from her protagonist to portray her with as much objectivity as she does her other characters. While Stafford's ironic detachment is evident in her depiction of the people in the Boston of Miss Pride, she identifies too closely with Sonie to apply the same standards of behavior to her as she does to others. This may help to explain some of the inconsistency in the tone of the novel, which alternates between a tendency to melodrama in the sections that deal with Sonia Marburg and her family and a tone of ironic detachment that characterizes the parts of the novel focusing on Miss Pride and the other inhabitants of Beacon Hill.

Despite these shortcomings, however, *Boston Adventure* is an impressive first novel. It demonstrates Stafford's brilliant use of language, her ability to create believable and interesting characters, her wit, and her ironic view of mankind. An American Jane Eyre, Stafford's Sonia Marburg takes her place among those female protagonists of the nineteenth- and twentieth-century female *Bildungsroman* who dream of a life very different from the one their circumstances permit them to live. Celebrating Stafford's achievement, Ihab Hassan wrote of *Boston Adventure* in 1955, "But whatever may be said of *Boston Adventure,* the sweep of its social intentions and the grip of some of its individual scenes put it on a par with any first novel by an American writer of this decade."[50]

Boston Adventure became a best-seller, and after it was published in 1944, Jean Stafford became a celebrity. She was interviewed for a radio program, received the *Mademoiselle* merit award, having been selected as one of *Mademoiselle's* "10 Women of the Year," and, much to her delight, finally had a substantial sum of money at her disposal from the sales of her novel. "It is fine that you all are in the big money," Allen Tate wrote to her and Lowell in October when they mailed him a check to repay the money he had loaned them.[51] Several months later Tate asked in a letter, "How does it feel to be rich?"[52] After she paid a trip to her in-laws, Stafford wrote to Cecile Starr that she felt "more thoroughly, more icily, more deeply disliked than ever" by the Lowells, though Cal's parents conceded that it was "a damned good thing" he had married someone who made money from her writing.[53]

In May of 1945 Philip Rahv wrote to Allen Tate, "Jean seems to think that she may get the Pulitzer; it won't be good for her if she does."[54] Rahv did not spell out whether receiving this recognition would not be "good" for Stafford personally or "good" for her writing; however, his concern about the effect on her of receiving the Pulitzer Prize was needless since the Pulitzer Prize for fiction that year was awarded not to Stafford's female *Bildungsroman, Boston Adventure,* but to John Hersey's novel about World War II, *A Bell for Adano.* Nevertheless, Stafford had cause for celebration that year: 40,000 hardcover copies of *Boston Adventure* were sold within a few months of publication and 300,000 additional copies were distributed by book clubs and sold in overseas editions. Moreover, with the success of *Boston Adventure,* Stafford now felt confident enough to apply for a prestigious Guggenheim Fellowship to support the writing of a projected sequel to this novel.

The money Stafford had earned enabled her and Lowell to rent a spacious house in a rural section of Westport early in October. She described to Bill Mock, who had contacted her when he returned to the States from France, how jubilant she was to be able to move from "two frightful little rooms" in Bridgeport to "The Barn," a large house in a pretty location: "Now everything is over and we have a big house in the country and all the leisure we want and nearly all the money we want, because my book has done very well," she said with relief.[55]

In addition to writing to her friend Mock, Stafford also began to exchange letters with Joe Chay, the intellectual ex-Marine at the University of Colorado with whom she had once fancied she was in love. After filling him in on what had transpired in her life since she had left Boulder, she invited him to come visit her and Cal at their "wonderful house deep in the country," with its "nine acres, five bedrooms, four bathrooms, and the handsomest pig-sty in Fairfield County." As a further inducement, she said, ". . . I have developed into so ardent a cook that if I weren't honor-bound to write, I should spend all my time making the most complicated soups and stews, the sort that require a bag of every known herb together with calves' feet and twenty-four hours of steady vigil."[56]

Before she even had time to settle into "The Barn," Stafford took the train to New York City to hunt for a job for Lowell that he would find acceptable, and she managed to sprain her ankle so badly while rushing for a train that she was confined to bed for a week. During this time, the devastating news arrived that her brother, a member of the airborne field artillery in France, had been killed in an ambulance accident after being wounded on the battlefield. She told Joe Chay that she had seen Dick in July during his last furlough and now found it impossible to believe that he was dead. She felt sure, she said, that if she could go to France, she would find him there "alive and whole."[57] Although she and her brother had not been close in recent years, she had been very fond of him nevertheless. The news of his death revived in her vivid memories of the childhood experiences they had shared. Before long these memories would give rise to Stafford's second novel, *The Mountain Lion,* which describes the relationship of a boy and his troubled younger sister.

After learning about her brother's death, Stafford decided to pay a visit to her parents in Oregon. She wrote to her sister Mary Lee that as soon as her sprained ankle was healed, she planned to meet her in Denver and travel with her to Portland; meanwhile, she was arranging to have a Catholic priest say a requiem mass for Dick. "I am so glad, in this terrible thing, to be a Catholic," she said. "And you must believe, as we have all got to believe, that he is just somewhere else."[58]

En route to Oregon, Stafford met Mary Lee as well as Paul and Dorothy Thompson and their two small sons in Denver; then she and Mary Lee traveled together to Oregon. Six years had elapsed since Stafford had last been in Portland. During the summer of 1938, when she had spent the summer with her parents, she had doubted whether she would ever succeed as a writer; now her first novel had been published by a well-known publisher and had become a commercial and critical success. But if returning to Oregon as a successful writer made her feel more self-confident, the sight of her aging parents instantly evoked memories of her lonely childhood and unhappy youth. Dressed in a somber navy blue suit and coat, she attended mass each morning. Her evenings, on the other hand, were usually spent in the company of her sisters, the three of them consuming bottles of wine from the local Piggly Wiggly store.[59] Ill with bronchitis during most of her stay and unnerved by her reunion with her family, she was desperately anxious to return to Westport almost as soon as she arrived in Oregon. "It was a very difficult and a very sad journey, and we found our parents aged and broken almost completely," she told Bill Mock.[60]

Lowell's biographer, Ian Hamilton, has described some of the letters Jean Stafford wrote during the months she and Cal were living in Westport as "jaunty and contented, studded with fond anecdotes of married life."[61] Several of the letters she wrote that winter, however, can hardly be described as "jaunty" or "contented." After her visit to Oregon, for example, she reported to Alfred Kazin that she had found the Westport house to be in "shocking shape" and was obliged to spend several days cleaning up the mess that Cal had made in her absence.[62] And even though she herself urged friends like Alfred Kazin and Joe Chay to come and visit, she also complained how weary she was of entertaining visitors. She quickly discovered that "The Barn," like the Tates' home in Monteagle, was becoming a way station for friends and acquaintances: Albert Erskine and his new wife, Peggy, were in residence for a while, and various other people from New York, including Gertrude Buckman and Marguerite Young, came to spend the day, the weekend, or a week with her and Cal. "I have bad nerves and entertaining large numbers of people does me in," she wrote to Joe Chay, admitting, "Inevitably I drink too much."[63] Several weeks later, she described to him how depressing Christmas in Westport had been:

> Christmas was grim, our guests were unharmonious and made no effort to adapt themselves to one another. There were undercurrents that ruined all the season's joy, and all the drinking was too steady and we couldn't face New Year's so we stayed at home, but went the night before to a queer dinner party at a rich woman's house where all the ladies, after dinner, were obliged to get dressed up in our hostess's old evening frocks, to everyone's bewilderment. Afterwards we all sang Jingle Bells into a costly recording machine.[64]

In February she reported to Joe Chay that she was "on the wagon," reiterating that she had "filthy nerves."[65] And she complained that trying to clean the "foully dirty" large house and its many crannies was "an endlessly hopeless task."[66] Perpetually inundated with guests for whom she felt obliged to cook and keep house, tempted to drink too much at social gatherings, she said that she longed to live in more complete isolation so that she could settle down and begin writing again.[67]

With the exception of *Boston Adventure,* the only works by Stafford to appear in print between the winter of 1944 and the summer of 1945 were two short stories, "The Home Front" and "Between the Porch and the Altar," and a brief review of Eudora Welty's second volume of short stories, *The Wide Net.* This review, appearing in the winter issue of the *Partisan Review,* compared Eudora Welty's second collection of short stories unfavorably with her first one, *A Curtain of Green.* Stafford asserted that whereas she had found the earlier collection to be "an astute commentary on human behavior," *The Wide Net* revealed the author losing her humor and "warily picking her way through meanings . . . or rocketing out of sight in a burst of fantasy," leaving "fissures in her masonry" and writing "eight stories in a language so vague that not only actual words but syntax itself have the improbable inexactitude of a verbal dream."[68] It is obvious that Stafford soon regretted her harsh words about this book, for in 1945 she asked John Crowe Ransom whether he would consider letting her review Welty's novel *Delta Wedding.* "I am very anxious to make up for a foolishly worded review I did of The Wide Net in Partisan . . . ," she wrote to him.[69] She later declined to review this novel because she was too busy revising *The Mountain Lion;* however, in future years she would frequently praise Eudora Welty's writing. In 1975 Stafford wrote, "Just about every word Eudora Welty puts to paper delights me . . ."[70] Born in the same decade, these two women writers would both publish their fiction in the *New Yorker,* and though they apparently never became intimate friends, they corresponded with one another throughout Stafford's lifetime and saw one another from time to time when Welty came to New York.

A new undertaking that spring for Stafford was a part-time teaching position at Queens College in Flushing, New York. Between February and May of 1945 she commuted from Westport to Flushing one day a week to teach a course in short story writing. Once she had agreed to teach the course, however, she began to regret the decision, for she vividly recalled how trying she had found teaching at Stephens College to be. Unhappy memories of her teaching experience at Stephens became even more vivid when she encountered by chance a former student while she was having lunch with her publisher and some other people at the Ritz. The young lady in question came "bolloping" through the room and grabbed her wrist, Stafford informed Bill Mock. "You do not know what that encounter did to me," she added, explaining that she would never have consented to accept a teaching job if her former student had appeared twenty-four hours before she was hired to teach at Queens.[71]

A mark of Stafford's growing fame that spring was her receipt both of a one-thousand-dollar award from the National Academy of Arts and Letters and a prestigious Guggenheim Fellowship. The citation for the former stated: "To Jean Stafford, born in California so recently as 1915, for the subtlety with which she portrays not only the surfaces but the inner life of her characters in *Boston Adventure.*"[72] As for the Guggenheim, it was granted for a sequel to *Boston Adventure,* which Jean Stafford had said would be set in Germany and would be "an analysis of conversion to the Church" and a commentary on "English and American expatriates in Germany in the early days of the Third Reich."[73] Initially, both Stafford and Lowell had considered applying for a Guggenheim Fellowship that year, but Allen Tate dissuaded Lowell from applying, pointing out that no husband-wife team had ever received a fellowship in the same year and advising Cal that Jean should be the one to apply since her immediate chances were better than his.[74]

Six people wrote to the Guggenheim Foundation on Stafford's behalf: Howard Mumford Jones; Wilbur Schramm, professor of journalism at the University of Iowa; Caroline Gordon; Alfred Kazin; Lionel Trilling; and John Crowe Ransom. Of the six, the one woman, Caroline Gordon, was the most negative about Stafford's achievement. "I find many flaws in Jean

Stafford Lowell's first novel," Gordon's letter to the Guggenheim Foundation began. She did, however, describe Stafford as "a born novelist," and, in addition, she mentioned the "great poverty" Stafford had endured in her childhood, which had resulted in her being in poor health. Another of the people who expressed some reservations to the Guggenheim about Stafford was Wilbur Schramm. He did not question the excellence of her work but her financial status. "I am told . . . that Mrs. Lowell's husband is a wealthy man," he wrote. "That may or may not be true." However, he concluded, "Even if it is true, there may be some good psychological reason why Mrs. Lowell should be free, during this period of writing, from support by her husband or his family."[75]

In June of 1945, for the seventh time in five years, Stafford had to take down pictures, pack books, and roll up rugs, for she and Lowell were given sixty days to vacate "The Barn" when the owner sold the property. This time they headed north, searching the coast of Maine for a suitable summer place to rent and finally settling on a small furnished cottage in Boothbay Harbor. Although she thought Maine was "marvelous," Stafford described the place where they were living as "a horrid cottage in a horrid town overrun by horrid large summer people."[76] The fact that they could not accommodate more than one guest at a time in their "horrid cottage," however, proved to be beneficial to both Stafford and Lowell. By the end of July she had written a short story and had finished the first draft of a 105-page manuscript called "The Mountain Lion," which she originally had also intended to be a short story. "I have got an enormous amount of work done," she wrote to Joe Chay; "enormous, I mean, by comparison with what I did in Westport. It's marvelously cool, there aren't any interruptions by week-end visitors and neighborhood poker parties, and the cottage is so unattractive I'm not moved to any sort of domesticity."[77] Lowell, too, was busily writing both prose and poetry that summer. "At the moment he is doing an omnibus review for the Sewanee of all the rotten poetry that has come out recently and he's pretty cross most of the time," she told Ruth Stauffer.[78]

Although Lowell claimed that they intensely disliked the commercialism of Boothbay Harbor,[79] Stafford found the climate and the scenery of Maine so congenial that she decided to buy a summer house in some unspoiled Maine fishing village that "hadn't been blighted by Route 1."[80] Damariscotta Mills proved to be just the sort of village she had in mind. Located at the head of the Damariscotta estuary, seventeen miles from the sea, the town had a post office, a general store, a train depot, and the mills from which the village derived its name, but no antique shops or other tourist attractions. The hundred-year-old white clapboard house with green shutters, purchased with money Stafford had earned from *Boston Adventure,* was large and classical in style. Surrounded by beautiful old trees, it was situated on a hillside overlooking Damariscotta Lake. An angler like Lowell could not help but be pleased by the twelve-mile lake full of bass and salmon. Stafford knew that Lowell would also approve of the nearby Roman Catholic church, the oldest church of that denomination north of southern Maryland, with a bell Paul Revere was said to have made. There was a barn attached to the house that they hoped to convert to two large studios, and next door was the splendid Kavanagh mansion, crowned by an elegant octagonal cupola. Best of all, perhaps, were the meadows, the hemlocks, and the pristine air, reminding her of Colorado.

Having been forced to share her living space with boarders in the small Boulder house and having had a nomadic life ever since leaving Colorado, Stafford exulted when she was able to buy such an imposing house in Damariscotta with the money she herself had earned. "A house is really the only solution for anyone and certainly for me who desire to immobilize myself like an eternal vegetable," she wrote to Joe Chay that summer.[81] Although she still looked like a girl in her slacks and saddle shoes and braids, owning a house seemed a very grown-up thing to do. Now she would be mistress of her own domain, just like the two established women writers she had recently visited: Caroline Gordon and Katherine Anne Porter. Reflecting Stafford's own sentiments when she purchased the house in Damariscotta, her protagonist Cora Savage observes in "An Influx of Poets," "I was thirty now, and I had achieved at last what I had striven for from the beginning: a house and a lawn and trees."[82]

At the end of September, Stafford sent a jubilant letter to Peter and Eleanor Taylor describing the house in Damariscotta and their new neighbors. "The house is too wonderful to be believed or will be, eventually," she wrote. She reported that she and Cal had painted the kitchen woodwork, that they had had an oil burner installed by "a large blasphemous man," and that they had a cricket living on their hearth. Confessing, however, that she had been spending most of her days and evenings not writing but pondering "corner cupboards, wallpaper and slipcovers" or reading *House Beautiful* and the Sears Roebuck catalogue, she said that soon she was going to quit decorating and return to her manuscripts. Lowell's friend Frank Parker paid them a visit that month, and in addition to socializing with him, she spent time getting acquainted with her new neighbors. One of her neighbors, Mary Cabot, wrote little notes folded up in the shape of "an air-tight diaper" and had her daughter, an Anglican nun named Sister Geraldine, deliver them. Another neighbor, a very nice woman with six children, was the widow of the bishop of Vermont. Stafford and Lowell had also met Father Lynch, the priest at St.

Patrick's, who was "rather a disappointment, being unintellectual and interested principally in prize-fights." Extending an invitation to Peter and Eleanor Taylor to visit them the following summer, she exclaimed ecstatically, "I have never been so happy anywhere in my life."[83]

While essential repairs were being made on the house that fall and winter, Stafford and Lowell planned to go to Washington to see Hightower. Interned in China in 1943, Hightower had returned to the States for a brief period but was now being sent to Peking to head a research institute. From Washington they would proceed to Tennessee, where they expected to share a house near Monteagle for several months with the Taylors. However, they had to cancel their stay in Tennessee after they received an urgent communiqué from Caroline Gordon: "I am not sure that you will want to come to Sewanee in October. I shall not be there and I am not sure Allen will. We are getting a divorce in December. It all came up quite suddenly though, of course, we have had troubles on and off, like most married couples. It is his idea, not mine. . . . I do not bolster his ego in little ways, he says—I have too high an opinion of him, an opinion he cannot live up to." Assuring them that she was not bitter, "just awfully tired, but pulling out of it nicely, thank you," Caroline Gordon said that she attributed their trouble to the fact that Allen had reached that stage of life when a man "fancies that he can have a brand new life if he can only get hold of a brand new wife."[84] Stafford, who had earlier marveled at "the superb marriage of the Tates,"[85] must have been taken aback by this news, but she promptly invited Caroline to spend the winter in the house at Damariscotta. However, she must have been somewhat chagrined that Caroline, addressing herself not to Jean or even to Jean and Cal, had written, "Cal, I shall expect some good suggestions from you about my new book."[86]

That fall Gordon lived in the house in Damariscotta while Stafford and Lowell visited friends and relatives. In November Lowell underwent an appendectomy at New York Hospital. For a brief time Stafford stayed at the overcrowded Murray Hill Hotel, but after developing "a neurosis about the plumbing," she decided to move instead to her friend Cecile Starr's apartment until Cal was released from the hospital. Describing how awful the weeks in New York had been, she wrote to Bill Mock: "The last two weeks in New York were so confused—I spent most of my time on the metropolitan transportation system getting from West 10th Street to East 58th—that I can't remember anything I did or anyone I saw. I have no recollection of ever eating anything but I do recall an interminable string of old-fashioneds which would stretch to the moon."[87]

After Thanksgiving, Stafford returned to Damariscotta alone. She was looking forward to a pleasant reunion there with Gordon. Instead, the reunion turned out to be one of the most traumatic experiences of Stafford's life, for a battle royal erupted between these two volatile women when Gordon began to interrogate her about what she knew about Allen's infatuation with a certain young woman. Instead of bringing Caroline and Jean closer together, Allen's infidelity caused a permanent rift between them. In a letter Jean Stafford wrote to her sister Mary Lee, she recounted the upsetting events that had occurred the preceding evening:

> I had the most ghastly experience of my life last night. Caroline had been interrogating me about Allen and the girl and she got out of me a great deal that I had never intended to tell her. At dinner she began abusing me and saying that I had been a busybody and that since I had told her these awful things, there was no hope of reconciliation . . . and that I had thereby ruined the lives of two of the most valuable artists the world has ever known. . . . And finally, she made me cry. She went on, screaming recriminations at me and suddenly she threw a glass of water in my face. I was on the verge of telling her to leave my house forever, but I said nothing and then she said, "I'm going to break every goddamned thing in the goddamned house" and she began throwing everything she could lay her hands on—dishes, glasses, pitchers, bottles of mayonnaise, peanut butter, the sugar bowl, a jar of maple syrup, ten million other things. Maybe she wasn't aiming at me but they were all flying about my head and made her even more passionately intent on destroying my house and I thought, on destroying me.[88]

Terrified, Stafford ran to Mrs. Cabot's house next door. Mrs. Cabot's daughter first called a doctor, and when he couldn't come, called the sheriff. Gordon later insisted that she had merely had a "girlish tantrum," but when Stafford told her that she would not permit her to remain in the house, Gordon began screaming at her again. Furious that Jean had gotten both her neighbor and the sheriff involved in their squabble, she telephoned Allen Tate in New York. Stafford admitted that the part she herself had played in this fracas was "awful, hideously humiliating" to Caroline, and she said she feared that Caroline and Allen would "plot some awful revenge" against her. "I shall never be convinced," she said, "that she didn't intend to kill me." She was afraid that when Cal returned to Damariscotta, he would either not believe her or would take Caroline's part, but she was relieved that Cal did believe her and forgave her for what she had done. Mortified nevertheless because the "scandal" was being discussed all over the village, she feared she might be obliged to sell her wonderful house. The "scandal" probably brought back unpleasant memories to her of an earlier "scandal" in her life, the suicide of Lucy McKee. The fight with Caroline Gordon so unnerved her that she told Mary Lee, "Cal will protect me and if I crack up I will go to a sanitarium."[89]

Just as Stafford had predicted, Caroline Gordon and Allen Tate were soon reconciled and returned together to Tennessee. When Stafford wrote a letter of apology, admitting that what she had done was "awful" but also "not deliberately awful,"[90] Gordon burned the letter after hastily perusing it. Gordon told Lowell, who acted as intermediary between the two women, that what Jean had done "put her beyond the pale" within which they all moved, and though she did not deny that some water "must have flown" in Jean's direction, her thoughts, she said, were not at the time of Jean since she had, for the moment, forgotten Jean's existence.[91] In the future, Jean Stafford and Caroline Gordon would try to be cordial to one another, but Stafford would never forget the night she was attacked by the woman who had once said she thought of Jean and Cal as her "children." Perhaps Gordon's sympathetic portrait of a vulnerable young woman writer from the West in *The Strange Children* was, in part, an attempt to make amends to Stafford for what had occurred that night in Maine.

Damariscotta and its environs is the setting for a number of Stafford's works: "The Hope Chest," "Polite Conversation," "A Country Love Story," "An Influx of Poets," *The Catherine Wheel,* and a beautifully written sketch of the region called "New England Winter" that appeared in *Holiday.* In "A Country Love Story," she speaks of a house like her own, which, though "old and derelict," has beautiful "lines and doors and window lights" as well as a cricket on the hearth. The two characters in this story, a writer who is recuperating from an illness, just as Lowell was recuperating from his appendectomy that winter, and the writer's wife, May, rejoice in their house and the views it affords of river, lake, woods, meadow, and a nearby mansion. Stafford and Lowell's own initial joy about their house and its surroundings is reflected in her description of May and Daniel: "Together, and with fascination, they consulted carpenters, plasterers, and chimney sweeps. In the blue evenings they read at ease, hearing no sound but that of the night birds—the loons on the lake and the owls in the tops of trees. When the days began to cool and shorten, a cricket came to bless their house, nightly singing behind the kitchen stove. They got two fat and idle tabby cats, who lay insensible beside the fireplace and only stirred themselves to purr perfunctorily."[92]

In "New England Winter," Stafford also reminisces about living in Maine during the winter, a season she asserts is "long, magnificent, as exciting to the eye, as tonic, as any natural splendor in the land." The splendid old houses of Damariscotta, its general store where "it was possible to buy bread and beans and overshoes," and the snow that made each morning look like Christmas all appear in her Currier and Ives recollection of the winter she spent in Maine:

There must have been overcast days, but I recall only brilliant skies and blinding sun on the undulant reaches of snow and sky, inebriating alpine air, as fresh to city lungs as spring water to a thirsty throat. The sun was hot like mountain sun and the southern rooms of our house at high noon took so much warmth from it that they were like solaria. This house had plumbing and electricity but no central heating, and we spent a good many of our waking hours feeding the voracious stoves. There were dreadful times when the banked fires went out during the night and we awoke to a cold as cruel and crippling as if no part of the house had ever been warmed; the walls and floors seemed stiff and aged like neglected bones. We were such greenhorns that the first fierce cold caught us unawares and one morning I got up to find icicles hanging from all the bathroom taps and great tumors and hideous fractures in the pipes . . . During the time the plumber was making replacements at a snail's pace, we depended on the well for our water . . .[93]

It is true that this retrospective view of the winter she and Lowell spent in Damariscotta is colored by nostalgia. Nevertheless, despite the fact that it was difficult to keep the house heated and that, after the pipes burst, water had to be toted from the well and they had to use the privy in the barn, she seems to have enjoyed the adventure of living there. "But I have never been in such topnotch shape in my life and do not even complain of the cold, a transformation in myself I do not altogether understand," she wrote to Allen Tate at the beginning of January.[94]

Yet during the course of the winter, the relationship between Jean Stafford and Robert Lowell became more and more strained. As May and Daniel in "A Country Love Story" do, they began to argue over trivial matters, and Lowell frequently retreated to his study, leaving her to spend her days and evenings alone. She revealed one source of tension to Cecile Starr: "I have reached the age when I do not want to meet any new people. . . . We are continuously being summoned to swimming, dancing, cocktail and dinner parties and as you may well imagine, Cal is always extremely difficult and makes me make up some horrendous lie or makes me go alone with an equally horrendous excuse for him . . ."[95] After attending one social event alone, a tea party given at the Kavanagh mansion by the neighborhood "grande dame," Mary Cabot, Stafford chortled, "Imagine a bogus Cabot talking to a bogus Lowell!"[96]

In her humorous short story, "Polite Conversation," Jean Stafford describes how a couple who are both writers deal with their neighbors. Margaret Heath makes "polite conversation" with a bishop's widow who has eleven children and with an Anglican nun who frequently visits "her truculently unwell mother in an ancestral dwelling . . . at the top of the hill."[97] Listening to the women gossip about people in the town as they make plans for various social activities, Margaret Heath looks with longing at her house across the road and pictures her husband "lying on his couch reading either the memoirs of Saint-Simon or the New English Dictionary, while she, poor martyr, listened to these hell-for-leather crusaders scheming and facetiously arguing."[98] No doubt Stafford's neighbors recognized themselves immediately in this story so closely paralleling her own life in Damariscotta Mills.

If Stafford was vexed when Lowell abdicated his responsibilities to her and their new community by withdrawing into the solitude of his study, he, in turn, was critical of her behavior, objecting to the bills she was running up with masons and carpenters to refurbish the house, and dismayed over her frequent trips by taxi to the state liquor store at Bath to purchase the alcohol on which she seemed to be growing more and more dependent. In his poem "The Old Flame," which was published in 1961, Lowell would refer to those days in their house in Maine:

> . . . how quivering and fierce we were,
> there snowbound together,
> simmering like wasps
> in our tent of books!

The speaker of these words, driving past the house "on top of its hill" that he and his former wife had once occupied, recalls how she kept summoning a taxi to transport her to the liquor store; addressing her ghost, he says:

> Poor ghost, old love, speak
> With your old voice
> Of flaming insight
> That kept us awake all night.
> In one bed and apart . . .[99]

Lowell's poem "The Mills of the Kavanaughs" also appears to be a meditation on the conflicts that arose between him and Stafford in Maine. The speaker in the poem, to whom he gives the name of his first fiancée, Anne, sits in the garden playing solitaire, as Stafford was wont to do. Dressed in "blue jeans," perhaps a cryptic reference to Jean Stafford's state of mind as well as her habitual apparel that year, Anne reflects on her marriage to wealthy Harry Kavanaugh, who had played "Prince Charming" to her "Cinderella" by rescuing her from a life of poverty. Ian Hamilton points out the connection between Lowell's poem and Stafford's "A Country Love Story." Both works deal with a husband who is suspicious of his wife. The nature of Daniel's suspicions is never specified in Stafford's story, though Stafford does describe an imaginary lover May conjures up to help relieve her terrible isolation. In

Lowell's poem, however, when Anne dreams of making love with a "boy" who is "not black / Like Harry," her husband actually accuses her of infidelity and tries to strangle her. A further connection between the two works is that both mention the noise of a snowplow outside the couple's window.[100] Citing these connections, Hamilton observes that it is tempting to read Lowell's "The Mills of the Kavanaughs" as a parable of his marriage to Stafford and a reflection of his jealousy.[101] Also reflecting their marital strife, Stafford's "A Country Love Story" is a poignant tale about despair, isolation, and loss. The story concludes with May contemplating the disintegration of her marriage and "rapidly wondering over and over again how she would live the rest of her life."[102]

In December Jean Stafford and Robert Lowell received an invitation from Delmore Schwartz to come and stay with him in his Cambridge apartment whenever they liked for as long as they liked. Tired of having to keep the pipes from freezing and distracted by having workers continuously tramping through their house, they decided to accept Schwartz's offer. Lowell needed time to put the final touches on his new volume of poems, *Lord Weary's Castle,* which was scheduled to be published that fall by Stafford's publisher, Harcourt, Brace, and Stafford sought to escape from the din of the workers so that she could complete the revision of *The Mountain Lion.* Schwartz assured them that his Ellery Street apartment had "two floors, two typewriters, beautiful pictures, too many books," and that it would afford them adequate privacy and solitude.[103]

Although they were both eager to leave Maine that winter, Stafford and Lowell had a number of reservations about spending several months at Schwartz's apartment—she because they would be required to appear at the Lowells' and he because he never had felt completely at ease with Delmore Schwartz. In "An Influx of Poets" Stafford would later describe the somewhat uncomfortable relationship between Cora Savage's husband and the Jewish poet Jerry Zumwalt, a character based on Delmore Schwartz. The narrator of this story, Cora Savage, says that her husband, anti-Semitic "by heritage and instinct," had remarked soon after they first met Jerry Zumwalt, "I would never have a Jew as a close friend," and she observes that the two men had never been close in the way her husband "was close to friends from boarding-school and college days."[104] But whatever their reservations about staying with Schwartz were, both Stafford and Lowell welcomed an opportunity to be in a warmer and quieter place than their house in Maine; perhaps, too, they hoped to mitigate the growing tension between them by spending time with their congenial host.

"We are down here now in Cambridge partly for the society of our excel-

lent and charming host and partly to escape the carpenters who are laying a
new floor in the kitchen," Stafford wrote to Joe Chay from Cambridge.[105]
Their "excellent and charming host" said of their ménage that the sound each
morning of two typewriters and of Lowell's pencil might lead one to conclude
that "this was not a household but a literary movement."[106] Stafford helped
Schwartz select a tiger kitten named Oranges, and she took on herself the
time-consuming task of keeping the apartment in order, not an easy job in the
cramped space she was sharing with her untidy host and her equally untidy
husband. In his poem "To Delmore Schwartz," Lowell later wrote about the
troubles they had had keeping the furnace lit, about Delmore's "antiquated
refrigerator" that "gurgled mustard gas," and about the quarts of gin they had
consumed.[107] Despite many distractions, Stafford managed nevertheless to
work "like mischief" on *The Mountain Lion* during the months they spent in
Cambridge, and her proximity to Boston proved convenient for buying wallpaper and making other "wild purchases" for the house in Maine.[108] Dealing
with her in-laws while she and Lowell were living in Cambridge, however,
proved to be as unpleasant as she had anticipated. She said of one visit to them,
"I have not been so persistently needled since before we were married." She
complained that the Lowells had made derogatory remarks about her family,
had commented that "Bobby" looked too thin and "not at all well," and had
asked them why they preferred staying with Delmore Schwartz rather than at
the Lowells' far more comfortable house on Marlborough Street.[109] Stafford
was unnerved by these comments, but it was Delmore Schwartz's visit with
them to Marlborough Street that ultimately poisoned the air in his Ellery
Street apartment. Invited by Cal to dinner at his parents' house, Schwartz,
who was sensitive to the point of paranoia about being Jewish, found the
Brahmin atmosphere there intimidating. He especially resented it when
Lowell pointedly mentioned that he had had a Jewish relative named Mor-
decai Myers, whose portrait was hanging in the Lowells' drawing room. According to Schwartz's biographer, James Atlas, "Things were never the same
after that evening. Delmore baited Lowell mercilessly, made fun of his parents' home, and tried to destroy the marriage by circulating vicious rumors.
Finally Lowell swung at Delmore, Jean Stafford had to separate them, and
soon afterwards the Lowells left for Maine."[110]

Stafford returned to Damariscotta alone. She spent most of the spring supervising the workers at the house, while Lowell chose this time to minister to
his spiritual needs at a Trappist monastery and also visited with friends in
New York. Stafford was pleased to see "her" house taking shape as walls were
repapered and the furnishings she had purchased in Boston were put in place,
but when he returned, Lowell began to criticize her bad taste or to erupt in

anger about the money she had lavished on the house. One piece of furniture, built by a local cabinetmaker to her specifications, would accompany her wherever she lived during the rest of her life: it was an oversized, handsome desk, with pigeonholes for letters, a place for her typewriter, and ample shelves for rows of reference books she wanted to have within reach.

But if she was delighted with how the desk had turned out, it also served as a constant reminder of how little writing she was actually doing that spring. The only work by her to appear that year was a short story called "The Present," which was published in the April issue of the *Sewanee Review*. She must have been pleased that the Olympian Allen Tate, who had rejected an earlier story of hers, had found this one enough to his liking to publish it in the journal for which he served as editor. After her recent contact with the Lowells, she also must have taken a perverse pleasure in being able to publish in Tate's prestigious literary journal a story that painted an unflattering portrait of a complacent and insular woman who was, like her mother-in-law, a member of the upper class. With the revisions of *The Mountain Lion* still not completed, however, Stafford was frequently anxious and morose, especially since the money she had earned from *Boston Adventure* was all too quickly being consumed by the house.

The novel Stafford was revising was also a source of anxiety. "My new book seems hideously pallid and loose-jointed and to escape the thought of it I have been visited lately with my really neurotic sleeping, hours and hours of such oblivion that I don't even dream," she wrote to Cecile Starr in March.[111] As she reworked her novel, which portrayed a relationship like the one she had had with her brother Dick, she could not help but feel she had been betrayed or abandoned by all the significant men in her life: her father, her brother, Hightower, and even Lowell. Writing about Hightower to Bill Mock the following spring, she said wistfully, "I've seen him several times and there seems to be no possibility of establishing any rapport. It grieves us equally, and it makes us both feel old."[112]

The arrival of Lowells' parents at Damariscotta on Memorial Day heralded what Stafford would subsequently describe as "the most ghastly awful summer" she had ever lived through.[113] When the Lowells departed, the "influx of poets" began, and soon the strain of trying to complete the revisions on her novel as well as doing the shopping, cooking, and tidying up became unbearable. By the end of June, Stafford was already wondering what the next winter would bring. She confessed to Bill Mock:

Already I have commenced to brood about the job of closing the house and often I wonder why on earth we ever took this householding upon our-

selves—it has ruined us financially and has ruined me physically and we are
both hard at work to make ourselves so eccentric that we will be left alone by
the absolutely *good* neighbors we have.[114]

She also described to Mary Lee how depleted she felt:

I am suffering from years of accumulated fatigue, not only from working so
hard but from spreading myself too thin and knowing too many people.
Being a writer and being married is a back-breaking job and my back is now
broken. I've now decided that writers shouldn't be married and certainly
women writers shouldn't be unless they are married to rich, responsible husbands who fill their house with servants.[115]

Lowell was rich—or his parents were—but he was not "responsible," and the
only servant in the house was Jean Stafford herself.

In her autobiographical short story, "An Influx of Poets," Stafford described that "awful" summer when "every poet in America" came to stay with
them. Her narrator, Cora Savage, says:

It was the first summer after the war, when people once again had gasoline
and could go where they liked all those poets came to our house in Maine and
stayed for weeks at a stretch, bringing wives or mistresses with whom they
quarrelled, and complaining so vividly about the wives and mistresses they'd
left, or had been left by, that the discards were real presences, swelling the
ranks, stretching the house, *my house* (my very own, my first and very own) to
its seams. At night, after supper, they'd read from their own works until four
o'clock in the morning, drinking Cuba Libres. They never listened to one
another; they were preoccupied with waiting for their turn. And I'd have to
stay up and clear out the living room after they went soddenly to bed—
sodden, but not too far gone to lose their conceit. And then all day I'd cook
and wash the dishes and chop the ice and weed the garden and type my
husband's poems and quarrel with him.[116]

In a sympathetic portrait of her friend Jean Stafford that appears in *Poets in
Their Youth,* Eileen Simpson speaks of the visit she and her husband John
Berryman paid to Stafford and Lowell that summer. Her account reveals how
accurately Stafford later portrayed the ambience and domestic arrangements
of the household in Damariscotta in "An Influx of Poets." Many literary
people did visit that summer, including the Berrymans, the Rahvs, the Black-
murs, Patrick Quinn, and Robert Giroux, as well as Lowell's friends Frank
Parker and Blair Clark. When Simpson accompanied her hosts to St. Patrick's
on Sunday, Stafford confided to her that Cal insisted on focusing on the aspects of Catholicism she found least compelling: spiritual exercises and reli-

gious retreats and good works. She said that she found his insistence that she too adhere to these practices "maddening and enervating."[117] Just as Cora Savage does in "An Influx of Poets," Stafford typed her husband's poems, draft after draft after draft,[118] and she cleaned the house, weeded the garden, and cooked three meals a day for their visitors. Cleaning up after meals was a particularly time-consuming chore since water had to be pumped and heated each time. She devoted many hours to cooking tasty meals for their guests, frequently preparing such dishes as crab ramekins and strawberry shortcake, but when her guests sometimes offered to assist her, she declined their help, insisting that she found it easier to do the work herself. "I am faced with a dinner party for nine people on Tuesday and am cross as hell about it," she complained to Mary Lee that August.[119] While Lowell and Berryman discussed poetry, a genre with which Jean Stafford never felt completely comfortable, she would sometimes take a piece of oiled chamois out of a drawer near her chair and run it over the already highly polished surface of the furniture.[120] A meticulous housekeeper, Stafford kept the vases filled with fresh flowers,[121] and she set the table for breakfast each night before she retired, a habit, she said, that dated back to the time when her mother had run a boarding house.[122] No doubt Stafford was thinking of Lowell's hostile reaction to her own housekeeping obsessions when she had Cora Savage observe: "My nesting and my neatening were compulsions in me that Theron looked on as plebeian, anti-intellectual, lace-curtain Irish. . . . My pride of house was the sin of pride."[123] Yet Jean Stafford insisted that were it not for her, Lowell would have gone for days without sleeping or eating or bathing.[124] Coming as he did from an affluent household where cooks and maids quietly and unobtrusively performed the mundane tasks upon which daily life depended, Lowell was not able to understand how hard it was to keep a big house functioning without servants to do the bulk of the work. Furthermore, having rebelled against the bourgeois amenities, he found Stafford's need to live in an attractive and orderly household irritating, though along with the guests he eagerly partook of the meals she prepared.

The parallels between Jean Stafford's life and that of her protagonist Cora Savage are striking. Yet one crucial difference between them is that Cora Savage is not a writer but a schoolteacher. Remarking on this difference after she had read "An Influx of Poets" when it was published in the *New Yorker* in 1978, Jean Stafford's friend Nancy Gibney wrote to her: "But great as you are, Madam, I have for once a bone to pick. This story must be read as autobiography, not fiction and I wish you had written it as such. Cora Savage, like hell, heavenly as her name is. Robert Lowell is up against precisely Jean Stafford, no hopeless school teacher . . . but a blazing genius, with better looks and taste and sense than he has, and the achieved success he only longs for." [125] A devoted friend and staunch champion of Stafford's, Gibney expressed the belief that Lowell, whether consciously or subconsciously, had been committed to Stafford's destruction. The fact that Jean Stafford was a writer rather than a teacher had made her situation that year even more unbearable than that of her protagonist. A writer herself, Gibney could well appreciate, as did Eileen Simpson, how impossibly difficult it had been for Stafford to satisfy her need to be both a model housewife and a first-rate writer. According to Simpson, Stafford chose to position her desk in the downstairs hall between the parlor and the kitchen rather than in a more secluded place. She had explained that she wanted to be able to keep an eye on her neighbors as she worked at her desk. But whatever her original motive had been for placing her desk in so public a place, once the visitors began to arrive that summer, she found herself unable to sit down at her desk to work without constant interruptions. Finding it impossible to get any writing done, suffering from insomnia, and drinking constantly to alleviate her anxiety, she grew more and more fearful about the future. Cal was not drinking that summer, but she insisted that being in a "bone-dry" house gave her "the wim-wams." [126] She resisted his attempts to control her drinking by stowing a glass of sherry behind the cookbooks in the kitchen, and she carried a flask in her large shoulder bag so that she could escape to the bathroom and swallow down some whiskey during boring visits with the neighbors. According to Simpson, another symptom of Stafford's depression that summer was the way she dressed: day after day, she would appear in the same checked slacks and baggy black sweater, and her shoulder-length hair hung limply about her face. [127] In late August Stafford described herself as "a hopeless mess" to Bill Mock, and she said portentously, "I am really on the verge of something and as soon as I have cleared the house I shall close it and go away." [128] Earlier that month, Lowell had written a despairing letter to Peter Taylor in which he had described Jean's frenzied behavior and had announced his intentions of parting from her, at least temporarily. [129] But despite the fact that her behavior grew increasingly more erratic every day, Lowell remained in Damariscotta with her.

The final chapter of this melodrama got under way just before Labor Day, when Stafford took a brief trip to Cambridge. While she was gone, Delmore Schwartz's former wife, Gertrude Buckman, arrived at the house in Damariscotta. Having been invited to come and see Jean and Cal in Maine, Gertrude was surprised to discover that Jean was away, and she was taken aback when Lowell darkly hinted that Jean's purpose in going to Cambridge was not to see the dentist, as she had claimed, but to visit Delmore Schwartz. Gertrude Buckman's version of what transpired during her visit to Damariscotta is somewhat different in detail from the way Stafford described the arrival and departure of a character named Minny Rosoff, who is based on Gertrude Buckman, in "An Influx of Poets." However, as Stafford says of Minny Rosoff in the story, Gertrude did arrive by seaplane, some friends having given her this trip as a birthday present; she did spent a good deal of time alone with Lowell even after Stafford returned from Cambridge; and she did begin to fall in love with Lowell by the time she departed from Damariscotta.

Initially, it had been Stafford's idea to invite Gertrude to visit them rather than Lowell's. Several years earlier, Gertrude Buckman and Jean Stafford had been introduced by Harold Shapero, whom Jean Stafford had met at Yaddo, and during the fall when Lowell was in jail, the two women had seen one another frequently. In fact, Stafford had thought well enough of Buckman to recommend her to her editors at Harcourt, Brace for the job of condensing *Boston Adventure* for a paperback edition. However, when Stafford began to suspect that Lowell was falling in love with the dark-haired, petite, charming, intelligent Gertrude, she became frantic. Later she would refer to Buckman as "the clever quicksilver, the heartless fey, the no-woman, the bedeviller" and "the stunted cowbird who came and ruinously fouled" her nest.[130] Describing to Peter Taylor how she had felt during Gertrude's visit, Stafford said that she had disliked the way Gertrude had flattered Cal about his poetry; she had been jealous when Cal, who was annoyed that she herself had never learned to swim, had gone swimming with Gertrude "early in the morning . . . and then in the afternoon, and then before dinner, and then late when the moon was full"; she had been distressed when Cal and Gertrude took walks to the village together, leaving her to rest at home; and she had been outraged when Gertrude criticized the way she had furnished the house and, even worse, told her what she had done wrong in *The Mountain Lion*. Remembering that Cal had seemed to agree with everything Gertrude said, Jean Stafford observed bitterly, "I was wormwood."[131]

Although Stafford claimed that Gertrude had lingered on at Damariscotta, Buckman insists that she stayed on because Jean implored her to do so. Night after night Jean would remain in the kitchen, "drinking herself into a stupor," but when Gertrude announced that she wanted to leave, Jean entreated her not to go. "How was I to know that she was feeling what she described in the story? Towards her I was perfectly innocent. I left soon after, feeling very unhappy myself," Buckman said. Almost forty years later, Buckman vividly recalled Stafford's way of telling a story with relish, as she took "long deep puffs of a cigarette, long deep sips of her drink, giving herself time to frame her sentences coming up, embroider them, dramatize them" while talking "slowly, deliberately, vividly, very entertainingly." She also remembered that her friend Jean was a harsh critic of others, a person who "would be ready to do anyone in for the sake of a good phrase, however malicious."[132]

Although Stafford laid the blame for the dissolution of her marriage on Gertrude Buckman, it is evident that Buckman played but a minor role in Lowell's decision to part with his wife. Many months would elapse, however, before Jean would be willing to acknowledge that Gertrude alone could not be held responsible for the breakup of her marriage. She would also recall the dreadful nights after Gertrude's departure. Having stopped drinking, Stafford was even more morose than she had been before, and she felt like "an angry, wounded child." One evening she went so far as to mutilate herself by grinding out her cigarette on the back of her hand, bringing back memories of acts of self-mutilation she had committed when she was a child. During their last night in Maine, after Lowell had gone up to bed, she burned old letters in the fireplace, but soon became terrified when she thought she saw Father Lynch in a tree beside the arc light in front of Kavanagh.[133]

"When the House Is Finished Death Comes"—this was the title Stafford originally gave to her poignant short story about a difficult marriage, "A Country Love Story." As she closed the windows and locked the door of her house in Damariscotta for the last time that fall before she left for New York, Stafford felt that death was in the air. In the autobiographical short story "An Influx of Poets," the death of a marriage is symbolized by the death of Cora Savage's cat and her kittens, put into a gunnysack weighted with stones and dropped into the lake by Cora's husband. Then, as Cora Savage locks the door of her house for the last time, she hears the hum of the taxi's motor, "the only sound that broke the silence of that absolutely azure and absolutely golden early autumn day."[134] Jean Stafford's marriage to Robert Lowell also ended on a "golden autumn day" when she left Damariscotta. Before long their house, which had been such a source of pleasure and pride to her, would be occupied by "a new landlord, a new wife, a new broom."[135]

Stafford once observed, ". . . the amenities of society, arbitrary and often absurd, beset us at every turn and it is only in larger things that one's will is really free."[136] Beset by social amenities that summer, Stafford discovered how completely depleted she felt. Having identified with her intellectual father during much of her lifetime, she found herself transformed into an avatar of that bitter drudge, her mother. If the "joking lad" she had married had left her "for the seraphim and saints,"[137] as Theron Maybank leaves Cora Savage in "An Influx of Poets," she herself, depressed, bitter, often preoccupied with domestic rather than literary matters, had also changed during the course of her marriage to Lowell. The last night in Maine she felt that something was coming, something she "could smell . . . like the air before a hurricane."[138] As she departed from Damariscotta the next day, she ruefully was forced to acknowledge that her Boston adventure had come to a dismal end.

Eight

The Bleeding Heart
Fall 1946–Summer 1949

If you like love and fame
Shop early, get your shots
Don't spit and pass with care—
Avoid at all costs
Death, breakdown, despair . . .
—ELEANOR ROSS TAYLOR, "TO A YOUNG WRITER"

The period of the wildest weeping, the fiercest delusion is over.
LOUISE BOGAN, "EVENING IN THE SANITARIUM"

ALTHOUGH JEAN STAFFORD told Bill Mock that in the fall she was planning a "bang-up treat," a trip to Bermuda, this "chi-chi spree" never materialized. Instead, in "perfectly dreadful nervous shape,"[1] she left Damariscotta for New York City with Lowell and lived with him briefly in a shabby apartment in a place called Slaughter Alley. Lowell had informed Gertrude Buckman that he and Jean were planning to separate, but several days later Stafford arrived at Buckman's apartment and announced they were not going to separate after all. The reconciliation of Stafford and Lowell was short-lived, however, and by the beginning of October she had moved into a hotel. Hoping that she might be able to salvage her marriage if she allowed Lowell to continue to see Buckman, she arranged on one occasion for the three of them to go to the Bronx Zoo together; but Lowell was annoyed when he learned of these plans, and in place of this outing he arranged to have dinner with Gertrude and Jean at her hotel. She said that at dinner she was infuriated when Cal and Gertrude not only made pointed remarks about overly possessive people but left soon afterward "very much like two married people obliged to dine with a boring relative."[2]

If living with Lowell was difficult, Stafford soon discovered that living alone was worse. Her friend Cecile Starr, at whose apartment she stayed for a brief time after the separation, has observed that to Stafford marriage, even at

its worst, represented "roots, home, a safe place"; when the marriage collapsed, she collapsed as well.[3] Soon after her arrival in New York, Stafford
began again to consume large quantities of alcohol, and despite the efforts of
her friends to make her stop drinking or at least to limit her alcoholic intake,
she continued to carry one or two bottles of whiskey with her wherever she
went. Alarmed at the state she was in, her friend and editor Robert Giroux
suggested that she go to see Carl Binger, a well-known New York psychiatrist
whose popular books on psychiatry had been published by her own publishers. Reluctantly, she agreed to do so, but she refused to put herself under
his care when he stipulated that he could not take her as a regular patient
unless she stopped drinking and recommended that she be admitted to Payne
Whitney Psychiatric Hospital for a short stay.[4] At the end of September she
had written to Mary Lee: "I have finally had to face the fact that I am very ill
and I now must face a long and arduous and tormenting cure, but it is the only
way out of my despair. I am full of self-hatred and disgust for I have always
scorned people who could not help themselves to become adjusted . . ."[5] Yet
even though she acknowledged that she needed professional help, she was
unwilling to accept Dr. Binger's advice.

Without any daily routines to sustain her and despite the support of her
friend Cecile Starr, Stafford's emotional and physical condition deteriorated
with alarming rapidity. Finally, on the recommendation of another well-
known psychiatrist, Gregory Zilboorg, she agreed to go to a sanitarium in
Detroit. When she arrived there, however, she discovered that the ornate
building, formerly the residence of a motor magnate, evoked painful memories of Yaddo. Observing that its windows were barred, that the bedrooms
had no doors, and that the patients all looked "strange and wild-eyed," she
fled. "I knew somehow," she said, ". . . that if I let the night fall I would be
there for good."[6]

That night she took a sleeper to Chicago, though she had no idea what she
would do once she arrived there. Discovering that she had no cash left and
realizing that she would not be able to cash a check in a city where no one
knew her, she became even more distraught and began to think she had no
alternative but to go up to the nearest policeman and say, "I am an irresponsible person" and insist that he lock her up. At last she remembered that her
publishers had a branch office from which she could wire the New York office
for money, and with cash in hand, she was later able to purchase a ticket for
Denver, where she was met by Mary Lee.

The days Stafford spent with Mary Lee proved to be more upsetting than
comforting, however. Later, recounting her harrowing trip to Lowell, Stafford said, "My sister was heartbroken at the spectacle of me." Alarmed by

Jean's unkempt appearance and evident anxiety, Mary Lee suggested that she seek help from a local physician whose father had taken care of the Stafford children. "He remembered how I had been in college, restless, plunging into work, into getting honors because . . . we were so poor that I could not express myself in the way I really wanted to, with friends, by going to dances, by learning to *do* things," she told Lowell. The five days she spent with her sister were tense ones: Mary Lee maintained that Jean's drinking was morally reprehensible and called her "selfish," but Jean insisted that she hated to drink, that drinking made her "unspeakably miserable," but that nevertheless she was unable to control her drinking and that she did not understand why she felt compelled to destroy herself. She said that she had become very angry when Mary Lee had repeatedly urged her to stop drinking. "'Quit drinking for my sake,' she'd say until I wanted to scream at her," Stafford wrote to him.[7]

Advised by the physician in Denver to call Dr. Zilboorg, she did so, and Dr. Zilboorg urged her to return to New York immediately. En route to New York, she stopped in Chicago again and called Morton Dauwen Zabel, a literary scholar whom she had gotten to know at Yaddo, but she discovered that in her present state it was as impossible to communicate with him as it had been to communicate with anyone else. As she waited for her train after they parted, she bought a dollar edition of *Boston Adventure,* though she had not been able to read anything for weeks. Full of self-pity as she relived this experience when recounting it to Lowell, she wrote: "I went into the women's room and tried to read it there and when I could not, the tears poured out and in a perfect rage I threw it in the trash container. In a way, it was a little suicide."[8]

In the weeks that followed her return to New York, Stafford went from analyst to analyst, unable to find a psychiatrist whom she felt she could trust. Dr. Zilboorg declined to see her again, and when she refused to go to another sanitarium that he recommended to her because she had heard dreadful things about the place, he firmly told her that he did not want her to continue telephoning him as she had been doing. Furious at being rejected by him, she wrote to Mary Lee that he had turned out to be "the worst kind of bastard."[9] Moving from hotel to hotel, each more shabby than the one that preceded it since her funds were rapidly dwindling, she was terrified that she would be seen by one of her literary acquaintances. Once, at a restaurant, she thought she saw Mary McCarthy across the room and left immediately before she ordered dinner. Even more distressing was meeting Delmore Schwartz by chance in Washington Square Park. In terrible shape himself, Delmore told her that she had "been among strangers for a long time." She wrote to Lowell that it seemed to her Delmore himself was "*the* stranger," that he epitomized

all the strangers in whose midst she had lived for years and years.[10] Unable to
eat and only able to sleep when she managed to obtain sleeping pills, disheveled, unbathed, and usually inebriated, she began to resemble the derelicts she
had observed in Dorothy Day's hospitality house near the Bowery, where she
had done volunteer work. She later described to Lowell how she would leave
her hotel room each day to go downstairs to the bar and would sit there drinking until it closed at three in the morning; then she would go back to her
"gruesome little room" and drink applejack, "waiting for the next day to
come, thinking of nothing but insanity and suicide." One of the only people
who was a source of comfort to her was Cecile Starr. "If it had not been for
Cecile, I would have killed myself," she said.[11]

Although Stafford had toyed with the idea of going to Ireland to write
some stories for *Harper's Bazaar* and had even managed to secure a passport,
she now realized that she was in no shape to travel. Desperately anxious to
find some physician who would be able to help her, Robert Giroux finally
asked Henry Murray, an elderly psychiatrist from Boston who was spending
the year in New York to write a book on Melville, if he would meet with her.
After talking with the kindly Murray for three hours in Central Park, Stafford felt that at last she had found a sympathetic doctor whom she could trust
and who did not frighten her. She was pleased because Murray praised her
writing instead of looking impatiently at his watch or appearing disinterested
when she revealed that she had no money, as she claimed the other psychiatrists had done. "He is old and wise and says I don't need analysis and I *do*
need sleep and a new life. . . . I wish he were our father," she wrote to Mary
Lee.[12] Murray was about to return to Boston, but realizing that she was in dire
need of someone to look after her, he suggested that she go to stay with the
Taylors in North Carolina. When she insisted that she did not want to jeopardize her relationship with these dear friends by going there in the state she
was in, he tried to persuade her to enter a psychiatric hospital. At first she
resisted this course of action that both Murray and Cecile Starr recommended.
Instead, she asked Father Dougherty, a priest who had been her spiritual
mentor as well as Lowell's, what he thought she should do and was advised by
him to go to a convent in New Jersey that was run by German nuns. The nuns,
however, would not agree to let her stay in the convent. Subsequently, with
grim humor, she summarized what she had actually done or had been advised
to do or had contemplated doing that fall:

> I have since the 21st of September been analyzed, been in a sanitarium in
> Detroit, had a police ambulance in Denver, been in Brazil, been in a sani-
> tarium in White Plains and one in Providence and now one outside of Boston;

> I have sold my house and mortgaged my house, and lived in my house; I have
> gotten a job in Germany and one in Palestine and one in New York and have
> been in a medical hospital in New York and one in Nashville and it seems
> small wonder that I am tired.[13]

Her doctor bills alone, she said, were enough to send anyone to an institution,
and she told Mary Lee how outraged she had been when a Freudian analyst
had informed her it would take four years, "six days a week at fifteen dollars a
day and no vacations," to analyze her since she was such a complex person.
Disgusted by "that whole Park Avenue outfit," she said she was planning to
expose them in a story that would "boil the skin off all of them."[14] As she read
her sister's angry words, Mary Lee might well have been reminded of her
father's diatribes against the "scoundrels" that had been responsible for his
financial disgrace.

Adding to Stafford's woes that month was the fact that Lowell, not unexpectedly, had sent her a letter asking for a divorce. To make matters worse, he
announced that he would not sign over the title of the house in Maine to her, a
house they had purchased with the money she had earned, unless she agreed
in writing not to contest the divorce or ask for alimony. When she finally met
with Lowell, she told Mary Lee that "he was exactly as cold, exactly as beastly,
just as much a Lowell as he always was" and always would be. Dismayed to
learn that Lowell had decided to leave the church, she said bitterly: "He has
left the church having used her up just as he has left me now that he has got all
he needs out of me. We together supported him through those first two books
and now that he has really arrived he does not feel any need for us and he feels
no gratitude . . . In my hysterical frenzy I felt such hatred for him that I really
wished the world would be rid of him and of all his kind, all the Olympian
Bostonians."[15]

Increasingly suicidal as the days passed, she alarmed Mary Lee when she
wrote to her, "I am going to name you in case anything should take place and
you know what that means."[16] At last, at the end of November, though she
still felt that it was shameful to admit to being mentally ill, she agreed to be
hospitalized at the Payne Whitney Clinic, with the stipulation that Robert
Giroux would arrange to have her released if she found being a patient there
unbearable. The doctor who admitted her tried to reassure her by telling her
that she would probably be well enough to be discharged in eight weeks, but
the trees were in leaf again by the time she was released in June of 1947.

"The loony bin," "Luna Park,"[17] and a "high-class booby-hatch"[18]—this
was how Jean Stafford flippantly referred to Payne Whitney. Hearing the
screams of the severely disturbed patients on the floor above hers during her

first terrifying night in the hospital, she found it hard to believe that she had been judged ill enough to be put in such company. It was one thing to write convincingly about the incarceration of Sonia Marburg's mother in a mental hospital in *Boston Adventure,* and quite another matter to find herself in similar circumstances. But though she later said she was as "shy as a wildcat and as watchful," she nevertheless obeyed the numerous rules and regulations of the hospital.[19] At first she was annoyed to discover that her bureau drawers and closet were locked, that she could not have cigarettes or matches in her room, that she was not allowed to keep a nail file, and that pens and pencils were taken from the room promptly at five each evening. However, before long she confessed that she was experiencing a growing sense of relief that she was "safe behind innumerable locked doors."[20] Three weeks after she was admitted to the hospital, she told Bill Mock that she was no longer unable to sleep or eat and found it "wonderful" not to be drinking.[21] A high protein diet, vitamins, and sedatives helped to improve her physical condition, and as a result, when Eileen Berryman visited her, she found Jean looking far better than she had at Damariscotta. Not only did she look healthier, but her hair was neatly combed and in place of the baggy sweater and pants that were her daily attire in Maine, she was wearing a skirt and blouse. Her psychiatrist insisted that she pay attention to her appearance, Stafford said, and she somewhat sheepishly remarked, "For dinner I put on pearls—like a Smith College girl."[22] Although she complained to Mary Lee about the indignity of having to make needlepoint pin cushions in occupational therapy and of being encouraged to play "ineffectual games of pool or gin rummy" for recreational therapy, she also emphasized that it was usually possible for her to become the detached observer and to be "overwhelmed with the humor" of her situation. Describing her daily activities, she wrote:

> The first thing we do is go out to a small courtyard where we walk round and round as fast as the mischief for half an hour. A high grill separates us from the free world and you feel that at any moment the passersby will toss us peanuts. Here we mingle with the gentlemen: the Ambassador from Portugal, the ex-associate editor of Fortune . . .[23]

Since Stafford had so little money of her own, most of her medical bills were left unpaid, even though Cecile Starr's wealthy uncles, Milton and Alfred Starr, generously loaned her some money during this period. Rather than having a private doctor, she was assigned to a twenty-eight-year-old female resident in psychiatry. Despite her youth, Mary Jane Sherfey immediately impressed Stafford, who found her to be someone she both admired and trusted and with whom from the first she had a great deal of rapport. What she appreciated especially about Dr. Sherfey was her thorough professionalism. Unlike some of the other psychiatrists she had seen, Dr. Sherfey did not, to impress her, make constant literary allusions or pamper her "in any shoddy way." Their relationship, Stafford said, was cordial but appropriately formal, and the fact that she did not feel obliged to be competitive with Dr. Sherfey put her at ease.[24] A young woman in what was then a male-dominated profession, Dr. Sherfey perhaps was better able to empathize with her patient's feelings of insecurity and her role conflicts than most male psychiatrists could have done. Keenly interested in the psychosocial implication of female sexuality, Dr. Sherfey would later postulate that the female capacity for multiple orgasms gave rise to the male's need for dominance and control.[25] Stafford soon became so dependent on Dr. Sherfey that she described her intense attachment to her therapist as an "addiction" that she had substituted for alcohol.[26] Nevertheless, she was a bit skeptical about her therapy sessions. She told Mary Lee that in part because she was born with "a monstrous talent for exaggeration" and in part because she was a writer of fiction, she was never quite certain whether she was telling the truth when she described her past experiences to her doctor.[27]

During the trying months that followed her admission to Payne Whitney, Stafford was forced to confront a number of painful issues: her impending divorce; her difficult relationship with her family; her feelings of jealousy and anger toward Gertrude Buckman; her fears about the effect of her impending divorce on her friendship with the Taylors, the Berrymans, and the Jarrells, who were also friends of Lowell; the dismantling and sale of her beloved house in Damariscotta; and her future status as a writer and a divorced woman. After several months of therapy she was able to admit that she had been "one sick girl for thirty-two years," and she said that she took pride in the fact that she had worked hard in her therapy sessions to understand herself, to learn patience, and to break herself of the "habits of impulsiveness and sudden starts of fear and anger."[28]

Most of the letters Stafford wrote to Lowell right after she was hospitalized dwelled on Lowell's abandonment of her and his infatuation with Gertrude Buckman. She saw Gertrude as almost completely her opposite: uninterested in domesticity; able to play the piano, to swim, and to fish; skilled at pleasing men. Moreover, she felt that even though Gertrude was talented, she was not an artist and therefore did not "go through the very disturbing and very difficult-to-live-with vexations and agonies of creation."[29] Fearing that everyone had heard about Lowell's affair with Gertrude, she imagined that Gertrude was gloating triumphantly. "I am sure," she wrote, "that Gertrude

Buckman feels properly set up that she has bagged the best poet and sent his wife into the bin—particularly since I was given to understand that it is generally supposed that Gertrude came *after* the fact and that I went completely off my nut with no other provocation than my bad heritage, and that these days I breakfast, so to speak, in my strait-jacket."[30]

Although Stafford's letters to Lowell from the hospital were filled with hostile comments about his treatment of her, she nevertheless initially harbored the hope that somehow she and he might be reconciled. However, she also told Peter Taylor that she had gradually come to understand what a mistake it had been to marry a man so much like the father she had "worshipped" as a child but by whom she later felt betrayed. Comparing the two men, she wrote of Lowell: "He was economically and domestically irresponsible as my father had always been. He read his poems aloud to me, as my father had read his stories for the pulp magazines. His manners were courtly or uncouth, and he was slovenly, as my father was." She acknowledged that her father did not have Lowell's wit or his brilliance, but she equated them nevertheless, observing that both were "violent men in every way."[31] Expressing her great disappointment that Lowell had never gone to meet her family, she went on to say that, had he done so, he would have witnessed for himself the poverty and barrenness of her parents' lives. Then he might have understood why living in gracious surroundings had become so terribly important to her. Willing to concede that she had been gauche in the way she went about acquiring all the material things that she associated with gracious living, she insisted nevertheless that Cal's behavior as well as her own had contributed to their unhappiness: if she had married someone who more and more came to represent the father she had grown to despise, Lowell, in turn, had treated her alternately as if she were his mother or someone like Delmore Schwartz, whom he had suddenly decided he no longer liked. "It was as if four people lived in our house: your mother and my father, both of whom were battling for the souls of us, the innocent children, poor Cal and Jean," she said to Lowell, pointing out to him that he too was not altogether "well."[32] At the time she wrote this letter, a very lengthy one in which she reflected on her past and their marriage, she insisted that the psychological problems of each of them had contributed to their difficulties; nevertheless, she probably would not have predicted that very soon Lowell himself would become a patient at Payne Whitney.

In December, just before Stafford's second novel, *The Mountain Lion,* was scheduled to appear, a poem by Lowell called "Her Dead Brother" was published in the *Nation.* Having dedicated her novel to Cal and to her brother Dick, her own "dead brother," Stafford was livid when she read Lowell's poem, which hinted at an incestuous relationship between a brother and a sister. The narrator of the poem and her brother come from a well-to-do family very different from the Staffords; however, Stafford detected a resemblance between these figures in the poem and the brother and sister in her own novel, who in turn were fictionalized portraits of herself and her brother. Perhaps Stafford was unduly sensitive about what people might conclude from the poem about her and her brother, but Lowell's depiction of the pair picnicking, bird-watching, and horseback riding among the hemlocks is indeed reminiscent of her own descriptions of Ralph and Molly Fawcett in *The Mountain Lion.* After she had read Lowell's poem, she wrote to him: "'Her Dead Brother,' appearing in The Nation a week before the publication of my book with its dedication, with its theme of latent incest, at a time when you have left me and I am in the hospital seems to me an act of so deep dishonor that it passes beyond dishonor and approaches madness. And I am trembling in this presence of your hate."[33]

Just as Stafford was beginning to feel somewhat better, Mary Lee wrote to her to tell her that their mother had malignant melanoma. Believing that she ought to rush to the bedside of her critically ill mother, she nevertheless explained to Mary Lee why she could not do so: "If I come now, sick with my grief over Cal and all the ruin of my life, I would start to drink again and this time I would succeed in what I was trying to do before, I would, that is, drink myself to death."[34] By the time Mary Lee received this letter from her sister, Ethel Stafford had already died. Granted permission to leave the hospital to attend her mother's funeral in Oregon, Jean Stafford met Mary Lee in Denver and traveled with her to Portland. According to her sister Marjorie, Jean's appearance had undergone a remarkable transformation since her last visit to Oregon in 1944 after Dick's death: no longer dressed in drab clothing, she wore bright, fashionable dresses, black fishnet stockings, high heels, and makeup. During this visit she did not drink anything stronger than coffee,[35] despite the fact that she was "nearly overpowered with the desire to drink" when she got from her father the usual "monstrous self-justifications" for having behaved "in a really scoundrelly fashion" during her childhood. "I try to see under the bad taste to the poverty beneath and under the inhumanity to the misfortune but it seems as willful and as senseless as it ever did. My father has never been so boring; his larger-than-life size conception of his role in mother's illness maddens me in the terrible and familiar way," she commented in a notebook she was keeping during her hospital stay.[36] She told Lowell, however, that even though she had dreaded going to Oregon, she was surprised to discover in herself an inexplicable feeling of joy, "a kind of spiritual and consuming rapture," during the journey to and from Portland. Commenting on this beatific experience to Lowell, she explained that somehow freed of guilt when her mother died peacefully, she was overcome with a feeling of love for her and remembered that it was her mother who had supplied the only sweetness she had experienced during her unhappy childhood.[37]

During Stafford's stay in the hospital, Lowell's second volume of poems, *Lord Weary's Castle,* and Stafford's second novel, *The Mountain Lion,* were published almost simultaneously, his dedicated "To Jean" and hers dedicated "To Cal and Dick." Both books were applauded by the critics. Stafford had enough generosity of spirit to tell Lowell how proud she was that his book with "these wonderful, these beautiful, these splendid poems" had been dedicated to her.[38] She was probably chagrined, however, when Lowell and not she was awarded a Pulitzer Prize that April, an honor she herself would not receive until twenty-three years had elapsed. Despite the fact that *The Mountain Lion* was judged by most critics to be an even more accomplished novel than *Boston Adventure,* it was not as great a commercial success as the earlier novel had been, and the Pulitzer Prize in fiction that year was awarded to *All the King's Men,* a novel written by Lowell's mentor and Stafford's boss at Louisiana State University, Robert Penn Warren.

A *Bildungsroman* like *Boston Adventure, The Mountain Lion* is written more in the vernacular mode of Mark Twain than the Jamesian mode that Stafford had adopted for her first novel. It describes the childhood and adolescence of Ralph Fawcett and his younger sister, Molly, who spend their earliest years in California and subsequently go to live on their uncle's ranch in Colorado. Both children are sickly and unsociable, and Ralph sometimes fears that his younger sister—a thin, freckled girl with "an ugly little face framed by black hair"[39]—is going crazy because she says and does peculiar things such as wearing a Halloween mask on the school bus because she fears she is going to be kidnapped. Fatherless, the two small children rebel against the values of their genteel mother and their two older sisters, Leah and Rachel. They identify not with their deceased maternal grandfather, a successful button manufacturer from St. Louis, but with their mother's stepfather, Grandpa Kenyon, an adventurer who swears and drinks bourbon from a bottle he stows away in his valise. Jean Stafford writes about Grandpa Kenyon: "He had been everywhere in the world and hunted every animal indigenous to the North American continent: deer, antelope, moose, caribou, big-horn, and every game bird you could name. He had caught wild horses in Nevada and had tamed them 'into the gentlest little benches a man ever saw.' He had killed rattlers as long as a man is tall; he had eaten alligator and said it tasted like chicken."[40]

During his annual summer visit to the Fawcetts in California, Grandpa Kenyon collapses and dies, and after his funeral, Ralph and Molly are sent to spend the summer at the Colorado ranch of Grandpa Kenyon's son, Uncle

Claude. At first, the children are afraid most of the time, finding the mountainous landscape forbidding. Gradually, however, Ralph begins to enjoy the masculine, rugged, outdoor world of Uncle Claude. He learns to ride a horse, and he becomes interested in hunting: "He wished he would be hiking by himself in the mountains one day and suddenly come on a lion's den. He would shoot the mother and the cubs and then take Uncle Claude up to see. He could just hear Uncle Claude suck in his breath and say, 'Well, I'll be a son-of-a gun.'"[41] Uncle Claude is eager to initiate his nephew into the male rituals of hunting and riding but is so mean to Molly that she seldom joins him and Ralph in their escapades. Instead, she stays at home to write or to help the housekeeper in the garden.

The remainder of *The Mountain Lion,* like Carson McCullers's *Member of the Wedding* or J. D. Salinger's *The Catcher in the Rye,* focuses on the theme, so prevalent in twentieth-century American novels, of the coming of age of a troubled adolescent protagonist. Stafford's novel, however, has not one but two protagonists, one male and the other female. Like other male-female double *Bildungsromane* by women writers, such as George Eliot's *The Mill on the Floss,* Willa Cather's *My Antonia,* and Joyce Carol Oates's *Them, The Mountain Lion* contrasts the coming of age of a male and a female character in a patriarchal society. As Ralph and Molly enter adolescence, they become more and more estranged from one another. Sent to spend the year at Uncle Claude's ranch while their mother goes abroad with their older sisters, Ralph and Molly follow very different paths: Ralph's life expands to encompass the outdoor world while Molly retreats more and more into herself. One of the most significant moments in the novel occurs when Ralph and Molly are traveling to Colorado by train. Like most fourteen-year-old boys, Ralph is preoccupied with sex, and as the train enters a tunnel, he whispers to his sister, "Molly, tell me all the dirty words you know." Emphasizing the significance of this moment, Stafford writes, "Ralph's childhood and his sister's expired at that moment of the train's entrance into the surcharged valley."[42] Desperately clinging to the innocence of childhood, Molly has tried to deny the realities of sexuality. Embarrassed by her body, she wears a bathing suit in the bathtub and prefers to think of herself not as flesh and blood but as "a long wooden box with a mind inside."[43] In describing Molly's fear that a "slender snake might come right through the faucet,"[44] Stafford also suggests Molly's morbid fears of being sexually violated. Although Ralph's licentious thoughts arouse in him feelings of guilt, sexuality nevertheless represents intriguing possibilities to him. But for Molly, sexuality is threatening. Dreaming of being a writer like Mark Twain or one of the other male writers from whose works she frequently quotes, Molly rejects her own femaleness. She does not identify either with her mother or with her two older sisters, whose only mission in life seems to be to attract suitable beaux, and she is disappointed when the housekeeper's daughter, a tomboy like Molly, suddenly becomes a flirtatious young woman who exchanges her dung-stained jeans for a dress and begins to talk about her beaux just as Molly's sisters do. After Ralph whispers to her in the tunnel, Molly adds his name to her long list of unforgivable people, "a list that included almost everyone."[45]

Recalling her own unhappiness as she was about to begin writing *The Mountain Lion* in 1945, Stafford wrote to Lowell from Payne Whitney, "Gradually I became Molly. I was so much Molly that finally I had to write her book . . ."[46] In light of Stafford's identification with Molly Fawcett, it is significant that the novel concludes with Molly's death, though in real life it was Stafford's brother who was killed and his sister who survived. Earlier in the novel, Molly had expressed the wish that she "had yellow hair like Leah's and Rachel's and the lion's." She also wished that "she could go to London and become a famous writer. She wished she did not have to wear glasses. She wished she were only four feet five."[47] But her wish to go to London and become a writer is as futile as her wish to alter her appearance, for at the end of the novel Ralph accidentally shoots Molly instead of the golden-haired mountain lion. "A friend loveth at all times, and a brother is born for adversity"— this is the passage from Proverbs that Stafford chose as the epigraph for *The Mountain Lion*. But it is the sister rather than the brother who appears to have been "born for adversity" in the novel, for Molly, who wished to have golden hair like that of Goldilocks, is killed by her brother. The violent ending of this novel, which concludes with the death of Stafford's surrogate, Molly, suggests that she wished it had been she who had been killed and her brother Dick who had survived.

To date, *The Mountain Lion* has received more critical attention than any other volume of fiction that Stafford published. When it appeared in 1947, Howard Mumford Jones described it as a "beautifully modeled tale,"[48] and the reviewer in the *New Yorker* said that it was "written wittily, lucidly, and with great respect for the resources of language."[49] Even that formidable critic Philip Rahv commended Stafford for her achievement. "Here for once is a novel about childhood and early adolescence which goes beyond genre painting, overcoming the limitations of personal biographical experience and converting its theme to the larger and more fundamental uses of literary expression," he wrote to her after the novel was published.[50] In his discussion of *The Mountain Lion* in *Pioneers and Caretakers,* a study of American women writers, Louis Auchincloss describes Molly as "one of the memorable children of American fiction."[51] And when the novel was recently reissued, Maureen

Howard wrote that she was delighted by Stafford's uncanny ability to render convincingly the playful discourse of the children in the book, as well as the sparse, direct speech of the laconic rancher, Uncle Claude.[52] Blanche Gelfant, Barbara White, Melody Graulich, Mary Ellen Williams Walsh, and I have all focused on gender issues in this novel whose setting is the West but whose plot is very different from that of the archetypal Western novel as conceived by male writers like James Fenimore Cooper and Zane Grey.[53] As Blanche Gelfant has pointed out, in Stafford's novel, gone is the mythical West that once accommodated the figure of a roving hero intent on leaving corrupt civilization behind and escaping to the territory ahead. Molly's death shatters Ralph's dream of the innocent life. But if Ralph fails to emerge as the archetypal Western hero, what Gelfant calls "the great masculine myth of the West" excludes Molly completely. She points out that a girl like Molly—intellectual, physically unattractive, "wedged between the cult of violence and the cult of virginity"—must be destroyed, for she is not merely extraneous or intrusive but "actively threatening to the ritual of male initiation."[54]

Stafford undoubtedly took some comfort from the flattering comments of people whose opinion of the novel she respected. However, in her letters to Lowell she repeatedly emphasized that her failed marriage had erased any pleasure she might have derived from her success as a writer. When Lowell told her that Randall Jarrell had liked her novel, she replied: "What do I care if Randall likes my book? Or anyone else? Why should it console me to be praised as a good writer? These stripped bones are not enough to feed a starving woman. I know this, Cal, and the knowledge eats me like an inward animal. There is no thing worse for a woman than to be deprived of her womanliness. For me, there is nothing worse than the knowledge that my life holds nothing for me but being a writer . . ." She said she resented the fact that Lowell had a second marriage to look forward to, while she, who had never regarded her writing as being as important as his, had "nothing left but to be a writer, and only a writer."[55] And in response to his expressed wish that she would be recognized as one of the best novelists of her generation, she wrote: "I want you to know that would mean to me absolutely *nothing*. It could not happen and even if it could, it would not make the days here less long nor would my loss of you be made up for. I respect myself as a workman and a human being and what I have done, I have done to save myself for myself. I shall be grateful for whatever praise I get, but I shall never be so confused as to think this is life or that, if one looks closely, it bears any resemblance to life."[56] Coming from a woman who had labored so long and hard to become a success as a writer, this was, indeed, an astonishing statement.

That winter two additional works by Stafford were published. "The Hope Chest," which was selected for an O. Henry Award, appeared in *Harper's* in January of 1947, and "A Slight Maneuver" was published the next month in *Mademoiselle*. The first of Stafford's works of fiction that is set in Maine, the former story describes the solitary Christmas of a desperately lonely eighty two-year-old spinster. Rhoda Bellamy had retreated to Maine from Boston with her wealthy parents after she had made a debut that turned out to be a complete fiasco. Having had no other beau in her life but her dear Papa, she is now so alone in her old age that she cajoles a young country boy into giving her a kiss in exchange for an ugly Christmas wreath she had agreed to purchase from him for a quarter. Although the story is little more than a sketch, it successfully blends pathos and humor. "Old and cold" Miss Bellamy is pitiful in her isolation, but she is also shown to be a despicable autocrat who takes pleasure in manipulating powerless individuals like her housemaid and the boy who sells her the wreath. Witchlike and full of spleen, she thinks, "I will eat you, little boy, because once upon a time I, too, had pink cheeks and a fair skin and clear eyes." Stafford's portrait of this scion of the upper class is hardly a complimentary one; nevertheless, at the story's end we sympathize as much with this lonely old woman who "nursed her hurt like a baby at a milkless breast" as we do with the young boy who desperately wants to flee after he has been forced to kiss her "bone-dry cheek." [57]

Stafford admitted to Lowell that she frequently made jokes about those situations that wounded her most, acknowledging that half of her being was really "a mass of buried injuries." [58] Using wit and irony in her fiction to conceal her pain, she exposed the peccadilloes and the cruelty of those individuals who had wounded her. The wit and irony that characterizes much of her fiction are very much in evidence in the second story she published in 1947, "A Slight Maneuver." This story, which appeared in *Mademoiselle*, describes the contempt a young woman feels for her fiancé, who has allowed himself to be completely dominated by his autocratic aunt. As William Leary has astutely observed, this work also has a subtext, for in it Stafford has expressed her own hostility both to Lowell and to his domineering mother. [59] Reversing Easterners and Westerners, Stafford pits Theo, a feisty young female protagonist from the East, against two Westerners: a submissive young man named Clyde Tompkins and his controlling but "illiterate" aunt. [60] These figures are thinly disguised representations of Stafford, Lowell, and Lowell's mother. The spineless Clyde Tompkins, "caught between the two women in his life, is unable to be mannerly to the one without offending the other." [61] When Clyde takes the reluctant Theo to the Carlsbad Caverns, as his aunt has advised him to do, Theo realizes that he is weak and that he values peace with his aunt more than making his fiancée happy. Herded with Clyde and the other tourists through the Carlsbad Caverns, Theo finds that she is as repelled by Clyde as she is by this "vagary of the earth," which she has been forced to explore against her will.[62] In "A Slight Maneuver" Stafford succeeded in venting her spleen against the West, Lowell, and, most of all, her meddlesome mother-in-law. As she was contemplating the end of her own marriage, Stafford wrote a story that concludes with the rupture of a relationship: by the time the tour of the Carlsbad Caverns is over, Theo realizes that she and Clyde have also reached the end of their romantic journey.

With the gradual improvement of her health, Stafford was allowed to leave the hospital for limited periods of time. She once attended a party at Cecile Starr's apartment, knowing full well that she would be going to a place where there was bound to be a good deal of drinking going on. She found, however, that it was less difficult for her to abstain from drinking alcohol than it was to confront former friends of hers and Cal's like Caroline Gordon and Randall Jarrell. Even more painful than the evening at Cecile Starr's was the trip she made to Maine to arrange for the sale of the house in Damariscotta and the storage of its furniture. The sight of her lovely house, abandoned now except for the ghosts who inhabited it, so unnerved her that on her second night there, after trying unsuccessfully to reach Dr. Sherfey by phone, she began to drink again. As a result, for some time after she returned to Payne Whitney, she was not permitted to leave the hospital grounds.[63]

Although the trip to Damariscotta caused a temporary setback, soon her state of mind began to improve. In a letter she sent that spring to her former neighbor in Damariscotta, Mrs. Booth, she managed to sound fairly cheerful and optimistic. Admitting that the sale of the house was terribly painful for her, she wrote, "Damariscotta especially breaks my heart because I had meant to live there all the rest of my life. I loved that house deeply and I cannot imagine now ever having or so much loving another." She mentioned a visit she had paid recently to the Berrymans in Princeton, and she indicated that she expected to be discharged from the hospital as soon as she had located an apartment and found a job. But for the time being, she said, she welcomed the haven her hospital room provided: "My room is light and pleasant and I have a splendid view of the East River whose traffic is wonderfully interesting. The company I keep is stunningly boring but for the most part I avoid it and stay in my room reading and writing and pondering how I am going to extricate myself from this morass." She informed Mrs. Booth that gradually she was recovering her hope and that in fact there were some days when she did not even think about the horrors of the past year, which seemed the longest of her life.[64]

Stafford's lack of money was very much on her mind as she contemplated leaving the hospital with bills unpaid and no one to support her. She told Cecile Starr how distressed she was that Lowell had offered to pay her only a mere five thousand dollars over a period of ten years. "This amounts, I think, to about $40 a month and I cannot help feeling like a hard-up seamstress of 1800," she said.[65] When Lowell suggested that she get a job to support herself, she was irate, pointing out to him that it would be as irksome for her to get a job as it would be for him to do so.[66] After Lowell was awarded the Pulitzer Prize, a Guggenheim Fellowship, and one thousand dollars following the publication of *Lord Weary's Castle,* she wrote to him at Yaddo, where he was spending the summer: "Cal, you are base about money. I know how much you have in prizes (which are tax-free) and royalties and gifts from your parents and your trust fund . . ." She pointed out that earlier, when she had temporarily withdrawn her claims for alimony payments, he had not yet received these awards. Moreover, she had hoped at that time that *The Mountain Lion* would sell more copies than it did. Now, however, she realized that he could well afford to help her out financially.[67] In May, after returning to the hospital from an expedition to search for an apartment, she wrote in her notebook, "I determine suddenly that if I should marry again, I shall not marry a poor man," and walking along Sutton Place, she imagined somewhere within one of the handsome houses she passed there was a "red room" where she would be able to work.[68]

The tone of Stafford's letters to Lowell after their separation varied from letter to letter. Initially, when they focused on Gertrude Buckman, her anger and hurt were evident; when her letters dealt with money, they were either coldly businesslike or scolding; and when, on occasion, she voiced the hope that despite everything she and Lowell might reconcile their differences, she was conciliatory. But as the months passed and a reconciliation seemed increasingly unlikely, she appeared to be intent on preserving their friendship for one another even if the marriage was over. "I am only saying, let us love one another as deeply and as perpetually as we can for there is so terribly little love in the world, and you and I are so starved for it," she implored him.[69]

The June 2, 1947, issue of *Life* contained a feature article entitled "Young U.S. Writers." Both Jean Stafford and Robert Lowell were included in these ranks. A photograph of Stafford shows her standing in front of a lion's cage at the zoo. Smartly dressed in a suit, carrying a shoulder bag and wearing black gloves, her shoulder-length blonde hair neatly arranged, she is turning her face away from the camera and is not smiling. The accompanying text comments: "Most brilliant of the new fiction writers is Jean Stafford, 31, wife of Pulitzer Prize winning poet Robert Lowell. In *Boston Adventure* she wrote about Boston bluebloods with such insight that critics promptly compared her to Proust. Her latest, *The Mountain Lion,* which tells in Freudian terms of a Colorado childhood and adolescence, is even better."[70] On the verge of divorcing the "Pulitzer Prize winning poet" when she read the *Life* article, the dejected Stafford might have exclaimed, using one of her own favorite expressions, "In a pig's valise!" Although she was probably the envy of many an aspiring young writer, she was much less triumphant than anyone reading about her in *Life* would have imagined. Having begun work on two novels during her hospital stay, "the one to escape the other," she remarked that she disliked the heroines of both, who were, as they had always been, herself. "I can write only of loneliness—when I don't, I offensively attack—only of half-mad separateness," she commented in her notebook on June 9.[71]

It is interesting to note that, whereas a number of Stafford's contemporaries, including Robert Lowell, Sylvia Plath, and Anne Sexton, described their hospitalizations in mental hospitals in their work, she did not make extensive use of her sojourn in Payne Whitney for her fiction. The description of a mental hospital in *Boston Adventure* antedated her own breakdown and hospitalization, and though one of her characters in *The Catherine Wheel* briefly mentions that a friend once wrote to her about being a patient in a sanitarium, nothing more is said about this. Although it was Stafford's usual practice to base her fiction on her own life, her stay in Payne Whitney was so painful that she could not bear to recreate it in her stories or novels.

Stafford did, however, write a poignant albeit highly stylized account of her illness and recuperation in an article that appeared during the fall of 1947 in *Vogue.* Bearing the title "My Sleep Grew Shy of Me," this essay, written in poetic prose, speaks of her intractable insomnia; her growing recognition that she was "*really* sick";[72] the counsel she received from a wise psychiatrist; her convalescence; and the wonderful moment when she realized with amazement that "the tempest" was truly over and that sleep had truly come back to her "like a dove wearing in its beak the olive branch."[73] Using St. Teresa of Avila's *The Interior Castle* as a model for this anatomy of her own melancholy, she imagined herself moving from illness to recovery through seven mansions, as St. Teresa imagined the soul progressing through seven mansions before it finally found a haven of peace. Nowhere in this essay does Stafford allude to her difficult childhood, to her separation from Lowell, to her alcoholism, or to her hospitalization. Instead, she focuses on her journey, with her wise psychiatrist as a guide, from the "exterior wasteland" where she kept "a violent vigil" to the "safe place" where she now sleeps. Asserting that she has come to honor "the good practice of psychiatry" as she had honored only religion and the arts in the past, she maintains that the intentions of psychiatry are "profoundly moral in the most splendid and intelligent sense because it aims to create happiness."[74]

When one compares "My Sleep Grew Shy of Me" with the entries Stafford made in her notebook during the late spring and the summer of 1947, it is evident that the tone of the article is far more optimistic than that of the journal entries. On May 30, for example, she brooded, "I do not remember how one starts again and this is the hardest time of all, since I have left behind no life lines." On July 25 she described a trip she had taken to Ocean City with Cecile Starr to visit Cecile's aunt and uncle. In Trenton, she had thought she saw Cal across the tracks waiting for a train, only to discover that she had been mistaken. On July 28 she recorded the fact that she had dreamed she never visited her parents, although they lived in Westport, a town where she frequently visited friends, and experiencing a "torment of guilt," she awoke to discover that her dream had been prophetic: that very day a letter arrived from her father, "heartbreaking, relentlessly pitiful." She commented that she thought of him as a "sad, senile child" and observed that he would probably live on and on. And on July 31 she wrote, "I am unbearably depressed by the life of everyone I see and by the dirt and the danger and the quotidian disappointment of New York which I hate, yet fear to leave . . ."[75]

Stafford's letters to Lowell during this period also reveal her profound anxiety about leaving the security of the hospital and being on her own once more. She feared that her separation from Lowell would cause a rift between her and people like Robert Giroux and Peter Taylor, who formerly had been close to both her and Cal. Comparing her situation with his, she wrote to Lowell: "I leave the hospital, therefore, without money and without friends and this is harder for a woman than for a man. A man who is called a scoundrel remains, to most people, attractive, but a woman who is called a bitch is shunned. A woman who has spent nearly a year in a hospital with a sickness of spirit has, with the people she has known before, an ineradicable black mark. Who would wish to know me. Because I am defeated and miserable, I cannot be appealing." About to be released from the hospital, she maintained nevertheless that she would continue to be sick until she found someone else to love her and take from her some of her misery; she insisted that she wanted to marry again and have a child before it was too late; and she also expressed the hope that she would, perhaps, find her "red room" and that in time all the warfare between her and Lowell would stop.[76]

Because there was an acute shortage of apartments in New York City now that the war had ended, Stafford had great difficulty finding an affordable place to live. She finally rented an apartment consisting of one large room, a kitchen, and a bath at 27 West 75th Street, half a block from the Metropolitan Museum of Art. The museum would serve as the setting for "Children Are Bored on Sundays," the first of her short stories to be published in the *New Yorker*. She was pleased to have found an apartment in so convenient a location, but on the day she moved in, she discovered, much to her chagrin, that her apartment was situated over a music school for children: ". . . within minutes of the departure of the moving van, the fiddles started being used like buzz-saws and the pianos started getting walloped, the horns began to neigh and nicker, and some persevering criminal of ten began, without success, to learn the piccolo obbligato from *Stars and Stripes Forever*." Her windows all faced blank walls, and when she looked down, all she could see was a fenced pen inhabited by two large gray dogs that "howled like Bugle Ann as soon as Piccolo Pete began."[77] The only compensation for living in this building was the fact that one of its other inhabitants was the writer Sax Rohmer, creator of the adventure stories featuring the notorious trafficker in dope and jewels and white slavery, Dr. Fu Manchu. Invited to drink champagne and talk shop with this mild, elderly, bald little Englishman whose stories about Oriental villains had thrilled her during her childhood, she discovered that "there wasn't a hint of the Orient in his digs" and that he and his Cockney wife, "Tories as doctrinaire as Iowa Republicans," were living in New York rather than England because they could not abide the Labor government of Clement Attlee.[78]

One month after she left the hospital, Stafford reported to Lowell that she was feeling well, despite the fact that she still had occasional bouts of insomnia. Three times a week she saw Dr. Sherfey for therapy, though she admitted that she had been ignoring Dr. Sherfey's strong recommendation that she abstain completely from drinking wine, beer, or liquor. At first she was kept busy setting up her new apartment, a chore that included packing up carton after carton of Lowell's books, which he had requested that she ship to Boston. She informed him that at the last she had been unable to manage one carton containing the complete works of his ancestor, James Russell Lowell, but assuring him that she needed these books the way she needed "a hole in the head," she offered to ship them later. She admitted annoyance over the fact that it was she rather than he who had to pack up the forty cartons of his books but was concerned that he would be cross with her for not packing them well. It is evident that even at this juncture she feared incurring his displeasure.[79]

During the months that followed, Stafford struggled to establish a daily routine for herself, but for the most part she found New York City a not very congenial place in which to live by one's self, especially since she had few meaningful relationships to sustain her there. "I am on the wagon, wear spectacles, am reading Dickens (one night I made myself some fudge and read half of Great Expectations—oh, he's such an awful writer)," she wrote to Lowell. She admitted to him that she was lonesome and still missed him but reported that nevertheless she was "as they say, 'making an adjustment.'"[80] She said she was in touch with some of their former friends, including Robert Penn Warren and his wife, the Thompsons, the Berrymans, and Cecile Starr, and she mentioned that she had also attended some literary gatherings. At one of these she had met Graham Greene. Wishing perhaps to arouse Lowell's jealousy, she said Greene had subsequently written that he could arrange for her to rent a "divine cottage" in Ireland and promised to introduce her to "the best pub-keepers, ex-gun-men, poker-playing priests, and an attractive doctor."[81]

Another male acquaintance whom she mentioned to Lowell was Alfred Einstein Cohn, an eminent sixty-eight-year-old cardiologist who was associated with the Rockefeller Institute. An intellectual with wide-ranging interests, Dr. Cohn not only wrote about medicine but about art, education, and literature. Stafford happily reported that Dr. Cohn had taken her to tea at the Plaza and had invited her to a party to celebrate the publication of one of his books. She found it pleasant to be invited to tea by avuncular men of taste and intelligence such as Dr. Cohn and the Melville scholar, Henry Murray, though she said candidly to Lowell, "I cannot truly feel that this life of being made over by men old enough to be my father and grandfather is the right one, but it is a pleasant and very *safe* stop-gap."[82] When she expressed an interest in learning more about science, Dr. Cohn made arrangements for her to study botany and genetics, the subjects that had most interested her brother. "I find scientists much more interesting than writers and my favorite word is 'skeptical,'" she told Lowell. Several days a week she met privately with a friend of Dr. Cohn's at Columbia University. One of the reasons she wanted to study at Columbia was that she hoped being on a campus would help her to recall her own college days for the novel she was then trying to write, but much to her disappointment, she met only the geneticist, who instructed her in his own laboratory, and her interest in slime molds and plasmodia rapidly waned. Soon she found herself trying to explain to Lowell why she had decided to give up her studies at Columbia: "I was not understanding Whitehead and was feeling sick with guilt for not doing so (as I was always guilty for not reading the Catholic Apologetics even after you'd given up trying to improve my mind) so that I was getting no writing done."[83] But even if her scientific education at Columbia University was short-lived, for several months her studies there provided some structure for her life and enabled her to focus her attention on what she saw through her microscope rather than on her own misery.

While Stafford found even the most casual social encounters difficult now that she was "on the wagon," she nevertheless accepted an invitation to deliver a lecture on the psychological novel at a symposium that was held at Bard College at the beginning of November. One of the inducements to speak at this symposium was that Lionel Trilling was also to appear on the same program; the other, that she would be paid, however modestly, for participating. Describing the ordeal of appearing in public at Bard to Lowell, she wrote: "I went to Bard to lecture and nearly died of terror (for no humane reason Mary McCarthy and Bowdoin [sic] Broadwater came and sat in the front row grinning like cats) and then I was almost killed in the automobile that took me—failed, rather, to take me to the station. I hated it all and vowed never again to leave my red room for public appearances."[84] She later reported that Mary McCarthy, a member of the faculty of Bard that year, had commented "with all her ignited ice" that the speech had had "a great deal of charm." What she felt like retorting, Stafford said bitterly, was that to be a "charming woman" was her principal ambition. Still desperately insecure about her intellectual abilities, always anticipating that she would be slighted by those people who had more power or prestige than she did, ready to attribute dark motives to someone else's casual pleasantries, she found public occasions such as the conference at Bard unnerving. Following the conference and her subsequent meeting with Mary McCarthy, she told Lowell, "And it is, at last I realize, better by far to talk only to the monkey in the zoo who impudently picks his nose in my presence and to go, like a lonely cloud, to the planetarium, than to burst my loneliness all apart in that awful process known as 'spreading Jean too thin.'"[85]

A characteristic maneuver of Stafford's to disarm those who might be critical of her efforts was to belittle them herself before someone else might do so. Thus she wrote to John Crowe Ransom following her lecture at Bard: "There is a matter that I must take up with you that I don't want to do at all. Lionel Trilling and I recently went to Bard College to give something called 'A Conference on the Novel.' We both lectured and then there was an interminable discussion. Anyhow, the Bard people want us to publish our lectures. Mine is so foolish and unmeaning that I am ashamed to show it to anyone, but I am obliged to and I promised them I would write and ask you if you would take a look at it."[86] Her comments both to her friend Dr. Cohn and to Lowell about her lecture were similarly self-deprecating. After sending the original copy of the text for the lecture to Dr. Cohn, she described it as "this product of my intransigent stupidity,"[87] and once Ransom had agreed to publish the lecture in the *Kenyon Review,* she informed Lowell: "Uncle Ransom is printing the lecture I gave at Bard and I am thoroughly unhappy about it because it is so awfully bad and I think he is off his trolley to use it—either that or he wants publicly to humiliate me. He wrote to me a very nice note on a penny postal saying that it was 'belletristic,' if not 'academic.' I dread your reading it."[88]

These self-deprecating comments are painful to read, particularly since her essay "The Psychological Novel" is very good indeed. Its excellence suggests that John Crowe Ransom accepted the essay for publication in the *Kenyon Review* not merely to extend a kindness to Lowell's former wife, who had once held a dinner party in his honor, but because he liked it. Stafford's essay advances no startling literary theories, and it lacks the quotations from authoritative sources and the numerous explanatory footnotes that usually characterize academic articles. Nevertheless, it is learned without being pedantic, and it is written with clarity, grace, and wit. In this essay she insists that *all* novels are "psychological," that they are "concerned with emotional motivations and their intellectual resolutions, with instincts and impulses and conflicts and behavior, with the convolutions and complexities of human relationships, with the crucifixions and the solaces of being alive." She maintains that she has no sympathy for novelists who borrow "the vocabulary of psychology rather than its methods of analysis and deduction," or novels that are merely compendia of clinical details of the "vile or the strange or the perverse," nor does she approve of novels that are "forthrightly and ungraciously autobiographical."[89] Nevertheless, she asserts that good writers must be good psychologists whose task is not to cure or to condemn but to preserve their ironic detachment.[90]

Whereas Stafford's previous contribution to the *Kenyon Review* had appeared under the name Phoebe Lowell, this "belletristic" essay is a Jean Stafford product from start to finish. In it, as in her other essays, she intermixes the objective and the personal; refers both to texts favored by the literary establishment, such as Chekhov's "Ward No. 6." and Henry James's "The Jolly Corner," and to popular works like *The Snake Pit* and *The Lost Weekend;* briefly digresses to relate an amusing anecdote that is pertinent to her topic but not essential to her argument; and alternately uses the elevated, formal diction of the scholar and a more colloquial style. She speculates, for example, that Henry James might be "prophetically pulling the wool over [Edmund] Wilson's eyes"[91] and says that Dickens can be considered a "great" writer "when he is not being a goose."[92] Perhaps Mary McCarthy and Bowden Broadwater *were* "grinning like cats" during her lecture at Bard, as Stafford had alleged, for this lecture is not only insightful but humorous as well. Whether she is poking fun at the editors of a new periodical called *Neurotica*

or decrying the "humorless narcissism" of Thomas Wolfe, Stafford's observations are always astute as well as amusing.

That fall and winter, Stafford devoted some of her time to working on her
novel about Lucy McKee's suicide for which she had submitted a fifty-six-
page summary along with her application for the renewal of her Guggenheim
Fellowship. She told Lowell that she had decided the novel was to have a
happy ending for her protagonist, Joyce, who, she admitted, was but another
version of her fictional personae, Sonie and Molly. "I imagine it couldn't have
been the book I mean it to be if I hadn't gone all apart that way and got cured
of my life-long sickness," she explained.[93]

In addition to working on the novel, she also wrote "Children Are Bored
on Sunday," an enormously accomplished short story that wittily caricatures
the New York intellectuals, depicting them from the point of view of a vulnerable young woman who is recuperating from an illness, as Stafford herself
was at that time. During the winter when the story was written, Stafford told
Lowell that she had declined an invitation to the Rahvs' to meet Arthur
Koestler because she "had already been to that party upward of a hundred
times."[94] In "Children Are Bored on Sunday," which takes its title from a
popular French song, her protagonist, too, has scrupulously been avoiding
parties given by the New York literati, parties crowded with composers and
painters and writers who "pronounced judgements in their individual argot,
on Hindemith, Ernst, Sartre, on Beethoven, Rubens, Baudelaire, on Stalin
and Freud and Kierkegaard, on Toynbee, Frazer, Thoreau, Franco, Salazar,
Roosevelt, Maimonides, Racine, Wallace, Picasso, Henry Luce, Monsignor
Sheen, the Atomic Energy Commission, and the movie industry."[95] Con-
valescing from an unnamed illness, Emma recalls how she had succeeded in
ingesting small quantities of food that autumn only by "flushing the frightful
stuff down with enormous drafts of magical, purifying, fulfilling applejack
diluted with tepid water from the tap."[96] On this Sunday when the events of
the story take place, she wanders from room to room of the Metropolitan Museum of Art and observes two "first-generation Metropolitan" boys, products
of a New York City upbringing, who spend their Sundays in museums.
Though she believes that her own upbringing in a small town, amidst lilac
bushes and hollyhocks, was in some ways superior to that of these urban children of immigrants, she nevertheless feels like a "rube" in comparison to them
and laments that her own childhood "had not equipped her to read, or to see,
or to listen, as theirs had done."[97]

Suddenly Emma comes upon a New York intellectual named Alfred
Eisenburg, with whom she had flirted at one of those literary parties she now
avoids. Terrified when she sees someone she had known before she became ill,

she decides that "today's excursion into the world had been premature."[98] The
story concludes on a more positive note, however, for Emma recalls having
been told that Alfred "was having a very bad time of it with a divorce, with
poverty, with a tempest that had carried off his job, and at last, with a psycho-
analyst, whose fees he could not possibly afford." Relieved to have discovered
in this New York intellectual a fellow sufferer, someone whose pain is compa-
rable to her own, she agrees to go have a drink with him, "a honeymoon of
cripples," a "nuptial consummation of the abandoned," hoping nevertheless
that during their rendezvous in some unfashionable bar he will "lay off the
fashions of the day and leave his learning in his private entrepôt."[99] Giving her
protagonist the same name as Jane Austen's energetic but sometimes mis-
guided protagonist, Stafford reveals in this story not only her identification
with the unhappy Emma, but the way in which she herself had metamor-
phosed from a "rube" to a highly sophisticated if self-educated writer, one
who could introduce the names of Titian, Holbein, Rembrandt, Dali, Botti-
celli, Seurat, Vermeer, and Klee as well as Palestrina, Copland, Hindemith,
Baudelaire, Sartre, and Racine into a single story. Although Stafford might
have despaired of becoming a real intellectual and might have feared that she
was a dilettante rather than a true scholar, in "Children Are Bored on Sunday," as William Leary has argued, she does not merely compile an impressive
list of names but also skillfully uses the paintings she mentions to parallel the
emotions of her protagonist.[100]

It was "Children Are Bored on Sunday," a story which so trenchantly ana-
lyzes the clash of cultures, the subtle differences between "rubes" and "intellectuals," the perspectives of outsiders and insiders, that launched Stafford's
career at the *New Yorker*. For the next ten years Stafford's stories would regularly appear in the same magazine she had once longed to read. A former
"rube" himself, Harold Ross, founder and editor of the *New Yorker*, had
grown up in Colorado, as Stafford had done. He was a brilliant editor, but he
was also considered by those who knew him to be unintellectual or even at
times positively anti-intellectual.[101] Receptive to the work of writers who were
not yet established, Ross valued style above all, preferring prose that was
simple, direct, colloquial. A man who was humorous and anecdotal, Ross
published the humorous stories and essays of writers such as James Thurber,
S. J. Perelman, and E. B. White in the pages of his magazine. Although writers for highbrow quarterlies like the *Partisan Review* in the thirties were disdainful of the *New Yorker*, a decade later the situation had changed: even Edmund Wilson and Dwight McDonald had begun to write for the *New Yorker*
and, as Irving Howe has noted, other writers too began to realize "that publishing a story in the *New Yorker* was not a sure ticket to Satan."[102] Even if

Lowell made snide remarks about the *New Yorker* and its ruination of writers,[103] Stafford certainly had no cause for being defensive about publishing her work in a magazine that also published stories by Nabokov, J. F. Powers, John Cheever, John Updike, and Peter Taylor, whose work was introduced to the editors of the *New Yorker* by Stafford. From its inception the *New Yorker* had always been more receptive to women writers than the quarterlies had been. Among its contributors were Dorothy Parker, Sally Benson, Cornelia Otis Skinner, Shirley Jackson, Sylvia Townsend Warner, Rebecca West, Eudora Welty, Anne Sexton, Emily Hahn, Janet Flanner, Mollie Panter-Downes, Edith Oliver, Pauline Kael, and Penelope Gilliatt.

For Stafford, even more significant a person than Harold Ross at the *New Yorker* was its fiction editor, Katharine White, to whom she would later dedicate her *Collected Stories.* Twenty-two years older than Stafford, Katharine White quickly became not merely a literary mentor but a confidante and advisor. A member of an old, well-connected Boston family and a graduate of Bryn Mawr, Katharine White had the impeccable credentials Stafford longed to have. She wore elegant clothes, and she was refined in manner and speech. What differentiated Katharine White most from Stafford, however, was the older woman's self-confidence. Divorced from her first husband, the father of her daughter and son, she had later married *New Yorker* writer E. B. White. In an era when most women did not attempt both to raise children and have a career, Katharine White was an exception. "I live a very full home life, and I hold an editorial position that is as exacting a full-time job as any I see about me," she wrote in 1926.[104] From its inception, she too had played a crucial role in shaping the *New Yorker.* According to E. B. White's biographer, Scott Elledge, it was primarily Katharine White who promoted the kind of story with which the magazine has become identified: one that eschews a formal plot, focusing instead on the nuances of character and situation.[105] The fact that many of Stafford's stories followed this model might have had something to do with White's response to the stories Stafford first submitted to the magazine. Between 1948 and 1978 Stafford would publish twenty-two short stories in the *New Yorker,* the great majority of them appearing during the period when White served as its fiction editor. As William Leary has pointed out, White became more attached to Stafford than most editors do to their writers; White's friendship and support were as important to Stafford as was the sound advice on literary matters that White gave her.[106] Often failing to maintain satisfying and long-lasting relationships with other women, Stafford nevertheless maintained a close relationship with her editor at the *New Yorker,* who treated her like a daughter. White offered sympathy during Stafford's divorce from Lowell in 1948 as well as her divorce from her second husband,

Oliver Jensen, in 1953; she invited her to parties at her home; she introduced her to *New Yorker* writer A. J. Liebling, who was to become Stafford's third husband; she and Stafford commiserated with one another about their frequent physical ailments; and she buoyed up Stafford's flagging spirits by repeating to her favorable comments that writers such as Mary McCarthy and Elizabeth Bishop had made about her fiction. Affirming how much she valued the fact that Stafford had dedicated her *Collected Stories* to her, White, shortly before her death, wrote to her, "I now feel that my chief or only claim to fame is that you dedicated that wonderful collection to me." [107]

On those days when her writing was going well or when she was planning to have dinner with a good friend like Eileen Berryman or to go to the theater with her editor Robert Giroux, the "gentlest man" she had ever known, [108] Stafford felt more optimistic about her future; on others, when she could no longer bear the cacophony of the instruments from the music school or when ghosts from her youth in Boulder filled her room as she worked on her novel about Lucy McKee, or when she longed to purchase a rare book or an antique silver spoon she could no longer afford, she was morose. Her visits to Dr. Sherfey, however, provided a necessary source of support to her, especially when familiar symptoms threatened to erupt with new virulence. In February, for example, after learning that her nephew had accidentally shot himself, all but removing his right arm, Stafford began once again to suffer from insomnia. Her sister Mary Lee, she told Eileen Berryman, was "rather spectacularly going to pieces" and wanted to come east to visit. But even though Stafford had often turned to Mary Lee for support in times of trouble, she did not feel strong enough herself to see Mary Lee now; instead, she urged her to take her nephew to a specialist. Writing to Eileen Berryman to explain why she had failed to visit the Berrymans in Princeton as she had promised to do, Stafford described how her nephew's accident and her sister's distress had affected her: "I have had another seizure of insomnia and last night I slept not at all in spite of the fact that I took ten phenobarbitals over a period of a long, nightmarish time, and when I got to my interview with Dr. Sherfey today I was as irresponsible as a cat in a catnip patch so that she told me I could not do anything but go home and go to bed." In a postscript to this letter, she added, "I feel compelled to state here that I frisked myself of all the rest of the phenobarbitol [sic] at Dr. Sherfey's office today." [109]

Two events that boosted her spirits that spring were her receipt of a National Press Club Award and the renewal of her Guggenheim Fellowship. When she first learned that she might be a recipient of the National Press Club Award, she wrote to Lowell, who was then working at the Library of Congress in Washington: "If a rumor I have heard from Milton Starr via

Cecile is true, I shall be in Washington in April to be feted—together with others, among them Rebecca West—at a dinner for being an industrious lady writer or some such and *maybe* we could meet."[110] In another letter she described to Lowell the new red shoes and little mitts she had bought to wear on the night of April 3, when she was to be presented to Harry and Bess Truman at the award ceremonies. "I am trying *so* hard to be a woman," she commented.[111] After this event took place, she would frequently describe her meeting with the president, recalling how she had summoned up the courage to tell him about the cowboy out west who had asked her what she did for a living. "I'm a writer," she had replied. "That's nice," said the cowboy. "That's something you can do in the shade."[112]

In her application to renew her Guggenheim Fellowship that year, Stafford had described her projected novel, tentatively called *In the Snowfall,* as "a novel of about 150,000 words, set in the thirties and dealing with the suicide of a young woman who is symbolic of a whole generation: a class that has been removed from reality by excessive intellectuality and a generation that has been dislocated by the depression." Once again, as she had done when she had applied for a Guggenheim Fellowship before, she asked Howard Mumford Jones to recommend her. He did so, stressing her sense of humor as well as "a kind of passionate veracity" that was evident in her writing. "I think there are very few novelists of her years who have shown both the performance and promise she has shown," he concluded. Robert Giroux, who also wrote a letter of recommendation on her behalf, said that she brought to American letters what he considered "potentially the greatest new talent in a decade," and he mentioned that the style of her new novel would be a fusion of the baroque style of *Boston Adventure* and the sparer style of *The Mountain Lion.* And John P. Marquand, another person who wrote on her behalf, not only endorsed her new project himself but asserted that Henry Canby, Christopher Morley, Dorothy Fisher, and Clifton Fadiman all agreed with his assessment of her talent.[113]

Henry Allen Moe wrote to Stafford in April to notify her that her fellowship had been renewed and to ask her when she wanted her payments to begin. She replied, "Because I am so harassed with personal problems, I shall not be able at this moment to tell you when I should like my fellowship to begin. I beg your indulgence for I am involved in a divorce which obliges me to be out of the city (but not, happily, out of work) for six weeks. May I write you when I have done the gruesome thing which is called 'establishing residence'?"[114] Soon after the letter was mailed, she boarded a plane bound for the Virgin Islands, where she would remain until her divorce from Lowell was granted. She told Lowell that she expected to be back in New York about

June 7 and hoped to see him before she left for Ireland to write an article for the *New Yorker.* "Perhaps we can meet . . . with affection and tranquility," she said, playfully admonishing him that during the trip he was planning to Boston that weekend, he should avoid being "devoured by the Radcliffe girls."[115]

While she was in St. Thomas awaiting the divorce, Stafford tried to sound fairly cheerful in her letters to Lowell, but her sojourn in the Virgin Islands was hardly the enjoyable "holiday" that Ian Hamilton has described it as being.[116] The five windows of her room at the Hotel 1829 in the town of Charlotte Amalie on the island of St. Thomas commanded "a prospect of sea and sky and white hillside, houses with red roofs and the blackest natives that ever were,"[117] but the charm of this "overdone landscape" of hibiscus and palm trees and "picture post-card beaches" quickly began to pall. To John Berryman, who had sent her a book of his poems on the eve of her departure, she complained about being ill with a mysterious fever: "I lie under a sheet on a Sears Roebuck bed in the best hotel in town and watch the lizards slither into my laundry bag that hangs on the wall and do not even care, I am so sick and so homesick, so truly miserable. This is the third week of my quarantine and each day I wonder why Cal and I, who are now so fond of one another, could have come to such a pass." She said that she was revolted by the divorcées-to-be who drank gin and Schweppes on the galleries; the whimsical innkeeper who used to live in Paterson, New Jersey; the hypochondriacal ladies whose doctors had told them to come there after their bronchitis and their hysterectomies; the wastrels who began drinking at eleven each morning; and the cruise boats carrying Rotarians.[118] In a letter to Cecile Starr she also complained about the "silly-ass women" awaiting divorces and the "awful awful men." Two colonels from the regular army, "great fat drunken things who slapped their thighs and guffawed," had spent an hour with her making distasteful anti-Semitic remarks, she said, exclaiming, "Oh, how deeply I hate the man in the street."[119]

Disinclined to spend a lot of time on the beach because she was afraid of getting sunburned and did not swim, she was delighted one day when Nancy Flagg Gibney, a writer for *Vogue,* and her husband Robert, who was also a writer, came to her hotel and invited her to have lunch with them. Nancy Gibney later vividly recalled their first meeting: "In person she looked like a pretty redhaired girl who had taken one hell of a beating . . . She rose above it. Her smashed nose was appealing. Her blue eyes blazed with a wild Western humor, and she had a delightful figure, slender and plump, like a Fragonard."[120] In his journal, Robert Gibney also noted his impressions of Stafford. "Jean Stafford," he wrote, "is remarkable for the way she seems rooted in the dead center of a personal hurricane. These winds clutch at her hair and crumple her clothes, but you feel the steadiness of immovable balanced forces under this harassed exterior." [121] Jean Stafford and the Gibneys subsequently became lifelong friends. "For all three of us it was love and jokes at first sight," Nancy Gibney remarked.[122]

Before the Gibneys departed, they invited Stafford to spend the next weekend with them on Henley Cay on the isle of St. John, where they had been camping out for the preceding sixteen months rent-free in a storehouse filled with lumber. Despite her nervousness about having to cross rough water in a small boat to reach them, Stafford was delighted to receive this invitation from such a charming and urbane couple, but during the trip by boat that weekend, she almost began to regret that she had accepted the Gibneys' invitation. In 1975 she would describe that harrowing trip between St. Thomas and St. John in an article in *Esquire:*

> . . . the skipper told me, the only passenger, that he had been as drunk as a
> billy goat for four days and had been having a whale of a time scaring the
> living daylights out of his voyagers. His condition was conspicuously un-
> changed. When we cast off at eight a.m., he sent a boy below for a bottle of
> rum and two beat-up tin cups and I drank faster than he did while he told me
> that this tide rip where the Caribbean joined the Atlantic was likely the most
> perilous stretch of water in the seven seas . . .[123]

Once she was on shore, she relaxed, however, and did not even mind sleeping, along with the Gibneys' five cats, on what ordinarily served them as a bed: a thin cotton mattress on top of stacked lumber. Describing her adventure to Lowell, she wrote of her carefree hosts: "They live in a shack with nothing at all and they spend their entire time (and they've been here a year and a half) reading when they are not looking at fish through diving masks. They fish and they swim and they are probably the happiest people I've ever seen. I couldn't have asked for better conversation." [124]

The weekend at the Gibneys' was a pleasant interlude, but it hardly made up for the long days spent working out the terms of the divorce settlement with her lawyer and then waiting for Lowell to sign the divorce papers. She told Lowell that the least disagreeable grounds for divorce appeared to be desertion; if she merely claimed incompatibility, she would be forced to say damaging things about his character that would not be pleasant for either of them.[125] Coaxing him to sign promptly the papers that would grant her the sum of six thousand dollars, to be paid in a single installment, she wrote:

> I am the only divorcee-to-be on the island who is married to a civilized man;
> or alas, perhaps I should state it another way and should say I am the only one
> whose husband wants to get rid of her as quickly as possible. But seeing them

all, I cannot help feeling that in spite of all my hideous behavior in the first year of our separation, we have behaved better on the whole than most people I know.

I want us both to marry again, don't you? We'll be so much wiser and so much calmer. It is my ambition to live the rest of my life at a low pitch.[126]

One of the most difficult things about the six weeks she spent in the Virgin Islands was the fact that this was the first time she had been separated from her therapist, Dr. Sherfey, on whom she had become very dependent. Having to deal with the psychological pressures of her impending divorce and finding herself in the company of people who had little to do and who consequently spent a good deal of time drinking, Stafford began to drink heavily again. After receiving a candid report from her patient about her activities, Dr. Sherfey was alarmed, especially when she read about Stafford's weekend at the Gibneys'. "Your first letter sounded like bad news," she wrote to Jean Stafford. "You have a perfectly terrific job to do staying away from those perfectly charming, perfectly indolent and perfectly urbane people. They really are not much different from the same type here. Try to rise above them and build a barrier between yourself and them, and stay away from coca-cola as if it were rattlesnake venom. Remember, you do not have to associate with them and have an excellent chance to test out your powers of independence from other people."[127] Dr. Sherfey was so alarmed by Stafford's letter that, on the same day she wrote her own letter, she also dispatched this telegram: "Pull yourself together and take it easy and say no to everybody. Live your life not theirs. Nothing is more important. I expect you to do it. Keep writing."[128] Although Dr. Sherfey did not mention the word *alcohol* either in her telegram or her letter, her intent was clear: she wanted her patient to avoid the company of people like the Gibneys for whom relaxing and drinking were synonymous. In a subsequent letter, written a month later, Dr. Sherfey assured her that there was no harm in taking something like phenobarbital to help her sleep, but she added, "Alcohol and Jean Lowell is another story." In response to Stafford's negative remarks about the tropics, she said with humor, "Not to like the tropics is no deep-seated neurotic manifestation stemming from an unresolved oedipus complex," and reminding her that she had a tendency to be hypochondriacal, she suggested that the physical malaise Stafford had described was probably caused by tension rather than "some obscure tropical fever." Then, revealing how much this difficult but fascinating patient had come to mean to her, Dr. Sherfey concluded, "Remember, transferences work both ways, and I sincerely want you back in one piece."[129]

During her stay in the Virgin Islands, Stafford got very little reading or writing done. She did begin to read Dante for the first time, no doubt remembering how Lowell and Robert Penn Warren used to lock the door in the office of the *Southern Review* from twelve to two to read Dante together. It is not clear whether she actually wrote "Pax Vobiscum," a story that appeared in the *New Yorker* the next year, while she was in St. Thomas, but it is obvious that she incorporated her own negative impressions of the island into the story. Although she was willing to concede that her impressions of the Virgin Islands were colored by her own melancholy circumstances,[130] instead of dwelling on the lush beauty of the island, she writes in this story of a "horrid stillness" lying over the island; of "puny" cats who have fed on the lizards and sleep "stupefied"; of tall guinea grass that hisses; and of wood doves that "sing sadly."[131] Sitting idle as they wait for their divorces, the white women who have come to the island spend their "six weeks' quarantine, with nothing in the world to do but bathe in the sun and sea, and drink, and haunt the shops for tax-free bargains in French perfume."[132] But there is a darker side to the life on the island, which pits rich whites against poor blacks, masters against houseboys, islanders against temporary visitors, men against women. A woman named Mrs. Otis from Massachusetts comes to understand this darker side of island life when the best friend of her genial host invents a grizzly tale to amuse the guests: he claims to have served a perfectly cooked ten-and-a-half-pound black "pickaninny" who had perished in a fire. This tall tale provokes laughter from the guests, but Mrs. Otis identifies with the black houseboy she fears has overheard the vicious tale. After reading this bleak story in the *New Yorker* the following year, Dr. Sherfey, attributing the morbid tone of the story to the state of mind of its author, wrote to Stafford: "The degree to which you can write *only* about the hidden pathological tortures of man's soul is the degree of your own pathology. The degree to which you can write about those aspects of life which make it good is the degree to which life has become good to you and after all, that is the only purpose of our relationship."[133] Later, when the story was reprinted in Stafford's *Collected Stories* under the title "A Modest Proposal," Stafford chose to emphasize its connection with the satirical essay of Jonathan Swift.

When Stafford departed for the Virgin Islands, Chris Merillat, an editor from *Time* whom she had been dating that spring, accompanied her to the airport, and he met her at the airport on her return. But even though she brought a photograph of him to the Virgin Islands and placed it conspicuously on the bureau in her hotel room, she had no illusions that he was in love with her.[134] Nor did she still wish she was married to Lowell once the divorce had been granted. In June she met Lowell briefly in New York and learned that he was no longer seeing Gertrude Buckman. "He is an altogether magnificent creature and I am so glad that I never have to see him again that I could dance," she told Peter Taylor. "He has a new girl in Washington (very much older than he, natch)." [135] To Lowell she plaintively wrote, however, "I find *no* advantages in not being married, not one. I think it is infinitely *more* complicated besides being the most miserably lonely nightmare I've ever known. What fun is it for a girl to meet Dr. Cohn on Tuesday at the Plaza and the rest of the time to see fairies and get passed at by the husbands of one's friends." [136]

With her return to New York, the old struggles began again: how to divide her time between work and socializing; whom to see and whom to avoid; above all, how to get through days of unbearable loneliness and disconnectedness. "I am now divorced, at loose ends, trying as hard as I can to pull my life together into some sort of order, but it is a vast undertaking," she wrote to Joe Chay in July. She explained that she would not be going west since each visit there had been "more dreadful" than the one before, and agreeing with an observation he had made that she could not run away from her past much longer, she remarked, "Alas, alas, I live within it and if I *could* run away it would be ever so much better for me." [137]

Although ordinarily she hated to travel, she found it a pleasant distraction that summer to visit Newport, Rhode Island, on assignment for the *New Yorker.* After she had settled into her hotel, "a white, summery Victorian assemblage of wings and balconies," [138] she began to wander the streets of the quaint town, stopping first to read about Newport's history in the Redwood Library and Atheneum, an elegant Greek Revival building tastefully furnished and filled with books and with portraits of local and national statesmen. She visited the famed Touro Synagogue, the Cliff Walk, and the "magnetically monstrous" mansions of Newport, whose expansive lawns, she said, go right down to the ocean and whose windows "command a prospect of all this gallant scene of endless breakers and vine-covered promontories and shaggy reefs and violet bays and spinnakers of yachts bellied by a wind that is not felt on land, where tea is being poured." [139] Later, in one of the very mansions whose exterior she had admired, she was served tea in an extraordinary drawing room filled with priceless porcelain and silver and gold. Though she admitted that at times the "glass of fashion" in Newport has given back "an image dreadfully embossed and hideously overlaid with affectation," she stoutly maintained nevertheless that every effort should be made to preserve Newport's splendid mansions and monuments. [140] The piece she wrote about Newport, one of three travel pieces she would write for the *New Yorker* during the next sixteen months, is a wonderful example of her exquisitely fluid prose style and her ability to pile detail upon detail to make a place come alive. "Practically everybody here is in transports of jealous despair over the wonders of your Newport piece. What a job!" Brendan Gill wrote to her from the *New Yorker* offices the week the article appeared.[141]

Two short stories by Stafford were published in September of 1948, "The Bleeding Heart" in the *Partisan Review* and "A Summer Day" in the *New Yorker*. The protagonists of both stories are displaced young people who find themselves in a threatening, alien environment. Rose Fabrizio, a "Mexican girl from the West," lives alone in a rented room in Concord, Massachusetts, and dreams of being adopted by an elderly gentleman she sees in the reading room of the public library. However, her illusions are shattered when she discovers how grotesque his life really is. His neck is disfigured by an ugly wen, and he lives with his senile mother and her malevolent parrot in rooms that smell of ordure. When he invites Rose to a movie, she flees in panic from this "elderly roué" who has asked her to call him "Daddy."[142] Jim Littlefield, the orphaned eight-year-old Cherokee Indian who is the protagonist of "A Summer Day," also finds himself in an alien environment when he is sent from Missouri to a desolate Indian orphanage in Oklahoma after his grandmother dies. Hot and thirsty after a long train trip, he dares not drink the water in the orphanage when he learns that many of the children have become ill after doing so, and although he has been planning to run away as soon as night falls, he is so exhausted by the heat and his sorrow that he lies down on the "sickly grass" in the yard and falls asleep.[143]

Grim evocations of loneliness and despair, both "The Bleeding Heart" and "A Summer Day" appear to reflect Stafford's own profound feelings of alienation and despair during the period when the stories were written. Soon after these stories were published, she told Bill Mock, ". . . I still write to no one, seeming unable to shake off the melancholy that lies on me like a disease." She complained that she felt "stifled by the terrible rush of time," the sense that she was growing older "without ever maturing." A recent visit to Greenwich Village had made her fear that she was beginning to resemble the many "aging adolescents" she observed there, "all gone to seed, all embittered and self-despising." Even though the spectacle of these wasted lives depressed her inordinately, she mused, "But if one is rootless, where does one go to live *but* New York?"[144] Although she wrote cheerfully to Lowell that fall about her social activities—seeing Randall Jarrell at a cocktail party for the Sitwells, having dinner with Elizabeth Bishop, attending the Yale-Princeton football game, watching the election returns with "the big wheels at Time Inc.," planning a trip to Boston in December with Alfred Kazin—in truth she was desperately lonely most of the time.[145]

As she wrestled with her novel *In the Snowfall* that winter, producing draft after draft of prose that dissatisfied her, she sometimes blamed her lack of productivity on the fact that her apartment was so noisy. To escape the sounds of the children from the music school practicing the piccolo, she would take her notebooks to a small private library nearby, but she found that instead of writing, she spent most of her time there reading novels by Edith Wharton. In Stafford's essay called "Truth and the Novelist," she itemizes the numerous ruses she invented to avoid having to sit down and write, from visiting the chimpanzee at the Central Park Zoo to walking across the Brooklyn Bridge. "There were some stretches when I wrote for ten hours a day," she said, "but these were followed by long intervals when I avoided the sight of the manuscripts on my desk as if they were the source of a physical pain and I fled my rooms, seeking a fresh affection but firmly convinced that I was really looking for a way to write this novel which had been scheduled for publication numerous times."[146] The noise in her apartment finally drove her to seek a quieter one, and at last she found a larger but more costly apartment that had a fireplace, large bookcases, and a view of the East River. After she moved into her new apartment at 32 East 68th Street, however, she was further distracted from working on her novel since, to pay the rent, she felt she had to work instead on short stories.

Discouraged by the fact that she seemed unable to make any real progress on her novel, Stafford sometimes feared that her counseling sessions with Dr. Sherfey had damaged her creative abilities. "There are times," she wrote to Mary Lee, "when I feel that it's psychiatry that has destroyed my gift, but perhaps the gift isn't gone yet, I don't know. If it *has,* God knows what will become of me because that is the only thing in the world I have."[147]

Beginning to plan a trip to Europe not only to write some articles for the *New Yorker* but to refresh her memory about certain places she wished to include in her book, she sought a way to escape temporarily from New York. All of her traveling plans temporarily came to a halt, however, when she learned that Lowell had suffered a mental breakdown and had been admitted to Baldpate, a small private mental hospital in Massachusetts. At Yaddo that winter Lowell's behavior had become increasingly erratic, and he had organized a movement among some of the artists there to oust its director, Elizabeth Ames, who he claimed was a Communist sympathizer. He had also become obsessed once again with Catholic ritual during this period, and he had begun to claim that his marriage to Stafford was still valid since the Catholic Church did not recognize civil divorce. Rumors of Lowell's odd behavior and heavy drinking had reached Stafford in December, prompting her to write to him at Yaddo, "Is it true that you are drinking too much and going to pieces . . .?"[148] By April his behavior had become so bizarre that Allen Tate felt obliged to warn Elizabeth Hardwick, with whom Lowell had become intimate at Yaddo, about Cal's capacity for violence. "Cal is dangerous; there are definite homicidal implications in his world, particularly toward women and children. He has a purification mania, which frequently takes homicidal form. You must not let him in your apartment," Tate wrote to Hardwick on April 4 after Lowell had paid him a visit.[149] Subsequently, while visiting Peter and Eleanor Taylor in Bloomington, Indiana, Lowell became so disruptive that Peter Taylor summoned Lowell's mother, Merrill Moore, and Lowell's friend, John Thompson. They finally managed to get him on a plane bound for Boston and then had him admitted to Baldpate.[150]

After hearing the news of Lowell's breakdown and hospitalization, Stafford wrote to Mary Lee, "I am going to stay here where Dr. Sherfey is and finally somehow liberate myself from my guilt over that poor boy." She told Mary Lee that Lowell's breakdown confirmed her own suspicions that neither she nor Cal was completely to blame for the failure of their marriage. ". . . it was not my fault and it was not his fault . . . we both had been sick from childhood and neither of us was to blame," she said, asking Mary Lee "completely to forgive Cal."[151] According to Ian Hamilton, Allen Tate later claimed that Stafford was responsible for spreading the word to the New York literati about Lowell's breakdown. If these allegations were correct, her behavior at this time is nevertheless understandable. Having suspected that most people believed the breakup of her marriage to Lowell was her fault rather than his, she could not have helped feeling somewhat vindicated when Lowell's breakdown made public what she had suspected all along: that Cal was not merely a high-strung genius but an individual with psychological problems that were, perhaps, more serious than her own.

In June Stafford began to make final preparations to sail for Europe. "My book goes so badly that I am in despair half the time and my insomnia has returned full force," she wrote to Mary Lee on June 10.[152] Her still unfinished novel had been causing her so much anxiety that she welcomed a trip to Europe on assignment for the *New Yorker*. Just before she sailed on the *Coronia* on July 21, she announced to Mary Lee, "I mean to make a fundamental change in my life when I return, but where I shall go and what I shall do, I don't know."[153] Meanwhile, her itinerary was planned: she would attend the Edinburgh Festival and would also revisit Germany to see firsthand what changes the war had wrought in the country where she had spent her Wanderjahr thirteen years earlier. The week after she sailed for Europe, Lowell married Elizabeth Hardwick in Massachusetts; and by the time Stafford returned from Europe the following fall, he was a patient in the same psychiatric hospital where she herself had been a patient for almost a year.

Nine

The Catherine Wheel
Fall 1949–Spring 1952

Man's life is a cheat and a disappointment;
All things are unreal, unreal or disappointing . . .

—T. S. ELIOT, *MURDER IN THE CATHEDRAL*

. . . all that she had had, and all that she had missed were lost together, and were twice lost in this landslide of remembered loss.

—KATHERINE ANNE PORTER, "THEFT"

WHEN JEAN STAFFORD sailed for Europe during the summer of 1949, she still did not feel completely secure about her status as a writer. Nevertheless, she was no longer the novice who had arrived in Europe in 1936 with aspirations to become a writer but grave doubts about whether she would ever succeed. She had published two well-received novels, twice had been the recipient of a prestigious Guggenheim Fellowship, and had also published short stories and articles in literary quarterlies such as the *Partisan Review,* the *Kenyon Review,* and the *Sewanee Review* as well as in more popular magazines such as the *New Yorker, Mademoiselle,* and *Vogue.* In 1949 alone three of her stories appeared in the *New Yorker:* "The Cavalier" in February, "Pax Vobiscum" in July, and "Polite Conversation" in August. The latter two stories were products of her marriage to Lowell, while "The Cavalier" was the first of a series of stories that referred back to her first trip to Europe and the months she had spent in Heidelberg in 1936 and 1937. The protagonist of "The Cavalier," a lonely American college student from Arizona, goes to Heidelberg to study Anglo-Saxon, as Stafford herself had done in 1936. Now, in 1949, thirteen years after her *Wanderjahr,* she would be able to revisit the very places in Heidelberg that she had recently described in this story. Once she had fulfilled her obligations to the *New Yorker* by writing an account of the Edinburgh Festival, she would finally have the opportunity to retrace her steps through Heidelberg, as she had longed to do ever since she had left this quaint German city in 1937.

In an article entitled "Why I Don't Get Around Much Anymore," which appeared in *Esquire* in 1975, Stafford presents her "case against travel": "Getting there is about as much fun as riding a condemned roller coaster and *there,* if revisited, is unrecognizably altered for the worse or, if seen for the first time, is having an unseasonable heat wave or a general strike." Admitting that she is a nervous traveler at best, she points out, however, that after returning from each of her trips, she always realizes that, despite inevitable mishaps along the way, she has been "exhilarated and ennobled" by the things she has seen. As a result, she says, she is always able to persuade herself that her assorted misadventures en route had "really been larks."[1]

The two articles in the *New Yorker* describing her trip abroad in 1949 reflect her ambivalence about travel, focusing as they do both on its pains and pleasures. The first article, "Letter from Edinburgh," summarized the events that took place at the "multi-ring circus" of the Edinburgh Festival. She complained about the "costly, incompetent, well-intentioned hotels, slowly serving tattle-gray food that would stop a clock in Liggett's"; the "three hours daily of total abstinence" when the pubs and the wine merchants' shops were closed; and the vulgarity of local songs and souvenirs—tobacco pouches in the shape of bagpipes, powder pouches in the shape of tam-o'-shanters, pillows with appliquéd figures in kilts and balmorals, embroidered with the legend "Frae Bonnie Scotland."[2] Although she described many things she found offensive in Edinburgh, she also spoke positively about the handsome ancient buildings; the demonstrations put on by the Queen's Royal Lancers and the Scots Guards; and the various performances of plays, music, and ballet she attended. "One knows with certainty that the festival is here to stay forever," she concluded, "getting better and better, and if the nettles tease and sting, they do so in a garden full of songbirds."[3] Though the article ends with a flourish, most of the writing is somewhat perfunctory, suggesting that she was less enthralled by Edinburgh than she had been by Newport and would be by Heidelberg. The only time we glimpse the writer herself in this piece is when she observes about a popular Scottish love song she had heard: "This is the sort of thing that chills the blood of a person who at the age of five had to wear a taffetta Mackenzie hair ribbon and sing 'Comin' thro' the Rye' for the pleasure of a Presbyterian pastor in California recently uprooted from Dundee."[4]

More successful than the "Letter from Edinburgh" is the "Letter from Germany" that appeared in the *New Yorker* in December. Beginning with a description of a rat who invaded her sparsely furnished room in Nuremburg, Stafford provided a moving portrait of postwar Germany, depicting the "massive havoc of Frankfort, Darmstadt, and Wurzburg," their buildings "mangled, chewed up, smashed to smithereens." Amidst the rubble she noted testaments to the past: a free-standing staircase, "snarls of steel, scabby with black rust," the "exposed entrails of a burst tower" that rose "in a wrathful tangle above the tops of the surrounding linden trees."[5] The devastation is emphasized by the comparisons she makes throughout between the splendors of prewar Germany that she had observed in the thirties and the ruins she witnessed when she returned there in 1949. Although she was aware that there were Germans who were still viciously anti-Semitic and that almost no German was willing to admit culpability for the atrocities of the past, she believed, nevertheless, that it was easy, even normal, in the face of the ruins she encountered everywhere, "to slip into pity for this beat-up nation" that was "uncomfortable, impoverished, impaled on ugliness."[6]

Heidelberg alone, with streets unmarred by rubble, seemed reassuringly familiar, its landmarks vividly recalling to her the year she had spent there, but she sensed that a great transformation had taken place in this city as well. At the Hotel Haarlass, on whose veranda she and Hightower used to drink beer as they watched the Nazi limousines and the Reichswehr lorries speeding by on the highway, the spirit of the patrons was "as flaccid as the tablecloths, the gaiety was as thin and insubstantial as the keys to the hotel bedrooms . . . and hope, ambition, and faith were as ragged as the ruins."[7] Just as she began her "Letter from Germany" with the horrifying image of an invading rat, so she concluded the piece with another horrifying reference to a living creature: a monkey she saw in the zoo at Frankfurt who was being put into the mouth of a hideous rhinoceros. Powerful indeed is the image of the monkey breaking away, trailing its leash behind it, and of its master, yelling furiously as he raced after the monkey "through the bright sunlight, between the brilliant flowers, underneath the lovely weeping-willow trees."[8] The image of the master and the monkey suggests both the sadism of the Germans and their misery after the war.

Stafford's return to Germany also resulted in two short stories with a German setting, "The Maiden" and "The Echo and the Nemesis." In "The Maiden" she focuses on the coexistence of German brutality, civility, and opulence. At a dinner party given by Americans who live in postwar Heidelberg, the guests sit at a table laden with lovely relics of the past: cut-glass wine decanters embossed with silver, heavy silverware, and Dresden china fruit plates.[9] Stafford's protagonist, an American journalist named Evan Leckie who has just arrived in Heidelberg after spending a month in Nuremburg, is almost able to forget the havoc he has witnessed and the squalor of the Occupation as he observes his hostess's resplendent dinner table and her beautiful garden. However, the illusion of peace and harmony is shattered when one of the guests, a German lawyer who claims to have been an enemy of the

Third Reich, describes the day twenty years earlier when he had proposed to his wife: after witnessing the execution of his first client, he had called up his sweetheart and insisted that they get married immediately since he was already appropriately dressed in a Prince Albert and a top hat. Although earlier in the evening Leckie had empathized with the German lawyer and his lovely wife and had wondered "what Eumenides had driven this pair to hardship, humiliation, and exile" from Nuremberg, he now comprehends what a great gulf separates Americans from those Germans who "joyfully dance a *Totentanz.*"[10] If the gleaming wine decanters on his hostess's table represent the elegant trappings of German civilization, the great knife of the guillotine is a reminder of the brutal underside of German life. Calling the guillotine in her story "the Maiden," the name given to the guillotine she had just seen in Edinburgh, Stafford establishes in this chilling tale a subtle connection between decapitation and defloration, between innocence and guilt, between life and death.

It is the Heidelberg she remembered rather than postwar Heidelberg that Stafford uses as the setting for "The Echo and the Nemesis," another of her stories that was included in Martha Foley's *Best American Short Stories* series. Just as the stories of Henry James such as "Daisy Miller" and "The Aspern Papers" are enriched by their European settings, so this memorable psychological tale is enriched by its descriptions of Heidelberg, where two Americans, Sue Ledbetter and Ramona Dunn, have come to study philology at the university. The story focuses on the psychological problems of Ramona, a compulsive eater who invents a beautiful dead sister, representing the thin self she has buried under layers of fat in order to avoid sexual entanglements. In this memorable short story, there is yet another pair of doubles: Ramona and her friend Sue. These two characters appear to represent, respectively, the reclusive Jean Stafford and the Jean Stafford who had longed to be popular. Ramona enjoys talking about "the vagaries of certain Old High Franconian verbs . . . or the linguistic influence Eleanor of Aquitaine had exerted on the English Court," while Sue, a serious student as well, nevertheless longs "for beaux and parties, and conversations about them."[11] In an article she called "The Art of Accepting Oneself," which appeared in *Vogue* two years after "The Echo and the Nemesis" was published in the *New Yorker,* Stafford speaks of her own conflicting states of mind: "Ever since they graduated from baby talk to shape words, my two minds have been in steadfast dispute over the custody of their spawn of satellite minds; ceaselessly they argue such issues as country life versus city life, the east versus the west, society versus solitude . . ."[12] "The Echo and the Nemesis" dramatizes these two conflicting selves by contrasting the attitudes of Ramona and Sue.

Several other issues that were important in Stafford's life are dramatized in this story. Ramona's compulsive overeating may allude to Stafford's own dread of getting fat and also her own addiction to alcohol. Drawing, perhaps, on her own craving for alcohol, Stafford writes of Ramona, who obsessively devours a third piece of cake to calm her nerves:

> Did Sue have any idea what it was like to be ruled by food and half driven out of one's mind until one dreamed of it and had at last no other ambition but to eat incessantly with an appetite that grew and grew until one saw oneself, in nightmares, as nothing but an enormous mouth and tongue, trembling lasciviously? Did she know the terror and the remorse that followed on the heels of it when one slyly sneaked the lion's share of buttered toast at tea? [13]

Another function of the double protagonist in this story is to contrast the face Jean Stafford saw in the mirror at the time the story was written with that of her earlier self when she first visited Heidelberg. Ramona's photograph of her "twin sister," a young girl with "pensive eyes" whose face "wore a look of lovely wonder and remoteness, as if she were all disconnected spirit," [14] is similar to the one in Stafford's own graduation photograph, taken before her beautiful face was irreparably damaged in the car accident. And Ramona's face, whose "thin, fair skin" is "subject to disfiguring afflictions, now hives, now eczema, now impetigo," as well as her "fine, pale hair that was abused once a week by a *Friseur* who baked it with an iron into dozens of horrid little snails," [15] is an accurate if uncharitable representation of what Stafford looked like during the period in which the story was written. A parallel story to Henry James's "The Jolly Corner," this remarkable short story shows Stafford's persona confronting an earlier version of Stafford herself.

Although Stafford had told Mary Lee before she departed for Europe that she meant to make "a fundamental change" in her life after her trip abroad,[16] she felt as rootless and as impoverished as ever when she returned to New York. Furthermore, though she produced draft after draft of the opening chapters of *In the Snowfall,* she still felt dissatisfied with what she had written. Later, recalling her frustrating struggles to write this novel, she said:

> . . . as I worked on the suicide story, I accumulated twenty pounds of manuscript and destroyed an equal amount. I completed two versions, one in the first person and one in third; I tried and rejected the omniscient observer; I made an effort to imitate Dostoevsky's method in *The Brothers Karamazov,* the use of a fellow citizen to record the lives of the principals. By actual count, I wrote twenty-three versions of the first chapter with twenty-three different accentuations. But the book continued to be a mess, heavy, flat, oppressively factual and cumbrously emotional. Something ailed my prose, and all my

rhythms were off; I was writing about people I knew as well as I knew myself, about a setting that was as immediately before my senses as the room in which I sat at my typewriter, about a sequence of events that I had thought about and talked about a hundred times. And even so, every page, every sentence, bore the signature of a prevaricator . . .[17]

She realized several years later that she had had so much difficulty writing this novel because she was too close to her material, too wrenched by memories of her unhappy years in Boulder and especially the suicide of Lucy McKee, to be sufficiently detached.

Lonely, depressed, and frustrated by her failure, she gladly accepted whatever social invitations came her way in order to escape the solitude of her apartment. It was at one of the many parties she attended that fall that she met a tall, handsome, affable, recently divorced man who seemed to have all of the "right" credentials. A Yale graduate and the son of a college professor, Oliver Jensen was then a very well paid member of the *Life* editorial staff. Physically, he reminded her somewhat of Lowell,[18] and if he lacked Lowell's brilliance and intensity, she nevertheless found Oliver Jensen to be a pleasant and attentive companion. Oliver Jensen, in turn, thought her "marvellously amusing and handsome"[19] and very intelligent. In his company, Stafford felt more desirable and coddled than she had felt in some time. Instead of bemoaning her fate as a solitary woman in her letters to Lowell, as she was wont to do in the past, she now reported exuberantly how much she had enjoyed the Yale-Princeton football game at the Yale stadium.

Having made prior arrangements to go to Paris and Rome that fall, Jensen left for Europe in November. Stafford's loneliness after his departure prompted her to write to Elizabeth Ames, the director of Yaddo, to see if it might be possible to spend some time there that winter. Complaining about how difficult she was finding it to get any work done in New York, she said:

> I have finally given up: I *cannot* work in New York. I live like a hermit and that doesn't work—I'm not gregarious, but I also cannot bear total solitude—and this year the difficulties have been aggravated by my knowledge that Cal is just at the end of my street in Payne Whitney and that at any moment I may encounter him or his wife. I accomplished next to nothing since I've been back from Europe and I'm almost desperate. The book simply *must* be done by April and since it is so nearly in shape, I'm sure a month of quiet in the country would do the trick.[20]

Ames warmly invited her to join the small community of artists who were in residence at Yaddo that December, but Stafford delayed her departure from New York because she was suffering from asthma and also had to have

some additional procedures performed on her nose. On December 27, she finally boarded the train for Saratoga Springs. "I am bringing my ice-skates in
the hope that there will be someone there who can teach me to use them," she
wrote to Ames.[21] As it turned out, her stay there was to be so brief that she
never ventured forth on the ice.

Stafford was less ill at ease at Yaddo than she had been during her first stay
there in 1943, but she did not find the artist colony any more conducive to
getting her writing done than before. By the middle of January, unnerved by
her inability to settle down and make any progress on her novel, she invited
Jensen to come and pay her a visit. She told him that she realized "knights in
shining armor still must inhabit a practical world"; nevertheless, she hoped
that he could arrange to get away from the city for a few days.[22] Shortly after
she wrote to him, an incident occurred that made her even more anxious to see
him: one of the guests at Yaddo, a North Carolinian whose "psychopathology"
was exacerbated by the benzedrine and alcohol that he consumed "in stun-
ning quantities and at a rate faster than light," almost went "totally off his
rocker." Stafford explained to Jensen that witnessing this man's behavior had
left her badly shaken: "I should warn you, if I have not already done so, that
my middle name is Psychosomatic and when I am badly frightened, as I was
the other night, I go into asthma, insomnia, fits of trembling and an inability
to eat. Violence really makes me sick, and the world has got to stop being
violent right this minute." Only his "clowning letter" and the anticipation of
seeing him, she said, had reminded her that "all of life is not hideous and that
Yaddo doesn't constitute the world . . ." What she preferred to think was that
"there is only one world, flower-filled and filled with sun, where Eintritt to
hobgoblins is bestimmt verboten."[23]

According to Jensen, "things moved much too fast" after he arrived at
Yaddo; and in retrospect, he believed that he and Stafford had been "foolish
and impetuous" when they decided impulsively to leave Yaddo together and
get married in New York City.[24] Just as she had left the University of Iowa
impulsively in 1938 and had married Lowell impulsively in 1940, so Stafford
left Yaddo in the middle of her term of residency there, without notifying
Ames of her intentions. Jensen later confessed to Mary Lee that he had decided to marry her sister despite the fact that Dr. Sherfey had tried to warn
him that Jean was not stable enough to take such a step. "But ardour transformed each of us, in the other's eyes, into the image we had sought," he commented sadly.[25]

On January 28, 1950, Jean Stafford and Oliver Jensen were married in New
York City in the chapel of Christ Church, a handsome Methodist church located on Park Avenue. A large group of their friends attended the wedding

reception, which was given by Lowell's friend from St. Mark's and Harvard, Blair Clark, and his wife Holly. Blair Clark provided a tangible link with the past since he had also been present when Stafford had married Lowell in 1940. Writing to Lowell before the wedding to inform him of her forthcoming marriage, Stafford observed pensively, "This letter is impossible to write, since there lies behind it so very much emotion and so very much memory and about all I can say is God bless us all." [26]

Immediately after the wedding, Stafford and her "knight in shining armor" left the cold Northeast for a honeymoon in Haiti, a world that was literally "flower-filled and filled with sun." From the Hotel La Citadelle in Port Au Prince, she wrote to Ames at Yaddo: "This isn't going to be more than a note because Oliver and I are still dazed and amazed at what we have done and it will be weeks yet before I shall alight. It is really only to tell you that I am indescribably happy as I never dreamed I could be and my joy is at once heady and grave. Oliver is everything to live for and to be healthy for." [27]

Stafford's description of her honeymoon in "Enchanted Island," an article published in the May issue of *Mademoiselle,* is full of good cheer. Most of the article is devoted to her recollections of her "land-locked" childhood in the foothills of the Rockies, during which she inhabited in her fancy "an island in the bright blue sea," but she begins the article with a vivid description of the throng of natives in Port Au Prince. In the same issue of *Mademoiselle* there is a photograph of Stafford and Jensen sitting on deck chairs on a patio overlooking a stretch of beach in Jamaica, where they went after leaving Haiti. Sporting a straw hat anchored firmly in place by a checkered bandana, Stafford is gazing at her attentive husband.

After they returned from their honeymoon, Stafford and Jensen lived temporarily in his apartment in Manhattan. Like a society matron announcing her daughter's marriage, Stafford sent to friends and even casual acquaintances an engraved announcement of her marriage as well as a card announcing that "Mr. and Mrs. Oliver Jensen" would be "at home after the fifteenth of February at 222 East Seventy-first Street." Intent on informing all of the people who might have known about her separation from Lowell, her breakdown, or her divorce that she had at last begun her life anew, she sent an announcement of her marriage to Oskar Diethelm, the head of psychiatry at Payne Whitney, and to Lowell's friends at the *Kenyon Review.*

Almost immediately, Stafford realized that her precipitous marriage to Jensen had been a mistake. Recalling their unhappy union, her friend Dorothea Straus would later write, "She and Jensen were like a couple cast in a performance of *Who's Afraid of Virginia Woolf* for summer stock. The play was to have a short run." [28] Had Stafford realized how short-lived her marriage to

Jensen would be, she might have spared herself the trouble and expense of sending out those engraved announcements.

Since she finally recognized that she would never be able to complete *In the Snowfall,* settling into her new life as Mrs. Oliver Jensen was, at first, a welcome distraction. Her unsuccessful struggles with the novel were the subject of a lecture she gave at Wellesley College that April. This talk would serve as the basis for two different articles that she published subsequently, "Truth and the Novelist" and "Truth in Fiction." At Wellesley she described the difficulties she had encountered in writing a novel based on "a nightmare incident" in her life, and her decision ultimately to burn the numerous drafts she had produced when she reluctantly was forced to conclude that the work, despite all the effort she had expended on it, was "pedestrian, malicious, and transparent, with lies told right and left." [29]

Even though Stafford failed to complete *In the Snowfall,* she was beginning to attract a good deal of attention as a short story writer. In May of 1950, one of her finest short stories, "A Country Love Story," appeared in the *New Yorker.* Included in the O. Henry Prize stories of 1951, "A Country Love Story" is one of her best and best known short stories. Especially after it was reprinted in Robert Penn Warren and Albert Erskine's excellent, widely circulated, and frequently reprinted anthology, *Short Story Masterpieces,* the story reached a wide audience. Set in Damariscotta Mills and focusing on despair and loss, "A Country Love Story" is related in theme and setting to *The Catherine Wheel,* the novel Stafford began that year after she finally had laid the still uncompleted manuscript of *In the Snowfall* aside.

During the summer of 1950, Stafford and Jensen rented a house in Wilton, Connecticut, while repairs were being made on a large old colonial house they had purchased in Westport, Connecticut. Stafford had married someone who reminded her of Lowell; now she was also planning to live in a house that resembled her dream house in Damariscotta. She was able to complete some short stories that summer and also made headway on a new novel she had begun, but her work was interrupted when her sister Mary Lee arrived for a three-week visit. This was the first time that a member of Stafford's family had visited her since she had fled the West in 1936. Although she was closer to Mary Lee than to any other member of her family, the visit could not help but arouse both bitter memories of her past and feelings of guilt about her father, whom she had not visited since her mother's death in 1947. Dividing his time between his two eldest daughters, this raging Lear had continued to be a source of tribulation to his family. In her letters to Jean, Mary Lee spoke about both how difficult he was and how sad observing him made her feel. Stafford was probably touched when her father had deerskin gloves made for Oliver from a deer he himself had killed; she probably chuckled when she read in her father's letters to her his invective about the "Boobiana" of the West or about the "S.O.B.'s" who were responsible for the economic problems of the country; she might even have been faintly amused when he asked her if she would recommend a literary agent to him or suggest which publisher might be interested in his manuscripts; however, she could not bear to be reminded of the fact that she was derelict in her duties to her aging father. Hence, she must have been annoyed when Mary Lee wrote not only to thank her and Oliver for their hospitality but to urge her to visit their father.

Always anxious about her lack of productivity, Stafford undoubtedly was pleased that December when two of her short stories were published: "The Nemesis" (later renamed "The Echo and the Nemesis" in her *Collected Stories*) appeared in the *New Yorker* and "Old Flaming Youth" in *Harper's Bazaar*. The latter was the first of six short stories by Stafford that had a Western setting and a female narrator. Although she did not choose to include "Old Flaming Youth" in her *Collected Stories*, it is similar in tone and style to stories such as "The Healthiest Girl in Town," "Bad Characters," and "A Reading Problem" that appear in this volume under the heading "Cowboys and Indians and Magic Mountains." Mary Ellen Williams Walsh has pointed out that as these other stories do, "Old Flaming Youth" reveals the influence on Jean Stafford's prose of Mark Twain in her use of vernacular and her commentary on the cruelty human beings can inflict on one another.[30] Set in a dreary town in the West, the story describes the encounter between two middle-class sisters, Sue and Janie Thomas, and the much less affluent Ferguson twins, who had "quit high school in their sophomore year because they didn't like to get up early in the morning."[31] The twins care for their cantankerous old grandfather all day while their mother, a divorcée who owns a millinery shop, is at the store. Stafford once observed to Lowell that as a result of her own troubled relationship with her father, in almost all of her stories "the father is either dead or cruelly driven away."[32] This story, however, abounds with father figures. Although there are two absent fathers, for both the Ferguson twins and the narrator are fatherless, Sue and Janie have an irascible stepfather whom they both dislike; and the Fergusons have a doddering old grandfather to whom they behave in a heartless fashion. It is clear that at some level these images of the father as absent, irascible, and doddering are bound up with Stafford's visions of her own father in his various guises. Sue and Janie turn in desperation to the Fergusons, the only girls their age who live nearby, seeking an alternative to school, which bores them, and wanting to avoid their dinner table, at which their irritable stepfather "every single night would fly off the handle about something."[33] The friendship is terminated, however, when one of the twins steals a gold bracelet from Janie and, more important, when the narrator and her sister witness how the grandfather is first mistreated by his heartless granddaughters and then is exiled to the County Home, an "awful poor farm out beyond the city limits where they still didn't have electricity and not a single tree or flower grew for miles around." [34] Reflecting Stafford's ambivalent feelings about her own father, this grim story, with its mixture of comedy and despair, is reminiscent not only of Mark Twain but of the stories of Flannery O'Connor and Malcolm Purdy. Buried now in the pages of *Harper's Bazaar,* "Old Flaming Youth" deserves a better fate than it was granted when Stafford chose to omit it from her *Collected Stories.*

During the summer of 1951, Stafford finally, with much trepidation, arranged to go to Colorado to see her father at Mary Lee's. She found the ten-day visit with him as harrowing as she had anticipated. Writing to Oliver from Hayden, she said the visit was so distressing that she needed to see Dr. Sherfey as soon as she returned to Connecticut: "I cannot wait to get home—indeed, I am almost wild—and I think maybe at last I shall be able to convey to Dr. Sherfey and to you exactly what the blight has been that has twisted and hallucinated me all my life, and perhaps you, Oliver, will finally understand my unnatural feelings towards my father—seeing him again, I am amazed that all of us did not commit suicide in our cradles. Maybe at last I'll get rid of some of the poison." [35]

So upset was she by this visit that she entered the hospital for a brief period after she returned east. Although she was ostensibly hospitalized because a hammertoe had caused her unbearable pain when she was out in Colorado, a letter she wrote to Mary Lee suggests that more than her toe and her grief about her father had caused her to retreat to the hospital, for in her letter she made snide remarks about Oliver as well. "He is in his proper element: he is Operating. Talking into two telephones at once, going to three cocktail parties a day, having dinner with important people late in the afternoon," she observed, and as she contemplated having to leave the hospital she said with despair, "I don't want to go. . . . I never want to leave this simplicity and the utter freedom of this small space in which there is nothing superfluous." [36] It is evident that at this juncture in her life, sequestering herself in a hospital room had begun to seem more appealing than living in the same house as Oliver Jensen.

The house in question was an elegant colonial built in 1810. It was located on Long Lots Road in Westport and was surrounded by four acres of land, replete with a small rose garden, peony beds, a large raspberry hedge, and a barn. Writing to Caroline Gordon from the hospital in September, Stafford described the house as "rather like the one in Damariscotta except that it is bigger and that for the most part it works," but she complained that the summer had been "a maddening procession of workmen," and she admitted that she was in the hospital "as much as a result of short temper as anything else."[37] Oliver Jensen later confided to Mary Lee that he had offered to purchase the house in Westport if Jean would agree not to divorce him, as she had been threatening to do almost from the first.[38] Although the house reminded her of the one in Damariscotta, this house was purchased not with Stafford's money but with Oliver's, and despite its spacious rooms and bucolic surroundings, she never enjoyed it as much as she had the other. At first, the idea of leaving New York City's "ceaseless bray and blast," its "abominable dirt," and its "ubiquitous coagulations of mortal creatures" had seemed attractive to Stafford. However, as she soon realized, Westport was hardly "the country." It is true that in its environs "there were farms with cows and silos, venerable houses and venerable stone walls; there were woods and dingles and rills, wild roses, song-birds, demure churches, tulip trees and fields of fragrant hay"; nevertheless, she soon grew to detest the "galloping contemporaneity of the hinterland" that also included "spanking new progressive schools, spanking new shopping centers and acres and acres of spanking new split-level ranch houses, in which dwelt former city dwellers with their spanking new children."[39]

In addition to criticizing Westport's subdivisions, she also complained about having to attend the stylized parties of the gentry, at which overdressed people inevitably ate too much, drank too much, stayed up too late, and engaged in "aimless prattle."[40] As did her contemporaries John Updike and John Cheever as well as her next-door neighbor in Westport, Peter De Vries, Stafford wrote trenchant satirical stories about the kind of social gatherings that typified the social life among the affluent exurbanites of Westport. Though Stafford's "Maggie Meriwether's Rich Experience" is set in France and "Beatrice Trueblood's Story" is set in Newport, it is evident that the groups of wealthy, sophisticated, but often tedious people she describes so wittily and venomously in these stories were types she observed firsthand at the parties she and Oliver regularly frequented in Westport.

It would be erroneous to conclude, however, that Stafford was disenchanted with everyone she met in Westport. Though she was often heard to make disparaging comments about the "station wagon set" there,[41] she formed close, enduring friendships with several people, especially with Peter De Vries and his wife Katinka. Very fond of the De Vries's daughter Emily, who died of leukemia several years later, she named one of the characters appearing in a number of her short stories Emily Vanderpool. In turn, a character resembling Stafford appears in Peter De Vries's *The Tunnel of Love* in the guise of Terry McBain, a young woman with hair "like corn silk" and a "full if somewhat pulpy mouth." [42] De Vries's character frequently spouts expressions that were favorite expressions of his neighbor, Jean Stafford, including "ish kabbible" and "none of its beeswax," and Terry McBain is writing a memoir about her father, a "wonderfully picturesque" salty character like John Stafford who "sues everybody" and is "always grumbling about the way things are." [43]

In Westport, Stafford also met the wealthy and sophisticated writer Anne Morrow Lindbergh. In an article she later wrote for *McCall's* about Anne Morrow Lindbergh and her celebrated husband Charles, Stafford would describe them before the kidnapping of their baby as having been "blessed with every goodliness that humankind is heir to." [44] Initially, she was intimidated by this wealthy, well brought up, and well-educated woman. On one occasion, having invited Lindbergh to tea, Stafford was so intent on doing things right when she entertained this pedigreed daughter of a diplomat and wife of a celebrity that she rushed over to Mary Lou Aswell's house to borrow linen tea napkins for the occasion. [45] But despite the differences in their backgrounds, Lindbergh and Stafford saw one another rather frequently during this period. Lindbergh said that she found Stafford to be "an extremely sensitive and perceptive woman and writer," recalling that they had commiserated about the way outside activities often prevented them from writing. [46]

Being a friend of someone never deterred Stafford from telling anecdotes or even making malicious comments about that individual. As her good friend Howard Moss, poetry editor of the *New Yorker,* was later to observe about her, "Funny and sharp about people, she loved gossip." [47] But if she sometimes made disparaging comments to others about her new friends in Westport, she nevertheless spent some pleasant moments in their company. She relied upon them not only to drive her into town but also to provide emotional support for her.

After Stafford had settled into the house in Westport, furnished mostly with antique pieces Jensen had acquired from his Yankee grandmother, she began to experience conflict between her role as wife and hostess and her role as a writer, just as she had in Damariscotta. While her cat, George Eliot, enjoyed the spacious surroundings and soon gave birth to a litter of six kittens fathered by an outside cat named Robert, Stafford herself discovered much to her chagrin that along with the large house came the responsibility for entertaining guests for dinner and long weekends. Thus she complained to Mary Lee about Oliver and his houseguest, Albert Erskine, who often came to spend the weekend with them:

Oliver is going cruising for ten days beginning two weeks from today and I am looking forward to a real holiday of no meals to cook. I am sick to death with everything connected with the mechanics of living and lately have commenced to rebel to the extent of cooking my own breakfast and letting Oliver and houseguests (who do not cease even though the frost has come) shift for themselves. I cannot help feeling vexed that these two huge things expect continual service all the while they are discussing the neurotic manners of modern women writers.

She also mentioned in this letter that she had stopped drinking and consequently had begun to decline invitations to many of the social functions they were expected to attend:

I will not go places where I know the only way to endure is to drink and this means that I go nowhere except to doctors who are the only people who make good sense to me. It is not the drinking that I mind, it is the intolerable boredom that I resent—the evening lasting until one or two. So Oliver stays in town frequently till all hours and I come out on the earliest possible train and get into bed with George Eliot and Silas Marner purring at my feet. It is not what I would call a full life but I am glad of the quiet.[48]

Just as Stafford, in several of her short stories, had described marital tensions similar to the ones she had experienced when she was Mrs. Robert Lowell, so she described disintegrating marriages like hers and Oliver's in stories that appeared in print during the fifties. In "The Connoisseurs," for example, a mismatched couple named the Rands soon discover that "on almost everything they found they were in obstinate and fundamental disaccord."[49] Donald Rand loves Wagner, Mary Rand, Bach; Donald Rand annoys his wife when he insists on reading passages from Toynbee aloud, and when she retaliates by reading to him passages from George Eliot's *Middlemarch,* he replies that "he had never had any respect at all for any woman novelist." Listing the issues about which the Rands disagree, Stafford writes: "They were disunited over the football games, psychiatry, capital punishment, modern furniture and progressive education. Their religious and political views were diametrically opposed, and they were pugnacious when they debated, as masochistically they often did, the Sacco and Vanzetti trial. Hardly a day passed when they did not inflame each other . . ."[50] By the end of this story, the Rands have amicably decided to part.

Marital discord is also the subject of "Beatrice Trueblood's Story." Although Stafford herself never suffered from hysterical deafness, as does her eponymous protagonist, there are many autobiographical references in the story. During her first marriage, Beatrice Trueblood recalls her "positively hideous childhood" of "the most humiliating squalor" during which she was subjected to the temper of a father who "could use his tongue like a bludgeon."[51] Overhearing each evening the invectives her parents hurled at one another, she had "miserably pushed her food about on her plate, never hungry,"[52] and often she imagined herself alone on a desert, far away from any human voice. Soon after she married Tom Trueblood (the name is perhaps a snide reference to the Brahmin Lowells), she had discovered that he was "obscene," he was "raucous," and he was also unfaithful.[53] Now, about to marry the "scrumptiously rich" though boring Marten ten Brink,[54] Beatrice begins to quarrel with him as well. Then, suddenly, she loses her hearing, having discovered what a torment their incessant wrangles are to someone like herself who "shuddered at raised voices and quailed before looks of hate."[55] When Beatrice decides that she "cannot and . . . will not listen to another word,"[56] she suddenly becomes deaf. Though she ruefully acknowledges that her deafness isolates her from other people, it also frees her from a relationship she has found intolerable. To the biographer, the tale is a fascinating one, for it reflects Stafford's view that her parents' marriage affected her own marital relationships. But the story is also a first-rate work of fiction, as the judges of the O. Henry Prize stories recognized when they included it in their 1956 volume. Stafford's witty depiction of the manners of the upper class in "Beatrice Trueblood's Story" reminds us once again of her affinities with both Henry James and Edith Wharton, and her use of deafness to symbolize her female protagonist's resistance to a badgering male also links her story to other fictional representations of female resistance to male oppression. In Barbara H. Solomon's anthology of short stories, *The Experience of American Women,* "Beatrice Trueblood's Story" takes its place among stories by American women writers such as Charlotte Perkins Gilman's "The Yellow Wallpaper," Mary Wilkins Freeman's "The Revolt of Mother," and Tillie Olsen's "Tell Me a Riddle," which also dramatize the ways in which a female protagonist reacts to a male who tries to dominate her.

No matter what her state of mind was or how often she was distracted, Stafford managed to work steadily on her articles, her short stories, and on her new novel, *The Catherine Wheel,* writing and endlessly rewriting. But Jensen recalls times when she would also be drinking steadily as she relived her unhappy childhood and her years with Lowell: ". . . there would be periods of black moods, and drinking, plus endless rehashing of her troubles with Lowell and after a while she came to disapprove of me too and my view on most subjects. Yes, she drank excessively—if you realize that a few drinks will suffice to start off an alcoholic, the same few drinks that, taken occasionally, will not do much damage to an ordinary person."[57] Seeking guidance about how he might deal more effectively with his wife's drinking, he finally wrote to her psychiatrist, Dr. Sherfey, in February of 1952. "Jean's attitude is that the whole thing is no business of mine, and that I should say and do nothing," he explained, assuring Dr. Sherfey that contrary to what his wife might insist, he did not regard alcoholism as a "moral" problem but a medical one about which he knew "nothing at all." Commenting about his wife's repeated bouts of depression, he said, "As of 1952 she is still heartbreakingly beset by drinking and the neurotic problems that underlie it. I believe you told me the latter would never disappear, but might be ameliorated, but they are not, and Jean's moments of dispair [sic] are terrible to watch, as she goes over and over her whole history of unhappy memories." [58]

Jensen wondered whether his wife's visits to Dr. Sherfey twice or more a week for therapy did not serve to make Jean dwell on unhappy past events. Painful as that process was, however, it also served to revive memories of her childhood and her first marriage that would enrich the short stories and the novel on which she was working. It is probably not coincidental that this period of intensive psychotherapy was also one of the most artistically productive periods of her life. In a talk that she gave at the P.E.N. Club in New York City in the spring of 1952, she discussed the positive effects psychotherapy can have on the writer: "I do not believe that 'artist' is synonymous with 'sufferer' or 'neurotic.' And I *do* believe, on the contrary, that psychoanalysis can prodigiously enrich an artist's insights, sharpen his sense of meaning, humanize his moral attitudes, validate his observations." About her own practices as a writer she observed wittily, "I would rather say that I *write* than that I *sublimate*. . . . I prefer to think of writing as an occupation, *not* a disorder." [59]

The prevailing tone of the work Stafford produced between 1950 and 1952 is one of alienation, loss, disgust, disillusionment, though there are always saving moments of humor and irony. "Man's life is a cheat and a disappointment"—Stafford chose these words from T. S. Eliot's play, *Murder in the Cathedral,* as the epigraph to her third novel, *The Catherine Wheel,* which was published in 1952. As Wanda Avila has suggested, to deal with life's inevitable betrayals Stafford often adopted "the stance of the ironic observer—reflective, objective, intellectually, and, above all, emotionally detached." [60] Whether she was writing about the stultifying dreariness of life in a small town in the West in "The Healthiest Girl in Town," or about the pains and joys of the holiday season in "Home for Christmas," or about jealousy and emotional deprivation in *The Catherine Wheel,* her work suggests that happiness is elusive or evanescent.

Stafford always maintained that no matter where she was, her roots remained in the semifictitious town of Adams, Colorado,[61] a place based on the

Boulder of her youth that serves as the setting for many of her stories. But if her own roots were in Colorado, she chose neither to celebrate the scenic magnificence of the Rockies nor to draw on the mythic images of heroic struggle that are evident in the male American Western literary tradition as formulated in the works of James Fenimore Cooper. Although one of Stafford's favorite protagonists, Molly Fawcett in *The Mountain Lion,* is reading Cooper's *The Pathfinder,* Stafford agreed with Mark Twain that Cooper had committed major literary offenses. Instead of Cooper's heroic images, the dominant images in Stafford's Western stories, as Mary Ellen Williams Walsh has observed, are images of "girls and young women trapped inside unpleasant houses, frozen in immobile positions, surrounded by the trappings of illness and death, often harassed by grotesque people."[62]

The oppressive environment of a small town is very much in evidence in Stafford's "The Healthiest Girl in Town," which appeared in the *New Yorker* in the spring of 1951. The narrator of this story recalls moving with her mother to the town in the West, whose "winters were so long and cruel that the sick compared the region to Siberia and their residence there to exile."[63] When she had first arrived in this town at the age of eight, she could not get used to the sight of the numerous consumptives who had come to this magic mountain hoping to be cured and carrying "the badge of their doom in their pink cheeks as a blind man carries his white stick in his hand."[64] An ironic twist in the story is that the alienation of Jean Stafford's narrator is symbolically represented by the little girl's own blooming health: in a town where illness is the norm, to be healthy is to be set apart from the majority of the inhabitants. It is her own profound isolation that leads the narrator to tell a fib about her father's death to the two rich girls for whom her mother works as a nurse. But if the narrator manages momentarily to get their attention by telling a lie when she confides to them that her father has died of leprosy, fear of exposure soon forces her to confess that she has not told the truth. Although the story ends on a positive note, with the narrator exulting in her own good health, she is no less isolated at the end of the story than she was at the beginning. Humorous, anecdotal, on the surface less profound perhaps than some of Stafford's other stories, "The Healthiest Girl in Town" reveals how desperate a young girl is to make an impression on others, so desperate, in fact, that she lies about the circumstances of her own father's death. Focusing on a storyteller who lies, "The Healthiest Girl in Town" may reflect Stafford's own apprehensions about retelling and perhaps even exaggerating painful events of her life in her fiction in order to write a story that would be of interest to her readers.

In "Home for Christmas," an essay that appeared in *Mademoiselle* in December of 1951, Stafford also recalls the painful experiences of childhood. She laments that she herself "started off on the wrong foot" on the first Christmas she was old enough to remember: ". . . the fact is that my partridge, the badge of my betrothal to this kingly, separate season, flew out of its tree on the very day it arrived, on the first Christmas that I remember," she writes, "and I have been looking for it ever since with a net and a salt cellar and a tenacity that makes my head ache."[65] She observes that in balmy California, in the chimneyless house where she lived as a young child, her older siblings failed to persuade her one year that Santa Claus could enter through the top of their house since she knew that the only way he could have entered was "through the solar tank and he would have been boiled alive."[66] She says, however, that even more traumatic than her feeling that she had been hoodwinked about Santa Claus was her loss of a pink silk bag her grandmother gave her that Christmas, a bag for which she has been searching ever since in the many places she has lived. Fifteen years after this article appeared, Stafford would refer to it as "a mushy article about Christmas, which I loathe,"[67] but except for the final paragraphs of the article, which describe Christmas as a day of return to "the passionate red, innocent white, green loveliness of infancy," the tone is elegaic rather than "mushy." "Home for Christmas" suggests the origins of Jean Stafford's disbelief in miracles and of her bitter feeling that fate had cheated her of life's most wonderful gifts.

In *The Catherine Wheel,* which was published in 1952, the Christmas carol "A Partridge in a Pear Tree" is also used to symbolize bitter disillusionment and loss. The chapter headings—"On the First Day of Summer," "My True Love Took from Me," "The Late Wedding Ring," "A Dream of a Dove"— parody the verses of the Christmas carol. Moreover, the only partridge to appear in the novel is a vain young man named James Partridge who asks one of the nieces of his hostess to sing "A Partridge in a Pear Tree," his favorite song because his name is mentioned in it.

Set in Hawthorne, a picturesque town in Maine still unspoiled by tourists that resembles the Damariscotta Stafford remembered so vividly, *The Catherine Wheel* describes a summer of betrayal from a dual perspective: that of a middle-aged, affluent spinster from Boston named Katharine Congreve; and that of Andrew, the twelve-year-old son of her cousins, Maeve and John Shipley. Andrew and his twin sisters, Honor and Harriet, have come to spend the summer with Katharine in Hawthorne, where each year from May to October she presides over her ancestral mansion, Congreve House. Just as Hawthorne resembles Damariscotta Mills, so does Congreve House resemble Kavanagh, the beautiful mansion that Jean Stafford and Robert Lowell could see from their windows in Damariscotta. Jilted in her youth by John Shipley, who chose her cousin Maeve instead, Katharine Congreve is given the opportunity to avenge the wrongs that were done to her, for John Shipley is now convinced that he should have chosen Katharine instead of her cousin Maeve. As the novel begins, we are informed that he has decided to leave Maeve and wants to persuade Katharine to begin life anew as his wife. Outwardly controlled and reserved, Katharine is consumed with corrosive feelings of anger—anger against her father, who had once seemed to prefer her orphaned cousin Maeve to her, anger at her mother, who was more interested in various social causes than in her own daughter; anger at Maeve, who robbed her of John Shipley's love; and anger at John Shipley, who has put his own needs first and tempted her to betray her love for his children by destroying his marriage. Twelve-year-old Andrew, too, silently nurses grievances against the world. He is angry at his irascible father; at his mother for always being too preoccupied to attend to his needs; at his older sisters, who usually ignore him; and this summer, at his former summer pal, a boy from town named Victor Smithwick, who has abandoned him to take care of an ill older brother. While Katharine Congreve plots revenge against Maeve, Andrew desperately longs for the death of Victor's brother. Guilt-ridden, Katharine is morbidly afraid that Andrew has discovered her secret desire to betray Maeve; and Andrew, in turn, is convinced that Katharine is aware of his death wishes for Victor's brother.

   The Catherine Wheel is both a fine novel and a fascinating document for the biographer. Taking her cue from Stafford's naming of the town where the events in the novel unfold, Jeanette Mann has remarked on the resemblance between this novel and the romances of Hawthorne, in which envy, guilt, and remorse play central roles.[68] The novel is also somewhat similar to Ford Madox Ford's *The Good Soldier,* for Stafford's novel, too, dramatizes the disparity between the elegant manners of the upper class and their destructive hidden passions. In naming Katharine Congreve's gardener Maddox, perhaps Stafford was hinting at her indebtedness to Ford. Another important literary source for *The Catherine Wheel* is Charles Dickens' *Great Expectations.* After Stafford and Lowell had separated, she asked him if she might borrow his volumes of Dickens for a year,[69] and she later reported to him that she had been reading *Great Expectations.*[70] It is probable that she drew on Dickens' portrait of Miss Havisham for her own portrait of Katharine Congreve. Just as Miss Havisham, jilted on her wedding day and in thrall to her past, immures herself in Satis House, so does Katharine Congreve immure herself in Congreve House after she is rejected by John Shipley. Stasis, whether symbolized by the stopped clocks in Dickens' novel or by Katharine's anachronistic horse-drawn carriage and coachman in *The Catherine Wheel,* is a controlling image in both novels. "*Not* changing is my only occupation,"[71] Katharine remarks. Plotting revenge against their enemies, Miss Havisham and Katharine Congreve alike are corroded by jealousy, and both die when their gowns catch fire. At the end of *The Catherine Wheel,* Andrew, a parallel figure to Dickens' Pip, survives the blaze that has taken the life of the older woman who played such an important role in his life.

One is reminded of Dickens, too, by the way in which Stafford introduces several weighty symbols, such as Katharine Congreve's tombstone decorated with the motif of the Catherine wheel. As a character explains in the novel, the Catherine wheel was the symbol of the intrepid martyr Catherine: "They tied her to a thing like that and set it spinning, but it broke before it killed her and then they chopped off her head."[72] Introduced first on the evening that Katharine Congreve is betrayed and later to symbolize her disintegrating consciousness, the Catherine wheel finally comes to represent the cross that Katharine Congreve bears in silence and her own ultimate martyrdom. Mixing humor, pathos, and melodrama, combining the lofty style of Henry James and the colloquial style of Mark Twain, *The Catherine Wheel* is Stafford's most complex novel.

In *The Catherine Wheel,* Stafford focuses not on one but on two protagonists, just as she had done in *The Mountain Lion.* However, whereas the earlier novel was based on Stafford's recollections of her own early childhood and that of her brother Dick, in *The Catherine Wheel* the dual protagonists represent, respectively, versions of Stafford's adolescent and adult selves. The town of Hawthorne, too, is obviously an amalgam of her memories of Boulder and her later impressions of Damariscotta. The original for the outcast named Em Bugtown, a town character in Hawthorne, for example, actually lived in Boulder when Stafford was a child, and Billy Bartholomew, the "blasphemous and long-winded blacksmith" who observes "the doings of his fellows with a misanthropic eye," is yet another fictional character resembling John Stafford.

During the period when Stafford was writing the novel, she was confronting in therapy sessions with Dr. Sherfey the painful memories of her childhood as well as her marriage to Lowell. In *The Catherine Wheel,* these two parts of her life are juxtaposed via the consciousnesses of Andrew and Katharine Congreve. Andrew Shipley is a rich prep school student from Boston, as was Robert Lowell, rather than a poor girl from the West like Jean Stafford, and the surname Shipley may be an allusion to Lowell's father, a naval commander. Nevertheless, Andrew's resemblance to Jean Stafford and to her other autobiographical personae, Sonie Marburg and Molly Fawcett, is apparent. The youngest in his family, as Jean Stafford was in hers, Andrew feels himself to be disliked by everyone. He hates the fact that his irritable father, another incarnation of John Stafford, "greeted the slightest mishap with a towering rage"[73]; he feels slighted when his mother responds only with polite interest to his discovery of the meanings of unusual words because she lacks intellectual curiosity and is preoccupied with housekeeping matters;[74] and he resents it when his older sisters either make fun of him or ignore him. As Stafford did, Andrew delights in using colloquial expressions like "in a pig's valise"; has nightmares and sleepwalks; spends his days in the public library reading the *New English Dictionary;* wishes he had an altogether different father; and feels dismayed, fearful, and guilty when he is forced to acknowledge his own "atrocious inner nature."[75]

In contrast to *The Mountain Lion,* in this novel Stafford chose a male rather than a female character to embody her younger self. While in doing so she might merely have been trying to create a character who at least superficially was different from Molly Fawcett, her use of a male protagonist to portray her earlier self might have psychological significance as well. As a young girl, the bookish Stafford preferred males like her father and her brother to females like her mother and her older sisters, and thus in thinking about herself at the age of twelve, it was as easy for her to represent herself in the guise of Andrew Shipley as it had been to see herself as Molly Fawcett. Always sympathetic to the plight of neglected children, Stafford identified with the "lost boy" Andrew Shipley just as she had identified with Molly Fawcett. "My theory about morality is my theory about children," she said in an interview soon after *The Catherine Wheel* was published. "The most important thing in writing is irony, and we find irony most clearly in children. The very innocence of a child is irony . . ."[76]

One crucial difference between Andrew Shipley and Molly Fawcett is that Molly Fawcett is killed at the end of *The Mountain Lion* whereas Andrew Shipley, another incarnation of Stafford's younger self, survives. It is to Andrew that the dying Katharine Congreve entrusts the sacred task of burning her diary with all its revelations of her secret life and hidden desires. In a letter to Lowell that Stafford had written when she was a patient at Payne Whitney, she had described how she had burned her old letters in the fireplace on their last night in Maine.[77] Recalling, perhaps, that terrible final night in her house in Damariscotta, she concluded the novel with Andrew feeding the pages of the dead Katharine Congreve's diary into the coal stove, "Leaf by leaf, without reading a word of them, . . . his big tears hissing and skittering away in minute bubbles on the iron lids."[78]

While Andrew Shipley exhibits many of the characteristics and attitudes of the young Jean Stafford, Katharine Congreve appears to be a fictional repre-

sentation of Stafford as an adult. Stafford indulged in a bit of fantasy by making Katharine Congreve the heiress of an affluent Bostonian's fortunes and
the mistress of a splendid mansion. However, far from glorifying her protagonist, she reveals Katharine's corrosive envy, her disintegration, and her
self-destructiveness. Like Stafford's mother, the mother of Katharine Congreve is an "extremely busy" woman who has "nothing at all in common with
her daughter."[79] More like Stafford's paternal grandmother than her mother,
however, Katharine's mother is devoted to various causes, from Baconianism,
to antivivisectionism, to health foods and rat control.[80] Katharine Congreve
identifies not with her mother but with her father, "a humanist, steadfastly
ironic," with vitally bright black eyes and coarse tight black curls like those of
John Stafford. The independently wealthy George Congreve, a "note-maker
for study's sake,"[81] does not jeopardize his family's livelihood by devoting
himself to intellectual pursuits, however. Hence, he is a far more sympathetic
character than various other characters representing John Stafford who appear in her fiction. But even in this novel she complements an idealized portrait of John Stafford with portraits of the irascible John Shipley and the "garrulous and tiresome and usually angry" Billy Bartholomew,[82] both of whom
also resemble her father in certain ways. Idolized by his daughter, George
Congreve gives her a statue of Minerva, goddess of wisdom and the arts, realizing that unlike other girls her age, his intellectual daughter would prefer
such a gift to one of clothes or jewelry. In her portrait of George Congreve,
Stafford pays tribute to the intellectual legacy her own father had bequeathed
to her even if he did do damage to her in other ways. Her portrait of George
Congreve may also owe something to her impressions of her surrogate father,
the affluent and cultured elderly cardiologist, Dr. Alfred Cohn. When Stafford described the statue of Minerva that George Congreve gave his daughter
Katharine, it is possible she was remembering that Dr. Cohn had sent a copy
of his book *Minerva's Progress* to her in 1946.

Given to "lapidary speech," as was Stafford herself, Katharine Congreve
enjoys many of the same pastimes that Stafford did: she loves flowers and once
took up the study of botany, as Stafford had done; she enjoys old-fashioned
pastimes such as playing Patience, doing needlepoint, and making potpourris
with sun-dried petals; she is a voracious reader of esoteric texts such as the
writings of Sir Thomas Browne; and she records her thoughts and feelings in
a diary. Though she is rather aloof, she is also generous to her relatives and
friends. Such details help make Katharine Congreve an attractive if somewhat eccentric character. However, Stafford also anatomizes unsparingly the
less savory characteristics of her protagonist, something she failed to do when
she described Sonie Marburg in *Boston Adventure*. Fiercely competitive with

other women, as was Sonie in *Boston Adventure,* Katharine comes to despise her cousin Maeve, who first became a rival for her father's affections and then stole her lover, John Shipley. Even before John Shipley fell in love with Maeve, Katharine was jealous of her and actually prayed that a skin disorder with which Maeve was afflicted would prove to be incurable. And now in middle age, as she contemplates being the cause of the breakup of Maeve's marriage to John Shipley, Katharine admits to herself: "The fact was that she had never really forgiven poor Maeve for anything though she had struggled to. Bending every effort of her will and intelligence, she had tried to love Maeve and failing, had come at last to this ultimate betrayal."[83] Into her description of Katharine's antagonism to Maeve, Stafford projected her own recollections of her competitive relationships with other women: with her sisters, with Lucy McKee, with Bunny Cole, and with Gertrude Buckman. The connection between the events in the novel and Gertrude Buckman's visit to Damariscotta that fateful summer of 1946 is evident, for example, in a passage in which Stafford describes Katharine Congreve painfully observing Maeve and John Shipley falling in love:

> As if it had been yesterday, she remembered her demeaning anguish when on idle afternoons, they begged her to read aloud to them *The Georgics.* . . . They sat the while demurely far apart, stealing glances and mouthing pet names. In the intoxication of their romance, furthered—even created—by this house, these grounds, this lake, this river that Katharine's father and grandfather and great-grandfather provided them with, in this lavish, extravagant Roman holiday, they had had energy and lunacy to spare and had showered her with it.[84]

In some of the most remarkable passages in *The Catherine Wheel,* Stafford describes her protagonist's mental disintegration. Just as women writers such as Sylvia Plath, Janet Frame, Doris Lessing, and Antonia White have recorded their own mental breakdowns in the pages of their fiction, so did Stafford draw on her recollections of the mental and physical torment she too had experienced in Damariscotta and later in New York. Insomniac and prey to momentary hallucinations, Katharine Congreve writes in her diary: "Poor, lonely, obsessed Katharine. For I am snatched by moments of hallucination when reality disgorges me like a cannon firing off a cannon ball and I am sent off into an upper air where there is no sound and my senses are destroyed by the awful, white, paining light. . . . At the same time that I rise, ejected from the planet into the empyrean, I plummet through the core of the world."[85]

One of the several books on psychology that Stafford owned was psychiatrist Karen Horney's *Self Analysis.* In this book Horney, a revisionist Freudian psychiatrist especially interested in the psychology of women, presented a case history of a patient named Clare. Focusing on the subtle pattern of female devaluation in a patriarchal society, Horney used the fictitious Clare's experience to explore the conflicts she herself had experienced in her lifetime.[86] In *The Catherine Wheel,* Stafford, too, used a fictitious character to explore her own conflicts, as she had done earlier in both *Boston Adventure* and *The Mountain Lion.* It is worth noting, however, that although Katharine Congreve has many intellectual pastimes, as did Stafford, she is not a writer. Rather, we are informed that, like her father, "she would read astutely and never write, observe wholeheartedly and never paint, not teach, not marry god."[87] During a trip to Germany in her youth, Katharine had begun to write a novel, but she was told by a German youth she liked, "You should take up the harp. Or paint ring-around-a-rosy on saucers." Just as Charles Tansley in Virginia Woolf's *To the Lighthouse* maintains that women should not paint or write, so this young German maintains "women should never try to write," and his teasing remarks about her novel make Katharine Congreve suffer "small fractures of the heart."[88] The only writing Katharine Congreve does as an adult is contained within the pages of her diary, and the diary, as she had wished, is destroyed by Andrew after she dies. Although Stafford never actually wrote a *Künstlerroman,* she incorporated into *The Catherine Wheel* many of the conflicts she had experienced as a woman and a writer.

Stafford's depression during the months she was completing *The Catherine Wheel* originated at least in part from the same tormenting self-doubt she had experienced during the months she was working on the final draft of *The Mountain Lion* in Damariscotta. Writing to Caroline Gordon just before *The Catherine Wheel* was published, she said, "Please do not read my new one coming out in January. It is not good," and she observed to this woman who had served as her mentor a decade earlier: "I really mean it about my new book. I feel like absolute hell about it and am ashamed of myself when I think how patiently you and Allen tried to teach me not to do the very things that I have done."[89] Perhaps she feared that the complicated plot and intricate style of her third novel would not appeal to Gordon, whose own prose was more spare, her use of symbolism less intrusive.

In addition to warning Gordon about the deficiencies of *The Catherine Wheel,* Stafford also wrote to other literary friends about the novel. Apprehensive that her latest novel would not meet with their approval, she confided to them that she was fully aware of its shortcomings. After receiving one of these self-deprecatory letters, Philip Rahv, dismayed by what he perceived to be a breach of decorum, told Allen Tate: "Jean seems to have sent out a round-robin to all her old literary friends warning them against her new novel. I, too, was the recipient of a confidential missive informing me that she herself thought little of the book and that therefore I was not to judge her by it. Literary manners are changing continually and Jean's procedure is really something new; she is trying to have it both ways."[90]

Yet another writer to receive a self-deprecatory letter from Stafford was Eudora Welty. Once Welty had read *The Catherine Wheel* and had also read some of the reviews of the book, she wrote to Stafford to tell her how sorry she was that Jean had had such bad feelings about the novel. Gently chiding her for being so insecure about her writing, she exclaimed, "Oh, Jean, it is full of goodness, and you don't need me to tell you so. I love all the detail and the splendor that belong to it—and the fine sustaining level and mood you set in it."[91] Another friend, the novelist Louis Auchincloss, who would soon include a chapter about Stafford in his study of American women writers, *Pioneers and Caretakers,* also tried to reassure her about *The Catherine Wheel.* "It may not be your best, but it's still better than anyone else's so why be ashamed of it. You're like a hard-boiled parent who wants all the children to be head of the class. Don't reject this latest; it has some of your best moments," he said.[92]

Not all of the critics were as charitable about *The Catherine Wheel* as Stafford's friends were. Although critics found much to admire in this novel, their response on the whole was less enthusiastic than the critical response to either *Boston Adventure* or *The Mountain Lion* had been. Philip Rahv, for example, thought this novel to be much less satisfactory than *The Mountain Lion,* which he had warmly praised. He described *The Catherine Wheel* to Allen Tate as her "worst performance so far." Although Rahv was willing to grant that she had "a fine narrative gift," he said that after reading the novel he wondered whether she would ever "get over her infatuation with the rich and well born," an infatuation he believed would "do her in."[93] Stafford was not privy to these remarks of Rahv. However, she must have been pained by Irving Howe's criticism of the novel in the *Kenyon Review.* While Howe credited her with being "a brilliant stylist," he felt that her style, "so fine and frequently so winning," ultimately served "to undermine the matter it was meant to reveal."[94] The reviewer for the *New York Times Book Review* was also disappointed with the novel, which she said "strains credibility, seeming manipulated and merely strange."[95] Another negative appraisal of the novel appeared in the *Times Literary Supplement,* whose reviewer felt the novel was too reminiscent of the fiction of Eudora Welty.[96] Instead of portraying the continuities between Welty's work and that of Stafford in a positive light, as critics had done, for example, when speaking of the relationship between the fiction of Turgenev and James, the reviewer maintained that *The Catherine Wheel* revealed "a decline in originality."

The reviews of *The Catherine Wheel,* however, were by no means all negative. Paul Engle observed that the novel provided "further proof of the fictional and psychological brilliance of the author," [97] and Walter Havighurst commended it for its "great restraint and . . . great beauty." [98] Subsequently, Ihab Hassan and Jeanette Mann published lengthy critical articles about the novel, both applauding Stafford's achievement. "*The Catherine Wheel* shows that Miss Stafford has caught the stride of her talent," Hassan wrote; he found the novel to be a "happy development in Jean Stafford's writing, from satiric wit, to irony and sensibility, from stylistics to poetry." [99]

Yet despite the fact that the majority of reviewers found much to admire in the novel, it has received little critical attention. After it was republished by Ecco Press in 1981 as part of its series called Neglected Books of the Twentieth Century, James Wolcott remarked, "What should have been an event became little more than a passing breeze." [100] The least well known of Stafford's three novels, *The Catherine Wheel* deserves to reach a wider audience. In an interview in the *New York Times* in 1952, after *The Catherine Wheel* was published, Stafford said that eventually she would like to fuse the style of *Boston Adventure* and the style of *The Mountain Lion.* [101] *The Catherine Wheel,* in fact, does attempt to fuse these two styles, the first represented by the consciousness of Katharine Congreve and the second by the consciousness of Andrew Shipley. The fusion of these two distinctive narrative voices contributes to the richness of the novel, as does Stafford's intricate use of symbolism. The Gothic elements remind one not only of Dickens but of Faulkner; her depiction of the genteel Bostonians who spend their summers in Hawthorne is reminiscent of James, Wharton, and Ford; and her portrait of the townspeople in Hawthorne as well as the unhappy Andrew Shipley suggests her indebtedness to Twain and to local color writers such as Sarah Orne Jewett and Eudora Welty. Yet despite these literary echoes, *The Catherine Wheel* does not seem to be merely a pale imitation of the works of others. Interweaving the western and the eastern strands of her life, as well as her life when she was a child like Andrew and her life as an adult, Stafford succeeded in creating a beautiful novel of childhood desolation and adult despair that is uniquely her own.

With the publication of *The Catherine Wheel,* Stafford again attracted public attention. On January 24 she was honored at a Book and Author luncheon at the Hotel Statler in Washington, D.C., along with Senator Robert Taft and the former U.S. attorney general, Francis Biddle. Robert Lowell's cousin, Harriet Winslow, who lived in Washington at the time, reported to him the next day that Jean had given a "short and amusing speech, well delivered." She said Jean had told her afterward that she was well and happy and had asked about him and Elizabeth Hardwick "with much interest." Lowell's cousin was quick to add, however, that she had heard Jean was still drinking too much, though she had appeared sober at the luncheon; and far from praising Jean Stafford's latest novel, she said she thought it "completely unreal . . . though certainly sumptuously well written in some ways, with a certain slack quality which augurs ill for her future." [102] It is probable that Harriet Winslow was no more pleased by Stafford's portrait of Boston society in *The Catherine Wheel* than her in-laws had been by her portrayal of their world in *Boston Adventure*.

In addition to being honored in Washington, another mark of Stafford's renewed visibility after the publication of *The Catherine Wheel* was the fact that she was selected as a judge for the 1952 National Book Award. The *Bridgeport Sunday Post* described her as "the only gentler sex jurist" to be selected as a judge. [103] Along with the other judges for the fiction category, Robert Gorham Davis, Brendan Gill, Lloyd Morris, and Budd Shulberg, she attended the award ceremony at the Hotel Commodore in New York City on January 29. The fact that James Jones's naturalistic World War II novel, *From Here to Eternity,* won the National Book Award that year suggests, perhaps, why Stafford's own reputation as a writer, and especially as a novelist, might have suffered a decline in the fifties, although she had been named one of the six best writers of the postwar era in 1949 in *Quick's* poll of leading critics. [104] During a decade that gave rise not only to Jones's war novel but to the fiction of ethnic male writers such as Ralph Ellison, Saul Bellow, Bernard Malamud, and Philip Roth, as well as to innovative works like William Gaddis's *Recognitions* and Jack Kerouac's *On the Road,* Stafford's *The Catherine Wheel* would begin to appear as old-fashioned as Katharine Congreve's horse-drawn carriage and as feminine as her protagonist's "mousseline de soie" evening gown. Being a woman novelist during this period, as James Wolcott has observed, might itself have had a negative effect on Stafford's literary reputation, for the prevailing literary values then were aggressively masculine ones, and novelists, critics, and readers alike tended to deprecate or ignore the achievements of women writers. [105] Only one work of fiction by a woman writer, Katherine Anne Porter's *Collected Short Stories,* received the National Book Award between 1950 and 1970.

To promote sales of *The Catherine Wheel,* Stafford went to Boston that March for what she subsequently described as "an agreeable meeting with half a dozen reviewers." [106] Pleased to be back in Boston for the first time in six years, she admitted to a reporter from the *Boston Globe* that she had only lived in or near Boston for a short time, though people always assumed she had been born and brought up there.

Much less to her liking than her Boston visit was a promotional luncheon she agreed to attend in a city in Connecticut where she said culture was on the rampage. Humorously describing this event during a talk she gave in Boulder that summer, she confided that her own five-minute speech after the luncheon had been a disaster, for she realized that no one in the audience had ever heard of her until that day; furthermore, even to her own ears, the speech she had prepared sounded "intellectual and rarified and snobby," causing "the faces which had first been thoughtful and then mirthful" to turn "to stone." The final humiliation she had had to endure was that no one bought a copy of her book, making her feel "exactly the same feverish humiliation" she had felt in grammar school when valentines were handed out and she either got none or a "scurrilous comic one" from her worst enemy. The fountain pen she was given as a gift for appearing on the program did not work, and the only compensation she received for the whole ordeal was the small profit she made by charging her publishers the round-trip Pullman fare though she had actually traveled by coach.[107] Stafford's witty account of this experience demonstrates not only her characteristic ability to convert her misadventures into amusing anecdotes but also her willingness to expose her own mortifying experiences to the scrutiny of others, whether to make them laugh, to kindle their interest, or to evoke their sympathy for her.

That winter and spring it became increasingly clear to Stafford that she could not continue to live with Oliver Jensen. "Things have been thick and tough ever since *The Catherine Wheel* came out," she wrote to Mary Lee. Although she claimed that she still had "great affection . . . and even some love" for Oliver, she said she could not abide the "monstrous mess of parties" they were obliged to attend and she found their "ceaseless quarrels" unbearable. In this letter, she neglected to mention, however, that a good many of their quarrels were about her drinking. To forestall any lectures from her older sister about leaving Oliver, she informed her that Dr. Sherfey was on her side. Her plan was to separate from Oliver as soon as he completed the book he was then working on, a pictorial history called *The Revolt of American Women*. She was anxious to leave him before the flowers and trees on their property would be in bloom, she said, for she feared that once spring arrived she would find it too difficult to part with their lovely Westport house. Meanwhile, determined to leave the place as spotless as Jensen's New York apartment had been when she had moved into it, she spent her days cleaning it from top to bottom with a "vilely neurotic" frenzy she feared she had inherited from her mother.[108]

Although she had originally intended to leave Oliver in March or early April, she remained in Westport until July, unable to summon up enough courage or energy to end this phase of her life and to abandon the security it provided. By the end of June she was so distraught that she was hospitalized briefly. A letter she wrote to an acquaintance during this time mentions that she really had no need to be in bed, suggesting that it was her state of mind rather than her physical state that caused her physician to admit her to the hospital.[109] In a note she left for Oliver as she departed for the hospital, she wrote, "Do not Worry, Do Not Worry." Describing her hospital stay as "a sort of sensible convalescence," she mentioned that her physician, Dr. Koteen, had advised her to take her manuscripts and her typewriter with her. Then, like a dutiful housewife whose first concern was her concern for her husband's welfare, she informed Oliver, "There is a beautiful steak in the ice-chest for you."[110]

One of the manuscripts Stafford might have been working on during her stay in the hospital was the short story "I Love Someone," which appeared in the first issue of the *Colorado Quarterly* that summer. The story's melancholy narrator, a middle-aged spinster who is living in New York City during the hot summer months, contemplates spending an "empty evening" alone, for she has failed to provide herself with company or anything interesting to do. Ruminating about the life of her married friends from Fairfield County and especially about Marigold Trask, a wife and mother who had recently committed suicide, she realizes that her married friends, too, were not impervious to suffering. Nevertheless, as she thinks of her own solitary existence, she concludes bitterly, "In my ungivingness, I am more dead now, this evening, than Marigold Trask in her suburban cemetery,"[111] and she envies the anonymous person who had scrawled I LOVE SOMEONE in chalk in a "fat, lopsided heart" on the city pavement beneath her window.[112] When the narrator observes two boys fighting in the street below, she is reminded that passion may also lead to violence, but she also acknowledges the sterility of her own solitary life. What is missing "at this banquet where the appointments are so elegant is something to eat," she thinks.[113]

Stafford herself was weighing the pros and cons of living alone when she wrote "I Love Someone." If she feared that remaining with Oliver in Westport might destroy her, as married life in Fairfield County had destroyed Marigold Trask, contemplating a solitary life in New York City as an alternative to her life with Oliver in Westport terrified her as well. Invited to participate in the Boulder Writer's Conference that summer, she had anxiety about returning there, but she was even more anxious about terminating her marriage as she considered what her life would be like if she divorced Oliver and had to survive on her own once more. All too vividly she recalled how badly she had fared after she and Robert Lowell had separated from one another.

Ten

In the Zoo
Summer 1952–Spring 1956

She is not at home in the world.

KATHERINE ANNE PORTER, "FLOWERING JUDAS"

IN "IT'S GOOD to Be Back," an article that appeared in *Mademoiselle* in July of 1952 just as Jean Stafford was packing her bags to attend the Boulder Writer's Conference, she described how exhilarated she felt whenever she returned to Colorado: ". . . I am freshly amazed by the Rocky Mountains, which I see first from the train at seven in the morning, darkly violet in the green and early light that has followed the furious sunrise, and when I leave the Union Station in Denver and for the first time encounter the inebriating air a mile above the level of the sea I wonder why on earth I ever left."[1] Not always so positive about Colorado, however, she more often chose to focus on its forbidding landscape and lonely plains than on its scenic splendors. Now, contemplating a rather extended stay in Boulder for the conference, she realized that Boulder's churches, graveyard, street corners, university buildings, and the Flatirons that loomed above the town would all remind her of her past.

In an interview with Stafford that appeared in the *Colorado Alumnus* after her stay in Boulder during the summer of 1952, a former acquaintance from her student days described her as "the same deadly serious gal with the same occasional far away look, . . . soft voice, the same little wisp of a smile that always faded back into seriousness." The title of the article, "You Can't Go Home Again," as well as the fact that this interview with one of the University of Colorado's most celebrated graduates was somewhat lacking in warmth suggests that she was unable to conceal her ambivalence about her homecoming.[2]

Stafford not only had mixed feelings about returning to Boulder during the summer of 1952; she was also disappointed by the conference, which she described to a friend from Westport as "very low-brow."[3] In a letter to Oliver Jensen, she complained as well about the tedium of having to read the manuscripts submitted by numerous untalented writers, and she said that she had developed bronchitis, a "humiliating circumstance for salubrious Colorado." She also mentioned how annoying she found it that people who claimed to have known her in the fourth grade kept on phoning to invite her to beefsteak fries. One of the people she saw during her stay in Boulder was Goodrich Walton, a former editor of her high school newspaper. He later recalled that they "did not get along" during the one evening she condescended to spend in his company, for they argued when he "accused her of writing about people with tea instead of blood in their veins." Walton said that, as a result of this meeting, their friendship came to an end and he never heard from her again.[4] More pleasurable to her were her encounters with old friends from the faculty of the university. She particularly enjoyed the company of her former professor, Joe Cohen. "My philosophy teacher has the same exciting effect on me he had when I first studied aesthetics under him," she remarked, and she observed that as a college student she had learned not only a great deal about philosophy but about the craft of writing from him.[5] She was dismayed to discover how many other people in Boulder wanted to take credit for having first recognized her talents as a writer. Although she was determined not to consume any alcohol during the conference, she found that without a drink to sustain her, she was unbearably bored by the round of obligatory social activities that had been planned for the conference. And though she herself was quick to criticize the other participants, she nevertheless feared they disliked her because she chose to remain "steadfastly aloof."[6]

In payment for being lionized by former acquaintances, Stafford had to deliver a major address at the conference, an event that she had dreaded from the moment she had been invited to participate. During her talk, which she called "An Etiquette for Writers," she reminisced about her student days in Boulder. She also commented on the pleasures and pains of earning a living as a writer. Candidly admitting in her opening remarks to "habitual and crippling stage fright," she said that the only reason she had agreed to speak on this particular occasion was that she had thought it was time to come back to Boulder to revisit the scenes of her early life and to thank her teachers for nourishing the better aspects of her character.[7] So traumatic did she find the experience of delivering this address that she wrote to Oliver afterward, "The nightmare is over and I have learned my lesson: I have appeared publicly for the very last time in all my life."[8] Although this was by no means the last public address she was to deliver, she continued to be apprehensive about speaking before large audiences during the remainder of her life, and each time she spoke in public, she vowed to herself that she would decline all future public speaking engagements.

Greatly contributing to her tensions and depression was the realization that once the conference was over she would have to decide what to do about her marriage. In the letters she wrote to Oliver from Boulder she referred to their repeated quarrels. She explained that when she had sworn to him that she would never entertain again, she was thinking how much she disliked their "extremely active social life." Far from blaming Oliver for all the problems of their marriage, however, she said guiltily, ". . . I cannot give you the kind of help that a wife should give a husband," and expressing regret that they seemed unable to resolve their differences, she observed: ". . . it is useless for me to say, the fault is mine and I will correct it. I cannot correct it because it goes in deep and is bound up with my writing so that I cannot in any way relinquish it. A woman so isolated by nature as I am, so terrified of any sort of possessiveness cheats when she marries and I shall not soon forgive myself even though I do not mean to cheat." Wishing to placate Oliver, perhaps, she conceded abjectly that she herself was in large measure responsible for the failure of their marriage. "I am all you say," she observed, "a liar, a breaker of promises, an alcoholic, an incompetent . . . a hypochondriac. Do you imagine that knowing this and knowing it full well—I can also love myself and wish to go on living, making your life an incessant disappointment?"[9] Admitting that she was an alcoholic was something she didn't ordinarily do, even to her closest friends. Although in future years she would make disparaging remarks about her second husband, sometimes referring to him as "that other man I was married to whose name escapes me at the moment,"[10] her letters to him suggest that she had had more affection for Jensen than she would later acknowledge. Nevertheless, she realized that she could no longer bear being married to him. It is probable that she would have had much less difficulty in deciding to part from him had a rupture with him not also meant that she would have to give up the comfortable house in Westport and the financial stability that her marriage afforded.

Early in November, on the publication day of Jensen's book *The Revolt of American Women,* Stafford staged a "revolt" of her own. Taking her clothes and her papers with her but abandoning her cats, she moved out of the house in Westport without leaving a forwarding address. According to Joan Stillman, she left the day after election day, when she learned that Jensen had voted for Eisenhower. An ardent supporter of Adlai Stevenson during the presidential campaign of 1952, Stafford had relentlessly attacked Jensen's more conservative political views and had accused him of being a Philistine.[11] "Jean left about a week ago," Oliver wrote to Mary Lee on November 18. "She gave me advance notice to be sure," he said, "but I did not entirely believe her until I came back to this house and found her gone. I believe that this time she is in dead earnest and I am very sad." Attributing their marital difficulties in large measure to Jean's drinking, he described her consumption of alcohol as a symptom rather than a cause of her persistent depression: "Her pessimism, catholic and profound, and her memory, which is photographic only, alas, in respect to unhappy things, hold her in thrall. She believes in disease but not in cures. She is convinced that she cannot live with me and also write . . ."[12]

In addition to informing Mary Lee about Jean's departure, he also told her that before Jean left for the Virgin Islands to secure a divorce from him, she was planning to have a hysterectomy since she had been found to have fibroid tumors. Although Jean's physician had not said that a hysterectomy was mandatory, Jean wanted to have the operation, he said, but he assured Mary Lee that Jean would not regret having to abandon the hope of having children since she had said many times that she did not want any. Jean was too much for him—perhaps for any husband—to handle, he claimed, and he sadly mused: "What in God's name is to happen to Jean, Mary Lee? I wish she could find some joy in life, some mode of existence sans all the violence, sickness, and mental self-torture. I can't provide them. Cal Lowell couldn't. Psychiatry, and it is not all nonsense whatever Jean thinks I believe, hasn't done much for her in six years. Catholicism couldn't help. She is 37 but the road is dark and the destination obscure." Willing to acknowledge that he too had made mistakes during their marriage, though rarely intentional ones, he observed mournfully that he would probably never feel the same way about anybody else as he had about Mary Lee's "remarkable, brilliant sister."[13]

After she left Westport, Stafford took the train to New York City, where she spent a "nightmarish, drunken week in the gloomiest but cheapest hotel in town," the Hotel Irving in Gramercy Square.[14] In a letter she wrote to a friend in Westport, she said that during this time she could not help recalling her weeks and weeks of "solitary boozing" before she had been admitted to Payne Whitney in 1946. On this occasion, however, she was admitted not to Payne Whitney but to the gynecology service of New York Hospital to have a hysterectomy. The week following the surgery was "Walpurgis and hideous," but by the end of November, in much better spirits, she said she was "again willing to be alive."[15]

Just before her departure from Westport, she had written to her friends the Gibneys, the couple with whom she had spent a weekend when she came to the Virgin Islands to obtain a divorce from Lowell: "I'm about to get a divorce again and while I dread the whole prospect and hate the idea of coming back to the Virgin Islands, I am even more repelled by Nevada, which is much too close to my outlaw father who, as he grows older, grows more peripatetic and more adroit in his blackmail."[16] By 1952 the Gibneys and their year-old son were living in a beautiful new stone house instead of the abandoned lumber shack they had formerly occupied in St. John. Stafford told them the only thing that consoled her about going to the Virgin Islands once again for a divorce was the prospect of spending some time with them and their baby. She admitted that she didn't understand babies very well but maintained that she sympathized with them nevertheless, especially when their parents didn't treat them with respect. "Then I know that sooner or later they're going to show up in the Virgin Islands on my business," she said, implying that her upbringing had contributed to her own psychological problems and, in turn, to the failure of both of her marriages.[17]

Eager to be supportive of their friend Jean, Bob and Nancy Gibney invited her to stay with them while she awaited her divorce. They were somewhat apprehensive about her visit since they realized that her health was fragile following her hysterectomy, that she hated hot weather, that her pale skin could not tolerate exposure to the sun, and that she had a fear of boating and swimming, the principal activities at Hawksnest.

Stafford neglected to inform her hosts exactly when she would be arriving. Long after dark and somewhat shaken, she arrived at Hawksnest on New Year's Eve, and she proceeded to entertain them and their two houseguests with tales of her assorted adventures aboard the *S.S. Puerto Rico,* a "filthy" cruise ship whose captain had been "drunk as a billygoat" during the entire voyage. She described most of the passengers aboard as "loathsome," said the crew had been "lazy and foul-mouthed," and maintained that the ship's doctor had "lurked about the passageways in his pajamas and wrapper." From the start, the trip had been a disaster. Feeling fairly cheerful when Robert Giroux had arrived in a rented Cadillac to escort her to the Brooklyn pier from which she was scheduled to depart, she was fuming by the time he left her because he had "used every Jesuitical ruse and trick" to make her sign a book contract with Harcourt, Brace that she did not consider to be in her best interests. During most of the journey she had been ill with bronchitis, her usual malady when she was under stress, and on the ship she had been unable to get any rest because of the heat, the noise, and the swarming mosquitoes.[18] She would later incorporate some of the more lurid details of this gruesome journey into "The Warlock," a tale describing the experiences of a woman who becomes ill while traveling alone on a cruise ship to Antigua. Terrified of the ship's doctor, a strange man more sympathetic to the voodoo medicine of the tropics than to modern medical practice, Stafford's protagonist fears for her life.

The morning after Stafford arrived at Hawksnest, Dr. Kling, a physician from New York who was one of the Gibneys' houseguests, told Nancy Gibney that Jean was too ill to be on an island where there was no doctor in residence. "She is like a raging fire—a bomb set to explode. She must return to New York and the best medical care. It is madness in her condition to be in this primitive place," he said about the new arrival, who was fast asleep on the living room couch.[19] His dire predictions proved to be wrong, however. According to Nancy Gibney, Jean's health appeared to improve remarkably during her stay on the island. An ideal guest, she remained in the guest room much of the day reading Evelyn Waugh or working on "In the Zoo," a story that would be published in the New Yorker the following September. For about an hour each afternoon she would emerge to spend time on the beach with Nancy and the baby, and then would not appear again until her hosts were ready for drinks and conversation. "The Gibneys' house is beautiful and is smack on the water on a long white beach where an elegant solitary white heron lives," she wrote to a friend, describing the Gibneys as "wonderful" and remarking that she loved them dearly.[20]

Initially, Stafford was delighted to be cossetted by the Gibneys, although she was suffering from insomnia and was also alarmed to discover how difficult it was for her to limit her drinking during her stay in the tropics. Several letters from Jensen proclaiming his love for her only succeeded in convincing her how "foolish" he was. She seemed less perturbed about the termination of her marriage than about what would happen to her belongings if he rented the house in Westport before her return.[21] Pleased to be far away from "awful Westport" and its Eisenhower supporters, she was concerned nevertheless about whether she would ever have a place of her own where she could settle in with her cat George Eliot, her first edition of George Eliot's Scenes of Clerical Life, and her spacious desk, which was a tangible symbol of her identity as a writer. "Often the thought of the future scares me," she admitted, "but for the most part I am calm as a vegetable."[22]

Stafford found the last week in the Virgin Islands the most trying because she was forced to leave her haven at Hawksnest and to remain in St. Thomas while awaiting a summons to court. "How I dread those last days, and the exposure to the Maughamish denizens of Charlotte Amalie with their awful little shops and their obstinately stupid minds," she wrote to Eudora Welty and Mary Lou Aswell before she left Hawksnest for St. Thomas.[23] As she had feared, St. Thomas "undid" her: she spent "a week of starvation induced by rage" in her "awful" room in a hotel named Bluebeard's Castle, drinking whiskey and worrying about how she would be able to support herself when she returned to the States.[24] Originally, she had considered sailing to Europe when the divorce was final, but she decided it was "harder to be broke abroad than . . . at home"[25] and planned instead to remain in New York until her finances improved. "I am anxious to get back and at the same time I am filled with dread because it seems to me that I am coming back to nothing," she wrote to Jensen, imploring him to be "kind, patient and forgiving" because she was "so sad."[26]

Despite her fear of airplanes, after the divorce was granted she decided to return to New York by plane since the trip by boat to the Virgin Islands had turned out to be very unpleasant. When she arrived in New York, she was so ill that her physician, Dr. Koteen, promptly readmitted her to New York Hospital for several days. From that refuge she wrote to the Gibneys that she did not know where she would settle but she was sure it wouldn't be New York.[27]

Stafford's strained financial circumstances were eased somewhat after the *New Yorker* generously gave her an advance; furthermore, a lawyer she had recently hired put pressure on Robert Giroux to see that she got an advance for a collection of her short stories that was scheduled to appear. Feeling a bit more solvent and unable to find an apartment to sublet, she moved into a "murderously expensive" Park Avenue hotel, the Sulgrave, after paying a brief visit to Peter and Eleanor Taylor in North Carolina. This reunion with two of her most intimate friends did not make her feel much more cheerful, however. She described the visit to the Taylors as "hopeless," observing to the Gibneys that "academic people on a Saturday night are worse than writers."[28]

Feeling depressed and uprooted after she returned to America, Stafford soon began thinking about resettling in Westport, the very town from which she had recently fled. Although she reported to the Gibneys in May that she was hard at work,[29] she soon announced, "New York is not for working people."[30] Distressed by the noise and the smell of her neighbors' dinner in the small New York apartment on East End Avenue that she had finally succeeded in subletting, she realized how much she missed friends in Westport like Katinka and Peter De Vries, Joe and Barbara Kaufman, and Joan Cuyler. When he learned that his former wife was looking for a place to rent in Fairfield County, Jensen was astounded since he had often been subjected to her tirades about Westport's "bourgeois bohemianism" and political conservatism. "I have always liked the landscape and the houses here," she explained. If she did decide to return to Westport, she said, she would only accept invitations to small, civilized dinner parties, maintaining that she had learned to dodge "all that hokum."[31]

Although she was dreadfully lonely in New York City, Stafford was alarmed when she learned that Mary Lee's son Jack was planning to visit her that June. Nevertheless, she took him to see whatever she thought a young man from rural Colorado might enjoy: the Broadway hit *Guys and Dolls,* which she found "too awful," the Empire State Building, Lindy's restaurant,

Times Square on Saturday night—and she complained afterward that, as a result, she was "a wreck." [32]

In August of 1953 Jean Stafford left New York for Connecticut. The writer Louis Kronenberger had offered to let her live in his house in Norwich for a month with two of his friends, Bernie Wolf and Fred Segal, providing her with a temporary refuge from the hot city. However, having recently been elected to New York's exclusive Cosmopolitan Club, an elegant meeting place and residential hotel for professional women, she worried what Louis Kronenberger's neighbor, Mrs. John Mason Brown, who was also a member of the Cosmopolitan Club, would say if she knew that she was living in the Kronenbergers' house with "two heterosexual men." [33]

Stafford's stay in Norwich was more short-lived than she had anticipated because the abundant greenery surrounding the Kronenbergers' farmhouse exacerbated her hay fever. By the end of August she had moved instead to a small, quiet hotel in Southport called the Pequot Inn. She found the inn so appealing that for a brief time she considered remaining in a cottage on its grounds rather than renting a place of her own in Westport. But even in these congenial surroundings she was not at ease, for a novella she had promised to contribute to a volume her friend Mary Lou Aswell was editing was still not completed. Though this novella, *A Winter's Tale,* was an abbreviated version of her early unpublished novel *Autumn Festival* rather than a new work, the task of revision was far more time-consuming than she had anticipated. Abjectly apologizing to Mary Lou Aswell for failing to meet her deadline, she said, "I'd rather die than tell you this . . . but this summer has been absolute hell." [34]

When arrangements to stay at the Pequot Inn permanently did not work out to her satisfaction that summer, she moved once again, this time to the top floor of a house at 24 Elm Avenue in Westport. While the apartment was very much more modest than the house she and Oliver had lived in, it was quiet and conveniently located in the center of town so that she did not have to rely on friends for transportation. The only other occupant of the house, her landlady, owned a dress shop and was away all day. "I never see her but when she comes in in the evening she calls upstairs, 'Good evening, Miss Stafford dearest,'" Stafford reported to the Gibneys. "It's not too bad but I don't intend to stay here after I've made my pile. Which has got to be soon since I'm poorer than I've been since adolescence," she said. She complained that she was "dead flat broke" and that never in her life had she been so depressed. She also described the final separation of her belongings from those of "O. J." as "one of the most harrowing experiences" of her life. Yet even though she said she was very depressed, the tone of this letter was surprisingly jocular, and though she claimed that she had sobbed for seventy-two hours, had remained drunk, hadn't bathed, had thrown up for a week, and had gotten a mild case of pellagra after she had packed up her belongings, her hyperbolical depiction of her sufferings was calculated to amuse the Gibneys as well as to arouse their sympathy. She concluded this description of her harrowing ordeal by asserting matter-of-factly, "Then I finally got my clothes to the cleaners and got a new sleeping tablet prescription and went on the wagon and now I am fine." [35]

Temporarily, a "mad autumnal tempest of creativity" allayed her anxieties. Relieved to find herself "writing like sixty six" once she had survived the strains of getting settled in her new quarters, she was delighted when this "fever of work" resulted in the sale of two new stories to the *New Yorker,* though the autobiographical novel she had begun still remained her "principal incubus." [36] She took comfort from the fact that despite the recent upheavals in her personal life, her career as a writer was still flourishing. *Children Are Bored on Sunday,* the first collection of her short stories, was issued in 1953, as was a second volume, *The Interior Castle,* which contained *Boston Adventure* and *The Mountain Lion,* as well as the ten stories that were also included in *Children Are Bored on Sunday.* Moreover, seven additional short stories—"The Violet Rock," "Life Is No Abyss," "I Love Someone," "The Connoisseurs," "Cops and Robbers," and "In the Zoo"—were also published during this period.

Children Are Bored on Sunday, issued jointly by Harcourt, Brace and Company and Random House in 1953, included ten short stories that had been published between 1945 and 1950 in the *New Yorker,* the *Partisan Review,* and *Harper's.* Among these stories are some of her most memorable ones: the title story, "The Echo and the Nemesis," "A Country Love Story," and "The Interior Castle." This volume of short stories would never earn a lot of money, for as William Peden has observed, in spite of the fact that short stories are enormously popular in periodicals, short story collections, with only rare exceptions, have been financial failures. [37] Nevertheless, *Children Are Bored on Sunday* increased Stafford's visibility as a writer and may well have helped to pave the way for the Pulitzer Prize she was to receive in 1970 for her *Collected Stories,* which included all ten of the stories in the first collection. The reviews for *Children Are Bored on Sunday* were mostly favorable. Describing the world of her fiction as "a limited one into which sunlight and fresh air never penetrate," with "the odor of death and decay" hovering over all, William Peden said that Stafford was "a skilled and disciplined artist who took great pains to write prose of admirable texture." [38] While several critics, on the contrary, thought that her intricate, embroidered prose was sometimes not as effective as it might have been, the overwhelming majority were favorably impressed by her achievement.

Among Stafford's stories that were published in 1952 and 1953 was "Life Is No Abyss," which appeared in the *Sewanee Review* in July of 1952. This story probably was a favorite of hers since she later chose to read it when she gave a public reading at the Y.M.-Y.W.H.A. Poetry Center in New York in 1967. Somewhat reminiscent of Welty's story in *A Curtain of Green* called "A Visit of Charity," a short story that also describes the visit of a young female protagonist to a public institution in which the elderly and infirm are incarcerated, "Life Is No Abyss" depicts the visit that twenty-year-old Lily pays to the poorhouse to see her octogenarian cousin, a bitter, cantankerous, and impoverished daughter of a Boston judge. Once well-to-do, Cousin Isobel had foolishly entrusted her fortune to her cousin Will, and he "madly and instantly" had "thrown her fortune to the four winds," leaving her penniless. Resembling one of the feisty elderly protagonists of Mary Wilkins Freeman, but somewhat less sympathetically drawn, Cousin Isobel exacts her revenge on the cousin who ruined her by making him feel guilty about her present state. Refusing the offers of various relatives to give her a home, Isobel prefers to feed upon her own wrath in the squalid surroundings she has chosen. Stafford unsparingly depicts how hateful the vindictive Isobel becomes when she is reduced to poverty. Nevertheless, morbidly in fear of being destitute herself, Stafford probably concurred with the sentiments voiced by her elderly protagonist, who says fiercely, "The lack of money is everything. . . . The lack of money is eternal punishment."[39]

It was also during this period that Stafford's stories about the Colorado of her youth began to appear in the pages of the *New Yorker*. Perhaps one of the inspirations for these local color stories was Sarah Orne Jewett's *The Country of Pointed Firs*. One of the books that Stafford sent as a gift to her sister Mary Lee that year, *The Country of Pointed Firs* focuses on female protagonists in a small, isolated town, depicting their rural milieu and their interactions with one another. Just as Willa Cather had begun to write about Nebraska after reading Sarah Orne Jewett's local color stories, so Stafford might have been inspired by Sarah Orne Jewett's stories to depict the life in a small Colorado town in her fiction. Stafford also admired the fiction of Willa Cather. After Knopf reissued *A Lost Lady* in 1973, Stafford wrote a very sympathetic review of Cather's novella. Having grown up herself in a West that had become tame and bourgeois and vulgar, she empathized with Cather's Marion Forrester, a woman who "lives in the wrong place at the wrong time, during the end of an era, the sunset of the pioneer."[40] As Willa Cather had done, Jean Stafford would reside in the East but also write about the town in the West where she had lived in her youth. While Stafford openly acknowledged her own debt to Mark Twain and Henry James, she appears to have owed a good deal as well to these two literary foremothers, Sarah Orne Jewett and Willa Cather, whose artful depictions of life in a small town she very much admired.

But if Willa Cather, born forty-two years before Jean Stafford, sometimes described in her fiction an earlier, more heroic era when the West was being settled, Stafford would depict in her Colorado stories an uninspiring milieu where the men on horseback were not dashing cowboys but rich polo-playing "dudes" from the East who "dressed in spotless riding trousers and expensive boots, short-sleeved white shirts, and rakish polo helmets";[41] where the adventurous past was represented only by "a clutter of seedy Western souvenirs";[42] and where the isolated outpost of adventurous prospectors for gold had given rise to a dreary town with "mongrel and multitudinous churches" and an ugly high school "shaped like a loaf of bread."[43] Although Polly Bay, the protagonist of Stafford's "The Liberation," admires the physical surroundings of Adams, Colorado, a town located in the foothills of the splendid Rocky Mountains, it is the provincialism of this town, its spiritual and intellectual desiccation, that prompts her to shout, "It's true—I hate, I despise, I abominate the West!"[44]

The three Colorado stories that appeared in 1952 and 1953, "The Violet Rock," "The Liberation," and "In the Zoo," all focus on female protagonists who suffer at the hands of their elders. As Stafford did, the youngest of these protagonists, Tess Vanderpool in "The Violet Rock," has two older sisters and an older brother. Tess enjoys most the company of her brother Jack: she wears his outgrown shirts and in the summer operates the popcorn machine with him in the park for the concessionaire. But Jack is not there to protect her when her sister Emily succeeds in convincing the little girl that the richest man in town has put a curse on her because she had "sassed him."[45] The "violet rock" in this charming if somewhat slight tale is described so vividly that people in Boulder who had read the story claimed the rock actually stood at the entrance to Boulder Canyon. Amused by their inability to distinguish fact from fiction, Jean Stafford told Oliver Jensen, ". . . this is an interesting fact to me since the violet rock, so far as I know, existed only in the mind of my sister Marjorie for a very brief time when we lived in Colorado Springs."[46] As Mark Twain had done, Stafford employs as narrator a child who speaks in the vernacular of the region; and as effectively as Mark Twain, she portrays the secret terrors of a naive child who is all too easily duped by her elders. For Tess Vanderpool, the small town in the West where she grows up is a place that terrifies her: she fears a corpse might be damming up the park "crick"; she suspects that miners who live on the outskirts of the town are "ready to carve up a girl into pieces if they took a mind to"; and she imagines that a house she must pass on her way home is haunted, its "long-dead, weed-ravaged garden . . . marking the graves of three horses, whose ghosts were heard trotting through Main Street invariably on a night when someone met a violent death."[47] But perhaps the grimmest aspect of the story is its depiction of the way a twelve-year-old preys on the fears and insecurities of her little sister. Because she herself is bored, the clever and volatile Emily frightens her sister Tess for her own amusement instead of offering to protect her.

The child Tess in "The Violet Rock" is unhappy in the western town where she lives. Similarly, Polly Bay, a thirty-year-old college professor in "The Liberation," dislikes the western town called Adams where she resides, and she fully comprehends "the claustrophobia that sent her sisters and cousins all but screaming out of town."[48] Feeling that "her own life had been like a dream of smothering," she is eager to leave Adams forever and go live in the East with the man from Boston to whom she has become secretly engaged. Her elderly uncle and aunt, with whom she has lived since her parents' death, insist that in leaving the West she is betraying the heritage of a family dating back to the first western migration. But leave she must to escape the stifling world of her hypochondriacal and chauvinistic relatives, even though she learns that her fiancé has died suddenly. The conclusion of the story is somewhat forced, perhaps. However, "The Liberation" successfully dramatizes the desperation of a young woman who feels trapped in the small town in the West in which she was raised. Fleeing for her life when she leaves the house of her relatives, Polly Bay realizes that she was in danger of remaining imprisoned forever in their musty, decaying ancestral home.

Of the three Adams stories published in 1952 and 1953, the darkest and most haunting is "In the Zoo." It appeared in the *New Yorker* in September of 1953 and subsequently received a three-hundred-dollar first prize in the O. Henry Memorial Awards of 1955. Thanks to the fact that "In the Zoo" has been reprinted in the widely circulated *Norton Anthology of Short Fiction,* it is today perhaps the best known of Stafford's short stories. The narrator of "In the Zoo" is an older incarnation of Polly Bay, the protagonist of "The Liberation." If Polly Bay has hopes of escaping physically and psychologically from Adams, the narrator of "In the Zoo" is forced to acknowledge in middle age that even though she succeeded in leaving Adams many years earlier, the years of desperation that she spent there left a permanent mark on her psyche. Born in the East but orphaned when she was eight and her sister Daisy was ten, the narrator and her sister had been sent to live with the "possessive, unloving, scornful, complacent"[49] Mrs. Placer, a girlhood friend of their grandmother. As she and her older sister observe a blind polar bear in the Denver zoo during one of their infrequent meetings, they are both mournfully reminded of a man named Mr. Murphy who was their only friend during their childhood when they were exiled to Adams.

In this story, begun soon after Stafford visited her father in Hayden during the summer of 1951, it is the mother figure, Mrs. Placer, rather than the father figure, Mr. Murphy, who plays the role of a Dickensian villain. The operator of a boardinghouse, like Stafford's own mother, "Gran" is forever dwelling on her own martyrdom and the slights she has had to endure. Life, according to Gran and her doleful boarders, is "essentially a matter of being done in, let down, and swindled."[50] In the corrosive atmosphere of the boardinghouse, the narrator and her sister are taught by Gran to be suspicious of others. As they begin to comprehend how mean-spirited their foster mother is, they grow to despise this woman who constantly reminds them that she has "sacrificed herself to the bone" for them.[51] Their only moments of happiness occur when they visit their friend Mr. Murphy, an alcoholic ne'er-do-well who plays solitaire all day and talks to a menagerie of bedraggled animals he has collected. When Mr. Murphy gives the girls a loving pup named Laddy, Gran appropriates the dog, renames him Caesar, and trains him to be a vicious cur who nips at the heels of strangers. The violence in the story escalates when Caesar kills Mr. Murphy's pet monkey, and Mr. Murphy, in turn, poisons Caesar.

At the story's conclusion, the narrator describes her trip back to the East after she has parted from her sister in Denver. She reveals that the attitude of mistrust instilled in her by Mrs. Placer has permanently altered her own perception of the world: she is suspicious of her fellow passengers on the train, and looking at the alfalfa fields through the train window, she imagines "they are chockablock with marijuana."[52] As Joyce Carol Oates has pointed out, "the story concludes with an extravagant outburst of paranoia that manages to be comic as well as distressing."[53] Just as Stafford recalled the bitter arguments of her own parents when she described the interminable wrangling of the Marburgs in *Boston Adventure,* so does she recreate her own feelings of horror and powerlessness during her childhood when she describes the reactions of the cringing narrator and her sister Daisy to the savage conflict between Mrs. Placer and Mr. Murphy, bitter antagonists who resemble her own mother and father. Sorrowfully remembering that her own beloved dog had been poisoned, that her mother had disliked the dog, that her father had often allied himself with her against her mother, she chose in this story to make the father figure, Mr. Murphy, a more sympathetic figure than the mother surrogate, Mrs. Placer. Convinced that her own upbringing had had a pernicious effect on her adult psyche, she created this brilliant, unforgettable, harrowing tale of childhood misery and adult regret.

Initially, as Stafford's life settled into a routine in her new apartment in Westport, she was happy to be relieved of some of the social obligations that had been a constant burden when she was married to Oliver Jensen. However, although she appreciated having more time for her writing, she discovered that she was frequently too lonely or anxious to settle down to work. As she wrote in "Divorce: Journey through Crisis," an article that was published in *Harper's Bazaar,* "The habit of being married is difficult to break," and though the person seeking a divorce often wants to be free of certain responsibilities, she may discover following a divorce that "it is grievous to be deprived of status, and of the disciplines and responsibilities of marriage . . ."[54] Now that she was in charge of her own schedule, she sometimes welcomed performing the very tasks she had found bothersome when she was married. "Is there anything I can do for you?" she asked the Gibneys, explaining, "I have to go to New York once a week (thank God) and would be delighted to run errands."[55] And though at first she rejoiced in being single, by February of 1954 she admitted to Nancy and Robert Gibney, "I think I would like to be married, or at least associated with someone, but I am still to [sic] apathetic to start the search."[56]

During her periodic trips to New York, Stafford would arrange to meet her friends—Bea and Allen Grover, Louis Auchincloss, Patricia McManus, Ann Honeycutt; people with whom she was friendly at the *New Yorker* such as Joseph Mitchell, Howard Moss, and Katharine White; or her new literary agent, James Oliver Brown, and her editor, Robert Giroux. Frequently suffering from real or imaginary ailments, she also paid visits to an assortment of physicians in the city and continued to see her psychiatrist, Dr. Sherfey, as well. Whenever the Gibneys were in town and on other occasions, too, she used the Cosmopolitan Club as her pied à terre. Being a member entitled her to be welcomed by a doorman into its elegant front hall with its gleaming black and white tiles and curved wrought iron staircase, to write letters on Cosmopolitan Club stationery, to secure a modest room for two-week intervals for a nominal sum, to have tea on the terrace, and to entertain her friends in its elegant dining room and sitting rooms. In college she had never been asked to join a sorority because she was "strikingly unpopular, unattractive, cantankerous, and dirt poor,"[57] though in retrospect she was not sure she would have joined a sorority even if she had been invited to do so. But remembering how it had felt to be excluded from a sorority, she now enjoyed belonging to the Cosmopolitan Club, where in order to be considered for membership one had only to be professionally accomplished rather than well-to-do or popular.

With the exception of an occasional trip to New York, she spent most of her time in Westport. When her writing was causing her too much anxiety or when she was feeling lonely and depressed, she would telephone friends in Westport to discuss a book she was reading or gossip about mutual friends or amusingly describe her latest ailments. Later, she would regret having revealed so much about her personal life to friends.[58] With the exception of Nancy Gibney, in fact, Stafford had few women friends with whom she remained intimate for a very extended period of her life, though wherever she was, she always found someone to serve as her confidante. Loathing the fact that she was so needy, she played the game Lillian Hellman once described as "the game of embrace-denounce." What Lillian Hellman wrote about Dorothy Parker would apply to Jean Stafford as well: desiring to charm, to be loved, to be admired "brought self-contempt that could only be consoled by behind the back denunciations . . ."[59]

Susanna Cuyler recalls that when she was five or six, she and her mother went to visit Jean Stafford in the Elm Avenue apartment. Ill, lying in a hospital bed she had installed in her bedroom, Stafford "held court" for her visitors. "Jean Stafford, when I was a child in Westport . . . was someone who assured me growing up was worthwhile, that the imprisonments of childhood would end. She was free," Susanna Cuyler reminisced in 1979 soon after Stafford's death. As an adult, Cuyler later came to appreciate her wit as well as her abilities as a writer. "I knew," she said, "she drank too much, was malicious, cruel, etc. but still what a laughter maker!"[60]

In the fall of 1954, Stafford summarized the events of the preceding summer to the Gibneys. She had remained in her freshly painted apartment in Westport, she said, and "except for loathing the summer people from New York," she had had a relatively pleasant though rather boring summer. One weekend she had accompanied Katinka and Peter De Vries to East Hampton, where "everyone seemed very rich and very corrupt," and she had also taken a trip to Gambier to visit Peter and Eleanor Taylor at Kenyon College. Describing this reunion with her friends as "disastrous," she remarked acerbically, "I have come to the conclusion that I dislike literary people more than *any* others and I particularly can't stand the ones that move about in groups. And as for academic society, oh, my God!" She also mentioned in this letter that her beloved cat, George Eliot, had been hit by a car that summer, sustaining a dreadful concussion; and that she had heard that Cal was back in Payne Whitney. Lowell's latest manic behavior, she said, closely resembled "immorality," his antics causing damage "from Cincinnati to Rome." The distressing news about Lowell, who had now decided he was in love with someone other than his second wife, Elizabeth Hardwick, as well as news that Oliver Jensen had recently gotten married for the third time, made her think with "dismay" about her own marriages to these two men. [61]

Delighted that she had recently earned more than ten thousand dollars from her writing during a twelve-month period, she began to spend some of it on new clothes and on furniture for her apartment. However, when her sister Mary Lee came for a visit during the autumn of 1954, Stafford began to feel guilty about her recent extravagance. Mary Lee's latest tales of woe about their father reminded her how little she herself had contributed to his upkeep over the years. Her sister Marjorie would later recall that whenever she asked Jean to make time to see their father, Jean became defensive and said she had no intention of "jeopardizing the edifice" she had built with her writing. [62] The almost eighty-year-old John Stafford had recently rediscovered a former college classmate and was considering the possibility of going to live with her in Los Angeles. Mary Lee urged Jean to encourage his courtship of Grace Finney, whose eccentricities matched his own. During Mary Lee's visit to Westport, Stafford complained to the Gibneys about her sister: ". . . she has contrived, in the gentlest and most ladylike way to make me feel like a heartless cad and the whole body of my lifelong guilt is sitting squarely on my chest. I *hate* family. When I was ten years old I walked out the back door and never went home again except for meals and I wouldn't have gone back for them if I'd been able to live on yucca and ladybugs in the mountains." Apologizing for writing them such a "wretched jeremiad," she exclaimed: "God damn it all to hell. I have been *so* happy, so productive, so healthy and at this point every bit of it seems to be gone. I have made a very interesting discovery that I am the only member of my family who was not neurotic and that's why they had to drive me into the bin." [63]

Between February of 1955 and January of 1956, Stafford published six new works of fiction in addition to a descriptive piece on the winter she had spent in Damariscotta that appeared in *Holiday.* The Jamesian *A Winter's Tale,* a retrospective account of a young woman's loss of innocence in prewar Heidelberg, was included in *New Short Novels,* edited by Mary Louise Aswell, and "Bad Characters," a humorous story about a childhood escapade in Colorado that is narrated by Emily Vanderpool, was published in the *New Yorker.* Four additional stories that are related to Stafford's life in Westport also appeared in the *New Yorker* during this period: "Beatrice Trueblood's Story," "Maggie Meriwether's Rich Experience," "The Warlock," and "The End of a Career." While Westport is not mentioned explicitly in any of these stories, both "Beatrice Trueblood's Story" and "Maggie Meriwether's Rich Experience" describe the kind of affluent people that Stafford encountered at elegant parties in Westport; "The End of a Career," a chilling tale about the desperate attempts made by an aging beauty to maintain her youthful appearance, is based on the experience of somebody she had heard about there; and "The Warlock" describes a voyage similar to the one Stafford took to the Virgin Islands to secure a divorce from Jensen. Both "Beatrice Trueblood's Story" and "The Warlock" were included among the O. Henry Award prize stories, the first in 1956 and the second in 1957. Although none of the works Stafford published during this period represents a radical departure from what she had written before, her fiction as well as her article in *Holiday* on Damariscotta are very accomplished works that reveal her versatility, her technical virtuosity, her wit, her irony, and the wonderful felicities of her prose style.

Stafford's friend Joseph Mitchell was later to observe about her decision to live in Westport, "She got off the train at the wrong place."[64] In one of her letters to Lowell that she wrote soon after her divorce from Jensen, she described the town as "absurd," and she said she was trying to pretend she was living in "a New England village instead of in the most vulgar suburb in the Western hemisphere."[65] It is true that she was quite productive during the time she lived there and that several of her short stories were inspired by her life in Westport, but in contrast to John Cheever, John Updike, and Peter De Vries, she never made the affluent suburban world a primary focus of her fiction, nor did she ever really feel at home there.

In July 1955, as Stafford's fortieth birthday approached, her anxiety about the future intensified. Pleased that her short stories had provided her with a steady source of income, she worried nevertheless about devoting her time to writing stories when she should have been working on the novel for which she had signed a contract. Moreover, always concerned about her health, she was distressed that for no apparent reason her eyes had begun to tear continuously. This annoying condition, which had developed soon after she returned from the Virgin Islands, still showed no signs of abating. Her "groper," Dr. Sherfey, speculating that the problem might be psychogenic in nature, pointed out that the tearing had begun soon after Jean Stafford's hysterectomy and immediately after she had become very attached to the Gibneys' baby at Hawksnest. After reading "Beatrice Trueblood's Story," a tale about a woman who becomes deaf, Dr. Sherfey pointed out that, since she had written a story about psychological deafness, she should be able to accept the fact that her own eye problems might be psychogenic in nature. The skeptical patient, however, insisted that Dr. Sherfey's explanation was "too neat," and, moreover, that even if her symptoms were psychogenic rather than due to a physical cause, she did not know how understanding the origin of the condition would help to cure it.[66]

Joseph Mitchell recalls that frequently when Stafford would arrive in Manhattan from Westport, she would telephone him from the train station and implore him to come to her rescue because she felt too filled with apprehension to move about the city on her own.[67] A sentence she wrote in a letter to the Gibneys during the summer of 1955 reflects how anxious and aimless she felt: "I feel as if I had my hat and coat on and were sitting uneasily in a railway station, not at all sure I want to get on the train," she said, describing a recent four-day stay at the Cosmopolitan Club during which she had spent most of the time "in a state bordering on rigor mortis." Endeavoring to remember "why on earth it is one ever gets up in the morning," she had never lifted her telephone except to order food. She assured the Gibneys that now she was somewhat more cheerful than she had been, but admitted, "I still feel as if I were put together with safety pins and have neither jokes or news to report."[68]

One cause for her agitation that summer—or perhaps a symptom of it— was the fact that she found herself to be suffering more and more frequently from writer's block. She complained to Katharine White that she had no ideas and did not know how she could continue to support herself unless she could keep on turning out marketable short stories. Anxious to be of assistance, White took her to lunch and told her about a tragic drowning that had occurred in New Hampshire many years before, an event she herself had always wanted to turn into a short story. In her youth, just after she had become engaged to Ernest Angell, the young man who was to become her first husband, Katharine White had visited her aunt's house after a summer outing. She and Ernest discovered that two of the Irish maids who worked for her aunt had gone swimming and had failed to return at the expected hour. Ernest soon found the maids' clothing in the boathouse but saw no other trace of the young women. More concerned about impressing her fiancé than about the fate of the "poor dead Irish girls,"[69] Katharine had rushed off to check the neighboring houses. Changing the locale of the story from New Hampshire to Colorado, Jean Stafford based a story she called "The Mountain Day" on the tragic incident Katharine White had related to her that day at lunch.

After Labor Day, Stafford took a brief trip to London, hoping that a change of scene would improve her spirits. Just before her departure she had seen Nancy Gibney in New York and had learned much to her distress that her friends, the Gibneys, had been having serious marital problems. She freely dispensed advice, but later apologized for her "drunken and intrusive behavior," writing from the *Liberté,* "My intentions are of the best and my performance is abominable." Comparing herself with Nancy's husband, Gib, she said: "I see so much of myself in Gib that that was another reason I shouldn't have gone on so long with you about him—I have looked on myself all my life as an orphan who had siblings and living parents and this is something like being an only child and have spent a great many of my years being involved in some aspect of rejection: dying a thousand deaths over being rejected or dying a million over rejecting." Much of this letter, however, was more cheerful than her previous ones. She said the ship was "a great pleasure" and expressed delight that she had been able to move from the "stygian and deeply interior broom closet" of a room to a large, airy outside cabin since the ship was half empty. The person occupying the adjacent cabin turned out to be a fellow writer from the *New Yorker* and former member of the crowd at the *Partisan Review,* Dwight McDonald, a "very funny man" whose company she enjoyed. Delighted to discover that in this environment she was able to concentrate on her writing for a period of three hours without interruption, she told Nancy Gibney that she might decide to stay in London indefinitely. The letter concluded with the kind of puns she and Nancy delighted in: "Chuck Roast and Tit Willow have led me to contemplate surgery for the removal of the skin of one's teeth, the bat of an eye, a frog in the throat, a bee in the bonnet." By the time she mailed the letter from the elegant Connaught Hotel, her jubilation at being back in the "supreme city" of London had changed to depression. In a postscript she wrote that she was "stupefied with a London cold." [70]

Stafford's stay in London was much briefer than she had anticipated. Worried about how much her stay was costing her, she soon decided to return to her Elm Avenue apartment in Westport, but she felt no more at home in this town of station wagons, barking dogs, and endless parties than she had in the past. Her writing was still at an impasse, and she was drinking far too much alcohol and consuming far too little nourishing food. Moreover, she was once again in a state of panic about her finances. It is evident that even though she was an established writer by 1955, her worries and her ways of dealing with them were not too different from those of the novice writer who had once contemplated her future with trepidation as she consumed cheap wine in her rented room in Concord in 1939. Her fears about her future multiplied when she discovered, in going over her financial affairs with her accountant, that she had earned less in 1955 than she had earned in any year since she had begun writing for the *New Yorker.* As a result, though she was tempted to visit Nancy Gibney during a "bleak, stale, ugly, nearly snowless winter," she did not feel she could afford to do so. "I keep hoping that some day I can arrange my life in such a way that I can accept such a pleasure as coming down to see you without being hampered by guilt or disease or impoverishment, which at this moment is acute . . . ," she wrote in January of 1956. [71]

In addition to her usual assortment of physical ailments, that winter she developed infectious hepatitis. "Now, threatened by relapse and by jaundice, I am on the wagon and for six months must eat 4000 calories a day (my average is 750) and lie abed half the time and get liver shots," she informed Nancy Gibney.[72] By February, though the hepatitis was under control, she had to have a cyst excised from the inside of her lower lip. "New York Hospital was her second home," Patricia McManus observed about her friend Jean's frequent hospitalizations.[73]

Despite illness and debilitating depression, Stafford managed to complete two stories for the *New Yorker,* and with the money she received in payment, as well as a tax refund, she paid a deposit on the *Mauretania,* intending to return to England. By the time she left for England, she would have undergone surgery for a neuroma in her foot; consequently, instead of "hotfooting" it across the Atlantic Ocean as she had done in her youth, she would be reduced to limping when she disembarked from the ship.

Between January and August of 1956, Stafford published four short stories: "The End of a Career," "A Reading Problem," and "The Mountain Day" in the *New Yorker,* and "The Matchmakers" (later renamed "Caveat Emptor") in *Mademoiselle.* Though none of the stories received the kind of accolades that had been bestowed on some of her earlier short stories, two of the four— "The End of a Career" and "A Reading Problem"—are outstanding examples of her achievement in this genre.

"The End of a Career," which dramatizes the desperate and ultimately futile quest of an aging woman to preserve her beauty and her youthful appearance, is an indictment both of the narcissistic woman and of a society that places a premium on feminine beauty and youthfulness. Like the doomed female protagonist in Hawthorne's "The Birthmark," Stafford's protagonist, who is symbolically named "Angelica Early," is willing to undergo a painful operation each summer in order to keep her angelic youthful appearance unblemished. Using an assumed name, she retreats to a clinic where a plastic surgeon planes away the surface of her skin with an electrically propelled steel-wire brush, causing her sickening pain. Desperately anxious to live up to her reputation as a great beauty, she decides that she wishes to die after a cruel remark by a stranger, which she overhears in an elevator, makes her realize that even if her face belies her age, her wrinkled hands reveal how old she really is. In this story about a woman whose frail ego is dependent on the affirmation of others, Stafford uses a telling analogy: desperate herself about her own flagging creativity during this period, Stafford wrote, "If my talent goes, I'm done for, says the artist, and Angelica said, if I lose my looks, I'm lost."[74]

"A Reading Problem," the third and last of the Emily Vanderpool stories to appear in the *New Yorker*, is similar to the earlier "Bad Characters" in its humorous evocation of the trials of a solitary, spirited young girl whose own isolation in a small western town leads her to befriend an unsavory character. In "Bad Characters," which was published in the *New Yorker* in 1954, Emily becomes the companion of an eleven-year-old petty thief named Lottie Jump, and in "A Reading Problem" she makes the acquaintance of a purveyor of patent medicines and evangelical preacher named Reverend Gerlash. Seeking a quiet place to read, Emily rejects the mountains in the winter because of the cold, in the spring because of the wood ticks, and in the summer because of the snakes. The public library also proves to be unsuitable, as does the lobby of the downtown hotel, and when Emily finally retreats in desperation to the visitors' waiting room of the jail, she is once again uprooted after the sheriff locks up some foul-mouthed moonshiners. On her way home, the frustrated Emily encounters Evangelist Gerlash and his bedraggled daughter Opal. Stafford wonderfully portrays the shenanigans of the Bible-toting evangelist and his pathetic, half-starved daughter. "I could eat a bushel of roasting ears. We ain't had a meal in a dog's age—not since that old handout in Niwot," Opal says, hoping that Emily will get her parents to invite them to dinner.[75] In her author's note to a volume of her short stories that she called *Bad Characters,* Stafford acknowledged that she "often occupied" the skin of the stubborn Emily, who was "a trial to her kin." She said that although she herself had wanted to be a road agent when she was young, she didn't have a chance; and as was true of her protagonist, the bookish Stafford always felt unwanted. Emily is exiled from the jail, afraid of the snakes in the mountains and in the way in the living room where her mother and her aunt are forever cutting out Butterick patterns. Seeking a quiet place to read, she is finally forced to retreat to the cemetery to study for an upcoming Bible contest.

Because Stafford was having great difficulty inventing plots for new stories, she took little comfort from the fact that she had had four stories published in 1956. When the *New Yorker* rejected her latest submission, "The Matchmakers," she had additional cause for alarm. This was the first time in several years that she had been obliged to submit a story elsewhere. Katharine White told her that she found the love affair in the story between two disaffected college teachers to be unconvincing and felt, moreover, that the satirical portrait of life in a second-rate college was not original enough to warrant publication.[76] Based on Stafford's experience at Stephens College, the story was a reworking of some of the material she had intended to include in her early unpublished novel, *Neville.* Even more distressing than having the story rejected, however, was her inability to make any headway on her autobio-

graphical novel. Before she sailed for Europe that June, she wrote to Katharine White that the novel was hopelessly inchoate.[77] Though Jessyca Russell
had reported in the *Writer's Newsletter* in April that Stafford was finishing up
a new novel in Westport, Connecticut,[78] in truth, the completion of the novel
was nowhere in sight. Writing to Albert Erskine at Random House to tell him
how "ashamed" she was of her failure to complete it, Stafford said abjectly:
"The novel just isn't ready and just won't be ready—at this point I think,
ever. . . . It's partly the fault of hepatitis and partly the fault of poverty, so that
I keep having to leave the book and write a story, but it's mainly indolence,
stupidity and a fundamental lack of talent." She confessed to Erskine that she
was "full of neurotic fears" and often thought of suicide.[79] Had she realized
that this novel was destined to remain unfinished during the next twenty-
three years of her life, she might not have had the courage to squander her
rapidly dwindling capital on a trip to London.

Eleven

Life Is No Abyss
Summer 1956–Winter 1963

The beauty of the world has two edges, one of laughter, one of anguish,
cutting the heart asunder.

—VIRGINIA WOOLF, *A ROOM OF ONE'S OWN*

JEAN STAFFORD WAS so anxious to leave Westport and so loath to return to Boulder that she chose to receive in absentia the Norlin Medal from her alma mater that summer, even though it was her favorite professor, Joseph Cohen, who had proposed her for this honor awarded to an outstanding graduate of the university. On the eve of her departure for England in June, she wrote to Richard Ludwig, an American acquaintance who had helped her to locate a suitable flat in London, to tell him how pleased she was about the prospect of returning to Europe. She said she planned to write a story for the *New Yorker* about Germany but confided that, as usual, she was worried about her finances. Describing her plans for the coming months, she observed: "Where any single solitary cent of money to pay for this vast shenanigan is going to come from I am sure I don't know. The policeman is outside my house at this very moment waiting to take me to debtor's prison and put a big ball and chain on my leg and give me a crust of bread once a day and a Girl Scout folding cup of water."[1]

When she arrived in London, she was in dreadful physical and mental shape. She complained to James Oliver Brown that the flat she had rented at 20 Chesham Place in Belgrave Square was "undoubtedly the most loathsome in London" and that the continuous noise of pneumatic drills from a building site across the way was intolerable.[2] Drinking heavily, unable to eat or to get any writing done, she was soon being treated by both an internist and a London psychiatrist. "I am so *sick* of telling the same dreary story," she wrote to her friend Ann Honeycutt at the end of June about her visit to her new psychiatrist, remarking plaintively that she desperately wanted "a magic wand that works."[3]

Suffering from the familiar "food (absence of) and drink (superabundance of) syndrome," she was urged by her psychiatrist to go to a nursing home for a week. Instead, anxious to escape from the noisy flat, she eagerly accepted whatever social invitations came her way. One evening she had dinner with Freud's grandson, the photographer Walker Evans, and George Orwell's widow. Following their meeting, Sonia Orwell arranged for her to be admitted to the House of Lords, where she sat in the Peeresses' gallery and listened to a debate. "It's true, the ladies' room is a dream and I stole some letter paper from it," she wrote to Ann Honeycutt afterward. She also mentioned that she had spent several evenings with Dorothy Parker's husband, Alan Campbell, whom she had met up with by chance in the bar of the Hotel Connaught. Still married to *New Yorker* writer Dorothy Parker but temporarily separated from her, the handsome and very drunk Campbell had told Stafford that he would like to marry her even if she was a lot like Dottie. "Indeed!" Jean Stafford exclaimed in her letter to Ann Honeycutt, remarking that she had wanted to phone him that very night to ask him what he meant by this "gratuitous insult." She claimed to have been so upset by this incident that she developed a case of paroxysmal tachycardia and awoke to discover that a blood vessel had burst in her arm.[4]

Sometime that summer she revisited Heidelberg, but even though she was impressed anew by its physical beauty, she was taken aback by the hostility of the German residents of Heidelberg who had observed her getting out of a U.S. Army car. "My Blithe, Sad Bird," an O. Henry Award–winning short story that appeared in the *New Yorker* in April of 1957, grew out of this visit to Heidelberg. Like Stafford, the story's protagonist, an American revisiting Heidelberg after a lapse of twenty years, finds it largely unchanged except for the fact that American soldiers have replaced the S.S. men she remembers from her earlier visit. Embodying the changes that have taken place in Heidelberg since the war are an American whom Miranda had met there when she was a student and his former landlady. Both this friend and the German woman exist now on memories of happier times, and as Miranda contemplates the sad spectacle of their diminished lives, she sadly realizes that "nothing on earth could drag her here again."[5] Although Stafford did not choose to include "My Blithe, Sad Bird" in her *Collected Stories,* it is an effective tale that vividly contrasts the Heidelberg she had seen in 1936 and the one she observed two decades later. Since the story is the last of Stafford's works to deal with her sojourn in Heidelberg in 1936, her protagonist's observation that "nothing on earth could drag her here again" may also be seen as Stafford's rueful acknowledgment that the Heidelberg material was now exhausted and could no longer serve as a subject for her fiction.

Before Stafford had left for England, Katharine White had given her letters of introduction to various English writers, including the London correspondent for the *New Yorker,* Mollie Panter-Downes, and novelist Elizabeth Taylor. Subsequently, when Katharine White learned that Stafford was dispirited and ill, she added another name to the list of people in London whose company she thought Stafford might enjoy: *New Yorker* staff writer Abbott Joseph Liebling. Asking Stafford whether she knew him, White said: "He is—or was, two weeks ago—at Duke's [*sic*] Hotel in London. We found him the best sort of London companion. He is a strange man; often it is next to impossible to get into conversation with him, some people think. But he smiles like a Buddha and when he does talk, it is very good indeed. He is a gourmet who knows the best and least obvious places to eat, and he takes a gusty delight in the English music-hall humors and entertainments. I am very fond of him and I've written a note to look you up."[6]

Katharine White must have been astonished when she learned subsequently that the rotund, bald, near-sighted, avuncular Joe Liebling had fallen in love with Stafford and that she, in turn, had fallen in love with him. At the time that he and Stafford met, Liebling was separated though not yet divorced from his second wife, Lucille Spectorsky. Eleven years older than Stafford, Liebling was a close friend of Stafford's pal Joseph Mitchell, but though she had admired Liebling's pieces in the *New Yorker* for years, she had never been introduced to this brilliant writer who had produced trenchant analyses of American journalism in the *New Yorker's* regularly featured column "The Wayward Press," stirring accounts from the World War II battlefields, and vivid descriptions of boxing matches and other sporting events. Adept at incorporating references to Faust, Ahab, Sisyphus, Churchill, Orson Welles, Don Giovanni, Margot Fonteyn, Artur Rubenstein, and Kafka into a single article on prizefighting,[7] Liebling was a journalist's journalist, even though his books had never sold well.

Liebling's father, a Jewish immigrant from Austria, had become a successful furrier in Manhattan by the time his only son was born. Liebling attended public school, first in New York City and then in Far Rockaway. At the age of sixteen he entered Dartmouth College but was soon expelled for failing to attend chapel regularly. He then enrolled at Columbia University's Pulitzer School of Journalism, secretly hoping to become a writer of fiction rather than a journalist. Later he remarked that the school had "all the intellectual status of a training school for future employees of the A & P."[8] His favorite course at Columbia was not a writing course but one in Romance philology. In 1926–1927 he had the opportunity to learn about France firsthand when he attended the University of Paris. That year he also explored the French countryside and officially began his life as a celebrated gourmet and gourmand by liberally sampling the French cuisine from Normandy to the Parisian cafés of the Left Bank. Four years before he met Stafford, he had been awarded the French Legion of Honor for his writing. A great admirer of François Villon, Rabelais, Stendhal, and Camus, he impressed her with his knowledge of French literature and also French medieval history. His wide-ranging interests and his witty observations made him an excellent companion.

Liebling was spending the summer alone in London and was living at his favorite London hotel, the small, unassuming Victorian Dukes Hotel, situated on a dead-end street off St. James. By some quirk of fate, the hotel is located very near both the Stafford Hotel and a street called Catherine Wheel Yard. Liebling, who weighed close to 250 pounds and suffered intermittently from acute attacks of gout and renal colic, was already showing the ill effects of years of feasting and excessive drinking. He was not one to let his physical ills interfere with his pleasures, however. When he was not taking notes at Epsom for a piece he was writing on Derby Day or sampling the specialty of some out-of-the-way restaurant he had discovered, he could be found at a table in a modest club near Haymarket, exchanging gossip with old cronies he had met during the war. Sporting a newly purchased rolled up black umbrella and a stiff black derby like the one his father had worn when Liebling was a boy, this stout, bald man in owlish wire-rimmed spectacles might have been mistaken for a London barrister until his New York accent became audible when he began to speak.[9]

According to Liebling's biographer, Raymond Sokolov, Liebling had been "lunging at almost every woman who crossed his path that spring."[10] When a letter arrived from Katharine White urging him to contact Stafford, he phoned the London office of the *New Yorker* and was told that Stafford had just stopped in to pick up her mail. They arranged to meet for tea. She later said about their first meeting, "I was awfully, awfully timid about it. I'd been reading him for years. We had some booze in the lobby. I was so impressed; he was wonderfully amiable."[11]

It would be difficult to picture anyone more dissimilar physically to the tall, handsome Robert Lowell or the tall, handsome Oliver Jensen than A. J. Liebling, nor did he resemble the shorter, wiry men in her life: her father, Hightower, and Joseph Mitchell. If he resembled anyone it was her father-surrogate, Alfred Cohn, who was also bald, plump, and myopic. Over the years Dr. Cohn had continued to correspond with Stafford and had generously renewed her subscription each year to the *Times Literary Supplement.* Sometime before her departure for Europe, she had learned that Dr. Cohn had suffered a debilitating stroke, which had deprived him of the power of speech. In "De Senectute," an unpublished story she wrote about Dr. Cohn after his death in 1957, her protagonist Cora Savage speaks about a character named Uncle Julian in terms that might have been used to describe Liebling as well: "This plump, short, bald, myopic man was the most glamorous she had ever known, and she had preferred his facts to the fantasies of the Arabian nights."[12] Although Liebling was fascinated by plebian pastimes such as horse racing and boxing that the intellectual humanist, Dr. Cohn, might have considered frivolous, Liebling's intellectual interests, like those of Dr. Cohn, were broad; moreover, like Dr. Cohn, Liebling was more than willing to play the role of benefactor to Stafford. In one important respect, however, Liebling also resembled her father: he was a journalist, as her father had been in the days before he had married when he had worked as a newspaper reporter in New York City.

Just before she met Liebling, Stafford had written to Ann Honeycutt about her relationship with men: "On the whole, I'm more for adoption than marriage."[13] As Liebling began inviting her to accompany him to the races, introducing her to his friends, and treating her to wonderful food and vintage wines at his favorite restaurants, she soon discovered that here, indeed, was an interesting, generous man who seemed willing to "adopt" her. Writing to Ann Honeycutt after she had returned from a "sublime" day at the races with Liebling, she said that the cheese he had supplied had been delicious and that riding in the Rolls Royce he had hired for the occasion was "like riding in a house."[14] Amused to learn about her friend Jean's latest adventures, Katinka De Vries inquired, "Does Liebling take basket lunches with the foil-sealed tops of something vintage peering out of the top?"[15] Though Liebling was hardly well-to-do, he did things with panache. When she left for home early that fall, Stafford would bring with her several suits Joe had had his London tailor make for her. Even more appealing to her than his generosity was the fact that he did not criticize her for drinking too much, as Cal and Oliver had done. A person who habitually overindulged in food and drink himself, he could hardly afford to upbraid his amusing new companion for her tendency to overindulge. Though Stafford took delight in emphasizing that Joe was "positively ugly,"[16] she was also quick to point out how generous and amusing he was. Moreover, she herself at forty-one was hardly the beautiful young woman she had been when she had posed for the art classes in Boulder. Eve Auchincloss, who met Jean Stafford for the first time that summer in London, vividly recalls the impression Jean made on her: "She had a sort of squarish, shapeless body. At 41 she wasn't beautiful. Her head was often cocked to one side, with her eyebrows drawn up in a pleading sort of expression. She had very big hands and feet. Her hands were slightly shaky, as she would guide a cigarette to her lips. Her hair was lusterless, permanented in a funny frizz."[17]

When Stafford complained to Liebling about her noisy flat, he suggested that she move to a room at Dukes Hotel.[18] They continued to see one another frequently during the month of August, and though both were somewhat wary about committing themselves to a permanent relationship, they spent several days together in a house they rented in the town of Lewes. A playful poem Stafford sent to "Jo Jo, the Birthday Boy" suggests that it was her idea to go to Lewes. Drawing a heart inscribed with the message "I Love You" on the left-hand corner of a piece of paper, she wrote:

> The nug who dearly loves the birthday boy
> And beseeches for him supernal and eternal joy
> HAS A TENDER PLOY:
> Giddy & Giddy (EST AGTS.) have a house
> To let (in Lewes)[19]

The poem is puzzling since Liebling was actually born on October 18 and the letter was sent somewhat earlier; perhaps they decided to celebrate his birthday early because she would no longer be in London by October. Several months after their trip to Lewes, he would write to her from Rome, ". . . it is nearly as good as Lewes, until I turn out the light."[20]

It is clear from the letters Liebling sent to Stafford during their courtship that he wanted her to know he found her sexually attractive as well as intelligent and talented. On assignment in Algiers in September, he wrote to her, "We had a hell of a time at the races and in places, and I'd love to have you in an air-conditioned cabin where we could work out the form together."[21] And on October 16, having begun to read some of her fiction for the first time, he said: "I seem to have held a very great lady in my arms at all those race meetings. It was a very great honor! I've been reading 'Children Are Bored On Sunday' and really you are a better writer than almost anybody I know."[22] In November he told her that his London friends, the Charoux, had named a new kitten Jeanie for her and were about to adopt a poodle they planned to name Joe. Charoux, Liebling reported, had asked, "Is Cheanie in town? We could squeeze her good in," and in his letter Liebling remarked, "I could squeeze you good in, too."[23] In future letters he would sometimes playfully refer to her as "Cat" and to himself as "Poodlopoodlopoulos."

After Liebling left for Algiers, Stafford accompanied a friend of hers from the States, the poet John Malcolm Brinnin, to a gathering of poets that was being held in Belgium. With him she explored the gambling casino in the

Belgian town of Knokke-le-Zoute, which she used as the setting for her short story "The Children's Game." The garish buildings in the resort town inspired one of her typical satiric descriptions:

> They wandered, amazed, through street after street of these teratoid villas and they concluded that the architecture of Knokke-le-Zoute was unique and far more disrespectful to the eye than that of any other maritime settlement they had seen, worse, by far than Brighton or Atlantic City. . . . In gardens there were topiary trees in the shape of Morris chairs and some that seemed to represent washing machines. The hotels along the sea were bedizened with every whimsy on earth, with derby-shaped domes and kidney-shaped balconies, with crenellations that looked like vertebrae and machiolations that looked like teeth, with turrets, bow-windows, dormers and gables, with fenestrations in brick or bordered with granite point lace . . .[24]

Reading in the newspaper about the gathering, Liebling remarked playfully, "It should be a sure kill for you if you haven't fallen for another poet."[25] She did not fall in love with another poet there, but if Liebling had read her short story that was based on her trip to Belgium, he might have had another cause for concern. In "The Children's Game" she describes a woman in her forties who is introduced to gambling by a man she thinks she wants to marry. Having reached the conclusion that she is "not the sort of woman who could live alone satisfactorily," Stafford's protagonist is trying to decide whether she wants to marry the friend she has accompanied to Belgium. Hugh Nicholson, "associated various times and in various ways with films,"[26] superficially resembles not Liebling but Alan Campbell, who was a film writer. However, like Liebling, he is estranged from his wife; like Liebling, he enjoys horse racing; and like Liebling's, Hugh's amiability sometimes gives way to periods of remoteness when he seems "suddenly to disappear, although his flesh remained, in the middle of a conversation, in the middle of a dance."[27] With Hugh, who deliberately chooses to frequent the grubbiest places, Abby shares adventures similar to those Stafford shared with Liebling: ". . . they went to race meetings at the Hippodrome and rode in hansoms along the *digue* and ate cockles and mussels on the quays . . ."[28] But ultimately Abby comes to believe that Hugh is a masochist, and as she observes him at the roulette table, she senses that he despises himself for being a compulsive gambler. The story concludes with Abby telling herself, "Happy as the interlude had been . . . , it had been an aberration and . . . she belonged where she had originated . . ."[29]

Until Liebling left for Algiers, Stafford had been enjoying her stay in London so much that she began to consider remaining there for an extended period. "I want to stay in London for the rest of my life. The thought of Westport brings on vertigo and vomiting," she wrote to Ann Honeycutt.[30] And informing James Oliver Brown that she was thinking of renting a house in London with Eve Auchincloss and Nora Sayre, she observed, "I'm having *far* too good a time and never want to come home or work or do a blessed thing except to be pleased in just the way I'm being pleased."[31] Once Liebling left for Algiers, however, she changed her mind about staying in London, and by the beginning of October she had returned, very reluctantly, to Westport. "I do miss George [her cat] but apart from her I miss nothing in my Westport life and I think with tears of the Main Street with all those people on it to whom soon I must talk . . . ," she had written to Mary Lee as she contemplated her return to 24 Elm Avenue.[32]

Although Stafford had been gone from Westport for only four months, when she returned she felt completely disconnected from the people there. As a result, she found it objectionable that *Life* wanted to photograph her in Westport for an article they were planning on younger American women. "I am so insanely hostile right at the moment to Westport, Conn. that I don't want to be associated with it in any way. I am ashamed to live here," she wrote to James Oliver Brown in October.[33] Yet she was annoyed subsequently when a photograph of her did not appear in *Life,* for the *Life* photographer had insisted on taking shot after shot of her and her cat.

Instead of settling down to write once the distractions of England were behind her, Stafford was abashed to discover that she still found it almost impossible to resume her writing. That winter Farrar, Straus and Cudahy published five of her short stories in a volume called *Stories*. The book also included short stories by John Cheever, Daniel Fuchs, and William Maxwell that had previously appeared in the *New Yorker*. The volume, or so the Author's Note claimed, grew out of the authors' annoyance that reviewers of short story collections often looked at several collections in tandem, pitting one writer against the next. Hoping that their stories would complement rather than compete with one another, these writers had decided to publish a sampling of their works in a single volume. Although the volume received favorable reviews, Stafford could take small comfort from its appearance, for her own five stories—"The Liberation," "In the Zoo," "Bad Characters," "Beatrice Trueblood's Story," and "Maggie Meriwether's Rich Experience"— were not new ones, and the book was not a great financial success.

Upset that she had virtually stopped writing, Stafford attributed her lack of productivity in part to her separation from Liebling. Suffering intermittently from writer's block himself, Liebling was distinctly annoyed when she implied in her letters to him that she would not be able to write as long as they were apart. Since he could not return to the States and still claim the tax exemption allowed to American citizens who had spent most of the year living abroad, he felt that he could not afford to rescue her, nor did he want to take any responsibility for her writing problems. "I do love you," he insisted, "but I don't want you to con yourself with the notion that you can't write anything until you see me. That serves the dark Jeanie two ways—it gets her out of doing any work for an indefinite time, and it puts pressure on me to come lickety-split to save her . . ." Afraid that perhaps he was being too harsh or blunt, he added: "I want you to write because you're a great woman, and I love what you write, and because you'll never be happy—for more than one afternoon or one night at a time—unless you do your self justice. I'll not give you up, and I'll combine things to have you together with me as soon as possible, and I'll make love to you as much as I want, which is certainly as much as you'll want, and we'll see wonderful things together . . ." Then, not wanting her to miss the main point of the letter, he chided her once more, ". . . *please* don't have tantrums. They're not worthy of you. You're a great person, for Christ's sake."[34]

Whether she was so distressed by his letter that she deliberately delayed answering it or whether her reply was delayed in the mails, a letter that Liebling wrote on January 3 suggests that he was annoyed because he had tried unsuccessfully to reach her. "For two lovers who earn their living by precise language we have difficulty in practical communication," he said, adding irately, "Where the hell are you? (in Westport or New York?)"[35]

It is evident that she had not given him as full an accounting of her activities and plans during the holiday season as she gave to her friend Nancy Gibney, fearing perhaps that he would be bored with her descriptions of her rendezvous with people he had never met or that he would reprimand her for socializing rather than working. In a letter to Nancy Gibney dated December 18, however, she mentioned a trip to Cambridge; a party she had attended; an evening at the opera; and plans to spend Christmas Eve at Ann Honeycutt's with a troubled psychiatrist friend to whom she had been giving "a good deal of therapy." As usual, the Christmas season depressed her. "I'm filled with more venomous Christmasphobia this year than ever before and I've concluded that Scrooge's metamorphosis was wrong way to," she said gloomily. Nevertheless, she claimed that she was happier than she had been in a long time because she had finally succeeded in finding an apartment in New York and hoped to be settled in at 18 East 80th Street by the middle of January. She was also pleased to report that she was revising a long story; and most important, she said her relationship with her "friend abroad" was "a bit less tentative" than it had been.[36]

In the middle of January, just as Stafford was in the process of moving into her new apartment, Liebling arrived in town for a ten-day visit. "I was moving so that the confusion was perpetual but, on the whole, was sweet," she wrote to Nancy Gibney. Although Raymond Sokolov claims that after Liebling's visit everyone knew Stafford was Joe's "official girl,"[37] her letter, written after Liebling departed, suggests that she was still unsure of where the relationship was heading. She and Liebling did see one another constantly when he was in New York, and he gave her a Victorian pin in the shape of a horse as a reminder of the days they had spent at the races in England. However, after he left for Israel, his next destination, she remarked wistfully, "I don't know if I shall ever see him again."[38]

Liebling had asked her to join him in Europe that summer, but having had such "unlucky histories," they were both filled with trepidation about their relationship. Meanwhile, in his absence, she was still continuing to go out with other men. "I've a widower at the moment—a youngish one—and shall be glad to have him take me to dinner often since I'm in no danger of getting involved," she remarked, observing that "it was *so* luxurious to be back amongst men."[39] She also described an elegant Author's League party she had attended with Lillian Hellman's former husband, Arthur Krober, who, she said, was "a very nice, gentle, funny man."[40] In "New York Is a Daisy," an article Stafford published in *Harper's Bazaar* in December of 1958, she would speak of the joy she experienced when she returned to the "magical, mercurial streets" of New York. After living with a "multitude of exurbanites," she explained, she was "grateful for the amplitude of New York," for the accessibility of libraries and theatres and shops and services and saloons.[41] Living in New York also made it easier for her to attend the parties given by her many literary acquaintances. At one party she met T. S. Eliot and his new wife, who "looked like an amiable white English pudding," at another, Greta Garbo.[42] She also enjoyed getting all dressed up for the opera evenings that Robert Giroux regularly hosted or going to the opening of a play. In February she attended the opening night of Graham Greene's *The Potting Shed,* and at a party at George S. Kaufman's afterward chatted with Lillian Hellman, who had recently visited Nancy Gibney at Hawksnest. "Lillian Hellman is rough on the girls and eats the boys alive so I gather . . . I wouldn't want to tangle with her," Stafford remarked afterward.[43]

But if Stafford's active social life made her feel less isolated and lonely, her busy schedule also allowed her little uninterrupted time to write. By May, her mounting guilt and panic were so acute that she told Nancy Gibney she was "broke and scared silly and depressed and sick," observing that even though on the whole her extensive social life was "very good fun," this was no way to earn a living.[44]

Liebling's letters to Stafford during the spring and summer of 1957 were filled with statements about his love for her and his hope that they would be reunited as soon as possible. Nevertheless, even after it was feasible for him to return to the States without jeopardizing his financial status with the Internal Revenue Service, he did not hurry back to her, for his own work was going well and he did not want to risk losing his momentum. At the end of March he wrote to her from Jerusalem:

> I'm just warming up, and don't think much of heading home, now. If you want to stay on there through the summer, do, and I'll be along toward fall. I won't have many more wander years and I may as well suck the juice out of this one. It may be all for the best if we don't constrain each other to depart from our respective courses—we're stars of such fiery portent and Roman-candescent magnitude—and if I make you come to Europe when you want to be writing in Eightieth Street, or if you woo me to the Gideon Putnam Hotel when I want to be in Djerba, the one who concedes may catch with a slow burn difficult to extinguish.[45]

He insisted that he was not trying to bully her into coming to England unless she wanted to do so; nevertheless, his letter reflects his anxiety about how they would be able to manage to be together without putting the writing career of one or the other of them in jeopardy. He knew how important writing was to both of them, and having experienced writing blocks himself, he fully understood her anguish when she confided to him that her own writing was not going well. Although he attempted to sound lighthearted when he urged her to set a good example for him by being industrious, his concern about her recent lack of productivity is evident in his admonition to her: "If you don't finish at least one masterpiece before I see you, I'll whack your bottom. And give you homily grits for breakfast. I've had ten years of a non-writing wife who lectured me for not writing. At last I have a writer I can lecture . . . In my childhood I was tyrannized by Russian governesses. I have always wanted a talented, sensitive reprobate to tyrannize over. Be fecund, every second . . . Copy, copy, make it snoppy."[46]

Jean Stafford's letters to Liebling have not survived, but his letters to her reveal his desire to mollify her after he had written something to her that had evoked her ire, such as accusing her of being a hypochondriac, or criticizing her for not spending more time at her desk, or referring to her as a "waif." After she took umbrage at being called a "waif," he described himself as a "he-waif" and admitted that the only kind of women he attracted and that attracted him were waifs like himself.[47] In one letter he proclaimed his love for his "volatile cat," and in another he wrote: "We have a million things to talk about and perhaps—since no man and woman agree always—some to fight about, but it's much better done with our heads on the pillow and the Divine Apparatus of Reconciliation immediately available."[48]

One aspect of her life that Stafford did not care to discuss with Liebling was her alcoholism. Once again during the winter and spring of 1957 she had begun to drink heavily. Eileen Simpson has described a weekend Stafford spent with her in Princeton that year during which she "turned night into day": "After the guests I'd invited to dinner to meet her left, she poured herself a nightcap and curled up in a chair to talk. Nightcap followed nightcap until 6:00 A.M., when she was finally willing to go to bed. She slept, with the help of sedatives, until cocktail time. No, she wasn't hungry, she said when she got up. If she could just have a little drink . . ."[49]

At the end of June, Robert Gibney arrived in New York to seek professional help for his own drinking problem. Stafford spent a good deal of time with him, and though she was in no position to offer advice to a fellow alcoholic, she was pleased that after talking to her he decided to seek the help of a psychiatrist. "My days of doctoring are over," she told Nancy Gibney, "and I never was a good nurse." Insisting that Gib had been of more help to her than she had been to him, she remarked that he had paid attention to all her "woes and mopes."[50] After Gibney's death in 1973 she would describe to his son Ed how she and her "dear old chum" Gib had walked the streets of New York City during the summer of 1957 before she went to England "to nail Liebling" and had discussed what her strategy "to net this bird" should be.[51]

Even as she planned her trip abroad, she was still not sure she would be able to scrape up enough money for the fare. "London in August looks so remote that I shall probably cancel my reservation next week, being unable to raise the price of it," she wrote to Nancy Gibney on June 26.[52] So desperate was she that the previous day she had written to Oliver Jensen: "The other night, you may remember you said you hoped that if I were in need I would let you know. Well, I *am* in need, in desperate need . . . This has been a worrisome and barren year, the worst I have had in a long time . . ."[53] What she did not reveal to Oliver was that she needed the money to pay for her passage to England to visit Liebling. Glad to be of assistance to his former wife, Jensen generously offered to loan her some money immediately, and in August Liebling offered to send her several hundred dollars in the event that she did not have sufficient funds to pay her own way.

On August 3 work by both Jean Stafford and A. J. Liebling appeared in the *New Yorker*. "The New Yorker married us . . . in the August 3 number," Liebling wrote to her. "As you have it we complement each other, and it makes a fine New Yorker, but I wonder whether it's pure coincidence or matchmaking."[54] The story of Stafford's in this issue was "A Reasonable Facsimile." It humorously describes the relationship between the retired chairman of the Philosophy Department at Adams's Neville College and a "bright pushy whelp" who teaches at an obscure finishing school in Florida. The young man in question is so infatuated with Dr. Bohrmann that he begins to mimic Dr. Bohrmann's every gesture. Stafford claimed the idea for this story came to her when she was reading the Holmes-Laski correspondence, though she observed, "I cannot tell you how many people have been positively identified with my wholly fictitious Holmes and Laski."[55] But if the idea for the story originated in the Holmes-Laski correspondence, as she claimed, she probably had other models as well for the professor and the ambitious young man who idolizes him. She told Mary Lee that her portrait of the old professor was a composite portrait of her own former professors Wolle, Cohen, and West; and Mary Ellen Williams Walsh has suggested that in portraying the sycophantic graduate student it is quite likely Stafford was also drawing a satiric portrait of the youthful Robert Lowell, who had once pitched a tent on Allen Tate's lawn. Walsh observes that when Stafford later included this story in a collection called *Bad Characters,* she was subtly mocking her former husband, about whom she wrote in the Author's Note to the volume, "The strenuous young man in 'A Reasonable Facsimile' is not bad, he is merely poisonous."[56] Although this story is not as memorable as some of Stafford's other ones, "A Reasonable Facsimile," which was one of the O. Henry Award winners for 1959, is witty and amusing nevertheless.

Stafford finally left for England early in September. In a letter she sent to her literary agent from the Dukes Hotel, she said she was having "an altogether beautiful time" and joyfully described being met by Liebling in Southampton: "My arrival could scarcely have been more auspicious. It was a supremely sunny, rose-smelling day and I was brought up to London splendidly in a Rolls; my elevenses, brought in a hamper and consumed by a hedgerow, were caviar and cheese and a beautiful red wine. Halfway up, I longed for my first taste of a flattish, warmish English lager so we stopped at a pub called The Catherine Wheel."[57]

Far less jubilant when she next wrote to James Oliver Brown on October 5, however, she reported that Liebling had been dreadfully ill with the Asian flu. Since he was feeling somewhat better by the end of the week, they had flown to Paris to attend the big race at Longchamp and had enjoyed "a few glorious days of sun and gentle light," but after they returned to the "murk of London," Joe had suffered a relapse and was bedridden once again.[58]

In addition to having to cope with Liebling's poor health, Stafford was further depressed when she learned that her story "The Children's Game" had been rejected by the *New Yorker*, though she had twice tried to revise it to meet their objections. "I can't possibly tell you how sorry I am to send you this 'no' and how badly we feel if we misled you into all this extra work for nothing," White wrote to her apologetically. White said she suspected that one of the reasons the story's male protagonist was not developed fully enough was that Stafford had been constrained by having a real person in mind when she described this character.[59] Perhaps White was reluctant to publish the story because she recognized several of Liebling's traits in Stafford's Hugh Nicholson. Upset when the story was rejected, Stafford instructed James Oliver Brown to send it to *Mademoiselle*, which she said had heretofore paid her the best prices. She also told him that she had no objections to his sending it to the mass-circulation ladies' magazines such as *McCall's*, the *Ladies Home Journal*, and *Good Housekeeping*, but she was further depressed when these magazines and the *Atlantic Monthly* rejected the story as well. Under the title "The Reluctant Gambler," the story finally appeared the following fall in the *Saturday Evening Post*.

Another story of hers that was also rejected by the *New Yorker* was "The Scarlet Letter," the last of the Emily Vanderpool stories. In this work Emily's badge of humiliation is not a letter that she wears on her breast, as Hawthorne's Hester does, but a letter she receives as a commendation for reading that she sews on one of her socks. Katharine White judged Emily's character too odd to be convincing in this story. Once more, realizing how insecure Stafford had become about her writing, White tried not to be too discouraging when she notified her that the story had been rejected. Insisting that the *New Yorker* needed Stafford in the magazine and acknowledging that she realized how much Stafford needed an acceptance, she diplomatically tried to explain what she felt had gone wrong with the story: "Emily is a difficult character that way—to make her wild and free and funny and yet not *too* exaggerated calls for an awfully fine line in the way it is written, but you have done this so wonderfully well in the past—that I know you can again."[60]

It may be significant that Stafford's difficulties at the *New Yorker* coincided with Katharine White's retirement from the position of fiction editor, for as William Leary has pointed out, Stafford's association with the *New Yorker* was very much bound up with White.[61] Two weeks after White had notified Stafford that "The Scarlet Letter" had been rejected, she wrote to her again to inform her that she would no longer be serving as the magazine's fiction editor.[62] As Stafford later acknowledged by dedicating her *Collected Stories* to Katharine White, the older woman had played a major role in promoting her career as a writer of short fiction. When White expressed reservations about her latest creative efforts and then informed her that she would no longer be in a position to assist her in her capacity as editor, Stafford must have feared that her own future prospects at the *New Yorker* were uncertain at best. During the next two decades, in fact, only two stories by Stafford—"The Philosophy Lesson" and "An Influx of Poets"—would be published in the magazine. In 1960, in a letter to *New Yorker* writer Emily Hahn, Stafford expressed her annoyance with William Shawn, who had replaced Harold Ross as editor of the *New Yorker*. "Shawn is hopeless," she wrote. "They bought a story of mine three years ago and have never run it so I want it back to sell somewhere else, but it's been on Shawn's desk all this time and will doubtless remain there forever." [63]

In mid-November, Stafford and Liebling returned together from London to New York. "Jean Stafford is traveling by the same boat—a good companion," Liebling wrote to Joseph and Therese Mitchell, wanting perhaps to conceal the true nature of the relationship since he was still legally married to Lucille Spectorsky. [64] Soon after their arrival, Stafford and Liebling established themselves in separate quarters in the Fifth Avenue Hotel. Just as she had enjoyed frequenting Liebling's favorite haunts with him in London, so in New York she enjoyed eating with him at his favorite restaurants or attending a boxing match with him or joining him and his *New Yorker* cronies at Costello's, the bar on Third Avenue whose walls were adorned with James Thurber's drawings of meek men being chased by predatory women. "In life Jean was, in a sense, always playing a role," Peter Taylor has written of her. "She had many roles, roles like those in her written fiction—a grande dame, a plain spoken old maid, a country girl from the West, a spoiled rich woman, her diction always changing to fit the role." [65] At least initially, as she sat in Bleeck's with the crusty newspaper reporters and sportsmen who were Liebling's favored companions, she was content to play the role of Liebling's moll. As Sokolov has observed, Stafford "had her fancy, Jamesian side, but for Liebling she could whistle a more popular tune, with a rougher tongue." [66]

It is evident that Stafford's relationship with Liebling was a far happier and more symmetrical one than her relationship with either Robert Lowell or Oliver Jensen had been. Yet the two major problems that she had had before she met Liebling did not simply vanish: after she returned to New York she still was unable to make any progress on her novel; and she still continued to drink excessively. Eve Auchincloss recalls that sometime during this period Stafford phoned her at six o'clock one morning and pleaded with her to come to her aid. When Auchincloss arrived, she found the living room floor strewn with whiskey bottles and Jean in the bedroom hallucinating wildly during an attack of delirium tremens. [67]

Liebling, like Stafford, was noticeably unproductive after his return to

New York, and his dwindling output meant that his capital was dwindling as well. When his divorce from Lucille Spectorsky finally came through, he did not immediately take on the financial burden of supporting a third wife. Stafford's explanation for their delay in securing a marriage license was that they "kept getting too busy to get married,"[68] but it is probable that Liebling was having second thoughts about whether he wanted to marry again. Even though he was in love with Stafford, he certainly was not oblivious to her problems, nor could he ignore the fact that she had no financial resources of her own to draw on and could not be counted on to earn money from her writing in the future. He had had to pay Lucille Spectorsky a substantial sum of money for a farmhouse they had purchased in Lucille's name in the Springs on the eastern tip of Long Island, and now, alarmed by his own recent lack of productivity, he had good reason to be cautious.

It seems curious that in a letter Stafford wrote to Nancy Gibney during the summer of 1958, she made no mention at all of Joe Liebling. Instead, she described a weekend she had spent visiting friends in Great Barrington, where she was introduced to the art of table tapping: "Einstein said that the universe was closed; all the people we communicated with said that they didn't have much fun," she reported. Having consumed too much alcohol and slept too little, she came down with a strep throat and trench mouth when she returned, and after frequent applications of gentian violet, she said she looked "like Dracula after a seven course meal."[69] When she wrote this letter, she was about to depart for a six-week stay in Connecticut, where she would be living in the house of Katharine White's son, Roger Angell, but instead of expressing joy at the prospect of getting away from the city for the summer, she said morosely that she was "full of foreboding," without indicating what events had triggered her depression.

In 1958 A. J. Liebling's *Normandy Revisited* was published by Simon and Schuster. Although it received good reviews, only 3,500 copies were sold. Nevertheless, this beautifully written reminiscence of Liebling's visits to Normandy—when he was a student during the twenties, in the forties when he was a war correspondent, and in the fifties—was an achievement Stafford could admire and even envy. The publication of this book was a tangible reminder of how little she had produced in recent years. The only story published by Jean Stafford in 1958 was "The Reluctant Gambler" in the *Saturday Evening Post;* when her agent also submitted "The Scarlet Letter," the editors returned it, noting, "It is a mildly amusing monologue, but it is far too long and without any basic situation to give it point or punch."[70]

Although it was true that Stafford's career as a writer of fiction was languishing, she succeeded nevertheless at writing brief articles and reviews. In

November of 1958 she published "Divorce: Journey through Crisis" in *Harper's Bazaar,* and the following month "New York Is a Daisy" appeared in the same magazine. Drawing in part on her own experience, as she had done in earlier articles such as "My Sleep Grew Shy of Me," she produced articles that were gracefully written and that reflected her sharp eye for the telling detail or example that would bring a generalization to life. A wickedly humorous review of Jonathan Kozol's novel, *The Fume of Poppies,* which appeared in the *Reporter* in February of 1959, also helped to launch her once again as a book reviewer, a task she had not performed since the early forties. With increasing regularity during the last two decades of her life, she would publish book reviews for *Washington Post Book World, Vogue, Esquire,* the *New York Review of Books,* and the *New Yorker.*

Another source of revenue for her were the interviews she published in a number of magazines. In September of 1959, for example, she received five hundred dollars from *Horizon* for writing an article on the famed Danish author of *Out of Africa* and *Seven Gothic Tales,* Isak Dinesen. The two authors met on a chilly day in March at the Cosmopolitan Club during a visit that the elderly, emaciated, but undaunted Isak Dinesen paid to the States. In this article, Stafford summarizes Dinesen's life and work. Although Dinesen's dreamlike tales are very different from Stafford's own stories, the article reflects Stafford's admiration for Dinesen's exotic verbal tapestries.[71]

On April 3, 1959, after a courtship of almost three years, Jean Stafford and A. J. Liebling were finally married in a civil ceremony at City Hall in New York, with Joe and Therese Mitchell serving as witnesses. Stafford liked to call Joe Liebling her "first completely Jewish husband," referring to the fact that Lowell, whose grandmother's grandfather was Jewish, had always insisted he was one-eighth Jewish.[72] Following a celebration at Costello's, where much alcohol was consumed by the bridal couple and their guests, Mr. and Mrs. A. J. Liebling returned to their new apartment at 43 Fifth Avenue.

For Stafford, nest building had always served as a convenient excuse for not getting any writing done; so had travel. She did both in the spring and summer of 1959, first fixing up their new apartment and then accompanying Liebling on working trips to Baton Rouge and to England. The idea for the former trip had been born one evening when she and Liebling were drinking coffee with *New Yorker* editor William Shawn and his wife. Stafford began talking about the "high jinks" of Earl Long, the governor of Louisiana, who had recently been released from a mental hospital. Intrigued by Louisiana politics ever since she had lived there in 1940, Stafford described the erratic Long's recent strange behavior. Shawn realized that Long was precisely the kind of flamboyant character about whom Liebling loved to write and sent him to Louisiana to interview the governor. The book that resulted, *The Earl of Louisiana,* paints a colorful portrait of the bombastic, eccentric brother of Huey Long. For three weeks, in the steaming heat of a Louisiana July, Liebling followed Long about. Later, Stafford would vividly recall how on a day that was "as hot as Tophet" they had waited for three hours for a press conference with Long to begin. Afterward, Liebling managed to speak to Long alone, and Long, charmed by Liebling, invited him to bring Stafford to dinner at the Governor's Mansion. "The governor talked a blue streak to this interloper from New York," she said. She also observed that watching Liebling extract information from the garrulous governor taught her how to proceed when she subsequently was asked to interview the mother of Lee Harvey Oswald for *McCall's* in 1965.[73] Liebling's influence on her own prose is evident in her acerbic portrait of the loquacious mother of Kennedy's assassin, printed first in *McCall's* and then in book form as *A Mother in History*.

At the end of August, Stafford, Liebling, and Liebling's stepdaughter, Susan Spectorsky, sailed for England on the *Media*. Liebling was on assignment to cover the British general elections, and Susan, who had graduated from Radcliffe that June, was en route to Egypt to do graduate work in Arabic. "She was lovely to me," Susan Spectorsky said of her stepfather's new wife.[74] In a letter Stafford wrote to Ann Honeycutt from the ship, she happily described the sleeping as "marvelous" and the "booze" as "plenteous."[75] While Liebling went about his own work in London, Stafford paid two visits to the Isle of Arran in the Firth of Clyde off the coast of Scotland, from whence three of her grandparents had originated. Leaving Edinburgh in the "cold and sullen early morning," she traveled by train to the port of Androssan and then took a boat in a downpour to the Isle of Arran, which the gazeteers promised was "a Scotland in miniature," abounding in beaches, glens, moors, mountains, and trout streams. On the way to her first destination, the famed Broderick Castle, she encountered a freckled girl of about nine or ten with long sandy hair and bony, bare, scratched legs, about whom there was "something pressingly familiar": wearing roller skates, she looked like a replica of Jean Stafford as she had appeared in grammar school. Describing her visit to the Isle of Arran in an unpublished essay she called "Samothrace," Stafford remarked that she had felt as though she had come "face to face with the ghost of a still-born twin" of whom she had never heard. "It gave me the fantods," she said.[76] After she returned to the Dukes Hotel, she wrote to James Oliver Brown that the trip to Scotland had been "fantastically, thrillingly fruitful." In the burying ground she had found the familiar family names of Duncan, McKillop, and McKenzie, and in the records of a Katy McKillop, who lived on the island in a village called Glen Sennox, she had discovered a reference to her grandfather, Malcolm McKillop. "I felt that I had at last come home," she said about her visit to Arran, observing that a number of people had remarked that she truly resembled the Arranites. Excited by her journey to find her roots, she declared, "If I don't get a story out of this, I'm not and have never been a writer." [77]

When Liebling's stint in London was over, he and Stafford traveled to Greece, a country that delighted them both. They especially enjoyed visiting the Aegean island of Samothrace; there Stafford began to weave a fantastic legend linking the Isle of Arran and the Greek island. Inspired perhaps by the tales that Isak Dinesen had written about her own Danish forebears, she imagined that she was a descendant of Alexander the Great and that her own ancestors had migrated from Samothrace to the Isle of Arran. In "Samothrace," she makes the rather far-fetched speculation that some enterprising ancestor of Alexander the Great brought his household gods with him to Scotland, naming the village in which he settled there Corrie after the Greek name Core or Kore. When she chose to name the protagonist of *The Parliament of Women* Cora, it is possible that she was linking Cora Savage and the mythical Kore, or Persephone, daughter of the goddess Demeter.

Seeking an economical way to travel home, Stafford and Liebling boarded an American cargo ship at Piraeus and returned via Naples, Genoa, Marseilles, and Barcelona to New York. After they arrived in New York following this extended honeymoon, they both resolved to devote themselves to their writing. But during the remaining three years of Liebling's life, his productivity declined, as did Stafford's. After Liebling's death, she told his biographer: "During our marriage, which was short, I was *extremely* unproductive. It was a source of woe to Joe. I could never figure out why it happened. Perhaps it's too simple an explanation, but I was happy for the first time in my life. He thought that if I wasn't writing, it meant I was unhappy with him." [78]

Stafford's explanation for why she was so unproductive during the years of her marriage to Liebling does indeed seem too "simple." It is true that she was much happier during these years than she had been earlier, but there may also have been other reasons for her lack of productivity. One of these was the fact that, like many women of her generation, she had failed to resolve satisfactorily the conflicting imperatives of domesticity and a career. When she invested her energies in her private life, she found it difficult to set aside time each day to write. In contrast to Liebling, who had an office at the *New Yorker,* she did not have a place to work outside of the apartment, the "red room" she had once imagined where, undisturbed by household distractions, she could focus completely on her writing. During the intervals when she had lived alone—in Concord, in Westport, in New York—she was productive but also

very lonely; now that she had exchanged solitude for intimacy, she found she
was constantly being distracted during the time she tried to set aside for writing. Although Madella, Liebling's loyal housekeeper and excellent cook, continued to work for them after their marriage, like the beleaguered protagonist
of Doris Lessing's "To Room Nineteen," Stafford always felt mentally teth-
ered to the household. She was in charge of maintaining their apartment in
New York as well as the house in the Springs that Liebling had purchased
from his second wife. Her letters to Nancy Gibney between 1959 and 1963 are
filled with descriptions of the domestic chores she was doing: writing thank-
you notes for wedding gifts; getting rugs back from the dry cleaners; purchas-
ing new lamps from Bloomingdale's; trying to eradicate the inevitable cockroaches in their New York City apartment; packing up their belongings when
they moved from New York to the Springs and back again; and searching for
a new apartment after the landlord had informed them that costly renovations
had to be made on their building. As she contemplated having to make yet
another move, she said wearily, "I'm tired of making houses." [79] If there was
one Jean Stafford who relished domesticity and got real pleasure from helping
to maintain a meticulous and well-run household, that Jean Stafford was eter-
nally in conflict with Jean Stafford the writer, who needed uninterrupted time
to work on her manuscripts.

Another deterrent to her writing was their busy social life, both in New
York City and in the Springs. Not only did they dine out frequently with her
friends or Liebling's, but they often entertained lavishly at home, offering
their guests choice wines from Liebling's extensive wine cellar and rich epi-
curean delights he continued to savor despite his doctor's orders. Madella did
most of the cooking, serving, and cleaning, but Stafford devoted many hours
to planning and supervising the arrangements for their parties. Like the protagonist in Henry James's short story "The Private Life," she often wished she
had a double who could fulfill her social obligations while she sequestered
herself in her study to write. Describing a recent trip she and Joe had taken to
Cambridge, where he had served for a week as a "sort of conversationalist-in-
residence" at Harvard's Kirkland House, she announced to Nancy Gibney:
"Now we are going nowhere until we leave for the summer in Easthampton
and once we get there I refuse to see anyone in anybody's house including my
own. I've not done a tap of real work for years now and I'm beside myself with
shame and poverty." [80]

But if there were external causes for her lack of productivity, there were
internal ones as well, among them her insecurity, her alcoholism, and her
writer's block. As a result, she often chose to occupy herself with domestic
chores instead of sitting down at the typewriter. Her friend Joseph Mitchell

had written in *Joe Gould's Secret* about a Greenwich Village character who claimed for decades that he was writing a book, but when Joe Gould died, nothing could be found except a few unfinished fragments. Stafford, too, had allegedly been close to completing her autobiographical novel for years, but despite the fact that she produced draft after draft of various chapters of the novel, she was never able to finish it.

The reasons why Stafford could not complete *The Parliament of Women* are complex. One important reason for her failure to complete the novel was that she had already exhausted much of the material that she had wished to incorporate into this autobiographical account. Since her earlier novels and short stories also drew heavily on autobiographical material, she must have realized that if she were not to repeat herself, she would have to invent different incidents in this novel than the ones she had already included in her published fiction. She seems to have found it enormously difficult to describe Cora Savage, her protagonist in *The Parliament of Women,* in a way that would clearly differentiate her from characters like Sonia Marburg, Joyce Bartholomew, Molly Fawcett, or Emily Vanderpool, all of whom, as she admitted, were versions of herself. An even more serious problem, perhaps, was that she still could not bear to deal with two problematical issues in her life: her troubled relationship with her father and the suicide of Lucy McKee. In the past Stafford had either chosen to omit the father figure from her fiction or to represent him as a more respectable citizen than he actually was. Now, however, in a novel she had designated as "autobiographical," she felt compelled to portray him as he actually was—and found she could not.

How much Stafford's father still unnerved her is evident in a letter she sent to Nancy Gibney during the spring of 1960. She said that she had just learned her "dreadful father" was going to be visiting her nephew in Utica and hoped to see her, too. "If that old man were under my roof for three minutes, it would mean ten years in Payne Whitney for me—after my discharge from New York General for treatment of perforated ulcers and grave cardiac disease," she wrote. So dismayed was she by the prospect of seeing him that she decided to pretend she was going to be in the Virgin Islands on assignment during the time he would be in New York State. "Oh, God," she exclaimed. "Things were going so swimmingly and now I've been drunk and hysterical for two weeks." [81]

Although Stafford made almost no headway on *The Parliament of Women* between 1960 and 1963, she did manage to earn modest sums of money by writing articles, book reviews, movie reviews, and stories for children. In 1960, for example, a memoir called "Souvenirs of Survival" appeared in the twenty-fifth anniversary issue of *Mademoiselle.* Her friend Eve Auchincloss had solicited this personal account of what life had been like in Boulder during the Great Depression. Stafford often spoke bitterly about her impoverished youth; however, the tone of this essay is nostalgic rather than acrimonious. She does not mention her father, the boardinghouse, her desperate unhappiness and isolation during her high school and college years, or her envy of the rich, popular students on campus. Instead, she portrays herself as a member of a group of "landlocked, penniless, ragtag and bobtail" students who used to congregate in a local sandwich shop to discuss literature and drink watered-down beer.

Another article that she wrote during this period focused on the way various kinds of whiskey are produced, and it included recipes for a variety of cocktails.[82] Those who knew how much alcohol Stafford herself had consumed in her lifetime must have sighed when they saw this article by her. Although she realized that such an article would do nothing to enhance her reputation as a writer, it was easy to write and the money she earned from it helped to pay her bills. She was willing to undertake projects that would entail a minimal investment of time and effort, but when Peter Davison, the executive editor of the *Atlantic Monthly* and son of her former professor, Edward Davison, invited her to write a book on the Sacco-Vanzetti trial, she declined on the grounds that she was too deeply committed to take on such a project.[83]

In 1960 a book review she called "Rara Avis" appeared in the *Reporter.* Bringing to this review her own firsthand knowledge of the West, Stafford enthusiastically endorsed Isabella Bird's *A Lady's Life in the Rocky Mountains,* a book that had been published initially in 1870 and had been recently reissued. Stafford expresses great admiration for this indefatigable Englishwoman who became "one of the most remarkable peripatetics of her time," despite a spinal disorder that often caused her to take to her bed.[84] Summarizing Isabella Bird's travels through Colorado, she commends her ability to observe the inhabitants "with scrupulous impartiality and the landscapes with love."[85] As Stafford describes Isabella Bird's "restless, changing, kaleidoscopic West" full of Indians, hunters, trappers, and desperadoes,[86] she appears not only to admire but to envy this woman of the nineteenth century who had been fortunate enough to experience a West that was so different from her own "tamed-down native grounds."[87]

In addition to book reviewing, Stafford also began to generate some income from writing movie reviews between September of 1960 and May of 1961. Most of the movie reviews appeared in *Horizon,* a magazine with which her former husband, Oliver Jensen, was associated. Her forays into movie reviewing suggest that she was neither very much interested in nor well versed in the technical aspects of movie production; nevertheless, the reviews were written with her characteristic wit and thoroughness. In "Neo-realismo Revisited," for example, she not only reviewed recent films by Roberto Rossellini and Vittorio de Sica but also discussed other films belonging to this genre; and in her review of Satyajit Ray's *The World of Apu,* she compared this film with earlier films that Ray directed. Although she was not destined to become a Pauline Kael or a Penelope Gilliatt of film reviewing, her reviews demonstrate her formidable intelligence and perspicacity.

In connection with her film reviewing for *Horizon,* in the spring of 1960 she was sent to Reno to write a story on the filming of *The Misfits.* The assignment promised to be an interesting one for her and would also allow her to visit the ranch in Hayden. "My weekend in the bosom of my family wasn't really bad at all," she told Nancy Gibney after she returned east. "I like my sister in her own house but can't stand her in mine—I can slip back into my western girlhood with no trouble at all, but she is completely irrelevant to my eastern adulthood." She said that her stay in Reno, where she met the film's director, John Huston, as well as his scriptwriter, playwright Arthur Miller, was "rather fun, rather interesting, rather contaminating and deadly hard work in the blazing desert heat."[88] In 1973, in her review of Norman Mailer's biography of the female lead of *The Misfits,* Marilyn Monroe, she would describe her as she had looked on the set in Nevada. Stafford was disappointed when, after all her hard work, *Horizon* decided not to print her article on *The Misfits.*

Another new venture for Stafford during this dry period was the writing of two books for children. The first, *Elephi: The Cat with the High IQ,* is a charming story about a cat like Stafford's own cat Elephi. The fictional Elephi, a beloved pet of Mr. and Mrs. Cuckoo, lives in an apartment at 43 Fifth Avenue. Inventing an adventure for Elephi, Stafford includes herself, Liebling, their housekeeper Madella, and Charlotte, the wife of Liebling's friend Pierre Guedenet, in her narrative. Stafford, who was forced to pay frequent visits to her own dentist, writes that "poor cuckoo old Mrs. Cuckoo . . . was forever and a day going to the dentist"; and Stafford's affection for her own cat is revealed when Mrs. Cuckoo, after a grueling session at the dentist, lays her aching cheek on Elephi's flank and says, "A cat is a peerless poultice."[89]

Although her agent, James Oliver Brown, tried to discourage her from accepting a contract for a nonroyalty book,[90] for a fee of one thousand dollars she also agreed to contribute a volume to a series of fairy tales retold by distinguished contemporary authors such as Randall Jarrell, Elizabeth Bowen, John Updike, and Isak Dinesen. Her own contribution, *The Lion and the Carpenter,* includes four tales from *The Arabian Nights.* In this book, Shahrazad, the wife of a bloodthirsty king, saves her own life through her cleverness. Spinning wonderful tales for the king each night, she keeps him in such great suspense about how her story will end that he cannot bring himself to kill her as he had his former wives. "In time," Stafford writes, Shahrazad "became a habit with her husband, like steamy baths or thick sweet coffee, and he grew to love her dearly."[91] A celebration of the way in which a female storyteller's extraordinary narrative abilities save her life and win her husband's love, *The Lion and the Carpenter* illustrates the narrative skills not only of Shahrazad but of Stafford, too.

In addition to her writing, Stafford was involved in other professional activities during the years when she was married to Liebling. In March of 1960, for example, she participated in the arts festival at the Woman's College of the University of North Carolina in Greensboro, where her friend Randall Jarrell was teaching. "Last week I went to North Carolina to give a lecture at the Woman's College and doubt that the wounds will ever heal," she wrote to Nancy Gibney. No more charitable about academic women than she had been when she was a graduate student in Iowa, she remarked that the numerous cocktail parties at the college were "made up almost entirely of ladies who have been getting their Phd's for the last thirty five years and who share ranch houses with dogs with literary names (a vile dachshund named Dutchy, short for the Duchess of Malfi, a fox terrier named Ralph, short for Ralph Roister Doister) and are good as gold and as sad as Niobe."[92] On March 9 she delivered the opening lecture of the conference, "Young Writers," an event she said was "jammed principally because that phenomenal snow had fallen the night before and the girls had nowhere else to go." Her lecture included much of the same material as her earlier lectures at Bard and Wellesley, though she also incorporated new material from her satiric book review "The Eat Generation," contrasting the inept prose of the author with the more authentic diary entries of a young Greek man she had met recently on the island of Samothrace. It is of interest to note that her satiric barbs were also aimed at one of the new culture heroes of the sixties, the author of *On the Road,* Jack Kerouac. "The life of a writer," she said, "is an unceasing and daring pilgrimage. . . . It is not an aimless ramble like those engaged in by Mr. Kerouac's maudlin hoboes, but it is a journey with a mission—the search for an original grail of excellence and price."[93]

Another professional service she performed in 1962 was to serve as a judge for the National Book Award in fiction. This turned out to be much more traumatic than she had anticipated, for after the award was presented to Walker Percy for *The Moviegoer,* Gay Talese claimed that Stafford had persuaded the other judges to do so. Talese claimed that Liebling had brought the novel, which is set in New Orleans, to her attention after he had visited there to do research for *The Earl of Louisiana*. Outraged by Talese's allegations, she promptly made a public statement defending her actions,[94] having realized how persuasive Talese was when Percy wrote to thank "the Boston adventuress" for promoting *The Moviegoer*.[95] Much to Stafford's displeasure, this issue was revived again in 1971 when Alfred Kazin mentioned in an article that it was no secret Liebling had discovered *The Moviegoer* in Louisiana. Writing to the editors of *Harper's,* in which Kazin's article had appeared, Stafford reiterated that Liebling had had no influence on her decision, though she admitted, ". . . by and large our tastes were similar—we liked leg of lamb to be rosy, we were crazy about bad jokes, we both despised travel. He didn't like Henry James but I made no attempt to convert him; he did try to convert me to Hemingway, with a singular (and rather noisy) want of success. We were most fortunate in our general concord of affinity and prejudice."[96] In response to Kazin's allegations, she also sent him a letter in which she accused him of "slovenliness" unworthy of his scholarship for having "stated *hearsay* as gospel."[97]

Another source of concern in 1962 was her professional relationship with Random House. It was Random House that had given her an advance for her autobiographical novel nine years earlier. In 1962 Stafford asked to be released from her contract with them, however. Writing to her editor at Random House, her old friend Albert Erskine, for whom she had once worked as a secretary at the *Southern Review,* she observed crossly: ". . . I have an eccentric but uncradicable sense of being still your not very competent secretary, subject to scolding and I hate being scolded. . . . Nor can I help feeling that this has contributed to my block."[98] Refusing to be blamed for her writer's block, Albert Erskine retorted that, since becoming her editor nine years earlier, he had not seen even one sentence from her. He admitted that occasionally he had expressed interest in her progress on the novel but insisted he had never scolded her about the "nondelivery of any manuscript." He said, moreover, that he considered her remarks about feeling like a secretary to be "frivolous," but offered nevertheless to assign her to another Random House editor if the prospect of working with him was really a stumbling block for her.[99] Even after receiving his reply, however, Stafford was determined to sever her connections with Random House, probably because she felt so guilty about having failed to produce the novel she had promised. Once she broke with Random House, she finally succeeded in obtaining a generous advance of ten thousand dollars from Roger Straus and Robert Giroux at Farrar, Straus and Giroux for two books, one of which would be a work of fiction, the other her book on Samothrace. She then repaid Random House five thousand dollars plus interest for the advance she had received.

As 1963 began, Stafford could look back on almost four relatively happy years as Liebling's wife. They were finally settled in their new apartment at 45 West 10th Street, which was more modern and easier to maintain than their former apartment on Fifth Avenue, even if it did lack its elegance and spaciousness. Although at first she was reluctant to spend any time in Liebling's house in the Springs, referring to it with distaste as "himself's house," she soon grew very fond of the brown-shingled farmhouse. "Joe's house is really country. I look out my windows on cows and the Atlantic Ocean," she wrote to Nancy Gibney in 1959.[100] Soon she began to refer to the house as "my house."[101] By 1963 she had added to the furnishings of the small but comfortable house in the Springs, and she had become friendly with some of Liebling's favorite people who lived in the environs of East Hampton. These included the motherly Jeannette Rattray, publisher of the *East Hampton Star,* and her son and daughter-in-law, Everett and Helen Rattray; *New Yorker* cartoonist Saul Steinberg; and *New Yorker* writer Berton Roueché and his wife. On the thirty acres of meadowland belonging to the house, Liebling had planted a small vegetable garden and a garden of specimen roses from whose dried petals Stafford liked to make potpourris for their friends. Liebling was annoyed when she insisted on consulting the Ouija board, particularly after she had had too much to drink; and she was annoyed when he expressed his disapproval of some of her literary friends.[102] Nevertheless, they enjoyed spending time together, laughing at themselves or other people, and entertaining their friends. In 1973 she would write to Ed Gibney about her marriage to Liebling, "Gib, having seen me through two bad marriages, wanted me to have a good one. I did."[103] Ten years after Liebling's death she was still writing on stationery engraved with the letterhead "Mrs. A. J. Liebling," and the names Liebling and Stafford continued to appear on the mailbox at 929 Fireplace Road in the Springs long after both of them were dead.

For Stafford, 1963 proved to be a disastrous year professionally and personally. This was the first time since she had married Liebling that she had not published anything at all during a twelve-month period. Liebling, too, was suffering from a writing block, and that year both were plagued by ill health. Later, Stafford was to feel guilty because she had not been responsive enough to Liebling's condition when he had begun to show signs of slipping into a profound depression. "Depression was new to him," she said. "Looking back on it, I wasn't sufficiently sympathetic because I had always had depression with me."[104]

In May, Stafford remained in the States while Liebling flew to Algeria to gather background material for a piece he was writing on one of the authors he most admired, Albert Camus. Writing to her from Algiers on May 15 that he had had a bad attack of renal colic, which made him feel a hundred years old, he declared his love for her and said sadly that sometimes he thought she didn't really believe he loved her.[105] Three days later, he complained that he had not heard from her for two weeks. "Please don't forget me," he beseeched her.[106] And on May 25, after outlining a trip to France he hoped to take with her that summer, he observed, "Your letter indicated that I'd find you more of a wreck than I am. Well, we'll collapse in each other's arms."[107]

Although they were both worried about their finances, they left for Europe at the end of July, visiting Normandy, where Stafford's brother was buried, Mont St. Michel, and La Carelle. The last was a thirteen-hundred-acre country estate located in the Beaujolais region near Lyon. It belonged to the family of Jean Riboud, a fighter in the French resistance, a survivor of Buchenwald, a liberal like Liebling, and an enormously successful investment banker. Riboud would later become the president of the multinational corporation Schlumberger. He had gotten to know Liebling when both were living in New York in the forties and had remained a close friend ever since. For two weeks Stafford and Liebling relaxed at La Carelle with Riboud and his wife Krishna, luxuriating in the beautiful surroundings of the estate. They stayed in the twenty-six-room Romanesque château, furnished with elegant Louis XIV furniture, paintings, and sculpture. The château contained three libraries of precious leather-bound books, a capacious wine cellar holding rare bottles of old wine and champagne of the region, a billiard room, and a room in which the latest films were shown. On its grounds were beautiful gardens and a sanctuary for exotic birds and animals.[108]

Their next stop was Paris, but Liebling's depression only deepened there. "My surmise," Stafford said, "is that he knew he would never see France again."[109] His depression contributed to her own negative feeling about the trip. In a letter she wrote to Howard Moss from Paris, she spoke of the "unconscionably hideous miseries" of travel, "the binding narrowing of it, the ridiculous *waste* of it," observing, "I'm all for travel. (Travel, i.e. . . . in a pig's valise)."[110]

After they returned to New York, Liebling's mood did not improve. A photograph of Jean Stafford and A. J. Liebling that had appeared in the May issue of *Horizon* that year eerily seems to prefigure what lay ahead: Liebling, unsmiling, is seated on a rattan settee in the garden of the house in the Springs; on a second settee several feet behind him sits an unsmiling Stafford, an ever-present cigarette in her hand and her needlepoint in her lap; and behind them the bare, twisted limbs of a diseased apple tree are silhouetted against the ripe summer greenery. At their summer house, the caption says, "the Lieblings wile away their summer days trying not to work—that is, write."[111]

Just before Christmas, Liebling contracted viral pneumonia, and his condition worsened so rapidly that he was admitted to Doctor's Hospital on December 21. When his condition deteriorated still further and he experienced congestive heart failure as well as renal failure, he was transferred by ambulance to the intensive care unit at Mt. Sinai. Stafford, who was with him in the ambulance, believed that the delirious Liebling was having an impassioned conversation in French with Camus.[112] That evening, after leaving her husband's bedside, Stafford appeared at a cocktail party of an acquaintance. Although her presence there astounded those who were aware of Liebling's desperate condition, Dick Cavett, one of the other guests at the party, subsequently excused her highly unconventional behavior by attributing it not to her lack of devotion or concern for her husband but to her "highly developed penchant for seeking escape." Cavett and his wife, the actress Carrie Nye, who met her for the first time that evening, accompanied a very drunk Stafford back to her apartment. There, after fixing drinks for Cavett, his wife, and for herself, Stafford took out her Ouija board, consulted it, and began to wail, "My . . . brother Dick . . . *hates* being dead." The next day A. J. Liebling's obituary appeared in the *New York Times*.[113]

Quoting words from Yeats in his eulogy for his friend A. J. Liebling, Joseph Mitchell said at the funeral service at Frank E. Campbell's Funeral Chapel in New York that Joe Liebling "was blessed and could bless."[114] Among the mourners at the funeral chapel on December 30 was Liebling's distraught widow, Jean Stafford, who understood the full meaning of these words.

Some time after the funeral, Stafford arranged to have Liebling's ashes buried in the Green River Cemetery in East Hampton. His grave is marked by a simple granite headstone that Stafford had ordered from a stonecutter in Newport. Engraved with a fleur de lis, it is inscribed with a paraphrase of the words of Yeats that Joseph Mitchell had recited at Liebling's funeral: "Blessed—he could bless." In future years Stafford would bring autumnal bittersweet and holly or summer daisies and roses from Joe's garden to his grave.[115] The dedication to her next book, *Bad Characters,* which was published the following year, reads: "In memory of Joe with all my heart."

Twelve

The End of a Career
January 1964–Spring 1975

As Kate Croy observed and chose accordingly
deprivation made people selfish, left them
robbed of the last rags of character,
preyed and put upon, enmired in rancor . . .
—AMY CLAMPITT, "AN ANATOMY OF MIGRAINE"

Things grow grimmer and grimmer. Anger alone keeps me alive.
—JEAN STAFFORD, IN A LETTER TO JAMES OLIVER BROWN, 1967

IN A LETTER Jean Stafford had written when she was on her way to the Virgin Islands to secure a divorce from Oliver Jensen, she described herself as having been "gypped" by life.[1] Now, after having experienced some modicum of happiness, stability, and financial security as Liebling's wife, she felt that she had been "gypped" once again when, following their marriage of three years, he died at the age of fifty-nine. In July she would be forty-nine years old, but she still felt dislocated and rootless. Moreover, she was terrified about how she would earn her living in the future, for except for occasional articles and reviews, her writing had virtually come to a standstill in recent months. Now she would have to deal with tax problems in conjunction with the settlement of Liebling's estate; and though Liebling had left the house in the Springs to her, the upkeep and taxes on it were considerable. Thanks to her friend Eve Auchincloss, she could count on regular assignments to review books for *Vogue* and the *Washington Post Book World*. However, the income she could earn from this work would hardly be sufficient to meet all her expenses, and the time she would have to devote to book reviewing would be time she felt she should spend on completing her novel.

Overcome with grief and anxiety after Liebling's funeral, she retreated to New York Hospital, as she had done so many times in the past. The young internist who took care of her, Thomas Roberts, admitted her on January 11 with a number of nonspecific complaints, but found that in addition to suffering from reactive depression and alcoholism, she had chronic bronchitis and malnutrition, possible cirrhosis of the liver, and a gastric ulcer.[2] "I am incommunicado in a hospital and am in touch only with the lawyers . . . I implore you not to try to track me down," she wrote to Mary Lee on January 14. Fearing that Mary Lee would be impelled to come east if she knew she was in the hospital, she said firmly, "When I am sick, I know how to get help. When I am low in mind I want to be left alone, when I am working well I dare not interrupt."[3]

After she was released from the hospital two weeks later, Stafford tried to sublease her apartment in New York while she took temporary refuge in the apartment of Ann Honeycutt, who was going to be in Key West for the month. When Honeycutt returned, Stafford had decided she would go out to the house in the Springs, even though she feared she might find it cold and lonely there. Describing her depression after Liebling's death to Nancy Gibney, she wrote, "Nothing so unkind has ever happened before in my life and I can't believe it. I am half dotty, really, and catch myself in the woeful realization that he's not just at the Aletti in Algeria."[4]

Still uncertain about whether she wanted to move out to the Springs since she did not drive and feared being so isolated, she took a room at the Cosmopolitan Club after Honeycutt returned to New York, planning to stay there as long as they would allow her to do so. On April 5, however, she was readmitted to New York Hospital after experiencing acute chest pain. The diagnosis this time was alarming indeed: she had had a myocardial infarction and her gall bladder was acutely inflamed.

In a letter Stafford wrote to Lowell from the hospital, she told him that as soon as she was discharged she planned to return to her room at the Cosmopolitan Club. It is evident from her letter to Lowell that he had written to her at the hospital and had expressed some feelings of guilt about their past. Thanking him for his letters, books and flowers, she said gently, ". . . please never castigate yourself for what you call blindness—how blind we both were, how green we were, how countless were our individual torments we didn't know the names of. All we can do is forgive ourselves and now be good friends—how I should cherish that!"[5]

When she was released from the hospital, various people offered assistance, including Nancy Gibney, who wanted to come to the Springs to keep house for her, and Blair Clark, who said he would stake her to a maid for the summer. Warning Nancy Gibney that she was not very good company because she was terribly self-absorbed and terribly afraid, she described her current mental state with candor: "I wasn't afraid in the beginning when I knew by the number of doctors and the heart machines that I might die—I found, indeed, that giving up the ghost is the easiest thing in the world but the flesh won't turn loose—but now, with no interne nearby the slightest flutter and the smallest pain send me into a panic."[6]

By the end of June she had returned to the Springs for the duration, without having decided whether she should hunt for "a costly new nest" or remain in East Hampton, where she would confront a winter of "disintegrating isolation."[7] Then, quite unexpectedly, she was invited to be a fellow at the Center for Advanced Studies at Wesleyan University. The director of the center, Paul Horgan, an admirer of Stafford's prose style and originality, had also written about the West after moving to New Mexico in his youth. When Robert Giroux had introduced him to Jean Stafford several years before, Horgan was very much impressed by her charm, her intelligence, and her droll, acid wit.[8] A writer, scholar, painter, and bibliophile, Horgan had been awarded two Pulitzer Prizes, one for his two-volume historical study, *Great River: The Rio Grande in American History,* the other for his biography of Archbishop Juan Bautista Lamy, the priest about whom Willa Cather had written in *Death Comes for the Archbishop.* It was indeed a compliment to Stafford that Horgan, a man of erudition and exquisite taste, had issued an invitation to her to serve as one of several distinguished fellows at Wesleyan.

The invitation to spend the academic year at Wesleyan could not have come at a more auspicious time for Stafford. During her year-long stay at Wesleyan, she would be given room and board and a generous stipend of fifteen thousand dollars; even her postage stamps would be supplied free of cost. All that would be required of her would be her attendance at a dinner of the fellows on Monday evenings, at which one of them would present a paper, and in the spring term she would meet individually with a few students to critique their work. On the eve of her departure for Wesleyan, she wrote to Mary Lee, "I should be forced to work as I have not done for many years. The faculty is bound to be sophisticated and the boys are bound to be bright."[9]

With her cat Elephi as her only companion, Stafford lived in spare but adequate rooms in the Center for Advanced Studies during the week, and frequently returned to the Springs in a small chartered plane for the weekends. The fellows that year included Luigi Barzini, Jr., Herbert Butterfield, the Reverend Martin C. D'Arcy, S.J., René Dubos, Moses Hadas, Hiram Haydn, Sir Herbert Reed, and an old acquaintance from the literary circles she and Lowell had frequented: the brilliant, loquacious, amusing, and often drunk elder statesman of American letters, Edmund Wilson. The only female "fellow" that year, she socialized with the other fellows mostly at the Monday evening gatherings, though she did enjoy having drinks with Edmund Wilson and his wife Elena before dinner each day. When John Clendenning, a young scholar at Wesleyan, first met Stafford, he thought her a snob. "Soon I learned that this arch demeanor was merely a defense against depression, insecurity, and chronic illness," he later said. He, his wife Sheila, Edmund Wilson, Paul Horgan, and Father D'Arcy began to spend a good deal of time together. At the Monday evening gatherings, she and Wilson would play word games, and she always kept her liquor cabinet stocked with Johnny Walker for Edmund Wilson and sherry for Father D'Arcy. What John Clendenning remembered most vividly about Stafford was her laughter. "She hurled laughter at despair, and her laughter still rings in my ears," he said. He realized, however, that Jean, a lover of irony and paradox, "used laughter as a shield." [10]

In the center's annual report Stafford is quoted as saying: "This year has been instructive and profitable. I've learned what is going on in the academic world and, to add an altogether personal note, the appointment saved my life." But if the appointment "saved" her life by providing a place for her to live rent free, a community, and a generous stipend, she nevertheless was not successful in overcoming her writing block during the year she spent at Wesleyan. Summing up her year there for Nancy Gibney, she wrote: "The year at Wesleyan was deadly but I did get out of debt to New York Hospital and can't look at it as time wasted. I wrote not a word except for reviews and if it hadn't been for Edmund Wilson and Father D'Arcy (and the rather vast amount of money with innumerable fringe benefits such as free postage) I'd have cleared out. Middletown is the ugliest place in the United States." [11]

During the winter she was at Wesleyan, one unanticipated cause for distress was the arrival of Lowell, who had come to campus to see a production of Racine's *Phédre,* which he had translated from the French. Subjected once again to her former husband's criticism of her work and the way she had chosen to lead her life, she was both unnerved by his visit and furious at him for invading the sanctuary to which she had retreated. She agreed to sit next to him at the performance, but was annoyed when he kept grasping her hand. Afterward she complained to John Clendenning, "He simply would not let me go." [12] She would later observe to Nancy Gibney that after seeing Lowell she was prepared to say without any qualifications that she could not stand him. Repeating a story Blair Clark had told her about Lowell, she said that after meeting Jacqueline Kennedy, Lowell, who was smitten with Mrs. Kennedy's charms, had proclaimed that she was the most brilliant woman in America. Though she wasn't as talented or well read as either Jean Stafford or Elizabeth Hardwick, he said, she had something that neither of them did. "I figured that what she had that Lizzie and I didn't was an assassinated husband and if he didn't watch his step, we would be three peas in a pod," Stafford quipped.[13]

In the spring, Stafford briefly left Wesleyan to participate in the Writing Forum at the University of North Carolina in Greensboro, as she had done in 1960. The modest honorarium would pay for the trip to see her two friends, Randall Jarrell and Peter Taylor, both of whom were also scheduled to be on the program. Although she looked forward to her reunion with them, as usual she dreaded having to appear on a panel. Commenting on how much Stafford hated and feared public appearances, Peter Taylor later observed that she would desperately cling to another member of the panel and attempt to have a private discussion instead of addressing her remarks to the audience.[14] This visit to Greensboro was far less pleasant than her earlier one had been, for when she arrived, she was told that Randall Jarrell had had to be replaced on the panel because he was suffering from severe depression. The following October he died after being hit by a car on the highway. Many of his friends believed he had committed suicide.[15]

Another trip Stafford took that year was one to Fort Worth, Texas, to interview the mother of John Kennedy's assassin, Lee Harvey Oswald, for *McCall's*. Recalling that trip, she wrote the following year about the garrulous Mrs. Oswald: ". . . before I could open my mouth, she opened hers and she never shut it once during the three monologues she granted me. I spent a total of nine hours with her and according to a Dallas newspaper, I hold the record except for the long-suffering Warren Commission."[16]

Tape recorder in hand, Stafford conducted three interviews with Mrs. Oswald, the last taking place on Mother's Day and involving a trip with her to Lee Harvey Oswald's grave. Although the article based on these interviews, "The Strange World of Marguerite Oswald," consists mainly of quotes gleaned from Mrs. Oswald's remarks about her son and his place in history, Stafford's own response to the talkative, illogical, and badly educated "mother in history" is evident from the occasional editorial comments she interjects as well as from the remarks of Mrs. Oswald that she chooses to quote. Mrs. Oswald's lapses of logic are emphasized as she valiantly explains that her son Lee performed an act of heroism when he shot the "critically ill" president. Apparent as well are Mrs. Oswald's bad taste, her improper diction, and her solecisms. Without making many editorial comments, Stafford manages to show her subject in the worst possible light by describing the "carroty polyethylene" upholstery in the living room, the "fake flowers and fake grapes," and the framed print of Whistler's mother that was prominently displayed above the sofa. She also quotes her bizarre statements, displaying her poor grammar and malapropisms. Stafford mentions, for example, that Mrs. Oswald referred to someone as "Mayor Wagner's right-handed man"; she said that Kennedy was suffering from "Atkinson's disease"; and she observed about her son Lee, "All the news mediums said he was such a failure in life." Selecting the telling details that served to characterize a subject for whom she felt great antipathy, Stafford notes the copper scroll, with its "syntactically abstruse manifesto," that hung in Mrs. Oswald's living room:

> MY SON
> LEE HARVEY OSWALD EVEN AFTER HIS DEATH HAS
> DONE MORE FOR HIS COUNTRY THAN ANY OTHER
> LIVING HUMAN BEING.[17]

Months after her trip to Texas, Stafford said she could still vividly recall the sound of Mrs. Oswald's "atrocious voice." She observed that after spending three days in Mrs. Oswald's company, she was so unnerved by her non sequiturs that she feared she "was going to carry on a Texas tradition" by assassinating the mother of Kennedy's assassin.[18]

By the time Stafford returned to Wesleyan from Texas, she had to begin packing her manuscripts and belongings. During her stay at Wesleyan she had not made any progress on her novel. Nevertheless, no longer as frail or distraught as she had been when she arrived in the fall, she would return home in a much better frame of mind and in much better health; she had paid her bills at New York Hospital; and after becoming so friendly with Edmund Wilson, she felt she could ask him to recommend her for a grant from the Rockefeller Foundation. Beginning July 1, 1965, she was six thousand dollars richer, having been awarded the Rockefeller grant to continue work on her novel.

According to John Clendenning, during her stay at Wesleyan Stafford rarely mentioned the novel she was writing, and when she was asked to read a paper at one of the Monday evening gatherings in May, she chose to read a part of her essay "Samothrace" rather than an excerpt from her novel. When someone tactlessly revealed to her that a younger faculty member had referred to her and Edmund Wilson as being "washed up," she was extremely upset. "I think she feared that it might be true," Clendenning observed.[19] However, most people would not have guessed that her career as a writer of fiction was foundering. In October of 1964, her latest collection of short stories, *Bad Characters,* garnered a host of laudatory reviews from the critics. Calling her "one of our best writers," Gene Baro observed in the *New York Times:* "She makes the English language a weapon or a wand. She can build solidly in the tradition of Hawthorne or James. She can manage the deceptive simplicities and sleight-of-hand of colloquial style. Dry wit or zany humor are well within her range. She is an impeccable social observer, with a sense of telling detail." [20] And Joyce Carol Oates described this collection as "a triumph of style and imagination." [21] A few critics commented on Stafford's rather narrow range, but even the most severe critics applauded the brilliance of her prose, her wit, her irony, and her ability to create memorable characters.

Another tribute to her work was the fact that Louis Auchincloss included her in a study of nine major American women writers that was published in 1965. In *Pioneers and Caretakers* Auchincloss points out that Stafford's fiction contains the same elements of nostalgia for a vanished past that are evident in the fiction of the other eight writers he considers: Sarah Orne Jewett, Edith Wharton, Ellen Glasgow, Willa Cather, Elizabeth Madox Roberts, Katherine Anne Porter, Carson McCullers, and Mary McCarthy. [22] Observing that his impetus for writing this book in large measure grew out of his enormous admiration for Stafford's fiction, he said that he considered her writing to be as distinguished a contribution to American letters as the work of the other, better-known women writers whose work he also discusses in this book. [23] Although Stafford objected to being labeled a "woman writer," as did a number of other women writers of her generation, she could not have helped being flattered that Auchincloss placed her in the illustrious company of Jewett, Wharton, Cather, and Porter, all of whose work she herself admired.

The favorable critical reception of *Bad Characters,* the publication of the chapter about her work in *Pioneers and Caretakers,* and the grant from the Rockefeller Foundation all seemed to augur well for Jean Stafford's future. But Stafford herself knew all too well that every story included in *Bad Characters* had been published prior to 1958. Moreover, even though she had just received a major grant to finish her novel, she still had to resolve grave artistic problems before *The Parliament of Women* would be completed to her satisfaction.

It is true that for the first time since 1959 new stories by Stafford were published in 1964. One of them, "The Ordeal of Conrad Pardee," appeared, however, in the *Ladies Home Journal,* a magazine for which Stafford probably had little esteem. The story, a slight and rather tedious Jamesian comedy of manners, is really only an extended anecdote that illustrates once again the snobbishness of a Boston society matron. But in contrast to this story, the second story that appeared in 1964, "The Tea Time of Stouthearted Ladies," is a vintage Stafford story about the experiences of a young woman who spends the summer working on a Colorado dude ranch. The story was published in the one hundredth issue of the *Kenyon Review,* which was touted as a "family reunion" of the early writers for the journal, including Robert Lowell, Peter

Taylor, Robert Penn Warren, Randall Jarrell, and John Berryman, in addition
to Jean Stafford, and was dedicated to its founder, John Crowe Ransom. For
Stafford, the publication of this story in the *Kenyon Review* no doubt was a
mixed blessing. Although it is one of her most memorable and moving stories,
it deals with important autobiographical material that she might have intended to incorporate into *The Parliament of Women*. Once "The Tea Time of
Stouthearted Ladies" had been published in the *Kenyon Review*, however,
Stafford was no longer free to incorporate this episode in its present form into
her novel unless she wanted to run the risk of repeating herself.

One might have thought that after the death of her father, Stafford would
have found it easier to write about him, but this did not turn out to be true.
Before her departure for Wesleyan, she had confessed to Mary Lee: "I've not
written Dad about my going there; indeed, I've not written him at all. Each
time I contemplate a letter I feel so sick and sad that I find something else to
do. That so preposterous a life should be so endlessly prolonged is an unfath-
omable mystery."[24] When John Stafford suffered a series of small strokes, Jean
Stafford's sister Marjorie, with whom he had been living in Oregon, decided
he would get better medical attention at a nearby nursing home than she
could provide. After he died in 1966, Stafford observed that she viewed the
death of her very, very old and almost blind father as "necessarily merciful,"
but nevertheless described herself as being "mournful" and "confused." Unable to face going to the funeral, she sent her regrets to her sisters and remained in the Springs instead of flying to Oregon.[25]

As she had contemplated her return to East Hampton at the end of her year
at Wesleyan, Stafford had confided to Allen Tate that she had no idea what
she would do with the rest of her life.[26] At first she thought about finding an
apartment in New York, but concluding finally that such a move would be
both difficult and expensive, she decided to remain in the house in the Springs
instead. Although East Hampton was sparsely populated in the winter, she
knew and liked several people who lived there year-round or who drove
down from the city for long weekends. Included in her list of favorite East
Hampton residents during that period were Anne Freedgood, an editor at
Doubleday, and her husband Sy, to whom Stafford referred as her "Long
Island Gibneys";[27] the elderly editor of the *East Hampton Star,* Jeannette Rattray; Jeannette's son Everett and his wife Helen; and her neighbor, Eleanor
Hempstead.

Earlier in her life Stafford had longed for some Prince Charming who
would rescue her from her misery. On her own once again and facing financial difficulties, she still sometimes had fantasies about being rescued by some

rich, handsome man, as the following dream she transcribed for Louis Auchincloss in 1965 suggests:

> I marry Louis Auchincloss. I am standing on a staircase waiting for the rest of
> the wedding party and hear people saying that I seem to be a nervous bride
> and I should be considering that Joe has been dead for such a short time.
> Louis and I are in a city of canals. He says he must stay no longer or there will
> be no possibility of an annulment. Now I am alone, barefoot, wearing only my
> nightclothes. I have no money and am far from home and know that if I hire
> a boat-taxi to take me home there will be no one there to pay the fare but I
> hire one anyhow.

This dream of abandonment and loss concludes, nevertheless, with Stafford taking charge of the situation: rather than crying or wringing her hands when she is abandoned by her bridegroom, she summons a "boat-taxi" to take her home even though she has no money and knows that no one is at home to pay the fare.[28] In *Pioneers and Caretakers* Louis Auchincloss had written about Jean Stafford: "It would be natural to assume that a woman of such intense sensitivity and intellectual awareness might be vague and otherworldly . . . but she is sharply practical as a housekeeper, and can find a telephone booth in a block where one *knows* there was not one before . . ."[29] In her dream about Auchincloss, Stafford did "summon a taxi" to take her home, becoming her own rescuer despite the fact that she realized she had no money to pay the fare.

For the remainder of her life Stafford would struggle to earn enough money for taxi fare, though she was also not above accepting gifts from her more affluent friends. That year she made arrangements to have two guest cottages built on her property to rent to summer tenants. Furthermore, during the next decade, she would accept speaking engagements at Syracuse University, the Y.M.-Y.W.H.A., Barnard College, Pennsylvania State College, the University of Colorado, the State University of New York at Stony Brook, and Southampton College. Moreover, even though she often found the writing of book reviews and articles tedious, preferring the writing of fiction to the writing of expository prose, to meet her daily expenses she would turn out countless book reviews for various periodicals and newspapers. And though she had never enjoyed teaching and had also insisted that creative writing could not be taught,[30] in 1967 she would accept a position as a teacher of creative writing at Columbia University.

Alone in the Springs during the holiday season, Stafford found the Christmas of 1965 even more depressing than usual. "The new year has come in disastrously, following on the worst set of holidays I have ever known and the end of the world seems nigh," she lamented to Nancy Gibney on January 4.[31] She also informed her of her plans to visit Hawksnest if she survived the two professional engagements on her calendar: in January she was scheduled to introduce Edmund Wilson, who would be reading his poetry at the Y.M.-Y.W.H.A. in Manhattan, and in February she had been invited to Syracuse University to deliver a public lecture.

One of Stafford's incentives for going to Syracuse might have been the fact that Delmore Schwartz was then a member of the English Department there. Linda Sternberg Katz, a student at Syracuse University in 1966, recalls how impressed she was by Stafford's formidable intelligence and wit when she heard her speak before a large audience at Syracuse. If Stafford was nervous, as she usually was on such occasions, she managed nevertheless to appear very poised and self-confident. "I was knocked out of my socks," Katz observed.[32] But even if the lecture was well received, Stafford's reunion with Delmore Schwartz could not have been a happy one, for by 1966 he was deeply depressed, and his former paranoid tendencies had blossomed into full-blown mania. Five months later the fifty-two-year-old Delmore would die in New York City after suffering a heart attack in the shabby corridor of his last "home," the squalid Hotel Dixie near Times Square.

Stafford's intentions to visit Nancy Gibney that winter never materialized, for she was unable to travel after suffering an injury to her right arm when she returned from Syracuse. Serving as her amanuensis, Anne Freedgood wrote to Nancy Gibney to explain why Jean would be unable to make the trip: "Jean Liebling has asked me to write you because her right arm is paralyzed and she can't. The likeliest theory as to the cause of this is that her doctor hit a nerve when giving her a shot about ten days ago. . . . She will write you as soon as she can (write, that is) and undoubtedly relate to you her saga of 1966, which, although it is only mid-February, carries a load of disaster that would sustain a decade . . ."[33]

The injury turned out to be a radial thrombosis, and her arm was immobilized.[34] This injury prevented her from working on her novel; it also explains why no book reviews by Stafford appeared in *Vogue* in April or May, though they had been appearing almost every month since January of 1964. The year 1966 was another lean one for Jean Stafford. She published no new work except for a number of brief book reviews; a portrait of designer and artist Ward Bennett in *Art in America;* an article called "Truth in Fiction" in the *Library Journal;* and a slender volume entitled *A Mother in History* that was published by Farrar, Straus and Giroux. Even the last two items were not completely original, both consisting of material that had appeared in a slightly different form elsewhere: "Truth in Fiction" repeated much of the same material that was included in her 1951 *Harper's Bazaar* article, "Truth and the Novelist"; and a significant portion of *A Mother in History* had already been printed in her *McCall's* article "The Strange World of Marguerite Oswald." That March, after Peter Davison had come across a review Stafford had written on E. Nesbit's books for children,[35] he was so appalled by what he considered a waste of her talents that he sent the following memorandum to one of the other editors of the Atlantic Monthly Press: "Jean Stafford is a marvelous writer. She is also probably hungry (see *Book Week* for 3 /6/ 66) . . . where she is reviewing the *children's books,* for God's sake. . . . Why can't we get *her* as our book reviewer?"[36]

Even though *A Mother in History* included much of the material that had appeared in her article the preceding year, the book nevertheless succeeded in keeping Stafford's name alive for the public. Hugh Downs on the *Today* show conducted a fourteen-minute interview with her on February 24, 1966, and just as the publication of her article about Mrs. Oswald had stirred up a good deal of controversy when it appeared in *McCall's,* so did *A Mother in History* receive rather conflicting reviews. Stafford later wrote that after the article had appeared in *McCall's,* she was inundated with hate mail: "While I had, I thought, made no judgments, allowed Mrs. Oswald to be her own jury, and had been myself little more than the court stenographer, the spectators accused me of seeking to demolish the sacred throne of motherhood on which Mrs. Oswald was entitled to sit. On the other hand, I had also sought to enthrone a wicked woman who did not deserve the sacred name of Mother . . ."[37] *A Mother in History* also received its share of hostile reviews: while *Newsweek* described it as "a masterpiece of character study and a gem of personal journalism,"[38] *Time* called it "perhaps the most abrasively unpleasant book in recent years," remarking that "it required no writing talent at all";[39] and novelist John Gardner in the *Southern Review* criticized Stafford for her superciliousness, a charge that would be difficult to refute.[40] There was some truth to these assessments, for if Stafford allows us to view the mother of Kennedy's assassin at close range, she also shows no sympathy for her travails. As Mary Ellen Williams Walsh has observed, with the deft sleight-of-hand of the accomplished fiction writer, Stafford has created an unforgettable and quite funny portrait of a woman who is as memorable as the paranoid Granny Placer in "In the Zoo."[41] The reviewer in the *London Observer* said that Stafford, "with her knowing New York superiority and her lack of human sympathy," is "quite as chilling" a figure as the woman she interviewed.[42] It is quite possible that Mrs. Oswald reminded Stafford of her own mother, whose use of clichés she also had mercilessly satirized.

"Things grow grimmer and grimmer. Anger alone keeps me alive," Stafford wrote to James Oliver Brown in January of 1967,[43] and she observed morosely to Nancy Gibney, ". . . it is my profound hope that in ten years or so I will be dead." Stafford also informed her that, even though she had only herself and one cat to support, she felt so dreadfully poor that she had agreed to teach a creative writing course at Columbia the following fall, despite the fact that she disliked teaching. Remarking that she had been having anxiety dreams ever since she had accepted this position, she said that she was sure her students would want her "to discuss the meanings of *Moby Dick* and/or *Naked Lunch.*"[44]

On February 19, Stafford was one of two writers who read from their work at the Poetry Center of the 92nd Street Y; the other writer was Elie Wiesel. When Stafford's friend from the Springs, Gaylen Williams, the administrator of the Poetry Center, had invited her to speak there, Williams had explained the center's practice of having two writers appear on the same program. Although Stafford was asked to suggest another writer with whom she would like to appear, she did not do so and was finally paired with Wiesel, who recently had published a book about Soviet Jewry, *The Jews of Silence.* No two more dissimilar writers could have been chosen to appear on the same platform. The story Jean Stafford read that evening was "Life Is No Abyss," a work with which most of her audience would not have been familiar since it had originally been published in the *Sewanee Review* and had not been included in any of her short story collections. This tale of a feisty aging Boston Brahmin woman was indeed very different from Wiesel's account of the persecution of Soviet Jews. "For Miss Stafford, life . . . may be no abyss—but in what curious company to say so!" observed one woman who had been in the audience that evening.[45]

After renovations on one of the small buildings behind her house had been completed, Stafford sought tenants without children or musical instruments. That summer she rented the cottage to a most suitable tenant, a former professor of English history from Swarthmore College named Laurence Lafore. He had met her first in the fifties in London at a Cypriot restaurant that was a favorite of many writers. After Liebling's death, Lafore met her again at the home of mutual friends in Bridgehampton. "She was both polite and reticent, but she pulled no punches when it came to people or ideas she disliked," he observed. Although he sometimes felt somewhat intimidated by the fact that she was so outspoken, they got along well, and when she asked him whether he would like to rent her newly remodeled cottage for the summer, he decided to do so. He had recently joined the faculty at the University of Iowa but preferred to spend his summers in the East, so the arrangement worked out well for both of them. Occasionally they had dinner together in her house or his cottage. Once, they were both invited to have tea with some very distinguished elderly people named Dekay and their houseguest, the wife of the celebrated man of letters Van Wyck Brooks. Delighted by the witty talk, which reminded them both of the kind of brilliant conversation they might have heard in a Paris salon of Proust's day, Lafore and Stafford invited the Dekays and Mrs. Brooks to a dinner party. For days afterward, he and Jean talked about their "Geriatric Party," feeling that they had come a long way from Iowa and Colorado. Summing up his impressions of that summer, Lafore wrote:

> Laughter is what I remember most about that summer. Whenever she and I were together, we were likely to laugh practically uninterruptedly. She was exceedingly witty and satirical and, about some things and people, sometimes hilariously venomous. And she was, of course, more perfectly in charge of the English language, spoken as well as written, than anyone else I have known. It was her syntax and diction quite as much as her perceptions and judgments that delighted me. . . . She had no patience with current fashions in literature or life, and she was therefore in a position to see the absurdity of everything around her and to put it into epigrams.[46]

For Stafford, however, an otherwise pleasant if professionally unproductive summer was marred by health problems: early in the summer she was admitted to New York Hospital to be evaluated for severe arthritis in her neck; and in August, after experiencing intolerable pain in her legs, she was treated at the local hospital for what was said to be either lead or arsenic poisoning from the tree and vegetable sprays that had been used on her property. After describing her symptoms in detail to Nancy Gibney, she apologized for her jeremiad, remarking that the only cheerful news she had to report was that she had acquired a wig. Although she had no new clothes, the wig of luxuriant shoulder-length brown hair would accompany her to Columbia University, covering her own rapidly thinning hair that had been damaged over the years by dyes and permanents.[47]

"I dread Columbia and in certain ways I dread New York. In others I greatly look forward to being back," Jean Stafford wrote to James Oliver Brown early in September. She observed that she had been trying out her city shoes and admiring her "extremely successful" wig, but regretted she had nothing at all to put on between her feet and her head.[48] Planning to remain in the city except for occasional weekends in East Hampton, she said she had rented a small but immaculate apartment at 11 East 87th Street for the duration of the school year and would be moving there with her special desk and her cat Elephi on September 22.

The Master of Fine Arts program in creative writing at Columbia had just been established when Stafford was hired to teach a course in short story writing there in 1967. For a salary of $7,500 a year she would be expected to meet once a week with a seminar of approximately ten students and also to hold individual conferences with them. The other writer who had been hired to teach fiction writing was Edward Dahlberg. If Jean Stafford and Elie Wiesel made a strange pair when they appeared together at the 92nd Street Y, an equally strange pair were Stafford and Dahlberg. The only similarity between the author of *Bottom Dogs* and Stafford was the extensive vocabulary of both. A vagabond, a Communist, a verbose self-aggrandizer and self-deprecator, and a prophet of doom, the paranoid, elderly Dahlberg might well have reminded Stafford of her own father. Stafford, arriving at Columbia each day in her somewhat dated but very proper suits, gloves, and pocketbook, also contrasted markedly in appearance with the disheveled Dahlberg. Dahlberg, whose eccentric work was much admired by the Beat poet Lawrence Ferlinghetti, had never even heard of Stafford before he was introduced to her at Columbia.[49]

Stafford described the building in which her seminar met as the most appalling place she had ever worked in. Located at 440 West 110th Street, Myles Cooper was old and dilapidated, its windows loose and rattling, its elevators and drinking fountain usually not functioning, its temperature "either one hundred and eighty nine degrees or twelve degrees above zero."[50] She was displeased not only by the physical accommodations at Columbia but also by her students. "My students at Columbia all have B.A.s and how they ever got into the second grade I cannot dream. They are not only illiterate, they are cruelly ignorant, *willfully* ignorant and they resent correction; indeed they resent education," she observed irately,[51] also remarking that she was dismayed when one of her students said, "I have nothing to say about 'A Rose for Emily.' I read two paragraphs, and it didn't turn me on. I don't dig Faulkner."[52] Although many of her students liked her as a teacher, enjoying especially her anecdotes about the literary world, she expressed contempt for most of them and claimed she did not find teaching any more rewarding than she had on earlier occasions.

While the teaching job at Columbia paid her enough to cover her rent and her food, she nevertheless wrote very little during her stay in New York. Her active social life might have been one of the causes for her lack of productivity during the eight months she was teaching at Columbia. How much of her time was spent with friends is suggested by a letter she wrote to Con Edison to complain about her bill for the period beginning April 29, 1968, and ending on May 25. In this letter she listed her social engagements day by day and insisted she could not possibly have used up the $401.23 worth of gas for which they had charged her because during this period she had almost never cooked meals at home. She claimed that on April 29 she had dined at an elegant French restaurant with Liebling's affluent friend Jean Riboud, who frequently made business trips to New York without his wife; she had eaten at Gino's on May 30 with a colleague; on May 2 and 3 she had attended an arts symposium at Vanderbilt University, where she had appeared on a panel with Robert Penn Warren; on May 4 she had dined at the Princeton Club with Allen Tate and his "charming new wife"; on May 7 she had attended a dinner party at Eve Auchincloss's; on both May 9 and 10 she had dined with Jean Riboud; that weekend Anne Freedgood had driven her out to the house in the Springs; on May 13 she had had dinner in the city with Anne Freedgood and the widow of Moses Hadas; on May 15 she and Jean Riboud had attended a dinner party given by Joseph and Therese Mitchell; on May 16 she had had dinner at the Yale Club with Oliver Jensen; on the following day she had taken a shuttle plane to Boston, where she stayed at the Ritz as the guest of Philip Rahv's former wife, Nathalie; on May 20 she had had dinner at the Greenwich Village home of Liebling's nephew, John Stonehill, and his wife; on May 21 she had joined Allen Grover and his wife Bea for dinner and bridge; on May 22 she had had dinner with Ann Honeycutt; and on May 23 she had moved out of "that nasty apartment on 87th Street," returning to East Hampton, a peaceful change from New York City, where she had been "awakened at the crack of every blessed dawn by the racket of Con Ed's eternal, infernal pneumatic drills mucking up the streets of what used to be a habitable city."[53] For rhetorical purposes, Stafford may have chosen to emphasize in this letter to Con Edison how wealthy, distinguished, and influential her friends were, but even if she had been trying to impress Con Ed with her own importance, there is no reason to believe she also greatly exaggerated how many social engagements she had had during this period. She would recount her battles with Con Ed in a 1974 article in the *New York Times:* after receiving two checks as a refund from Con Ed, one for six cents and one for twenty-three cents, she framed them and hung them in her bathroom.[54]

Stafford welcomed the stipend she received for her teaching at Columbia and also enjoyed her proximity to friends in New York City. However, a number of distressing events occurred that year to depress her: in January, Anne Freedgood's husband Sy, who had been ill and depressed, perished in a fire in the Freedgoods' home in Bridgehampton; sometime that winter, Stafford's beloved cat Elephi died of a virulent virus that she claimed Elephi had contracted from breathing the noxious city air in her apartment; and her teaching was disrupted in April when student activists at Columbia, protesting the policies of the university, staged a sit-in, which in turn prompted the administration to summon the police to campus. Observing later that the disturbances at Columbia had both repelled her and bored her to death, she said tartly, "I have become very set in my ways, very conservative, very much down on the young . . . as a social class and I take no responsibility for slavery."[55] The following year she would again speak of her growing conservatism, describing herself as "reactionary and paranoid, racist and coploving and opposed in general to this so-called twentieth century."[56]

At the end of May she was delighted to return to her house in the Springs, but her stay there was short-lived. Early that summer she was again admitted to New York Hospital, where she underwent surgery to remove spurs on her spine that had begun to pinch nerves. Once more her writing hand was affected, the thumb and the forefinger virtually paralyzed by the pressure on the nerves.

In a letter she wrote that summer to the *East Hampton Star,* Stafford admitted she was "cross as a bear" a good deal of the time. In addition to expressing her annoyance at the summer people who flocked to the Hamptons, she proclaimed:

> I have it in for all public utilities, for all businesses, for all businesses that use computers, for all petitioners for all causes who come to my door, have the unconscionable brass to call me on the telephone, and fill my letter box with their matter. I am down on Mark Rudd, John Wayne, Cassius Clay, modern inconveniences, the United States postal service, The New York Times with its interminable essays which I believe are called "think pieces," and its wholehearted participation in the debasement of the English language.[57]

Frequently "cross as a bear" during the remainder of her life, she would often publicly lambaste individuals or groups whose behavior displeased her.

Although Stafford's neck was still causing her a good deal of pain by the end of the summer, she decided, nevertheless, to accept the invitation of Jean Riboud and his wife Krishna to visit them in France at La Carelle. She remained there for exactly one week, later describing the trip as a perfect one during which "not one mishap, not one delay, not one moment of inclement weather, not one cross word" had interfered with her pleasure. Arriving at La Carelle on a Thursday at teatime after being met and taken over the Juras in a private car the Ribouds had sent for her, she spent "a perfect week in a perfect house with perfect friends."[58]

Wearing a neck brace, she returned to Columbia University the following fall but soon discovered she disliked teaching there even more than she had the previous year. By the beginning of the second semester she had made arrangements for the novelist Lore Segal to assume her teaching responsibilities at Columbia, and with relief she returned to her house in the Springs. Though she complained that she was broke and would have to continue to write book reviews in order to pay for necessary repairs on the house, she enjoyed settling into the place where she now felt most at home. Writing to Nancy Gibney during a late winter snowstorm, she said contentedly, "I am enjoying the confinement because the snow is handsome and I have plenty of cigarettes and vodka, milk and top round ground, cat food, and so far, power for the furnace and telly."[59]

In addition to the dozen or so book reviews by Stafford that appeared in 1968 in *Vogue,* the *New York Review of Books,* and *Washington Post Book World,* her short story "The Philosophy Lesson" appeared in the *New Yorker,* the first story by her to be published in that magazine in more than a decade. "The Philosophy Lesson" describes the experience of a college student on a day when she is serving as a model in a college art class. Cora Savage, daughter of an anxious United Presbyterian mother and sister of Abigail, Evangeline, and Randall, learns on that day of the suicide of a medical student who was engaged to a rich young woman named Maisie Perrine. What misery had brought this boy, "rich, privileged, in love," to commit suicide, Cora wonders. "And yet, why not? Why did not she, who was so seldom happy, do it herself?"[60] Since the protagonist of "The Philosophy Lesson" bears the same name as the protagonist of *The Parliament of Women* and since the suicide of a student is an oblique reference to the suicide of Lucy McKee, it is reasonable to assume that this story, which includes many other autobiographical references as well, was originally intended to serve as yet another episode in Stafford's unfinished autobiographical novel.

A protagonist named Cora Savage also appears in two additional fragments of the novel, "An Influx of Poets," which was published in the *New Yorker* in 1978, the year before Stafford died, and "Woden's Day," which was published posthumously in an issue of *Shenandoah* that was dedicated to Stafford. Perhaps when she chose this name for her protagonist, she was recalling the Miss Savage from the West in Richard Eberhart's verse play about Robert Lowell. In addition, she may have chosen this name for her protagonist because Lowell had linked a character in *The Mills of the Kavanaughs* who resembles Stafford to the figure of Persephone or Kore, who is abducted by Pluto to Hades. In "The Philosophy Lesson" the name Kavanagh, in fact, is mentioned in reference to Cora's childhood in Missouri: Granny Savage had sometimes "driven over from Kavanagh to call."[61] In 1979, among the papers that were lying on Stafford's bedside table at the rehabilitation hospital where she was a patient prior to her death was an annotated copy of Lowell's *The Mills of the Kavanaughs.* Alongside a line in the poem referring to a former navy man, Stafford had written: ". . . old Mr. Bob Lowell, bossed by Char-

lotte, & despised and patronized by his son. He did, I know he did love me—
he thought I was a regular fella & he also though [*sic*] I was a pretty girl"; and
alongside a passage in which a boy recites "O dandelion, wish my wish, be
true" as he blows the fluff into the eyes of the girl who accompanies him,
Stafford had written: "I taught him this. He saw nothing of the natural
world—nothing!!"[62]

On January 3, 1969, a notice appeared in *Time* announcing that a new
novel by Jean Stafford, the first in seventeen years, was about to be published.
If Stafford heard about this announcement, she must have been mortified, for
it was not her long-promised novel, *The Parliament of Women,* but *The Collected Stories of Jean Stafford,* which would soon be published by Farrar, Straus
and Giroux. Nevertheless, the appearance of this book turned out to be a
major literary event, even though all thirty stories included in this volume,
except for "The Tea Time of Stouthearted Ladies" and "The Philosophy
Lesson," had appeared initially more than ten years earlier.

The book succeeded in attracting a good deal of favorable attention from
the critics. A new generation of readers was largely unfamiliar with the fiction
of Jean Stafford, but once again, after the book was awarded the Pulitzer
Prize for fiction the following year, Stafford became a literary celebrity. Her
increased visibility no doubt also helped her to obtain two grants that year, an
Ingram-Merrill grant and a Chapelbook grant.

The fact that *The Collected Stories of Jean Stafford* was dedicated to *New
Yorker* editor Katharine White immediately identified Stafford with the
magazine in which most of the stories initially appeared. The illustration on
the cover, too, linked Stafford with the *New Yorker.* Making use of a drawing
by Stafford's friend Bea Grover, the cover design superimposed a sketch of the
face of a youthful Jean Stafford on a collage of pages of her stories that had
actually appeared in the magazine. Katharine White immediately expressed
her delight with the new volume. When she received an advance copy of the
book, she wrote to Stafford, praising the way the stories had been grouped by
their geographical settings into four sections: The Innocents Abroad; The
Bostonians, and Other Manifestations of the American Scene; Cowboys and
Indians, and Magic Mountains; and Manhattan Island.[63] Gratified that such a
distinguished collection of short stories had been dedicated to her, White said,
". . . your collection contains some of the best short stories of our era and I feel
an unjustified personal pride in it because you dedicated the book to me."[64]

The laudatory reviews Stafford received for these stories to which she had
devoted a substantial part of the preceding twenty-five years must have been
gratifying indeed. Thomas Lask in the *New York Times* began his review by
proclaiming:

Everything that we desire from a collection of short stories, from the art of fiction, in fact, can be found in this gathering of Jean Stafford's work: a superior and controlled craftsmanship, human dilemmas uniquely individual, yet common to all of us, backgrounds and situations authentic in themselves and perfect for providing the skeletal structure of her tales, and those insights into human behavior and personality that we call wisdom.

At her best, Lask said, "she is flawless."[65] In the *New York Times Book Review* Guy Davenport also celebrated the publication of this volume of short stories, calling its appearance "an event in our literature." The two aspects of Stafford's work that Davenport emphasized were her sense of place, which he said gave such authenticity to her work, and her portrayal of the American woman as both the builder and the inhabitant of the "prison" of contemporary life.[66]

For Stafford, the success of her volume of short stories was personally satisfying. Moreover, the royalties from the sale of the book could be used to pay some of her household and medical expenses. In addition, she now felt in a better position to ask for some more money from her publishers. "I *will* have to have some money. Do you think we could get 3,000? Or, come to think of it, why not 5,000?" she wrote to James Oliver Brown on July 8.[67] By that date she had already spent a part of her recent earnings from the book on having the walls of her house in the Springs painted and repapered.[68]

Following the publication of her *Collected Stories,* Stafford not only received money but the honor of being elected to the American Academy and Institute of Arts and Letters. Housed in an elegant old building on West 155th Street in Manhattan, it has an inscription in memory of Mary Wilkins Freeman engraved above its front entrance. Stafford had confessed to Allen Tate that she was piqued each year to discover she had failed once again to be elected to the institute.[69] Finally, in January of 1970, she was notified that she had been elected a member. "How come she hasn't been elected long since?" novelist Glenway Westcott, a long-standing member of the institute, had asked another member, the poet Muriel Rukeyser, the preceding July.[70] In fact, Stafford had been turned down for membership once in 1959 and again in 1960; now at last her achievements were recognized by the academy as well as the critics. In May 1970 she was honored for her achievements as a novelist, short story writer, and essayist. Noting her outstanding accomplishments in each of these genres, the citation that was read at the inaugural ceremonies stated:

Both in fiction and expository writing, Jean Stafford is noted for her fieriness and her severity and her continuity in good work for so many years. There is always great emotion in her mind but she restrains it, in order to portray

realities distinctly and to express her judgment of them, beginning with a
novel about a superior Boston society, *Boston Adventure* (1944). Jamesian in
what was then a modern way, she has reduced, refined, shaped and sharp-
ened her narration. Now the over-all effect of her Collected Short Stories is
masterly.[71]

The same month that Stafford was elected to the American Academy and
Institute of Arts and Letters, she also learned that she had been awarded the
Pulitzer Prize for fiction. On May 4 Eve Auchincloss phoned her to tell her
the good news. Stafford said that at first she had not believed her, for she had
heard no rumors that her *Collected Stories* was even being considered for this
award; it was only after Robert Giroux confirmed the news that she was convinced her book had actually been selected as that year's winner. "I find it
awfully heartening that a writer as traditional as I can be recognized," she told
an interviewer, voicing the hope that giving the award to her might herald a
turning away from the kind of bad experimental writing that recently had
been in vogue. "Do we really need a poem about a banana that is set in type to
form the shape of a banana?" she asked.[72] During the preceding decade she
had been distressed to observe that a new kind of writer had begun to receive
attention. When her *Collected Stories* was said to be old-fashioned by several
reviewers, she had observed irately to Allen Tate: "I'm now getting very
snippy reviews—I'm not 'relevant,' I'm not involved with issues, I'm not a
Jew and I'm not a Negro, I deal only with the human heart and that has been
transplanted."[73]

Once she had received the Pulitzer Prize, she was besieged by reporters
from a number of local papers.[74] In these interviews she commented on her
work habits—from approximately eleven until three o'clock each day she
worked in her upstairs study on her fourth novel; her hobbies were reading,
gardening, making potpourris, doing needlepoint; she was subject to bouts of
compulsive housecleaning that were often a sign of depression; she enjoyed
preparing special dishes for friends, such as striped bass chowder and bar-
becued spare ribs with white beans; and she loved the Springs, where people
were urbane and the setting was bucolic. Several of her interviewers noted the
two white cards that were tacked on her back door. The first warned: "The
word 'hopefully' must not be misused at these premises. Violators will be humiliated"; the second announced: "We are at work and must not be disturbed.
If your business is urgent, please telephone. This does not apply to service
people or delivery men. It applies to time-wasting droppers-in and anyone
with a petition for or against any cause whatsoever." The cards were signed
"Liebling, Stafford, Stackpole." The last of these names is the name of a young
journalist in Henry James's *Portrait of a Lady* who is a loyal friend of James's

protagonist, Isabel Archer. Stafford gave this name to her imaginary secretary, a person who sometimes wrote scurrilous letters for her when, allegedly, she herself was out of the country or otherwise unavailable.

The success of her *Collected Stories* afforded Stafford the kind of visibility she had not enjoyed for a long time, and she was invited to give a number of guest lectures that year. In January of 1970, when the isolation of her house in the Springs began to depress her, she accepted an invitation as writer-in-residence at Pennsylvania State University's Institute for Arts and Humanistic Studies. Several years after her stay there she would describe her negative reaction to this experience and others like it. In her article "Why I Don't Get Around Much Anymore," she commented that she was often tempted to accept such invitations because she thought she would get to see a new part of the country and would be well paid for her efforts. Inevitably, however, she came to regret her decision: "I see no rain forests or striking geological phenomena or aboriginal Kansans in a native tattoo. I see only lecture halls, seminar rooms, and faculty clubs where dangerous cocktail parties and soirées are held: Next to summer vacationers in East Hampton academicians are the hardest-drinking crew I have ever met up with. I also see airports and motels. The honorarium does not begin to cover my medical expenses when I come home, and the things I have lost are irreplaceable."[75]

Her visit to Penn State was typical of the above. She complained that her room in their campus hotel, the Nittany Lion Inn, was unbearably cold; that the only chair in her room was uncomfortable; and that for two days a tenor from a Canadian opera company who was staying in the room next door practiced scales and sang arias from Wagner's *Ring* cycle at all hours, forcing her to retreat with a book to the ladies' room. Perhaps it was this last experience that prompted her to choose to read her short story "A Reading Problem" to the Comparative Literature Luncheon Club, for in this story the desperate protagonist retreats with her book to the town jail, the only place she can read without being disturbed.[76] Writing to Ann Honeycutt from the Nittany Lion Inn, she said that a quart of bourbon and a carton of cigarettes would help her to survive the remaining six days in this "meat cooler." However, she vowed after her stint at Penn State that she would "never, never, never, never" sleep in any bed but her own, "except for seasons in New York Hospital."[77]

It was fortunate that several of the other professional activities in which she had already agreed to participate did not involve travel or only required a trip into the town of East Hampton. In March she served as a judge for the Hopwood writing awards given by the University of Michigan, a chore that demanded only the reading of manuscripts sent to her home. She approved of the irony and inventiveness of one of the writers, Max Apple, and found a second writer's fiction to be somewhat promising, but she pronounced the work of the other ten candidates "thin and indolent," observing: "The preoccupation with everything disgusting under the sun; the grubbiness of the language, the listlessness of thought, the poverty of imagination, this fashionable and deadly and jokeless ennui depresses me to the point of tears."[78]

That March Jean Stafford gave a talk called "A Gallery of Improbable Women" at Guild Hall in East Hampton for their Writers of the Region series. From time to time during the remainder of her life she would appear at similar local events; she contributed a portrait a friend had painted of her to an exhibit at Guild Hall; and in 1973 she wrote a charming introduction to the catalogue for a Guild Hall art exhibit on flowers. In this piece, which is a perfect illustration of the way she characteristically mixed a colloquial and a formal writing style, as well as personal anecdotes and erudite references, she traces her own lifelong interest in flowers to her childhood in Colorado, describing how she had once been awarded a book called *The Language of Flowers*. Stafford's own fiction is enriched by her knowledge of flowers, as are the works of Shakespeare, Wordsworth, Proust, and Colette, whom she mentions in this essay. In addition to contributing to local cultural events, she aired her views about local issues in the *East Hampton Star*. And though she insisted that she liked to maintain her privacy, one summer she permitted her house in the Springs to be included in a house tour sponsored by Guild Hall.

Stafford frequently protested that the writing of articles and book reviews interfered with her "real" vocation, the writing of fiction. "I *must* stick to my own knitting until I have finished some of the work that I was set upon this earth to do, for otherwise, I won't go to heaven and as the intimations of my mortality daily grow more pointed, this is a matter that concerns me," she wrote to one individual who had asked her to write an article on a topic that did not interest her.[79] But it was the articles and book reviews she wrote for periodicals and newspapers that produced a steady source of income during the last decade of her life. On occasion she agreed to write something because she relished the opportunity to air her opinions about various matters that irritated her. "When such a big talent is frustrated," Wilfrid Sheed remarked about Jean Stafford, "it can rage in many directions."[80] Increasingly conservative in her last years, she inveighed against the recent "hysterical tantrums, the collective conniption fits on campuses and on the plazas of city halls." In an article that appeared in *McCall's* in January of 1970, she wrote: "The next ten years will undoubtedly be characterized by even more protest than the past five years have been, but let us pray devoutly that it will be inspired by reason and not by the frivolous impulse to make noise . . ."[81]

One target of her invective were those people who misused the English language. Expressing the wish that the seventies would come to be known as the "Age of Order," she decried the way in which the English language was being tainted by "rubbishy jargon and solecisms," by "incorrect usage and slothful imprecision" that she believed were symptoms of social disorder.[82] Whether she was inveighing against the "stultifying tedium" of encounter groups[83] or against gum-chewing bank tellers in miniskirts,[84] she used her wit and irony to attack those people and practices that aroused her indignation.

One group of protestors Stafford attacked repeatedly in her articles were the more vituperative members of the women's liberation movement, the "hordes of Dumb Doras and Xanthippes and common scolds" who had "raised such a hue and cry at the beginning that you couldn't hear the wood-winds for the crashes of the trees."[85] In an article that appeared in the *New York Times* the week she was awarded the Pulitzer Prize, she exclaimed: "The fustian and the hollering, the deification of Simone de Beauvoir and Betty Friedan, the strident jokelessness attendant on the movement are woefully unpropitious because they obfuscate a good many justified grievances."[86] As a college student, Stafford had objected to the lack of equality between the sexes. In a paper that she wrote called "The Utopian Woman," for example, she observed that most men discriminate against women, the sentimentalists arguing "that a woman's place is in the home with roses around the door and bouncing baby boys squalling around the threshold; the pietists shouting that a woman's place is in the home, making it sound more like a prison . . . and raging against the licentiousness of women, clearly seen in their wanton habits of dress and cosmetic."[87] It is also interesting to note that among the many books Stafford owned was Olive Schreiner's *Story of an African Farm,* a novel by the South African turn-of-the-century feminist whose work recently has been rediscovered by feminist scholars. This novel, which concerns a brother and sister in a rural community in South Africa, has some interesting parallels to Stafford's *The Mountain Lion.*

During the last years of her life, Stafford said she found it objectionable that some women received lower salaries than men who performed the same job and that women were not promoted as readily as men. Forgetting that in the past *Time* had not been willing to hire her because she was a woman, she insisted that she herself had never been discriminated against because of her gender,[88] but she did agree with the claims of feminists who maintained that women and men were often not treated as equals in the work place. She also declared that she was in favor of legal abortion, and she supported the estab-lishment of day care centers for working mothers. Stafford concluded, however, that no amount of legislation could alter what she believed were very real innate differences between men and women.[89]

One activity of feminists that especially aroused her ire was the attempt of feminist scholars to promote the work of women writers. Distressed by the proliferation of books by women about women, she insisted that the work of "the older stars"—Madame de Staël, Jane Austen, and Willa Cather—did not "need exegesis in terms of 'the new woman.'"[90] As a number of prominent women writers of her generation had also done, she argued that the work of women writers should be judged by the same standards as the work of men: "If women are not to be isolated, if they are not to be 'the Second Sex,' (what a self-defeating temper tantrum that title describes!) they are to be garlanded with the same variety of laurel as the men with whom they compete."[91]

From her caustic comments it is also evident that she disapproved of feminist interpretations of her work. In 1975, after reading Blanche Gelfant's reexamination of *The Mountain Lion* in the *New Republic,* for example, she observed snidely to Nancy Gibney that Gelfant had suggested "Ralph has to kill Molly in order to prove he is a male chauvinist pig."[92] Stafford would probably have been surprised, perhaps even dismayed, to discover what a major role feminist literary critics have played in championing her fiction during the last decade.

One misdemeanor of the group she referred to sarcastically as "Fem Lib" that aroused her ire was their use of the neologism *sexism,* a term which she described as "the most teratoid coinage so far" in the "heyday of odious neologisms."[93] A self-appointed guardian of the English language, she was also adamantly opposed to the use of the term *Ms.* In an amusing article in the *New York Times* that was sure to offend many feminists, she remarked in 1973:

> Whenever there comes in the mail a piece of first-class matter addressed to me as "Ms.," I slit the envelope open and if there is a check within, abstract it. Then when I reseal the envelope with Scotch tape (I like to do this when I have just finished changing a typewriter ribbon or have been out in the garden messing with the beets or scallions or other vegetables that grow underground—and you know what scotch tape is like when it is applied with grimy fingers) and circling the "Ms." in red, I write also in red: NOT ACCEPTABLE TO ADDRESSEE. RETURN TO SENDER, and put it back in my box.[94]

Although Stafford's most detailed response to the women's liberation movement, an uncompleted essay she called "Sisterhood," was never published, the articles that she did publish in response to feminism reveal her unwillingness to be identified with its more militant proponents.

In an essay called "Paradoxes and Dilemmas: The Woman as Writer,"

Margaret Atwood speaks about the many women poets and novelists in this country who have refused to identify themselves with the political activities of the women's movement. This group of women, Atwood says, "accomplished what they did by themselves, often at great personal expense," and she notes that "it would be fairly galling for these writers, if they have any respect for historical accuracy . . . to be hailed as products, spokeswomen, or advocates of the women's movement." Atwood also observes that many of those women writers who have transcended the limitations imposed upon women in general tend to regard themselves and to be treated by their male colleagues as "honorable men."[95] Atwood's observations are pertinent to a consideration of Stafford's attitudes toward other women and toward feminism. Growing up in a society that denigrated the achievements of women, Stafford identified with her father and her brother rather than her mother and sisters. Later, defining herself as an intellectual and trying to establish herself as a writer, she often made disparaging remarks about other women and liked to be considered "one of the boys." As Peter Taylor once observed, Stafford really didn't like most women, to which Eleanor Taylor replied that, if Jean really didn't like other women, it was because she was so much more intelligent than most of them.[96] The question of Stafford's attitude toward other women does, indeed, to use Atwood's words, pose a "paradoxical dilemma." Throughout her life, Stafford relied on the support of other women, including her mother, her sisters Mary Lee and Marjorie, Irene McKeehan, Evelyn Scott, Caroline Gordon, Cecile Starr, Katharine White, Nancy Gibney, Eudora Welty, Mary Louise Aswell, Dorothea Straus, Ann Honeycutt, Jeannette Rattray, Carrie Nye, and her loyal housekeeper, Mrs. Monsell, to whom she left the bulk of her estate when she died. Yet she was fiercely competitive with other women, frequently made snide remarks about them, and encouraged the flattery and attention of men. As her published comments about the women's movement suggest, though she supported some of the goals of the women's movement, she was not above making nasty comments about those "strident" feminists whose militancy she considered ill advised. She frequently declared that the "fem lib" movement "left her cold,"[97] and she publicly ridiculed some of its leading figures. Nevertheless, both her difficulty in dealing with her own unresolved role conflicts and her sympathetic fictional portraits of conflicted female characters are of great interest to feminist scholars today.

In addition to militant feminists, another group of people who were often subjected to Stafford's hostile barrages were her editors. Shana Alexander, in 1979 an editor at *McCall's*, was the recipient of one of her angry letters. Greatly displeased by the way someone at *McCall's* had edited her article on the Charles Manson murders, "Love among the Rattlesnakes," Stafford wrote an angry letter to Alexander after the article was published to complain about deletions that had been made without her permission. In defense of her practice of including many personal anecdotes and many examples in her articles, Stafford said: "Digression is integral to my style. Parenthesis is my middle name. And I have been assiduously at work on my style for a great many years. Style is the morality of language, and I look upon myself as a moral writer." Not only did she claim that the excisions had obliterated her irony and her humor, very important components of her style, but she objected to the fact that most of the exposition in the original manuscript had been removed without consulting her. Nostalgically recalling the days when Barbara Lawrence and Vivian Cadden had edited her profile of Marguerite Oswald for *McCall's*, she complained that in addition to having had her article mangled, she had also been meagerly paid for her efforts, especially considering the fact that she had had to put the article through her typewriter twice.[98] Shana Alexander observed that at the time she received this letter, she had never even met Jean Stafford, nor had she seen the manuscript in question. Much to Alexander's surprise, three years later when she invited Stafford to a party for writers from the Hamptons that she was co-hosting with *Newsday*, someone from the newspaper office called to tell her that Stafford had refused to set foot on her lawn. "The lady had a short temper but a long memory, both useful attributes in the writing trade," Alexander observed.[99]

Robert Silvers at the *New York Review of Books* was another recipient of one of Stafford's tirades. In 1971, after she discovered that some material in her review of Per Seyersted's biography of Kate Chopin had been deleted when the review was published, she angrily wrote to Silvers: "Why was I never sent the galleys? . . . no one has ever altered my work without my permission (that is, no respectable magazine has ever tampered with me; on certain occasions, when I have been obliged to write something to pay for a new roof or the repair of a pump, I have been outrageously mutilated by disrespectful and illiterate editors with tin ears) . . ." She was particularly irate because someone had written a letter to the editor accusing her of having failed to comment about an important aspect of Chopin's work. Stafford insisted that the omission was not due to her own lack of insight but to the fact that deletions had been made in the review she originally had submitted. Threatening that she might decide never to write reviews for the *New York Review of Books* again, she observed that the periodical had become more interested in politics than literature, whereas it was literature that was her own primary concern.[100] The review she wrote for the *New York Review of Books* the following year was the last review by her to appear in this periodical.

During the summer of 1970, Stafford's imagination was stirred by the activities of a group of hot-air balloonists who camped out in a field across from her house while they prepared to launch a transatlantic flight of the *Free Life* hot-air balloon. She became very friendly with the crew and sometimes shared with them a bottle of wine from Liebling's wine cellar. *New Yorker* writer Penelope Gilliatt, who was visiting Stafford at the time the balloon was scheduled to be launched, remembers Stafford's growing excitement as the hour of the launch approached. "I wish these birds would get off the ground because they're taking up too much of my time. . . . They are sweet, these maniacs, and so unconscionably *dumb,"* Stafford wrote to Oliver Jensen.[101] The voyage ended disastrously, however, almost before it had begun, and all the members of the crew perished. Although she had intended to produce an amusing Talk-of-the-Town piece about the balloonists for the *New Yorker,* she was so distressed after the disaster that she could not bear to write about it.[102]

One assignment for the *New Yorker* that Stafford did fulfill with distinction from December 1970 through December 1975 was the annual omnibus review of children's books for Christmas. Early each summer the annual cartons of children's books would begin to arrive. "Gosh darned sanitized pap! Give me the bad witches and demons, the scalding cauldrons and evil spells of the old days!" she would sneer about the majority of books she was sent to review.[103] As she contemplated these cartons in June 1971, she wrote in despair to Mary Lee, ". . . the children's books have begun to arrive and I look at all these cartons of rubbish and go faint and queasy. Still, I will do it—as much because I look at the reviews as a public service as because my roof must be replaced."[104] Never able to approach even the most mundane writing chore in a perfunctory way, she performed this task scrupulously, carefully selecting the treasures from the dross. "A balanced diet—such is my belief—should include magic, mystery, rambunctious nonsense, adventure that could come to pass, sentimentality (nothing like a good cry over 'Black Beauty'), tall tales, and history transformed by fictional apparatus into a party instead of a punishment," she wrote.[105]

During the summers, Stafford complained that East Hampton was overrun with tourists. "When the town becomes a summer resort, I stay in the house with the doors locked and the blinds drawn, snarling. . . . Throughout these suburban months the Radical Chic and the Beautiful People, conspicuously consuming, hold happenings in meadows, and fireworks extravaganzas on the dunes," she said.[106] But if she complained about the summers in East Hampton, she also dreaded the isolation winter would inevitably bring. Just before Christmas in 1970, assuming the persona of her imaginary secretary

Henrietta Stackpole, she wrote to her physician, Thomas Roberts, to inform him about her battles with insomnia and her problems with alcohol that winter. Henrietta Stackpole reported that her employer, Mrs. A. J. Liebling, was unable to sleep despite massive doses of chloral hydrate. With reference to her employer, she observed: "When she stays at home by herself, tends to her knitting, she is not a bad sort at all. Cross, to be sure, and hypercritical of all improper behavior. But she enjoys reading and writing which latter she does with a fair amount of facility. (And when her native stick-to-it-iveness prevails she can make enough money to pay her board at this high class establishment.)" At the close of this note, however, Henrietta Stackpole mentioned the issue that probably was the real occasion of this communiqué: her employer's consumption of alcohol. "If she stays away from John Barleycorn," Henrietta Stackpole wrote, "she is, in our opinions, an O.K. kid, and to tell you the honest truth, I think J. B. is basically the root of her problem. . . ."[107] No doubt Dr. Roberts, as well as Stafford's friends and neighbors, would have concurred that "John Barleycorn" *was* her greatest problem, though she usually did not discuss her drinking with others, especially after she married Liebling and stopped seeing Dr. Sherfey. From time to time she would take Antabuse in order to curtail her drinking, but in moments of stress or boredom, she would ask her host or hostess repeatedly to refill her glass, and when she was alone she often could not resist the temptation of taking a drink to lift her spirits or to help her sleep.

Contributing to her anxiety that winter was the prospect of having to give five lectures at Barnard College in March. Sometime in 1969, Elizabeth Janeway, a distinguished author and an active Barnard alumna, had suggested to the president of Barnard, Martha Peterson, that Barnard sponsor a series of lectures by an individual outside of academia who had been successful as an artist or writer. When the suggestion was greeted with enthusiasm, Janeway not only offered to select an appropriate speaker but to obtain funding for such an undertaking. A great admirer of Jean Stafford's writing, Janeway chose her to inaugurate the Barnard lectures in 1971. Although Janeway acknowledged that Stafford did not deal consciously with feminist issues in her fiction, she found in Stafford's work "a steady, unromantic concentration on the immediate lived experience of women."[108]

Stafford delivered a series of five lectures at Barnard between March 1 and March 15. Under the rubric "Tradition and Dissent," she spoke to a small audience of students, alumnae, and friends on topics entitled "The Felicities of Formal Education," "The Present Afflictions of the American Language," "The Teaching of Writing," "Sense and Sensibility," and "The Snows of Yesteryear." In her opening remarks, Stafford announced, "For the next two weeks I'm going to be talking on a number of subjects, although as I look back on what I've written, they all seem to be variations on the same subject: the upheaval of our traditions." Interweaving personal anecdotes about her family, her friends, her childhood in the West, and her experiences as a student and as a teacher, she spoke critically of the changes in manners and morals that she had witnessed during her lifetime. She claimed to be an optimist, in contrast to her father, a "man embattled from his bassinette" who had thought "the world was going to hell in a handbasket," but in these talks, she devoted more time to reminiscing about the past or criticizing the excesses of the present than to making optimistic predictions about the future.[109]

During her stay at Barnard, Stafford was amused to discover that Barnard's president had once been a student of her Kansas cousin, Margaret Lynn, author of a memoir about life on the frontier, *A Stepdaughter of the Prairie,* whose name Stafford had mentioned in the introduction to her *Collected Stories.* President Peterson later recalled with pleasure how entertaining and stimulating Stafford's lectures had been, though she commented on Stafford's evident nervousness as she addressed her audience at Barnard.[110] Though ill at ease on the lecture platform, Stafford enjoyed being the center of attention during the two weeks that she served as the Virginia Gildersleeve Professor-in-Residence. She was housed in comfortable quarters on campus and fêted at parties and receptions. At a dinner party given in her honor by Iola Haverstick, a friend she had met in Westport, she was surrounded by some of her favorite people: Robert Giroux, Dorothea and Roger Straus, and Jean Riboud, who promised to take her to the Muhammad Ali prizefight the following evening.

After she returned to the Springs, Stafford was plagued by ill health. In May she complained to Mary Lee about unbearable pains in her back that had forced her to resume wearing an orthopedic corset, a cervical collar, and elastic stockings. She said that, as a result, once again she was excoriating the driver of the automobile that had "mucked up" her life thirty-three years earlier. Although she had counted on finishing her novel during that summer, she feared that the weakness of the skeleton would invade the brain and make it listless.[111] She did not succeed in completing the novel, but she did continue to turn out well-written book reviews, and she was still capable of producing superbly written essays such as a lyrical description of beaches that she wrote for a book called *The American Coast.*

When Jean Stafford was able to find congenial summer tenants for her guest house and converted chicken coop, she did not feel as isolated as she had felt when she was alone during the winters. That summer, the son of Frank Sheed and Maisie Ward, Wilfrid Sheed, was her tenant, and in 1974 she in-

vited Craig Nova, a young man she had considered to be her most promising
student at Columbia, to be her writer-in-residence, providing that he help her
with the chores and drive her to town and to the nearby beaches. Whenever
her solitude became too oppressive during the rest of the year, she would invite a friend to spend some time with her. Just before Christmas in 1971, Lore
Segal, the writer who had taken over her class at Columbia, came out to the
house in the Springs to spend a week. Since both were serving as judges of
children's books for the National Book Award that year, they would meet for
dinner after a day of writing and would discuss that year's contenders "with
galvanizing disgust and anaesthetizing boredom."[112] Another writer who visited that winter was novelist Maureen Howard. "I spent that New Year's with
Jean Stafford Liebling out in her orderly house," Howard wrote in her memoir, *Facts of Life*. Once Howard's young daughter was asleep, the two women
sat together until five minutes after midnight. ". . . I remember there was no
rancor or bitterness in anything we said . . . Nothing sorrowful: I had gotten
through. Jean, scrubbing over the last pot, dismissed me, a gruff and uncom-
monly good friend," she said.[113]

Another strategy Stafford adopted to escape the solitude of the Springs
during the winter months was to attend committee meetings at the National
Institute of Arts and Letters. After she was appointed to the Award Committee for Literature in 1971, she would take a cab to the city from East Hampton
and charge the institute for her transportation and her lodging at the Cosmopolitan Club. "Forgive me . . . for being about as expensive to transport
from East Hampton as Eudora from Jacksonville," she wrote to Felicia
Geffen at the institute. Requesting one hundred and fifty dollars for her cab
fare, she explained, "I don't drive and I *cannot* manage the LIRR or, worse,
the LIRR station in New York, egress from which consists of 987 straight up
and straight down stairs through a dimlit labyrinth densely packed with Cut-
throats, Thimbleriggers and Widow Killers."[114]

In the spring of 1972, Stafford was feeling sufficiently well to undertake a
trip to Colorado. Her primary purpose in doing so was to receive an honorary
degree from the University of Colorado, but en route she also delivered a lecture at the University of Kansas and paid a brief visit to her friend Laurence
Lafore in Iowa City. Amused by an article Stafford had written for *Vogue* in
1971 about how an ideal guest room should be furnished, he had gone to great
lengths to furnish the guest room in his house with all of the items she had
recommended: a Thermos jug for water; a small beautiful vase filled with
flowers; a flashlight in case of power failures; a box of tissues; a scratch pad
and sharp pencils; a sewing kit and a small tin of safety pins; scissors; and a
box of lemon drops.[115]

Much to her surprise, Stafford found the ceremony in Boulder at which she was awarded an honorary degree to be both exhilarating and emotional, for she usually abhorred "the unconscionable tedium of such rituals."[116] From a distance, she said, the mountains "looked as handsome as ever," but she was astonished by the "vast swarming size of the town."[117] On May 24 she was awarded the degree of Doctor of Humane Letters "for her mastery of her craft, especially as the creator of a brilliantly rich and flexible prose."[118] The following day she gave a talk to the Associates of the Rare Books Room of the Norlin Library, where her papers are housed at present. In a printed version of this talk, which she called "Miss McKeehan's Pocketbook," Jean Stafford spoke fondly of her former English professor, Irene Petit McKeehan, the teacher who had first suggested to her that she might consider becoming a writer. "It would have been a good deal easier for me if she had touted me onto the beauty-parlor business or the F.B.I.," she observed. Confessing that most of the time she was "poorer than Job's turkey and his wife" and often suicidal because she was convinced she had never written a decent sentence in her life and would not ever write another line, she nevertheless expressed her gratitude to Miss McKeehan for having encouraged her to pursue a career as a writer. She went on to describe her writing habits: in her upstairs study she was a novelist and writer of short stories, while in her downstairs study she worked as a journalist "to make money to keep a roof over the upstairs ivory tower." It was her intention, she stated, to compile a book of her essays and lectures and angry letters to public utility companies. In memory of her professor, who always used to carry a large black leather handbag, she planned to call this collection *Miss McKeehan's Pocketbook*.[119]

In June of 1973, Stafford was awarded a second honorary degree, this one from Southampton College, where she delivered a commencement address about the value of a liberal arts education that was similar to the first of her Barnard lectures. Yet another honor she received during the last decade of life was an award in journalism for an article she had written in *Vogue* in 1973 on the editor of the *Washington Post*, Katharine Graham.[120]

While the honors that were bestowed on Stafford for her past achievements made her feel more positive about what she had accomplished to date, she nevertheless was in continual turmoil because *The Parliament of Women* remained unfinished. In an interview with Stafford that appeared in the *New York Times* on August 26, 1973, Alden Whitman reported that the only Pulitzer Prize–winning writer in the Hamptons was "glimpsing the end" of her first autobiographical novel "about Mommy and Daddy and Missouri and Colorado and Massachusetts and New York." She informed Whitman that she expected to turn her manuscript in to her publishers in mid-September, after which she and Robert Giroux, her friend and editor, her counselor and executor, would "live with it night and day." Hinting at the barely disguised portraits of actual people she had known that would appear in the novel, she said, "An American poet, with whom I was once closely associated, is petrified, and well he should be! I'm setting up the poets to a fare-thee-well." [121] But the novel never was published, and the only portions of it that were salvaged from the manuscript by Robert Giroux were a chapter about her father that was published posthumously in *Shenandoah* under the title "Woden's Day" and a portion of the novel set in Damariscotta and dealing with Stafford's relationship to Lowell that was published under the title "An Influx of Poets" in the *New Yorker* in 1978, several months before she died.

Meanwhile, Stafford continued to support herself by writing feature articles, book reviews, and introductions to books that were written by others. *Vogue* discontinued her monthly review in 1974; however, her book reviews continued to appear in the *Washington Post Book World* until 1976, when it ceased publication; her annual review "Children's Books for Christmas" appeared in the *New Yorker* until 1975; and between October of 1975 and October of 1976, she wrote a monthly book review for *Esquire,* as Dorothy Parker had done for the magazine between 1957 and 1964. Her reviews are witty, insightful, and sometimes exceedingly snide. A vitriolic review in *Esquire* of Susan Brownmiller's *Against Our Will,* in fact, gave rise to the kind of "hate mail" from outraged feminists that she had earlier described in her 1974 essay in *Esquire,* "Somebody Out There Hates Me";[122] and her review of Rose Kennedy's autobiography was so caustic and unsympathetic that the editors of the *Atlantic Monthly,* who had suggested that she review the book, ultimately decided to pay her for her efforts but not to print it.

Between 1975 and 1976 Stafford also contributed introductions to three books whose writers she admired: A. J. Liebling, P. G. Wodehouse, and Helen Hunt Jackson. A revised edition of a collection of Liebling's articles, *The Press,* includes a four-page introduction by Stafford in which she speaks about her late husband and his work. She was pleased to have a forum for writing about Liebling, and though she probably was not paid very much money for this introduction or for her introduction to Wodehouse's *Mulliner Nights* and Jackson's *Nelly's Silvermine,* she enjoyed writing about Liebling, about the comic capers of Wodehouse's characters, and about Jackson's Nelly, whose western childhood might well have reminded her of her own early years in Boulder.

Articles by Stafford continued to appear regularly in various periodicals and newspapers until she suffered a stroke in December of 1976. Nevertheless, she was always depressed about the sorry state of her bank account and about other matters as well. For a brief period in 1973 she enjoyed the company of Nancy Gibney, who sublet a house in East Hampton, but Nancy had to return to the Virgin Islands in November when Robert Gibney died unexpectedly there. Stafford's letters to her friend after Nancy left East Hampton were filled with depressing news about Everett Rattray's cancer; the death of Jeannette Rattray; the death of one of Stafford's cats; and her devastating health problems. In one letter she enclosed a newspaper photograph of a balding, bespectacled Lowell with long gray hair. "I enclose a new photograph of the reason we first met," she wrote. "Eve Auchincloss sent it to me saying, 'The Ben Franklin de nos jours. Yuch!' It's impossible to believe that this is the raving beauty I knew as a young man."[123]

As Stafford contemplated her sixtieth birthday in July of 1975, she glumly wrote to Nancy Gibney, ". . . I have accepted this as an uncontrovertible fact: the stars had it in for me and intend to carry the grudge until I die at the age of 120."[124] The following January, however, she reported cheerfully that "with rambunctious folly" she had appeared on the "Today" show, where she, Theodore Bernstein, Dwight ("the Jackass") McDonald, and Edwin Newman had discussed the plight of the English language in America. For her television appearance she wore "an absolutely smashing" felt burgundy hat with black grosgrain trim that Carrie Nye had given her for Christmas, a black turtleneck, a blazer, boots, and burgundy slacks. "Now and again I could see myself on the monitor and, if I do say so myself . . . thought I didn't look half bad," she said gleefully. However, she complained that the trip to New York was not worth the trouble since she had only been on the air about three and a half minutes, during which time the moderator mostly focused on her "old wheeze hopefully."[125]

In an effort to generate some capital to pay her outstanding bills, Stafford turned that year to the rare book dealers to negotiate with them the sale of some of the texts in Liebling's collection of rare books about sports. "The Pain was fleeting," she reported to Nancy Gibney after the book dealers had removed about half the books.[126] More traumatic, however, were her negotiations with Lowell about some of the books he had written. In August, ignoring how wounding such a request might be to her pride, she wrote to him:

> You don't know it, but you saved me this summer from being taken by the black Maria to debtor's prison (in which I fully believe) there to be fed moldy crusts and given smelly water to drink. With sorrow and regret, I sold my copy of *Land of Unlikeness* and blessed you from the bottom of my heart. I

knew, moreover, that you would not mind, indeed, you would be glad that you'd helped me out of a nasty pinch. And so, quite frankly, I want to make some more money out of you. May I? Can we collude as we were accused of doing when my head got busted?

She explained that what she wanted him to do was to inscribe all of the first editions she owned of his books, as well as her copy of the *Oxford Book of Verse,* which contained annotations in his hand of several of the poems in the volume. "Do you loathe me for this? Do I wound you? If you do, tell me and I'll stop," she said, adding, "I do *so* want to finish my novel. I do *so* hate to have to interrupt it to write reviews and articles. I wasn't put on the earth to be a journalist. I'm *sure* I wasn't." [127]

Lowell not only agreed to meet her in Boston to autograph copies of his books, but offered to give her some money in addition. "That was *not* intended to be a begging letter, but after considerable debate, I have decided to accept your generosity, hoping you can afford it," she replied. Since he mentioned in his letter to her that he had recently fainted after drinking when he was taking Antabuse, she confided to him about her own drinking problems:

> One of the principal reasons I have become so reclusive is that I don't want to drink, and I find that I can't not drink when I'm with people—I use booze as insulation against boredom and impatience, or to exalt my feeling of camaraderie to the point of mania. Moreover, it makes my stomach ache and brings on monstrous insomnia. If I drink alone—and sometimes I do occasionally—I fall down and break something—either an irreplaceable piece of something breakable or one of my bones. And on those occasions, my solitude becomes loneliness and I may plan a dinner party and telephone invitations. And then I have to cancel it with some heavily documented excuse . . . [128]

When Jean Stafford met with Robert Lowell in Cambridge, she brought with her not only her own copies of books Lowell had written but also several that her sister Marjorie had sent her. Frequently enraged by something her sister Marjorie had done—or failed to do—Stafford was furious when Marjorie mailed her an autographed book of Lowell's poems that he had sent to her parents, as well as an unsigned, tattered copy of *Boston Adventure.* In her long list of grievances against her sister, Stafford now included the fact that Marjorie had carefully preserved the first edition of Lowell's poems but not the books written by her own sister. Describing the distressing and frightfully expensive lunch she had had with Cal and his new wife, Lady Caroline Blackwood, during which the book signing took place, she wrote angrily to Marjorie: "Your sending to me that beat-up copy of Boston Adventure to sign made me feel that probably all my books have been lost or chucked out. I don't give a damn—I really don't because I don't give a damn about anything now except work, and secondarily, about the problems of my bones, my electricity bill, the heat and humidity of Suffolk County, the vexations of age, etc."[129] In a subsequent letter she told Marjorie that she couldn't help wondering why all Cal's books had been saved, while hers had not. Speaking of her own feelings of hostility to Marjorie, she observed to her, "From experience and observation, I have long been aware . . . that the relationship of sisters is more complicated than any other among blood ties. If it works well it works with wondrous beauty; if it works badly, it is hideous."[130]

One indication that Stafford was worried about how she would continue to generate enough income to maintain herself was her decision to acquire a different literary agent after working for so many years with James Oliver Brown. On the surface their relationship over the years had been a cordial one. However, from time to time he had gently chastised her for failing to pay him his commission for some piece of writing she had published without consulting him, and she, in turn, had expressed irritation about some of the writing projects he had proposed to her. On January 16, 1975, she wrote to Brown to inform him of her decision to terminate their professional relationship. "The novel is still miles and years in the future," she informed him candidly, and she sadly observed: "Our business relationship has been a happy one, our friendship a joy. But the first, I think has dwindled almost to the point of no return. And as I write you this letter, I feel you may well read it with relief."[131] On April 11, 1975, she and Brown officially parted company. For the remainder of her life Timothy Seldes at Russell and Volkening would serve as her literary agent. Perhaps Stafford guessed that the end of her relationship with Brown also signaled the end of her career.

Thirteen

In the Snowfall
Summer 1975–Spring 1979

Is there any balm in Gilead?
—JEAN STAFFORD, IN A LETTER TO THOMAS ROBERTS, APRIL 3, 1976

The snow was a benison. It forgave them all.
—JEAN STAFFORD, "THE PHILOSOPHY LESSON"

TO EVEN THE most casual of Jean Stafford's acquaintances it was obvious that her health was rapidly deteriorating. Though she was known to be a hypochondriac who kept the Merck manual on her desk alongside her dictionaries, she was nevertheless suffering from a potentially fatal heart and lung disorder, and by October of 1975 she weighed a mere 105 pounds. She herself recognized the gravity of her condition. After a visit to Dr. Roberts she wrote to him: "My last birthday, the 60th, turned me morbid. Heretofore no other anniversary has done so. I think I have not asked this of you before, but I do now implore you never to withhold anything from me. Our palaver about my probably appalling longevity may no longer be palaver. I have premonitions. I have a great deal of work to do before I am gathered to Abraham's scratchy bosom and I must not waste my time."[1]

Advised in the past by Dr. Roberts that she must stop smoking, she said that the very thought of having to do so had made her smoke six cartons right straight through,[2] but eventually her chronic bronchitis and emphysema had become so debilitating that in the hopes of finding a way to give up cigarettes she had decided to consult a psychiatrist who used hypnotism as a therapeutic modality. Afterward, paraphrasing Dewey Dell in Faulkner's *As I Lay Dying,* she said wryly to Joseph Mitchell, "He charged me a dollar and I don't think he did me a bit of good!"[3]

In May of 1975 Stafford was admitted to New York Hospital with a diagnosis of angina pectoris and chronic lung disease and was warned that she was in grave danger of having a stroke. "A heart attack is one thing, lung cancer is another, but a stroke simply won't do," she wrote to Nancy Gibney, revealing her terror even though she attempted to sound more lighthearted than she felt.[4] She was discharged on a regimen of home care that included using a machine she referred to as a "pulmonary toilet" to flush out her lungs, and four times a day she had to inhale oxygen from a tube attached to a pressurized tank.[5] Writing to Nancy Gibney from her "machine shop bedroom," she said, "I am so ghastly sick, so lonely, so abysmally broke . . . that bitterness is in my blood and brain." Her only consolation, she observed, lay in memories of laughing with friends like Nancy or Peter Taylor, "all of them far away— or dead."[6]

During the months that followed, Stafford was largely confined to her bedroom, where she performed for herself the duties of an intensive-care nurse as she scrupulously followed the health care routine her physicians had prescribed. The early American furnishings in her small white room were dominated by the tall green oxygen cylinders that stood at her bedside, and she complained that the breathing machine and blow bottles distracted the eye from the lithograph on her wall that her friend, cartoonist Saul Steinberg, had given her.[7] Her imaginary "red room" had now been replaced by the confining walls of her own white bedroom. Although she still continued to read the children's books for her annual *New Yorker* review, much of the day, too exhausted to work, she played solitaire or did the crossword puzzle or desultorily read the *New York Times,* "seething at all the stories datelined East Hampton" that talked about "the high life at Bobby Van's among the writers in this Radical Chic Leper Colony."[8] At first, after she had returned from the hospital, she had hired a practical nurse, but annoyed by the nurse's nonstop talking, she promptly fired her, and when her sister Marjorie offered to come east, she insisted that she was able to manage on her own. To reassure Marjorie, she mentioned that her devoted housekeeper, Mrs. Monsell, came in once a week to clean, and said that two friends regularly prepared appetizing meals for her from ingredients she herself would order from the supermarket. She was learning patience while she lay abed, she observed, and was enjoying the luxury of being able to read for pleasure, something she had scarcely found time to do during the last fifteen years when she had been obliged to read the books she had agreed to review for various publications. Although she emphasized how self-sufficient she was, she nevertheless remarked bleakly, "You can't supply me with the two things I desperately need—money and the strength to write."[9]

Initially, friends and neighbors offered whatever assistance they could. Her friend John Thompson, whom she had first met when Lowell brought her to Kenyon College, visited her and brought her food. "She used to scorch her big hands trying to cook supper," he said; "then she was persuaded to stop that and we fetched in food. Little of it would she eat. In contrast to her peer Isak, Ean-beaner made it on whisky and salted almonds rather than champagne & caviar."[10] Liebling's friends, Pierre and Charlotte Guedenet, who had moved to East Hampton after Pierre retired, often invited her to have dinner with them and frequently phoned her to offer their assistance; Howard Moss took her out to dinner and listened patiently to her habitual complaints about people who had offended her; and Steven Hahn, an electrical engineer who lived in East Hampton, spent long evenings listening to her anecdotes about the people she knew in the literary world. He also made recordings of her reading her short stories. Friends in New York City like Ann Honeycutt and Dorothea Straus helped to relieve her anxieties whenever she telephoned them—and she frequently did. Dorothea Straus remembered vividly her late-night conversations with Jean Stafford: "After an hour or so of gossip and book talk . . . I might point out the hour. But she was not easily deterred. I pictured her alone with her cat in the gray shingle salt-box filled with its orderly, well-tended clutter of Victorian furniture, bric-a-brac and keepsakes . . . upstairs and down, a profusion of desks, serious ones equipped with typewriters, as well as impractical antiques." When Dorothea Straus grew weary and suggested that the hour was late, Jean would say, "I'll hang up p.d.q." but would continue to talk. "It took a long time to dispose of the final victim, pickled in her special flavorsome recipe of brine," Dorothea Straus recalled with amusement.[11]

Although Stafford was usually annoyed by her sisters, she used to call them too when her isolation became unbearable. "When I called her, I was likely to find her in not so amiable a mood and our conversations were much shorter," her sister Marjorie observed, however.[12] In September of 1976 Marjorie and a friend stopped in New York City en route to Europe. Looking very frail and carrying a small oxygen tank to help her breathe, Stafford met Marjorie in Manhattan and took her to the Cosmopolitan Club, to which she referred as her "old ladies club." They both had dinner in the dining room and spent the night there.[13] The next day, in the private car she had hired to transport her from the Springs to the city, she and Marjorie drove to Kennedy Airport together.

Anxious to have someone nearby at all times, Stafford turned to a young couple she had recently met in East Hampton: Maria Robbins, a writer of children's books, and her husband Ken, who was a photographer. Describing Maria and Ken to Nancy Gibney as her "fine young slaves," she reported that Maria brought her delicious, nourishing food, and Ken assumed responsibility for making necessary repairs on the house and also drove her to town.[14] During the summer of 1976 she gave the Robbins an acre of land behind the converted chicken coop so that they could have a house built for themselves. Anticipating Nancy's reaction to the news that she had given away such valuable property, she wrote that she counted on Maria and Ken to succor her, "Numero Uno": "*Give* land! Are you daft? says everybody. No, I am not daft: I can't sell the land, I need strong young people near me, strong young people who will never invade. It is not an act of altruism but one of pure selfishness."[15]

"A writer who isn't writing is always a menace . . . ," Wilfrid Sheed has remarked in his portrait of Jean Stafford that appeared in *Shenandoah* after her death. He observed that Stafford "used some of her leftover talent to act the great lady, putting people down right and left and making wisecracks which were bound to get back to their victims in such a small playground."[16] His portrait of his friend Jean Stafford and the comments that various other friends and acquaintances have made about her suggest that especially during these last trying years she could often be tiresome, venomous about people she disliked, disloyal, demanding. Yet she was capable of great generosity, was courageous, and was still usually able to maintain her sense of humor. Noting some of the contradictory aspects of her character, Howard Moss said that he found her to possess "a special combination of the tart and the sweet," of decorum and outlandishness. "One of her qualities hardest to get down on paper," he observed, "was the young girl always present in the civilized and cultivated woman."[17] Alternately reticent and open about her past, she sometimes afforded her friends an intimate glimpse of her psychological turmoil. Sheed recalled, for example, one occasion when she had confided to him that she had dreamt eight nights in a row about coming down to family breakfast in Colorado. "If I have that dream again, I'll go ab-so-lutely crazy," she had exclaimed.[18]

Recalling how demanding Stafford often was during the last decade of her life, Ann Honeycutt remarked sadly, "She had managed to estrange everybody."[19] Eventually, even the most loyal of her friends found it trying to be in her company, especially when she had been drinking. Eleanor Hempstead, who was her neighbor in the Springs, remembered how difficult a dinner guest Jean Stafford had been. Aware of Stafford's desperate loneliness, she would sometimes invite her to a dinner party, but subsequently would regret that she had extended the invitation. More and more drunk as the evening wore on, Stafford would refuse to eat and would monopolize the conversation; then, when she had decided at last that it was time for her to leave, she would imperiously ask one of the other dinner guests to accompany her home and would invite that individual in to have drinks with her.[20]

In August of 1976, Stafford wrote to Nancy Gibney, "I am not sure how long I want to live." She mentioned that she had had two bad attacks during the preceding spring. After the second, she had summoned Hightower from Cambridge and had asked him to bring her a "Goering Instant Silver Bullet," but when he came to see her, he had not brought what she had requested. "My affection for Hightower didn't really diminish: I'd be fearful of the responsibility myself living, as we are obliged to do, in a cloud of unknowing," she said.[21]

The catastrophe Stafford had dreaded and feared most—a stroke—occurred on December 1, 1976. She was transferred from Southampton Hospital to New York Hospital to be treated for a stroke that had severely impaired both her ability to write and to speak. As Robert Giroux observed, "For one of America's most expressive and articulate users of the language, this was hell."[22] Several letters she laboriously wrote after her stroke reveal the severity of her impairment: she found it difficult to summon up the appropriate word or to spell the most common of words. Informing her sister Marjorie in February about her intentions to go to the Rusk Institute for therapy and rehabilitation, she wrote, "I am having to stay at least a weak [sic] in the city Monday–Friday. This, I regret to say, after for [sic] or five months. . . . I go now to one asylum and another";[23] and in July she wrote to Marjorie, "Don't call even until my marble are back."[24]

News of Stafford's stroke reached Robert Lowell just before he was scheduled to give a reading of his poetry at the 92nd Street Y. Included among the poems he read on December 8 were two about Jean Stafford: "The Old Flame" from his 1964 book *For the Union Dead* and a more recent poem from *Day by Day,* "Jean Stafford, A Letter." Before he read the second of these poems, he remarked to the audience about his former wife: "Men may be superior to women, but women always do better in college, I think, and are much more precocious. . . . She could punctuate, and do all sorts of things. . . . She is one of our best writers, and her talent developed early."[25]

No longer the pretty young woman in "Heidelberry braids and Bavarian peasant aprons" whom Robert Lowell fondly recalled in his later poem, the bedridden Stafford, emaciated, breathing laboriously, and deprived of her powers of speech, was distressed when Robert Giroux mentioned the new poem Lowell had read about her. Raising her bony arms, she managed to stammer, "The son of a bitch! Why doesn't he leave me alone!"[26] On September 12, nine months after he had read his poems at the 92nd Street Y, Lowell had a heart attack and died in a New York taxicab. Stafford was too ill to attend the funeral, nor did she ever sum up in writing her final impressions of their long, complex, and often trying relationship.

After the stroke, Stafford could no longer write the articles and reviews that had provided her with enough money to sustain herself. In February, without her knowledge, her friend—and sometimes "enemy"—Craig Claiborne circulated a letter among her friends and acquaintances asking for contributions to an account several people had opened for her in her bank in East Hampton. Five years after her death, he would reminisce fondly about his friend and neighbor in the Springs, "who was of course one of this nation's finest writers." She "had a passion for good food," he said, and was "a marvelous and inspired cook." He recalled the hours they had spent over tea, wine, and "more serious libations," during which they discussed eating habits, taste, and other matters concerning the preparation and consumption of food. She told him "wildly amusing stories" about Mrs. Jack Gardner, who had served champagne and donuts on the day her resplendent Boston home, Fenway Court, was opened to the public. Edith Wharton, who was one of Mrs. Gardner's guests, was heard to remark in French in the presence of her hostess that the refreshments were the kind "you would be served in a railroad restaurant," she said.[27]

Another person who tried to assist Stafford was Kurt Vonnegut, a fellow member of the National Academy and Institute of Arts and Letters. He called to see whether the institute would be able to contribute some money for Stafford's groceries and for the speech therapy she so badly needed. A memo describing Stafford's "dire straits" was sent to the members of the committee for the Artists' and Writers' Fund, and they not only agreed to send her a check for the maximum amount they awarded writers and artists who were in need of help, but said that if she needed more in a few months, they would send an additional sum of money to her.[28]

Ultimately, the only thing that saved her from the abject poverty she had feared ever since she was a child was the sale of 29.5 acres of her property in the Springs. From the sale of this property to relatives of Ken Robbins, Stafford received $115,000 in December 1977, a substantial sum, though hardly enough to compensate her for the loss of the land she and Liebling had loved or to allow her to live out the remainder of her life without financial worries. She used some of the capital she received after the sale of her property to repay Jean Riboud, who had sent her money after her stroke. "You need not have done it but you have forever a line of credit of $10,000, and not with a banker charging interest but with me—anytime you need it, let me know," he wrote to her after her check arrived.[29]

In addition to selling her land, Stafford hoped to generate some more capital from the sale of her papers to a research library. She had continued to maintain a close affiliation with the Norlin Library at the University of Colorado, and a sizable pile of her manuscripts had already been deposited in the library's Special Collections several years earlier. However, she was somewhat reluctant to turn her papers over to this library, her sentimental attachment to it notwithstanding, since she was anxious to get as much money as she could and felt that other libraries had greater financial resources than the Norlin Library did. Sometime after her stroke, she agreed to meet with the individual who was in charge of Special Collections at the Norlin Library, Ellsworth Mason, to discuss how she wished him to proceed. A Joyce scholar and a great admirer of her writing, Mason was very sympathetic to her needs and desires. When he learned about her stroke from Paul and Dorothy Thompson, he paid two visits to Stafford's house in the Springs, returning to Boulder each time with boxes of the manuscripts that she had carefully sorted. During her lifetime, Mason was not successful in finding a suitable buyer for her papers, but in the interim, he catalogued all the material he had received so that scholars would be able to assess what was available. Now a greatly expanded collection of Stafford's manuscripts and correspondence is a permanent part of Special Collections at the Norlin Library.[30]

During these dark months, one happy event in Stafford's life was the appearance of "An Influx of Poets" in the *New Yorker* in November of 1978. Realizing that *The Parliament of Women* would undoubtedly not be completed, Robert Giroux decided to extract this witty, insightful, and very bitter fictional account of Jean Stafford's stormy marriage to Robert Lowell from her unfinished novel, as well as material that was published posthumously as "Woden's Day" in an issue of *Shenandoah* that was dedicated to Stafford the autumn after she died. Perhaps Stafford would have been somewhat reluctant to publish such a nakedly autobiographical account of her marriage to Lowell while he was still alive, but by 1978 both Lowell and Delmore Schwartz, who is represented in the story by a character named Jerry Zumwalt, were dead, and the real Minnie Zumwalt, Gertrude Buckman, was living abroad. "An Influx of Poets" generated a good deal of interest, particularly among the people in the literary circles that Jean Stafford and Robert Lowell had frequented, and when this new story by Stafford appeared, many individuals, including Hightower, mistakenly concluded that she had made a remarkable recovery from her stroke and had begun writing again. However, telephoning her to congratulate her on her latest achievement, they realized immediately when they heard her garbled speech that she was still aphasic. Stafford was very pleased by all the attention that she received after the story was published; nevertheless, agreeing to allow the *New Yorker* to publish this excerpt from *The Parliament of Women* was tantamount to admitting that the novel to which she had devoted so many years of her life and which had caused her so much anguish would never be published.

In May of 1979 a letter to the editor describing the last year of Stafford's life appeared in the *East Hampton Star*. The writer of the letter, a woman by the name of Barbara Hadden, had prepared meals for Stafford after she had returned from yet another stay in the hospital in February of 1978. Urging her readers not to neglect those people in the community who desperately were in need of compassion and assistance, Hadden wrote about Stafford's depression and loneliness: "When I first met Jean I was struck by the fact that nothing was being done to rehabilitate her and that there were few people around to encourage her or to give her the support that she so badly needed. She was in deep pain and despair and felt very much alone." Convinced that Stafford's symptoms would improve if some special effort were made to ameliorate them, Hadden spent many afternoons with her encouraging her to converse; she also made arrangements for a speech therapist to work with her on her speaking and writing. Although Hadden realized as she came to know Stafford better how difficult she could be at times, she also admired her intelligence, her courage, her dignity, and her ability to maintain a sense of humor despite the fact that she was so ill and so frustrated by her handicaps. "It saddens me to think that in her despair, she may have turned people away from her," she wrote.[31]

Throughout her lifetime Stafford had had many friends, but she had grown to dislike some of the people whom she had liked initially and had alienated many others. She had no children, she was estranged from her sisters, and even those people whom she had considered to be her most intimate friends had neither the time nor the energy to assume full responsibility for her care; nor would Stafford have assumed the responsibility of caring for others if they had been in need. Resembling the sick, forgotten, elderly women whose plight Doris Lessing has recently described so movingly in her novel *The Diary of a Good Neighbor,* Stafford, ineluctably, became more and more isolated during the last months of her life. Ultimately, the only person on whom she felt she could depend was her "faithful and beloved cleaning woman,"[32] Josephine Monsell. Always appearing on schedule, Mrs. Monsell kept the house tidy, brought her a breakfast tray and the newspaper when she arrived at work in the morning, and greeted her cheerfully. "I used to tell her, 'Come on, Mrs. Liebling, the world is waiting for you,'" Mrs. Monsell recalled.[33] Longing to be mothered, Stafford was reminded perhaps of her own mother as she watched Mrs. Monsell go about her household chores. "She *is* rather like a typhoon, noisy and all over the place, but she does get things so nicely back into shape," she once wrote about "Mrs. M." in an article called "Suffering Summer Houseguests."[34]

Several of Stafford's friends have poignantly described her during the agonizing last months of her life. Dick Cavett recalled her excruciating late-night calls: often they ended with Jean, unable to utter the word she wanted to say, "snarling with disgust and slamming the phone down," he said; even worse though were the times when the phone rang and there would be no sound with the exception of a "kind of strangled croak and a hanging up."[35] Dorothea Straus's picture of Stafford before she died is equally chilling. The face of the once pretty young woman was now ravaged; her hair, formerly reddish blond, was dyed a harsh mahogany and was exceedingly sparse; and she was painfully thin and frail. A short time before she died, Stafford made her way to the Cosmopolitan Club, accompanied by the green oxygen cylinders. Dressed in a black silk dress with an uneven hemline that hung too loosely on her emaciated body, she met Dorothea and Roger Straus in the deserted club library one Saturday night. Her scarlet pumps and matching handbag made her look like a small-town librarian all dressed up for an outing in the big city, Dorothea Straus said. On the next occasion when they met, Jean was a patient in New York Hospital, to which she had been taken from the club. Still smoking incessantly despite her doctor's orders, she made a valiant attempt at conversation and chuckled with appreciation as Dorothea tried to cheer her up by telling her amusing anecdotes about people they knew. Despite the evident gravity of her physical condition, Stafford told Dorothea that she was thinking of selling her house in the Springs and moving to the city because she was weary of her solitary life.[36]

From New York Hospital Jean Stafford was taken to the Burke Rehabilitation Center in White Plains. Robert Giroux, who visited her there, took her outside in a wheelchair, but as soon as they were no longer in sight of the main building, she insisted on walking, and, much to his dismay, she took out a cigarette, though Dr. Roberts had explicitly warned her that smoking could be fatal. When Robert Giroux begged her not to smoke and refused to light her cigarette, she took a cigarette lighter out of her own pocketbook. Later, in her room, he noticed a student's green book bag near her bed and was surprised to discover that it contained some early poems Robert Lowell had written. Observing that the poems were annotated in her familiar script, Robert Giroux asked her whether she felt that she was the person to do an annotated edition of Lowell's poems. In answer to his question, she smiled and nodded yes.[37]

"Last week somebody I knew died," Stafford's friend Katinka De Vries wrote in a short story that was published in the *New Yorker* one year after Stafford's death. Katinka De Vries's narrator goes on to say:

> She had phoned to tell me where she was. "Come see me," she said. When I called back to say we'd be down very soon, she was gone. Now she stammers again, in my memory: "Call this a re-ha-bil-i-ta-tion center? Some re-ha-bil-i-tation. Conked out, didn't I?" . . . She may not be widely mourned, but I remember when she lived in our town, on our road, when she strolled toward our house with a basket of red raspberries slung over her arm, freshly gathered from the masses of tangled bushes in her yard, all the scents of summer in them.[38]

It is obvious that the "neighbor" about whom Katinka De Vries was writing was her friend Jean Stafford, who at the age of sixty-three had died of cardiac arrest on March 26, 1979, at the Burke Rehabilitation Center.

Long before her death, Stafford had ordered her own tombstone from the same stonecutter in Newport who had made the tombstone for Liebling. In doing so, she had replicated an event in her fiction, for in *The Catherine Wheel*, Katharine Congreve, too, orders her tombstone before she dies. Across the continent from her native California and thousands of miles from the Colorado of her youth, Stafford's ashes were buried on April 10 alongside those of A. J. Liebling in Green River Cemetery in East Hampton, where the artists Jackson Pollack, Ad Reinhardt, and Stuart Davis are also buried. Identical in size and shape to Liebling's, her gray granite tombstone is inscribed JEAN STAFFORD LIEBLING 1915–1979, and above her name a single snowflake is engraved. In choosing this symbol, perhaps she was recalling the "snows of yesteryear" that she remembered from her childhood in the Rockies, the snow Cora Savage contemplates in "The Philosophy Lesson." "She loved the snow," Stafford wrote about Cora. "When she had first heard of heaven, she had thought it would be a place where snow was forever falling and forever concealing the harshness of the world."[39] The story, which describes the suicide of a young student, concludes peacefully: "The snow was a benison. It forgave them all."[40]

Some of Stafford's friends were appalled that there were so few people at the graveside funeral service and that no one who had known her intimately had been asked to deliver a eulogy. Liebling's nephew, John Stonehill, recalled the gray afternoon when approximately twenty-five people gathered at the Green River Cemetery. Neither of her sisters was present, and after the undertaker read a psalm, two young women she had known in East Hampton spoke very briefly, mentioning some rather trivial details about her. Then the mourners, feeling pained and embarrassed, walked quietly back to their cars.[41] Comparing the small group of ill-at-ease people who gathered at that cemetery in East Hampton with the six hundred mourners who had attended the funeral of Robert Lowell in Boston's Beacon Hill the previous year,[42] Susanna Cuyler was distressed that this wonderful writer whom she had idolized had been treated so shabbily.[43] But even though someone who had attended her funeral had remarked that Jean Stafford, a lover of ceremony, would have been disappointed by her own funeral service, perhaps that individual was mistaken. Always attentive to housekeeping details, Stafford had ordered her tombstone and had determined where her ashes would be buried. "Under his fig tree in his own backyard and under the aspect of eternity: what peace awaits us all!" she had once written about the father of Katharine Congreve in *The Catherine Wheel*.[44] The gravesite next to Liebling's, the earth, the sky, and the peacefulness of death—these, rather than the burial service itself, were perhaps finally most important to her.

A key event in many novels is the moment when the deceased person's last will and testament, replete with surprising codicils, is read, as eager relatives and friends listen breathlessly for their names to be mentioned. Having used the events of her own life to fashion her fiction, Stafford appears to have wanted to write her own ending to her life as well, an ending that was as dramatic as the ending of a Victorian novel. When her will was probated, her family and friends were astonished to discover that in a final version of her will, signed in East Hampton in the office of her lawyer, Duane Whelan, on November 15, 1978, she had left most of her estate, including her literary remains, to her loyal cleaning lady, Josephine Monsell. "Jean Stafford left almost her entire estate to her maid. This is generous and fine, but it has the maid's other publishing type employers very nervous. They're afraid she'll quit polishing and retire," Liz Smith wrote in the gossip column of the *New York Daily News* on April 11, 1979.

A number of years earlier, Stafford had invited Robert Giroux and Everett Rattray to a formal lunch at her home. On that occasion she had asked Giroux to be her executor and Rattray to serve as the executor of the estate of A. J. Liebling. Both had agreed to do so, and the lawyers had then sent them copies of the clause in which they were named as executors. By the time she had her final will drawn up, however, Everett Rattray had died of cancer, and no mention was made of Robert Giroux in the most recent will. Instead, she made the following provisions: to Liebling's nephew, John Stonehill, she left several art works; to Paul and Dorothy Thompson, a Hogarth engraving; to Peter and Eleanor Taylor, the Belter Victorian settle and side chair that were treasured furnishings in her house in the Springs; to Thomas Roberts and his wife, silver serving pieces; to Nancy Gibney, her dresses; to Joseph Mitchell, a print and all of her books; and to her housekeeper Josephine Monsell, her house and the remainder of her property, including her literary rights. Although Giroux is convinced that in drafting the new will, the lawyer, Duane Whelan, somehow omitted the earlier clause naming him the literary executor, it was her cleaning lady and not her editor who became Stafford's literary executor.[45] Stafford's real intentions remain a mystery. Perhaps, as Giroux believes, she had never intended to make Mrs. Monsell her literary executor; or perhaps, in leaving most of her property to the motherly Mrs. Monsell, a woman who had taken care of her when she was ill but had never read her books, she was making reparations to her own mother, whose domestic contributions to the Stafford household Stafford had never appreciated sufficiently during the lean years in Colorado when Ethel Stafford's boardinghouse had enabled the family to survive; or perhaps, as Dick Cavett has conjectured, the will was Jean Stafford's "final mordant joke," one that allowed her to anticipate with glee the distress it would cause her editor and the members of her family, none of whom were mentioned in this document.[46] In her largely affectionate memoir of her youngest sister, Marjorie Stafford Pinkham has allowed herself one moment of bitterness during which she observes:

> Jean often spoke affectionately of her nephew Bob Frichtel, and told me she was going to name him her chief heir. It was astounding to hear of her last will and testament in which she not only did not name Bob, but bequeathed nothing to any of her family, no keepsake of any sort. She left her considerable estate, including all her literary rights, to her neighbor who was also her cleaning lady. It is impossible to figure out what was in her mind. She was a mystery, brilliant, diligent, capable of great warmth, but also capable of indifference and cruel coldness. Someone called her "a homesick writer." The pity is that she never acted like one.[47]

The eulogy Stafford would have appreciated most was delivered by her devoted friend Peter Taylor on November 13, 1979, at a memorial service for her that was held at the National Academy and Institute of Arts and Letters. In his tribute to this superb writer who had generously helped him to launch his own literary career, Peter Taylor said that after her death in March he had reread her work, for that was what he thought she would have liked her friends to do, and he was astonished anew by the brilliance of her writing. Emphasizing how private a person she had been, he insisted that it was her work that mattered to her most. "She wrote because she had to, and not for professional advancement," he said. Urging that she be remembered primarily for her artistic achievements, he commented:

One remembers Jean Stafford for her literary art, the art which she labored on for its own sake. One remembers her for her rages against stupidity and insensibility, for her expressions of passionate devotion to whatever of nobility and serenity can be salvaged from the ugliness of most lives, remembers her for her wit, for her humility, for her modesty, and for her responsiveness to one's own ideas and feelings. . . . [48]

Although Stafford died at the relatively young age of sixty-four, her life was full of adventures and misadventures. The road she traveled took her from the Pacific to the Atlantic, from Boulder to Heidelberg, from Boston to Louisiana, from Maine to New York, and en route she made many friends, and many enemies as well. Always troubled and angry, forever feeling dislocated, she searched for the "red room" where, untrammeled by want or responsibilities, she would be free to write her novels and short stories. Her literary output was slender: with the exception of the numerous book reviews and articles she was compelled to write in order to generate enough income to support herself, she published only three novels and forty-three short stories. Yet even though she was plagued by insecurity, by financial worries, by poor health, by an inability to resolve those self-destructive impulses that had their origins in her unhappy childhood and that persisted thoughout her life, and by role conflicts that were common to women writers of her generation, she managed nevertheless to write one truly outstanding novel, *The Mountain Lion*, two other novels that are notable for their style and their portrayal of female angst, and at least half a dozen memorable short stories. Barely a decade after her death, her work has been reissued and is being rediscovered by a new generation of readers.

Notes

Preface

1. Tillie Olsen, *Silences* (New York: Delacorte Press/Seymour Lawrence, 1978), pp. 218–223.

2. Alfred Kazin, *Bright Book of Life: American Novelists and Story Tellers from Hemingway to Mailer* (Boston: Little, Brown, 1971), pp. 174–175. Kazin writes, "In some writers the style is a leading character, as in Jean Stafford's elaborately written *Boston Adventure* and those brilliantly ungiving stories whose tightness of structure is at such variance with the usual theme of a young woman's inability to sustain relationships."

3. Maureen Ryan, *Innocence and Estrangement in the Fiction of Jean Stafford* (Baton Rouge: Louisiana State University Press, 1987), p. 9.

4. Elaine K. G. Benson, "Jean Stafford," *East Hampton Summer Sun,* April 20, 1979, p. 4.

5. David Roberts's biography of Jean Stafford, *Jean Stafford: A Biography,* published during the summer of 1988 by Little, Brown, appeared after this manuscript was completed.

1. The Shorn Lamb: 1915–1922

1. Jean Stafford, *Boston Adventure,* in *The Interior Castle* (New York: Harcourt Brace and Company, 1953), p. 10. Citations to works by Jean Stafford will omit the author's name after the first reference.

2. Marjorie Stafford Pinkham, "Jean," *Antaeus* 28 (Spring 1981): 1–3. Details about life on the Staffords' ranch in California have been derived from this source. See also Marjorie Stafford Pinkham, "A Look Backward at Covina and West Covina," *Mt. San Antonia Historian* 6 (Spring 1980): 78–90.

3. Jean Stafford, *The Collected Stories of Jean Stafford* (New York: Farrar, Straus and Giroux, 1969), p. 1.

4. Jean Stafford, *The Mountain Lion,* in *The Interior Castle,* p. 4.

5. *Collected Stories,* p. 172.

6. Ibid., p. 173.

7. *The Mountain Lion,* p. 204.

8. Jean Stafford, "When I Was Little," unpublished manuscript, Jean Stafford Manuscripts, Special Collections, Norlin Library, Boulder, Colorado (hereafter cited as Norlin).

9. *The Mountain Lion,* p. 11.

10. Jean Stafford to Carlos Baker and P. Albert Duhamel, undated, Norlin.

11. Jean Stafford, "Samothrace," unpublished manuscript, Norlin.

12. "Biographical History," pp. 495–497, courtesy Marjorie Stafford Pinkham.

13. "Samothrace."

14. *The Mountain Lion,* p. 49.

15. Ibid., p. 35.

16. Jean Stafford, "Home for Christmas," *Mademoiselle* 41 (December 1951): 108.

17. Jean Stafford, unpublished manuscript, Norlin.

18. "Samothrace."

19. Marjorie Stafford Pinkham, "The McKillop Family," unpublished manuscript, courtesy Marjorie Stafford Pinkham.

20. Harvey Breit, "Talk with Jean Stafford," *New York Times Book Review,* January 20, 1952, p. 18.

21. Jean Stafford, "Woden's Day," *Shenandoah* 30 (Autumn 1979): 14.

22. Jean Stafford, "Felicities of a Formal Education," unpublished manuscript, Norlin.

23. John Richard Stafford to Jean Stafford, June 3, 1963, Norlin.

24. Pinkham, "Jean," p. 11.

25. Jean Stafford, "California," unpublished manuscript, Norlin.

26. Jean Stafford, "Letter from Edinburgh," *New Yorker* 25 (September 17, 1949): 94.

27. "Woden's Day," p. 6.

28. Pinkham, "Jean," p. 9.

29. Jean Stafford, "Sisterhood," unpublished manuscript, Norlin.

30. Jean Stafford, unpublished manuscript, Norlin.

31. *The Mountain Lion,* p. 30.

32. Jean Stafford to Carlos Baker and P. Albert Duhamel, October 25, 1974, Norlin.

33. Jean Stafford to Robert Lowell, undated, Robert Lowell Papers, Houghton Library, Harvard University.

34. *The Mountain Lion,* pp. 130–131.

35. Jean Stafford, unpublished manuscript, Norlin.

36. Ibid.

37. *The Mountain Lion,* p. 31.

38. Jean Stafford, unpublished manuscript, Norlin.

39. Pinkham, "A Look Backward," p. 90.

40. Ethel Pratt to Charlotte Goodman, September 17, 1984.

41. "California."

42. *The Mountain Lion,* p. 212.

43. "Woden's Day," p. 18.

44. Jean Stafford, "Introduction," *The American Coast* (New York: Charles Scribner's, 1971), p. 19.

45. Marjorie Stafford Pinkham, "Jean Stafford's Family," unpublished manuscript, p. 21, courtesy Marjorie Stafford Pinkham.

46. "Woden's Day," p. 22.

47. "California."

48. Pinkham, "Jean," p. 17.

49. "Woden's Day," p. 16.

50. Jean Stafford to James Robert Hightower, undated, courtesy James Robert Hightower.

51. Pinkham, "Jean," p. 15.

52. *Collected Stories,* p. 425.

53. Jean Stafford, prospectus for *In the Snowfall,* unpublished manuscript, Norlin.

2. Cowboys and Indians and Magic Mountains: 1922–1936

1. Jean Stafford, "Going West," unpublished manuscript, Norlin.

2. Jean Stafford, "Disenchantment," unpublished manuscript, Norlin.

3. Pinkham, "Jean," p. 20. The details of the Staffords' life in Colorado Springs appear on pp. 18–21 of this article.

4. *The Mountain Lion,* p. 98.

5. *Boston Adventure,* p. 385.

6. Jean Stafford, unpublished manuscript, Juvenilia, Norlin.

7. *Collected Stories,* p. 198.

8. Jean Stafford, unpublished manuscript, Norlin.

9. Breit, "Talk with Jean Stafford," p. 18.

10. Prospectus for *In the Snowfall.*

11. Jean Stafford to Robert Lowell, undated, Robert Lowell Papers, Houghton Library.

12. Isabella Bird, *A Lady's Life in the Rocky Mountains* (London: Virago Press, 1982), p. 230.

13. Jean Stafford, "Enchanted Island," *Mademoiselle* 40 (May 1950): 140.

14. Prospectus for *In the Snowfall.*

15. Pinkham, "Jean," p. 22.

16. "Enchanted Island," p. 40.

17. Jean Stafford to James Robert Hightower, July 21, 1938, courtesy James Robert Hightower.

18. *Collected Stories,* p. 261.

19. *Boulder Daily Camera,* May 21, 1929.

20. *Boulder Daily Camera,* October 29, 1923.

21. See Katherine Harris, "Sex Roles and Work Patterns among Homesteading Families in Northern Colorado, 1873–1920, *Frontiers* 7 (March 1984): 43–49.

22. Quoted in William E. Paris, *Glory Colorado: A History of the University of Colorado 1858–1963* (Boulder: Pruitt Press, 1965), p. 174.

23. Ibid., p. 411.

24. *Colorado Clubwoman,* May 1936, p. 12.

25. Jean Stafford, "An Etiquette for Writers," unpublished manuscript, Norlin, p. 1.

26. Jean Stafford, "Varieties of Religious Experience," unpublished manuscript, Norlin.

27. Jean Stafford, "The Crossword Puzzle Has Gone to Hell," *Esquire* 82 (December 1974): 144.

28. *Collected Stories,* p. 263.

29. Wilfred Sheed, "Writer As Something Else," *New York Times Book Review,* March 4, 1973, p. 2.

30. "Etiquette," p. 32.

31. Jean Stafford, "Fame Is Sweet to the Foolish Man," unpublished manuscript, Norlin.

32. Jean Stafford to Marjorie Pinkham, undated, Norlin.

33. "Etiquette," p. 4.

34. Prospectus for *In the Snowfall.*

35. *The Mountain Lion,* p. 180.

36. Robert Berueffy to Charlotte Goodman, November 28, 1983.

37. "Beatrice Trueblood's Story," *Collected Stories,* p. 402.

38. *The Mountain Lion,* p. 180.

39. Ibid., p. 182.

40. Robert Berueffy to Charlotte Goodman, November 28, 1983.

41. John Ramaley to Jean Stafford, September 23, 1973, Norlin.

42. *Prep Owl,* April 3, 1931.

43. Ibid., March 11, 1932.

44. Interview with Goodrich Walton, July 27, 1983, Boulder, Colorado.

45. John Ramaley to Jean Stafford, September 23, 1973, Norlin.

46. Eileen Simpson, *Poets in Their Youth* (New York: Random House, 1982), p. 121.

47. *The Mountain Lion,* p. 143.

48. *Prep Owl,* April 24, 1931.

49. "The Tea Time of Stouthearted Ladies," *Collected Stories,* pp. 219–230.

50. Jean Stafford, "Souvenirs of Survival: The Thirties Revisited," *Mademoiselle* 50 (February 1960): 90.

51. Prospectus for *In the Snowfall.*

52. Jean Stafford, "Treasures and Pleasures," unpublished manuscript, Norlin.

53. Jean Stafford, "Venus," unpublished manuscript, Norlin.

54. *Collected Stories,* p. 362.

55. David Roberts, "Rediscovering Jean Stafford," *Boston Globe Magazine,* December 18, 1983, p. 8.

56. Jean Stafford, "Miss McKeehan's Pocketbook," *Colorado Quarterly* 24 (Spring 1976): 408.

57. Jean Stafford, "Profane and Divine Love in English Literature of the Thirteenth Century" (Master's thesis), Norlin.

58. "Souvenirs," p. 91.

59. Jean Stafford to Alex Warner, July 30, 1974, Norlin.

60. Lucy McKee, diary, Norlin.

61. Andrew Cooke to Charlotte Goodman, May 17, 1985.

62. Ibid.

63. Ibid.

64. *Boulder Daily Camera,* November 11, 1935, p. 1.

65. Jean Stafford, "Truth in Fiction," *Library Journal* 91 (October 1, 1966): 4561.

66. Jean Stafford to J. R. Hightower, undated, courtesy James Robert Hightower.

67. Prospectus for *In the Snowfall.*

68. Roberts, "Rediscovering Jean Stafford," p. 8.

69. Jean Stafford to Joe Chay, December 10, 1944, Norlin.

70. Prospectus for *In the Snowfall.*

71. Robert Berueffy to Charlotte Goodman, November 26, 1983.

72. Jean Stafford, *Tomorrow in Vienna,* unpublished manuscript, Norlin.

73. *Boulder Daily Camera,* June 17, 1936.

74. Robert Berueffy to Charlotte Goodman, November 28, 1983.

75. Jean Stafford to Joe Chay, July 3, 1948, Norlin.

76. Jean Stafford to Mary Elizabeth O'Rourke, February 12, 1969, Norlin.

3. Old Flaming Youth: 1936–1938

1. "Souvenirs," p. 175.

2. Ibid.

3. Jean Stafford to Martha Foley, August 23, 1936, *Story Magazine* Papers, Firestone Library, Princeton University.

4. Jean Stafford to Andrew Cooke, undated, Norlin.

5. James Robert Hightower to Jean Stafford, undated, courtesy James Robert Hightower.

6. Jean Stafford to Andrew Cooke, undated, Norlin.

7. Jean Stafford to Mary Lee Frichtel, undated, Norlin.

8. Jean Stafford, "Letter from Germany," *New Yorker* 25 (September 17, 1949): 82–83.

9. Jean Stafford to Andrew Cooke, undated, Norlin.

10. Ibid.

11. Interview with James Robert Hightower, June 6, 1983, Cambridge, Massachusetts.

12. "Letter from Germany," p. 85.

13. Jean Stafford to James Robert Hightower, June 28, 1938, courtesy James Robert Hightower.

14. Jean Stafford, *A Mother in History* (New York: Bantam, 1966), p. 70.

15. "Souvenirs," p. 175.

16. "Letter from Germany," p. 89.

17. Ibid., p. 86.

18. Jean Stafford to Andrew Cooke, October 28, 1936, Norlin.

19. Robert Berueffy to Charlotte Goodman, November 28, 1983.

20. Ibid.

21. "Souvenirs," p. 175.

22. Jean Stafford to Nancy Flagg Gibney, undated, courtesy Eleanor Gibney.

23. Robert Berueffy to Charlotte Goodman, November 28, 1983.

24. Jean Stafford, "It's Good to Be Back," *Mademoiselle* 42 (July 1952): 113.

25. Robert Berueffy to Charlotte Goodman, November 28, 1983.

26. Ibid.

27. Martha Foley to Jean Stafford, January 25, 1937, *Story Magazine* Papers, Firestone Library, Princeton University.

28. Jean Stafford to Martha Foley, February 5, 1937, *Story Magazine* Papers, Firestone Library, Princeton University.

29. "Miss McKeehan's Pocketbook," p. 410.

30. Jean Stafford to James Robert Hightower and Robert Berueffy, undated, courtesy James Robert Hightower.

31. Robert Berueffy to Charlotte Goodman, November 28, 1983.

32. Jean Stafford to James Robert Hightower, January 1, 1938, courtesy James Robert Hightower.

33. Jean Stafford to James Robert Hightower and Robert Berueffy, April 11, 1937, courtesy James Robert Hightower.

34. Edward Davison to Natalie Davison, April 25, 1937, Edward Davison Papers, Beineke Library, Yale University.

35. Jean Stafford to "Buck" and "Stephen," undated, courtesy James Robert Hightower.

36. Jean Stafford to James Robert Hightower and Robert Berueffy, undated, courtesy James Robert Hightower.

37. Ibid.

38. Jean Stafford to Natalie Davison, undated, Edward Davison Papers, Beineke Library, Yale University.

39. Jean Stafford to James Robert Hightower and Robert Berueffy, undated, courtesy James Robert Hightower.

40. Ibid.

41. Jean Stafford to Mary Lee Frichtel, undated, Norlin.

42. Jean Stafford to James Robert Hightower and Robert Berueffy, undated, courtesy James Robert Hightower.

43. Ibid.

44. Ibid.

45. Jean Stafford to James Robert Hightower and Robert Berueffy, undated, courtesy James Robert Hightower.

46. Jean Stafford, "Bessie's Debâcle," in Jean Stafford to James Robert Hightower, undated, courtesy James Robert Hightower.

47. Jean Stafford to James Robert Hightower and Robert Berueffy, undated, courtesy James Robert Hightower.

48. Ibid.

49. Ibid.

50. Robert Lowell, "Jean Stafford, A Letter," *Day by Day* (New York: Farrar, Straus and Giroux, 1977), p. 29.

51. Telephone interview with Frances Lindley, February 11, 1985.

52. Jean Stafford to James Robert Hightower and Robert Berueffy, undated, courtesy James Robert Hightower.

53. Ibid.

54. Ibid.

55. Jean Stafford to James Robert Hightower, January 1, 1938, courtesy James Robert Hightower.

56. John Crowe Ransom to Allen Tate, January 1, 1938, in Thomas Daniel Young and George Core, eds., *The Selected Letters of John Crowe Ransom* (Baton Rouge: Louisiana State University Press, 1985), pp. 236–237.

57. Robert Berueffy to Charlotte Goodman, November 28, 1983.

58. *Boulder Daily Camera,* August 3, 1937.

59. Jean Stafford, *Autumn Festival,* unpublished manuscript, Norlin.

60. Jean Stafford to James Robert Hightower and Robert Berueffy, undated, courtesy James Robert Hightower.

61. Ibid.

62. Jean Stafford to James Robert Hightower, September 13, 1937, courtesy James Robert Hightower.

63. Jean Stafford, "What Does Martha Mitchell Know?" *McCall's* 100 (October 1972): 31.

64. Jean Stafford to James Robert Hightower, September 29, 1937, courtesy James Robert Hightower.

65. Ibid., September 21, 1937.

66. Ibid.

67. Ibid., September 13, 1937.

68. Marion Israel to Charlotte Goodman, August 17, 1983.

69. William Mock to Charlotte Goodman, April 8, 1985.

70. Jean Stafford to James Robert Hightower, December 12, 1937, courtesy James Robert Hightower.

71. William Mock to Charlotte Goodman, August 17, 1983.

72. "It's Good to Be Back," p. 113.

73. Jean Stafford to James Robert Hightower, January 6, 1938, courtesy James Robert Hightower.

74. Ibid., January 1, 1938.

75. Ibid., January 7, 1938.

76. Jean Stafford to Whit Burnett, January 3, 1938, *Story Magazine* Papers, Firestone Library, Princeton University.

77. Jean Stafford to James Robert Hightower, February 4, 1938, courtesy James Robert Hightower.

78. Jean Stafford to Ford Madox Ford, February 1, 1938, Ford Madox Ford Papers, Olin Library, Cornell University.

79. Ibid.

80. Ford Madox Ford to Jean Stafford, February 11, 1938, Ford Madox Ford Papers, Olin Library, Cornell University.

81. Whit Burnett to Jean Stafford, February 28, 1938, *Story Magazine* Papers, Firestone Library, Princeton University.

82. Jean Stafford, "Prologue," unpublished manuscript, in James Robert Hightower to Jean Stafford, undated, courtesy James Robert Hightower.

83. Jean Stafford to Whit Burnett, undated, *Story Magazine* Papers, Firestone Library, Princeton University.

84. Jean Stafford to James Robert Hightower, February 9, 1938, courtesy James Robert Hightower.

85. Ibid., April 11, 1938.

86. Ibid., March 3, 1938.

87. Ibid., April 20, 1938.

88. Evelyn Scott to Jean Stafford, undated, Norlin.

89. Helen Thackaberry to Charlotte Goodman, March 2, 1981.

90. Jean Stafford to James Robert Hightower, April 26, 1938, Norlin.

91. Ibid., May 9, 1938.

92. Ibid., April 19, 1938.

4. I Love Someone: Summer and Fall 1938

1. Jean Stafford to James Robert Hightower, undated, courtesy James Robert Hightower.

2. Jean Stafford to William Mock, undated, courtesy William Mock.

3. Jean Stafford to James Robert Hightower, June 21, 1938, courtesy James Robert Hightower.

4. Jean Stafford to William Mock, undated, courtesy William Mock.

5. Jean Stafford to James Robert Hightower, June 29, 1938, courtesy James Robert Hightower.

6. Robert Giroux, "Hard Years and 'Scary Days': Remembering Jean Stafford," *New York Times Book Review,* June 10, 1984, p. 3.

7. Jean Stafford to William Mock, undated, courtesy William Mock.

8. Ibid.

9. Jean Stafford to James Robert Hightower, July 2, 1938, courtesy James Robert Hightower.

10. Jean Stafford to William Mock, undated, courtesy William Mock.

11. Ibid.

12. Jean Stafford to James Robert Hightower, July 31, 1938, courtesy James Robert Hightower.

13. Jean Stafford to William Mock, undated, courtesy William Mock.

14. Jean Stafford to James Robert Hightower, July 21, 1938, courtesy James Robert Hightower.

15. James Robert Hightower to Jean Stafford, undated, courtesy James Robert Hightower.

16. Jean Stafford to James Robert Hightower, July 21, 1938, courtesy James Robert Hightower.

17. Ibid., July 7, 1938.

18. Jean Stafford to William Mock, undated, courtesy William Mock.

19. Ibid., August 19, 1938.

20. Ibid., August 16, 1938.

21. Joseph Barber Junior to Jean Stafford, July 12, 1938, Atlantic Monthly Press Archives, Boston, Massachusetts.

22. Jean Stafford to James Robert Hightower, July 2, 1938, courtesy James Robert Hightower.

23. Jean Stafford to William Mock, undated, courtesy William Mock.

24. Jean Stafford to James Robert Hightower, July 14, 1938, courtesy James Robert Hightower.

25. Ibid., August 11, 1938.

26. Jean Stafford, "And Lots of Solid Color," *American Prefaces,* 5 (November 1939): 24.

27. Ibid.

28. Jean Stafford to William Mock, undated, courtesy William Mock.

29. Jean Stafford to James Robert Hightower, July 5, 1938, courtesy James Robert Hightower.

30. Ibid., April 14, 1938.

31. Jean Stafford to William Mock, undated, courtesy William Mock.

32. Ibid.

33. Jean Stafford to James Robert Hightower, June 25, 1938, courtesy James Robert Hightower.

34. Ibid., undated.

35. Ibid., June 28, 1938.

36. James Robert Hightower to Jean Stafford, August 5, 1938, courtesy James Robert Hightower.

37. Ibid.

38. Ibid.

39. Ibid.

40. Jean Stafford to James Robert Hightower, June 28, 1938, courtesy James Robert Hightower.

41. Ibid., July 5, 1938.

42. Ibid., July 7, 1938.

43. Ibid.

44. Evelyn Scott to Jean Stafford, July 10, 1938, Norlin.

45. Jean Stafford to William Mock, August 19, 1938.

46. Jean Stafford to James Robert Hightower, July 21, 1938, courtesy James Robert Hightower.

47. Jean Stafford to William Mock, August 19, 1938, courtesy William Mock.

48. Ibid., undated.

49. Jean Stafford to James Robert Hightower, August 4, 1938, courtesy James Robert Hightower.

50. Jean Stafford to William Mock, August 5, 1938, courtesy William Mock.

51. Ibid., August 19, 1938.

52. Jean Stafford to James Robert Hightower, August 4, 1938, courtesy James Robert Hightower.

53. Ibid., August 31, 1938.

54. Ibid., August 20, 1938.

55. Ibid., August 24, 1938.

56. Ibid., August 19, 1938.

57. Ibid., July 14, 1938.

58. Jean Stafford to William Mock, August 16, 1938, courtesy William Mock.

59. Jean Stafford to James Robert Hightower, September 19, 1938, courtesy James Robert Hightower.

60. Ibid., October 3, 1938.

61. Ibid., October 28, 1938.

62. Ibid., September, 30, 1938.

63. Ibid., October 3, 1938.

64. James Robert Hightower to Jean Stafford, October 7, 1938, courtesy James Robert Hightower.

65. Jean Stafford to James Robert Hightower, October 3, 1938, courtesy James Robert Hightower.

66. Ibid., September 30, 1938.

67. Ibid., September 23, 1938.

68. Ibid., October 18, 1938.

69. Ibid., October 3, 1938.

70. Ibid., September 30, 1938.

71. Ibid., October 15, 1938.

72. Jean Stafford to William Mock, October 20, 1938, courtesy William Mock.

73. Jean Stafford to James Robert Hightower, October 18, 1938, courtesy James Robert Hightower.

74. Ibid., October 28, 1938.

75. Ibid., November 3, 1938.

5. Boston Adventure: Winter 1938–Spring 1940

1. *Boulder Daily Camera,* June 6, 1932.
2. William Mock to Charlotte Goodman, April 8, 1985.
3. Evelyn Scott to Jean Stafford, undated, Norlin.
4. Jean Stafford to William Mock, November 27, 1938, courtesy William Mock.
5. Ian Hamilton, *Robert Lowell: A Biography* (New York: Random House, 1982), p. 60.
6. *Collected Stories,* p. 317.
7. Ibid., p. 319.
8. Jean Stafford to William Mock, November 19, 1938, courtesy William Mock.
9. Ibid., November 27, 1938.
10. A. O. Ogden to Jean Stafford, undated, Atlantic Monthly Press Archives, Boston, Massachusetts.
11. Jean Stafford to James Robert Hightower, July 25, 1939, courtesy James Robert Hightower.
12. Robert Lowell to James Robert Hightower, November 20, 1938, courtesy James Robert Hightower.
13. Jean Stafford to William Mock, November 27, 1938, courtesy William Mock.
14. Jean Stafford to James Robert Hightower, January 19, 1939, courtesy James Robert Hightower.
15. Jean Stafford to William Mock, December 2, 1939, courtesy William Mock.
16. *Boston Adventure,* p. 412.
17. *Collected Stories,* p. 156.
18. Ibid., p. 155.
19. Ibid., p. 148.
20. Ibid.
21. Jean Stafford to James Robert Hightower, December 13, 1938, courtesy James Robert Hightower.
22. Jean Stafford to William Mock, December 3, 1938, courtesy William Mock.
23. Ibid., December 14, 1938.
24. James Robert Hightower to William Mock, December 22, 1938, courtesy William Mock.
25. William Mock to Charlotte Goodman, April 8, 1985.
26. See Hamilton, *Robert Lowell,* p. 63.
27. Jean Stafford to William Mock, January 17, 1939, courtesy William Mock.
28. Quoted in Simpson, *Poets in Their Youth,* p. 120.
29. Quoted in Hamilton, *Robert Lowell,* p. 64.
30. Jean Stafford to William Mock, undated, courtesy William Mock.
31. A. O. Ogden to Jean Stafford, December 22, 1938, Atlantic Monthly Press Archives, Boston, Massachusetts.
32. Jean Stafford to James Robert Hightower, January 10, 1939, courtesy James Robert Hightower.

33. Ibid., January 20, 1939.

34. James Robert Hightower to Jean Stafford, January 26, 1939, Norlin.

35. Jean Stafford to Ruth Stauffer, January 29, 1973, courtesy Ruth Stauffer.

36. Ruth Stauffer to Charlotte Goodman, July 24, 1985.

37. Jean Stafford to William Mock, February 1, 1939, courtesy William Mock.

38. Quoted in Simpson, *Poets in Their Youth,* p. 125.

39. Jean Stafford to William Mock, February 7, 1939, courtesy William Mock.

40. Simpson, *Poets in Their Youth,* pp. 125–126.

41. St. Teresa of Avila, *Interior Castle* (Garden City: Image Books, 1961), p. 33.

42. Ibid., p. 28.

43. *Collected Stories,* p. 182.

44. Ibid., p. 192.

45. Ibid., p. 182.

46. Ibid., p. 187.

47. Ibid., p. 192.

48. Ibid., p. 193.

49. Jean Stafford to William Mock, February 1, 1939, courtesy William Mock.

50. Ibid., January 24, 1939.

51. Ibid., undated.

52. Ibid.

53. Jean Stafford to James Robert Hightower, June 14, 1939, courtesy James Robert Hightower.

54. Jean Stafford to William Mock, undated, courtesy William Mock.

55. Jean Stafford to A. O. Ogden, undated, Atlantic Monthly Press Archives, Boston, Massachusetts.

56. Hamilton, *Robert Lowell,* p. 41.

57. Robert Berueffy to Charlotte Goodman, November 28, 1983.

58. Jean Stafford to William Mock, April 18, 1939, courtesy William Mock.

59. *Boston Adventure,* p. 250.

60. Roberts, "Rediscovering Jean Stafford," p. 40.

61. Jean Stafford to William Mock, April 18, 1939, courtesy William Mock.

62. Richard Eberhart, "The Mad Musician," *Collected Verse Plays of Richard Eberhart* (Chapel Hill: University of North Carolina Press, 1962), pp. 138–139.

63. Ibid., p. 138.

64. Jean Stafford to William Mock, May 11, 1939, courtesy William Mock.

65. A. O. Ogden, May 25, 1939, Atlantic Monthly Press Archives, Boston, Massachusetts.

66. Jean Stafford to William Mock, June 5, 1939, courtesy William Mock.

67. Jean Stafford to James Robert Hightower, June 13, 1939, courtesy James Robert Hightower.

68. Ibid., June 27, 1939.

69. Ibid., July 5, 1939.

70. Hamilton, *Robert Lowell,* pp. 64–65.

71. Jean Stafford to James Robert Hightower, July 19, 1939, courtesy James Robert Hightower.

72. Ibid., undated.

73. Ibid., October 8, 1939.

74. Ibid., September 20, 1939.

75. Ibid., December 11, 1939.

76. Quoted in Simpson, *Poets in Their Youth,* p. 126.

77. Interview with Sylvia Berkman, October 12, 1982, Cambridge, Massachusetts.

78. Peter Taylor, "1939," *Collected Stories of Peter Taylor* (New York: Farrar, Straus and Giroux, 1969), p. 350.

79. Ibid., pp. 351–352.

80. Ibid., p. 352.

81. Giroux, "Hard Years and 'Scary Days,'" p. 28.

82. Jean Stafford to James Robert Hightower, December 17, 1939, courtesy James Robert Hightower.

83. Ibid., undated.

84. Mary Darlington Taylor, "Jean Stafford's Novel—A Superb Literary Accomplishment," *Bridgeport Sunday Post,* January 13, 1952.

85. Jean Stafford to James Robert Hightower, undated, courtesy James Robert Hightower.

86. Ibid., March 30, 1940.

87. Ibid., undated.

88. Ibid., April 2, 1940.

89. Henry James, *The Bostonians* (New York: Dial Press, 1945), p. 378.

6. Sensations Sweet and Sour: Summer 1940–Fall 1943

1. Jean Stafford to James Robert Hightower, April 23 [1940], courtesy James Robert Hightower.

2. Robert Lowell to Charlotte Lowell, undated, Robert Lowell Papers, Houghton Library, Harvard University.

3. Caroline Gordon to Charlotte Lowell, April 17, 1940, Papers of Caroline Gordon and Allen Tate, McFarlin Library, University of Tulsa.

4. Jean Stafford to James Robert Hightower, undated, courtesy James Robert Hightower.

5. Ibid., April 19, 1940.

6. Ibid., May 6, 1940.

7. Ibid., undated.

8. Ibid., April 9, 1940.

9. Ibid., undated.

10. Ibid., April 21 [1940].

11. Ibid., April 27 [1940].

12. Ibid., April 21 [1940].

13. Evelyn Scott to Jean Stafford, April 30, 1940, Norlin.

14. Jean Stafford to James Robert Hightower, April 21 [1940], courtesy James Robert Hightower.

15. Ibid., undated.

16. Ibid., April 23 [1940].

17. Ibid., April 20 [1940].

18. Ibid., April 27 [1940].

19. Ibid.

20. Ibid., undated.

21. Ibid., May 25, 1940.

22. Interview with James Robert Hightower, September 12, 1983, Cambridge, Massachusetts.

23. Jean Stafford to James Robert Hightower, June 6, 1940, courtesy James Robert Hightower.

24. Ibid., undated.

25. John Thompson, "Robert Lowell, 1917–1977," *New York Review of Books* 24 (October 27, 1977): 14–15.

26. Quoted in Hamilton, *Robert Lowell,* p. 55.

27. Jean Stafford to Peter Taylor, September 28, 1945, in Jean Stafford, "Some Letters to Peter and Eleanor Taylor," *Shenandoah* 30 (Autumn 1979): 51.

28. "An Influx of Poets," *New Yorker* 34 (November 6, 1978): 51.

29. John Crowe Ransom to Allen Tate, Spring 1940, in Young and Core, eds., *The Selected Letters of John Crowe Ransom,* p. 270.

30. Quoted in Hamilton, *Robert Lowell,* p. 74.

31. Ibid., p. 75.

32. Jean Stafford to Howard Mumford Jones, Howard Mumford Jones Papers, Houghton Library, Harvard University.

33. Jean Stafford, "An American Sampler," *Newsday,* May 13, 1973.

34. Jean Stafford, *The Catherine Wheel* (New York: Ecco Press, 1981), p. 143.

35. Hamilton, *Robert Lowell,* p. 75.

36. Jean Stafford, "Children's Books for Christmas," *New Yorker* 46 (December 5, 1970): 188.

37. Jean Stafford to Peter Taylor, June 1946, in Stafford, "Some Letters to Peter and Eleanor Taylor," p. 27.

38. Jean Stafford, "Baton Rouge," unpublished manuscript, Norlin.

39. Robert Lowell to Mrs. Arthur Winslow, quoted in Hamilton, *Robert Lowell,* p. 75.

40. Robert Lowell to Jean Stafford, September 11, 1976, Norlin.

41. Cleanth Brooks, "The Life and Death of an Academic Journal," Jean Stafford Manuscripts, Norlin.

42. Robert Penn Warren to Charlotte Goodman, undated.

43. Jean Stafford to Edward Davison, August 20, 1940, Edward Davison Papers, Beineke Library, Yale University.

44. Caroline Gordon to Jean Stafford, undated, Papers of Caroline Gordon and Allen Tate, McFarlin Library, University of Tulsa.

45. "Treasures and Pleasures."

46. "Baton Rouge."

47. Hamilton, *Robert Lowell,* p. 80.

48. Robert Berueffy to Charlotte Goodman, November 28, 1983.

49. Jean Stafford to Robie Macauley, undated, quoted in Hamilton, *Robert Lowell,* p. 78.

50. Ibid., p. 79.

51. Ibid.

52. Ibid., p. 80.

53. Quoted in William O'Rourke, "A Father's Father Figure," *Nation,* February 28, 1981, p. 245.

54. "An Influx of Poets," p. 49.

55. Ibid., p. 50.

56. Ibid., p. 49.

57. Jean Stafford to Peter Taylor, October 1941, in Stafford, "Some Letters to Peter and Eleanor Taylor," p. 30.

58. Ibid.

59. Wilfrid Sheed, "Miss Jean Stafford," *Shenandoah* 30 (Autumn 1979): 93.

60. Quoted in Simpson, *Poets in Their Youth,* p. 126.

61. Alex Eliot to Charlotte Goodman, January 21, 1987.

62. Caroline Gordon to Sally Wood, January 9, 1930, in *The Southern Mandarins: Letters of Caroline Gordon to Sally Wood 1924–1937,* ed. Sally Wood (Baton Rouge: Louisiana State University Press, 1984), p. 36.

63. Jean Stafford to Peter Taylor, October 1941, in Stafford, "Some Letters to Peter and Eleanor Taylor," p. 33.

64. Ibid., p. 30.

65. Ibid.

66. Jean Stafford, "Walpurgis Nacht," *Kenyon Review* 14 (Winter 1942): 108.

67. Jean Stafford to Peter Taylor, October 1941, in Stafford, "Some Letters to Peter and Eleanor Taylor," p. 32.

68. Giroux, "Hard Years and 'Scary Days,'" p. 29.

69. Hamilton, *Robert Lowell,* p. 82.

70. Evelyn Scott to Jean Stafford, July 26, 1941, Norlin.

71. Jean Stafford to Joe Chay, October 12, 1944, Norlin.

72. Caroline Gordon to Katherine Anne Porter, undated, Katherine Anne Porter Papers, Special Collections, University of Maryland Library.

73. Simpson, *Poets in Their Youth,* p. 127.

74. Jean Stafford to Peter Taylor, August 1942, in Stafford, "Some Letters to Peter and Eleanor Taylor," pp. 34–36.

75. Frederick Seidel, "Interview with Robert Lowell," *Writers at Work: The Paris Interviews* (New York: Viking, 1963), p. 342.

76. Fannie Cheney to Charlotte Goodman, February 13, 1985.

77. Caroline Gordon to Jean Stafford, undated, Papers of Caroline Gordon and Allen Tate, McFarlin Library, University of Tulsa.

78. Robert Lowell to Allen Tate, November 19, 1943, Papers of Caroline Gordon and Allen Tate, McFarlin Library, University of Tulsa.

79. Caroline Gordon, *The Strange Children* (New York: Cooper Square Publishers, 1971), p. 85.

80. Ibid., p. 86.

81. Ibid., p. 119.

82. Ibid., p. 31.

83. Ibid., p. 173.

84. Simpson, *Poets in Their Youth,* p. 201.

85. Caroline Gordon to Sally Wood, January 9, 1930, in Wood, ed., *The Southern Mandarins,* p. 52.

86. Gordon, *The Strange Children,* p. 153.

87. "Dream Journal," Caroline Gordon Papers, Firestone Library, Princeton University.

88. Ibid.

89. Ibid.

90. Eleanor Ross Taylor, *Wilderness of Ladies* (New York: McDowell, Oblensky, 1960), p. 15.

91. Eleanor Ross Taylor, "Early Death," *Virginia Quarterly Review* 61 (Autumn 1985): 664.

92. Eleanor Ross Taylor to Jean Stafford, July 31, 1943, Norlin.

93. Peter Taylor to Jean Stafford, September 6, Norlin.

94. Peter Taylor to Jean Stafford and Robert Lowell, undated, Norlin.

95. Jean Stafford to Peter Taylor, July 1943, in Stafford, "Some Letters to Peter and Eleanor Taylor," p. 42.

96. John Crowe Ransom to Elizabeth Ames, June 2, 1943, Yaddo Archives, Saratoga Springs, New York.

97. Jean Stafford to Eleanor and Peter Taylor, July 10, 1943, in Stafford, "Some Letters to Peter and Eleanor Taylor," p. 38.

98. Ibid., p. 40.

99. Ibid.

100. Caroline Gordon to Jean Stafford, undated, Papers of Caroline Gordon and Allen Tate, McFarlin Library, University of Tulsa.

101. Quoted in Hamilton, *Robert Lowell,* p. 87.

102. Ibid.

103. Jean Stafford to Eleanor and Peter Taylor, July 10, 1943, in Stafford, "Some Letters to Peter and Eleanor Taylor," pp. 38–39.

104. Ibid., October 1943, p. 42.

105. Ibid.

106. Ibid., October 1943, p. 45.

107. Alfred Kantorowicz to Virginia Spencer Carr, July 8, 1972, courtesy Virginia Spencer Carr.

108. Jean Stafford to Eleanor and Peter Taylor, July 1943, in Stafford, "Some Letters to Peter and Eleanor Taylor," p. 43.

109. Interview with Harold Shapero, March 26, 1985, Natick, Massachusetts.

110. Caroline Gordon to Jean Stafford, undated, Papers of Caroline Gordon and Allen Tate, McFarlin Library, University of Tulsa.

111. Jean Stafford to Eleanor and Peter Taylor, September 1, 1943, in Stafford, "Some Letters to Peter and Eleanor Taylor," p. 44.

7. An Influx of Poets: Fall 1943–Fall 1946

1. Hamilton, *Robert Lowell,* pp. 87–88.

2. Robert Lowell to Charlotte Lowell, September 7, 1943, quoted in ibid.

3. Jean Stafford to Mary Lee Frichtel, undated, Norlin.

4. John Crowe Ransom to Allen Tate, November 1, 1943, in Young and Core, eds., *The Selected Letters of John Crowe Ransom,* p. 312.

5. Jean Stafford to Eleanor and Peter Taylor, October 1943, in Stafford, "Some Letters to Peter and Eleanor Taylor," p. 45.

6. Ibid., December 22, 1943, p. 49.

7. Ibid., New York, 1943, p. 46.

8. Charlotte Lowell to Jean Stafford, November 10, 1943, quoted in Hamilton, *Robert Lowell,* p. 95.

9. Jean Stafford to Caroline Gordon and Allen Tate, undated, Caroline Gordon Papers, Firestone Library, Princeton University.

10. Jean Stafford to Eleanor and Peter Taylor, December 22, 1943, in Stafford, "Some Letters to Peter and Eleanor Taylor," p. 49.

11. Ibid., October 1943, p. 46.

12. Interview with Mary Lou Aswell, July 23, 1983, Santa Fe, New Mexico.

13. *Collected Stories,* p. 178.

14. Jean Stafford, Notebook, Jean Stafford Manuscripts, Norlin.

15. William Phillips, *A Partisan View* (New York: Stein & Day, 1983), p. 75.

16. *Collected Stories,* pp. 376–377.

17. Delmore Schwartz to Robert Lowell, December 15, 1945, in *The Letters of Delmore Schwartz,* ed. Robert Phillips (Princeton: Ontario Review Press, 1984), p. 223.

18. James Atlas, "Unsentimental Education," *Atlantic Monthly* 237 (June 1983): 87.

19. Phillips, *A Partisan View,* pp. 272–273.

20. Dorothea Straus, *Palaces and Prisons* (Boston: Houghton Mifflin, 1976), p. 67.

21. Philip Rahv to Allen Tate, December 4, 1945, Firestone Library, Princeton University.

22. Telephone interview with Sidney Hook, January 19, 1987.

23. Jean Stafford to Eleanor and Peter Taylor, November 1943, in Stafford, "Some Letters to Peter and Eleanor Taylor," pp. 47–48.

24. Jean Stafford to P. Albert Duhamel and Carlos Baker, October 25, 1975, Norlin.

25. *Collected Stories,* p. 375.

26. Jean Stafford to Eleanor and Peter Taylor, December 22, 1943, in Stafford, "Some Letters to Peter and Eleanor Taylor," p. 50.

27. Alfred Kazin, *New York Jew* (New York: Vintage, 1979), p. 102.

28. Randall Jarrell to Philip Rahv, August 1953, in *Randall Jarrell's Letters,* ed. Mary Jarrell (Boston: Houghton Mifflin, 1985), pp. 381–383.

29. Jean Stafford to Peter Taylor, February 11, 1944, quoted in Hamilton, *Robert Lowell,* p. 96.

30. Robert Lowell, "Between the Porch and the Altar," *Selected Poems of Robert Lowell* (New York: Farrar, Straus and Giroux, 1986), p. 18.

31. *Collected Stories,* pp. 407–414.

32. Robert Lowell, "Colloquy in Black Rock," *Selected Poems,* p. 5.

33. "The Home Front," *Children Are Bored on Sunday,* p. 11, in *The Interior Castle.*

34. Ibid., p. 113.

35. Jean Stafford to Cecile Starr, undated, courtesy Cecile Starr.

36. Ibid.

37. Jean Stafford to Eleanor Taylor, July 26, 1944, quoted in Hamilton, *Robert Lowell,* p. 98.

38. Jean Stafford, "Truth and the Novelist," *Harper's Bazaar* 85 (August 1951): 187–189.

39. Jean Stafford to Joe Chay, February 27, 1946, Norlin.

40. *Boston Adventure,* p. 168.

41. Ibid., p. 405.

42. Ibid., p. 333.

43. Elizabeth Abel, Marianne Hirsch, and Elizabeth Langland, eds., *The Voyage In: Fictions of Female Development* (Hanover: University Press of New England, 1983), p. 8.

44. *Boston Adventure,* p. 414.

45. Diana Trilling, "A New Talent," *Nation* 159 (September 30, 1944): 383.

46. *Boston Adventure,* p. 107.

47. Theodore Spencer, "Recent Fiction," *Sewanee Review* 53 (Spring 1945): 302–303.

48. Elizabeth Hardwick, "Boston: The Lost Ideal," in *Contemporary American Essays,* ed. Maureen Howard (New York: Penguin, 1984), p. 250.

49. Mary Ellen Williams Walsh, *Jean Stafford* (Boston: Twayne, 1985), pp. 56–58.

50. Ihab Hassan, "Jean Stafford: The Expense of Style and the Scope of Sensibility," *Western Review* 19 (Spring 1955): 191.

51. Allen Tate to Jean Stafford and Robert Lowell, October 23, 1944, Papers of Caroline Gordon and Allen Tate, McFarlin Library, University of Tulsa.

52. Ibid., March 17, 1945.

53. Jean Stafford to Cecile Starr, May 5, 1945, quoted in Hamilton, *Robert Lowell,* p. 102.

54. Philip Rahv to Allen Tate, May 7, 1945, Firestone Library, Princeton University.

55. Jean Stafford to William Mock, undated, courtesy William Mock.

56. Jean Stafford to Joe Chay, October 12, 1944, Norlin.

57. Ibid.

58. Jean Stafford to Mary Lee Frichtel, October 8, 1944, Norlin.

59. Jean Stafford, unpublished manuscript, Norlin.

60. Jean Stafford to William Mock, undated, courtesy William Mock.

61. Hamilton, *Robert Lowell,* p. 101.

62. Jean Stafford to Alfred Kazin, November 27, 1944, Berg Collection, New York Public Library.

63. Jean Stafford to Joe Chay, December 22, 1944, Norlin.

64. Jean Stafford to Joe Chay, January 11, 1944 [1945], Norlin.

65. Ibid., February 4, 1945.

66. Ibid., April 14, 1945.

67. Ibid., January 11, 1944 [1945].

68. Jean Stafford, "The Empty Net," *Partisan Review* 11 (Winter 1944): 14–15.

69. Jean Stafford to John Crowe Ransom, December 2, [1945], Kenyon College Archives.

70. Jean Stafford, "On Books to Read before Sleep," *Mademoiselle* 81 (February 1975): 156.

71. Jean Stafford to William Mock, January 26, 1945, courtesy William Mock.

72. Archives of the American Academy and Institute of Arts and Letters, New York, New York.

73. Jean Stafford, Guggenheim Fellowship Proposal, 1945, John Simon Guggenheim Foundation Archives, New York, New York.

74. Allen Tate to Robert Lowell, undated, Papers of Caroline Gordon and Allen Tate, McFarlin Library, University of Tulsa.

75. Caroline Gordon and Wilbur Schramm to John Simon Guggenheim Memorial Foundation, re Jean Stafford, 1945, John Simon Guggenheim Foundation Archives, New York, New York.

76. Jean Stafford to William Mock, July 15 [1945], courtesy William Mock.

77. Jean Stafford to Joe Chay, July 28, 1945, Norlin.

78. Jean Stafford to Ruth Stauffer, July 25, 1945, courtesy Ruth Stauffer.

79. Robert Lowell to Allen Tate, July 7, 1945, quoted in Hamilton, *Robert Lowell,* p. 102.

80. Jean Stafford to Joe Chay, July 28, 1945, Norlin.

81. Ibid., August 1, 1945.

82. "An Influx of Poets," p. 55.

83. Jean Stafford to Peter and Eleanor Taylor, September 28, 1943 [1945], Damariscotta, in Stafford, "Some Letters to Peter and Eleanor Taylor," p. 51.

84. Caroline Gordon to Jean Stafford and Robert Lowell, undated, Papers of Caroline Gordon and Allen Tate, McFarlin Library, University of Tulsa.

85. Jean Stafford to James Robert Hightower, undated, courtesy James Robert Hightower.

86. Caroline Gordon to Jean Stafford and Robert Lowell, undated, Papers of Caroline Gordon and Allen Tate, McFarlin Library, University of Tulsa.

87. Jean Stafford to William Mock, November 27 [1945], courtesy William Mock.

88. Jean Stafford to Mary Lee Frichtel, November 27, 1945, Norlin.

89. Ibid.

90. Jean Stafford to Caroline Gordon and Allen Tate, December 16 [1945], Caroline Gordon Papers, Firestone Library, Princeton University.

91. Caroline Gordon to Robert Lowell, undated, Papers of Caroline Gordon and Allen Tate, McFarlin Library, University of Tulsa.

92. *Collected Stories,* p. 136.

93. Jean Stafford, "New England Winter," *Holiday* 15 (February 1954): 40.

94. Jean Stafford to Allen Tate, January 4 [1946], Firestone Library, Princeton University.

95. Jean Stafford to Cecile Starr, undated, courtesy Cecile Starr.

96. Nancy Booth to Charlotte Goodman, April 14, 1984.

97. *Collected Stories,* p. 125.

98. Ibid., p. 127.

99. Robert Lowell, "The Old Flame," *Selected Poems,* pp. 101–102.

100. Robert Lowell, "The Mills of the Kavanaughs," *The Mills of The Kavanaughs* (New York: Harcourt, Brace & World, 1951), p. 13: "I heard/ the snowplow banging . . ."; and Jean Stafford, "A Country Love Story," *Collected Stories,* p. 143: "He slept, indeed, so well that he never ever heard the ditcher on snowy nights rising with a groan over the hill."

101. See Hamilton, *Robert Lowell,* pp. 182–187.

102. *Collected Stories,* p. 145.

103. Delmore Schwartz to Robert Lowell, December 15, 1945, in Phillips, ed., *The Letters of Delmore Schwartz,* p. 223.

104. "An Influx of Poets," p. 56.

105. Jean Stafford to Joe Chay, February 27, 1946, Norlin.

106. Delmore Schwartz to Helen Blackmur, February 2, 1946, quoted in James Atlas, *Delmore Schwartz: The Life of an American Poet* (New York: Avon, 1977), p. 248.

107. Robert Lowell, "To Delmore Schwartz: Cambridge 1946," *Selected Poems,* pp. 63–64.

108. Jean Stafford to William Mock, April 15 [1946], courtesy William Mock.

109. Jean Stafford to Cecile Starr, February 1946, quoted in Hamilton, *Robert Lowell,* p. 109.

110. Atlas, *Delmore Schwartz,* pp. 250–251.

111. Jean Stafford to Cecile Starr, March 11, [1946], courtesy Cecile Starr.

112. Jean Stafford to William Mock, March 6, 1947, courtesy William Mock.

113. Ibid., August 28, 1947.

114. Ibid., June 28, 1946.

115. Jean Stafford to Mary Lee Frichtel, June 13 [1946], Norlin.

116. "An Influx of Poets," p. 43.

117. Simpson, *Poets in Their Youth,* p. 131.

118. "An Influx of Poets," p. 43: ". . . if they changed an 'a' to a 'the' the whole sonnet had to be typed over."

119. Jean Stafford to Mary Lee Frichtel, August 16, 1946, Norlin.

120. Simpson, *Poets in Their Youth,* p. 132.

121. Ibid.

122. Ibid., p. 122.

123. "An Influx of Poets," p. 54.

124. Simpson, *Poets in Their Youth,* p. 134.

125. Nancy Flagg Gibney to Jean Stafford, January 2, 1979, Norlin.

126. Simpson, *Poets in Their Youth,* p. 132.

127. Ibid., p. 143.

128. Jean Stafford to William Mock, August 28, 1946, courtesy William Mock.

129. Robert Lowell to Peter Taylor, August 16, 1946, quoted in Hamilton, *Robert Lowell,* p. 115.

130. Jean Stafford to Robert Lowell, undated, Robert Lowell Papers, Houghton Library, Harvard University.

131. Jean Stafford to Peter Taylor, December 19, 1946, quoted in Hamilton, *Robert Lowell,* p. 117.

132. Gertrude Buckman to Charlotte Goodman, January 11, 1985.

133. Jean Stafford to Robert Lowell, undated, Robert Lowell Papers, Houghton Library, Harvard University.

134. "An Influx of Poets," p. 60.

135. Robert Lowell, "The Old Flame," *Selected Poems,* p. 101.

136. Jean Stafford, quoted in *A Woman's Notebook II* (Philadelphia: Running Press, 1981), p. 66.

137. "An Influx of Poets," p. 49.

138. Jean Stafford to Robert Lowell, undated, Robert Lowell Papers, Houghton Library, Harvard University.

8. The Bleeding Heart: Fall 1946–Summer 1949

1. Jean Stafford to William Mock, September 21, 1946, courtesy William Mock.

2. Jean Stafford to Peter Taylor, December 19, 1946, quoted in Hamilton, *Robert Lowell,* p. 119.

3. Cecile Starr to Ian Hamilton, September 30, 1981, courtesy Cecile Starr.

4. Cecile Starr to Charlotte Goodman, February 9, 1984.

5. Jean Stafford to Mary Lee Frichtel, undated, Norlin.

6. Jean Stafford to Robert Lowell, undated, Robert Lowell Papers, Houghton Library, Harvard University.

7. Ibid.

8. Ibid.

9. Jean Stafford to Mary Lee Frichtel, October 25, 1946, Norlin.

10. Jean Stafford to Robert Lowell, undated, Robert Lowell Papers, Houghton Library, Harvard University.

11. Ibid.

12. Jean Stafford to Mary Lee Frichtel, October 25, 1946, Norlin.

13. Ibid., November 1, 1946.

14. Ibid., November 8, 1946.

15. Ibid., November 19, 1946.

16. Ibid., undated.

17. Simpson, *Poets in Their Youth*, p. 150.

18. Jean Stafford to William Mock, undated, courtesy William Mock.

19. Jean Stafford to Robert Lowell, undated, Robert Lowell Papers, Houghton Library, Harvard University.

20. Jean Stafford to Mary Lee Frichtel, undated, Norlin.

21. Jean Stafford to William Mock, undated, courtesy William Mock.

22. Simpson, *Poets in Their Youth*, p. 150.

23. Jean Stafford to Mary Lee Frichtel, undated, Norlin.

24. Jean Stafford, "What Are Your Feelings about Me?" unpublished manuscript, Norlin.

25. See Mary Jane Sherfey, "The Evolution and Nature of Female Sexuality in Relation to Psychoanalytic Theory," *Journal of the American Psychoanalytic Association* 14 (1966): 28–128.

26. Jean Stafford to Robert Lowell, undated, Robert Lowell Papers, Houghton Library, Harvard University.

27. Jean Stafford to Mary Lee Frichtel, undated, Norlin.

28. Jean Stafford to Robert Lowell, undated, Robert Lowell Papers, Houghton Library, Harvard University.

29. Ibid.

30. Ibid.

31. Jean Stafford to Peter Taylor, November 26, 1946, quoted in Hamilton, *Robert Lowell,* p. 120.

32. Jean Stafford to Robert Lowell, undated, Robert Lowell Papers, Houghton Library, Harvard University.

33. Ibid.

34. Jean Stafford to Mary Lee Frichtel, February 3, 1947, Norlin.

35. Pinkham, "Jean," p. 28.

36. Jean Stafford, Hospital Notebook, Norlin.

37. Jean Stafford to Robert Lowell, undated, Robert Lowell Papers, Houghton Library, Harvard University.

38. Ibid.

39. *The Mountain Lion,* p. 92.

40. Ibid., p. 26.

41. Ibid., p. 113.

42. Ibid., p. 159.

43. Ibid., p. 177.

44. Ibid., p. 175.

45. Ibid., p. 178.

46. Jean Stafford to Robert Lowell, undated, Robert Lowell Papers, Houghton Library, Harvard University.

47. *The Mountain Lion,* p. 212.

48. Howard Mumford Jones, "A New Jean Stafford," *New York Times Book Review,* March 2, 1947, p. 5.

49. Unsigned review, *New Yorker* 23 (March 8, 1947): 109–110.

50. Philip Rahv to Jean Stafford, February 8, 1947, Norlin.

51. Louis Auchincloss, *Pioneers and Caretakers: A Study of Nine American Women Writers* (Minneapolis: University of Minnesota Press, 1965), p. 157.

52. Maureen Howard, "Fiction in Review," *Yale Review* 73 (Summer 1984): x.

53. See Blanche Gelfant, "Reconsiderations: *The Mountain Lion,* by Jean Stafford," *New Republic* 172 (May 10, 1975): 22–25; Barbara White, "Initiation, the Hunt, and the West in Jean Stafford's *The Mountain Lion,*" *Essays in Literature* 9 (Fall 1982): 194–210; Melody Graulich, "Jean Stafford's Western Childhood: Huck Finn Joins the Camp Fire Girls," *Denver Quarterly* 18 (Spring 1983): 39–55; Walsh, *Jean Stafford,* pp. 29–37; Charlotte Goodman, "The Lost Brother / The Twin: Women Novelists and the Male-Female Double Bildungsroman," *Novel: A Forum on Fiction* 17 (Fall 1983): 28–43.

54. Gelfant, "Reconsiderations," pp. 22–23.

55. Jean Stafford to Robert Lowell, undated, Robert Lowell Papers, Houghton Library, Harvard University.

56. Ibid.

57. *Collected Stories,* p. 119.

58. Jean Stafford to Robert Lowell, undated, Robert Lowell Papers, Houghton Library, Harvard University.

59. See William Leary, "Checkmate: Jean Stafford's 'A Slight Maneuver,'" *Western American Literature* 21 (Spring 1986): 99–110.

60. Jean Stafford, "A Slight Maneuver," *Mademoiselle* 24 (February 1947): 284.

61. Ibid., p. 285.

62. Ibid., p. 286.

63. Jean Stafford to Cecile Starr, undated, courtesy Cecile Starr.

64. Jean Stafford to Mrs. [Nancy] Booth, undated, courtesy Nancy Booth.

65. Jean Stafford to Cecile Starr, undated, courtesy Cecile Starr.

66. Jean Stafford to Robert Lowell, undated, Robert Lowell Papers, Houghton Library, Harvard University.

67. Ibid.

68. Hospital Notebook, Norlin.

69. Jean Stafford to Robert Lowell, undated, Robert Lowell Papers, Houghton Library, Harvard University.

70. "Young U.S. Writers," *Life* 22 (June 2, 1947): 76.

71. Hospital Notebook, Norlin.

72. Jean Stafford, "My Sleep Grew Shy of Me," *Vogue* 110 (October 15, 1947): 171.

73. Ibid., p. 174.

74. Ibid., p. 171.

75. Hospital Notebook, Norlin.

76. Jean Stafford to Robert Lowell, undated, Robert Lowell Papers, Houghton Library, Harvard University.

77. Jean Stafford, "The Polyglot Mr. Rohmer," *Rohmer Review,* 14 (1976): 1.

78. Ibid., p. 2.

79. Jean Stafford to Robert Lowell, undated, Robert Lowell Papers, Houghton Library, Harvard University.

80. Ibid.

81. Ibid.

82. Ibid.

83. Ibid.

84. Ibid.

85. Ibid.

86. Jean Stafford to John Crowe Ransom, undated, Kenyon College Archives.

87. Jean Stafford to Dr. Alfred Cohn, undated, Rockefeller Institute Archives.

88. Jean Stafford to Robert Lowell, undated, Robert Lowell Papers, Houghton Library, Harvard University.

89. Jean Stafford, "The Psychological Novel," *Kenyon Review* 10 (Spring 1948): 215.

90. Ibid., p. 221.

91. Ibid., p. 217.

92. Ibid., p. 227.

93. Jean Stafford to Robert Lowell, undated, Robert Lowell Papers, Houghton Library, Harvard University.

94. Ibid.

95. *Collected Stories,* p. 374.

96. Ibid., p. 380.

97. Ibid., p. 376.

98. Ibid., p. 377.

99. Ibid., pp. 380–381.

100. William Leary, "Pictures at an Exhibition: Jean Stafford's 'Children Are Bored on Sunday,'" *Kenyon Review* 49 (Spring 1987): 8.

101. William Shawn, quoted in Brendan Gill, *Here at The New Yorker* (New York: Random House, 1975), p. 390.

102. Irving Howe, *World of Our Fathers* (New York: Harcourt Brace Jovanovich, 1976), p. 605.

103. Robert Lowell to Peter Taylor, May 1, 1952, Robert Lowell Papers, Houghton Library, Harvard University.

104. Katharine White, "Home and Office," quoted in Scott Elledge, *E. B. White: A Biography* (New York: W. W. Norton & Company, 1984), p. 112.

105. Ibid., p. 182.

106. See William Leary, "Jean Stafford, Katharine White, and *The New Yorker,*" *Sewanee Review* 93 (Fall 1985): 584–596.

107. Katharine White to Jean Stafford, January 31, 1976, Norlin.

108. Jean Stafford to Cecile Starr, undated, courtesy Cecile Starr.

109. Jean Stafford to Eileen Berryman, February 7, 1948, University of Minnesota Library.

110. Jean Stafford to Robert Lowell, undated, Robert Lowell Papers, Houghton Library, Harvard University.

111. Ibid.

112. Quoted in Thomas Lask, Obituary, *New York Times,* March 28, 1979, Sec. B, p. 12.

113. John Simon Guggenheim Foundation Archives, New York, New York.

114. Jean Stafford to Henry Allen Moe, April 28, 1948, John Simon Guggenheim Foundation Archives, New York, New York.

115. Jean Stafford to Robert Lowell, undated, Robert Lowell Papers, Houghton Library, Harvard University.

116. Hamilton, *Robert Lowell,* p. 132.

117. Jean Stafford to Cecile Starr, undated, courtesy Cecile Starr.

118. Jean Stafford to John Berryman, May 17, 1948, University of Minnesota Library.

119. Jean Stafford to Cecile Starr, April 30, 1948, courtesy Cecile Starr.

120. Nancy Flagg, "People to Stay," *Shenandoah* 30 (Autumn 1979): 67.

121. Ibid., p. 65.

122. Ibid., p. 67.

123. Jean Stafford, "Why I Don't Get Around Much Anymore," *Esquire* 83 (March 1975): 114.

124. Jean Stafford to Robert Lowell, undated, Robert Lowell Papers, Houghton Library, Harvard University.

125. Ibid.

126. Ibid.

127. Mary Jane Sherfey to Jean Stafford, April 28, 1948, Norlin.

128. Ibid., telegram.

129. Mary Jane Sherfey to Jean Stafford, May 20, 1948, Norlin.

130. Jean Stafford to Dr. Alfred Cohn, undated, Rockefeller Institute Archives.

131. The story was printed in *Collected Stories* as "A Modest Proposal," p. 65.

132. Ibid., p. 66.

133. Mary Jane Sherfey to Jean Stafford, July 27, 1948, Norlin.

134. Jean Stafford to Cecile Starr, May 5, 1948, courtesy Cecile Starr.

135. Jean Stafford to Peter Taylor, June 26, 1948, quoted in Hamilton, *Robert Lowell,* p. 133.

136. Jean Stafford to Robert Lowell, undated, Robert Lowell Papers, Houghton Library, Harvard University.

137. Jean Stafford to Joe Chay, July 3, 1948, Norlin.

138. Jean Stafford, "Profiles: American Town," *New Yorker* 24 (August 28, 1949): 28.

139. Ibid., p. 35.

140. Ibid., p. 36.

141. Brendan Gill to Jean Stafford, August 24, 1948, Norlin.

142. *Collected Stories,* pp. 147–170.

143. Ibid., pp. 345–360.

144. Jean Stafford to William Mock, October 24, 1948, courtesy William Mock.

145. Jean Stafford to Robert Lowell, undated, Robert Lowell Papers, Houghton Library, Harvard University.

146. "Truth and the Novelist," p. 188.

147. Jean Stafford to Mary Lee Frichtel, June 10, 1949, Norlin.

148. Jean Stafford to Robert Lowell, January 1, 1949, quoted in Hamilton, *Robert Lowell,* p. 138.

149. See Hamilton, pp. 138–158.

150. Allen Tate to Elizabeth Hardwick, April 4, 1949, quoted in Hamilton, *Robert Lowell,* p. 156.

151. Jean Stafford to Mary Lee Frichtel, April 12, 1949, Norlin.

152. Ibid., June 10, 1949.

153. Ibid., July 5, 1949.

9. The Catherine Wheel: Fall 1949–Spring 1952

1. "Why I Don't Get Around Much Anymore," p. 114.

2. "Letter from Edinburgh," pp. 89–90.

3. Ibid., p. 94.

4. Ibid.

5. Jean Stafford, "Letter from Germany," *New Yorker* 25 (September 17, 1949): 83.

6. Ibid., p. 84.

7. Ibid., p. 91.

8. Ibid., p. 95.

9. *Collected Stories,* p. 63.

10. Ibid., p. 64.

11. Ibid., p. 35.

12. Jean Stafford, "The Art of Accepting Oneself," *Vogue* 119 (February 1, 1952): 174.

13. *Collected Stories,* p. 43.

14. Ibid., p. 51.

15. Ibid., p. 36.

16. Jean Stafford to Mary Lee Frichtel, undated, Norlin.

17. "Truth and the Novelist," p. 188.

18. Interview with Mary Lou Aswell, July 23, 1983, Santa Fe, New Mexico.

19. Oliver Jensen to Charlotte Goodman, May 23, 1984.

20. Jean Stafford to Elizabeth Ames, undated, Yaddo Archives, Saratoga Springs, New York.

21. Ibid.

22. Jean Stafford to Oliver Jensen, undated, Norlin.

23. Ibid.

24. Oliver Jensen to Charlotte Goodman, May 23, 1983.

25. Oliver Jensen to Mary Lee Frichtel, November 18, 1952, Norlin.

26. Jean Stafford to Robert Lowell, undated, Robert Lowell Papers, Houghton Library, Harvard University.

27. Jean Stafford to Elizabeth Ames, undated, Yaddo Archives, Saratoga Springs, New York.

28. Dorothea Straus, "Jean Stafford," *Shenandoah* 30 (Autumn 1979): 85.

29. *Wellesley College News,* April 20, 1950, p. 3.

30. Walsh, *Jean Stafford,* p. 23.

31. Jean Stafford, "Old Flaming Youth," *Harper's Bazaar* 84 (December 1950): 94.

32. Jean Stafford to Robert Lowell, undated, Robert Lowell Papers, Houghton Library, Harvard University.

33. "Old Flaming Youth," p. 182.

34. Ibid., p. 184.

35. Jean Stafford to Oliver Jensen, undated, Norlin.

36. Jean Stafford to Mary Lee Frichtel, September, 23, 1951, Norlin.

37. Jean Stafford to Caroline Gordon, undated, Caroline Gordon Papers, Firestone Library, Princeton University.

38. Oliver Jensen to Mary Lee Frichtel, November 18, 1952, Norlin.

39. Jean Stafford, "New York Is a Daisy," *Harper's Bazaar* 92 (December 1958): 126.

40. *Collected Stories,* p. 395.

41. Straus, "Jean Stafford," p. 85.

42. Peter De Vries, *The Tunnel of Love* (New York: Penguin, 1949), p. 133.

43. Ibid., p. 137.

44. Jean Stafford, "Anne Morrow Lindbergh's Ordeal," *McCall's* 103 (March 1973): 110.

45. Interview with Mary Lou Aswell, July 23, 1983, Santa Fe, New Mexico.

46. Anne Morrow Lindbergh to Charlotte Goodman, May 29, 1984.

47. Howard Moss, "Jean: Some Fragments," *Shenandoah* 30 (Autumn 1979): 77.

48. Jean Stafford to Mary Lee Frichtel, October 19, 1951, Norlin.

49. Jean Stafford, "The Connoisseurs," *Harper's Bazaar* 86 (October 1952): 234.

50. Ibid.

51. *Collected Stories,* p. 386.

52. Ibid., p. 402.

53. Ibid., p. 386.

54. Ibid.

55. Ibid., p. 401.

56. Ibid.

57. Oliver Jensen to Charlotte Goodman, May 23, 1984.

58. Oliver Jensen to Dr. Mary Jane Sherfey, February 22, 1952, Norlin.

59. Jean Stafford, "The Writer and Psychoanalysis," unpublished manuscript, Norlin.

60. Wanda Avila, *Jean Stafford: A Comprehensive Bibliography* (New York: Garland, 1983), p. xxviii.

61. "Author's Note," *Collected Stories,* p. [i].

62. Mary Ellen Williams Walsh, "The Young Girl in the West: Disenchantment in Jean Stafford's Fiction," in *Women and Western American Literature,* ed. Helen Winter Stauffer and Susan J. Rosowski (Troy: Whitston, 1982), p. 242.

63. *Collected Stories,* p. 199.

64. Ibid.

65. "Home for Christmas," p. 78.

66. Ibid.

67. Jean Stafford, "Truth in Fiction," *Library Journal* 91 (October 1, 1966): 4563.

68. Jeanette W. Mann, "Toward New Archetypal Forms: Jean Stafford's *The Catherine Wheel,*" *Critique* 17 (December 1975): 77.

69. Jean Stafford to Robert Lowell, undated, Robert Lowell Papers, Houghton Library, Harvard University.

70. Ibid.

71. *The Catherine Wheel,* p. 173.

72. Ibid., pp. 237 238.

73. Ibid., p. 21.

74. Ibid., p. 200.

75. Ibid., p. 300.

76. Alice Dixon Bond, "Fascination with Words Started Jean Stafford on Writing Career," *Boston Sunday Herald,* January 27, 1952.

77. Jean Stafford to Robert Lowell, undated, Robert Lowell Papers, Houghton Library, Harvard University.

78. *The Catherine Wheel,* p. 281.

79. Ibid., pp. 84–85.

80. Ibid., p. 62.

81. Ibid., p. 84.

82. Ibid., p. 121.

83. Ibid., p. 214.

84. Ibid., pp. 82–83.

85. Ibid., pp. 74–75.

86. See Marcia Westkott, *The Feminist Legacy of Karen Horney* (New Haven: Yale University Press, 1986), p. 9.

87. *The Catherine Wheel,* p. 84.

88. Ibid., p. 216.

89. Jean Stafford to Caroline Gordon, undated, Papers of Caroline Gordon and Allen Tate, McFarlin Library, University of Tulsa.

90. Philip Rahv to Allen Tate, March 10, 1952, Firestone Library, Princeton University.

91. Eudora Welty to Jean Stafford, undated, Norlin.

92. Louis Auchincloss to Jean Stafford, undated, Norlin.

93. Philip Rahv to Allen Tate, February 19, 1952, Firestone Library, Princeton University.

94. Irving Howe, "Sensibility Troubles," *Kenyon Review* 14 (Spring 1952): 345–348.

95. Alice S. Morris, "When Hatred Breaks the Surface," *New York Times Book Review,* January 13, 1952, p. 5.

96. "Searching and Findings," *Times Literary Supplement,* October 24, 1952, p. 689.

97. Paul Engle, "Jean Stafford's Fire Glows in Her New Novel," *Chicago Sunday Tribune Magazine of Books,* January 13, 1952, p. 3.

98. Walter Havighurst, "Tragedy of Isolation," *Saturday Review* 35 (January 26, 1952): 11.

99. Ihab Hassan, "Jean Stafford: The Expense of Style and the Scope of Sensibility," *Western Review* 19 (Spring 1955): 194–197.

100. James Wolcott, "Blowing Smoke into the Zeitgeist: The Well-Deserved Resurrection of Jean Stafford," *Harper's* 266 (June 1983): 58.

101. Breit, "Talk with Jean Stafford," p. 18.

102. Harriet Winslow to Robert Lowell, January 25, 1952, Robert Lowell Papers, Houghton Library, Harvard University.

103. *Bridgeport Sunday Post,* February 3, 1952.

104. "Critics Pick the Best Writers," *Quick,* February 1, 1949, pp. 35–36.

105. Wolcott, "Blowing Smoke," 57–59.

106. "An Etiquette for Writers," p. 10.

107. Ibid., pp. 10–11.

108. Jean Stafford to Mary Lee Frichtel, undated, Norlin.

109. Jean Stafford to Rev. Arthur MacGillivray, S.J., June 28, 1952, courtesy Arthur MacGillivray.

110. Jean Stafford to Oliver Jensen, undated, Norlin.

111. *Collected Stories,* p. 418.

112. Ibid., p. 415.

113. Ibid., p. 422.

10. In the Zoo: Summer 1952–Spring 1956

1. "It's Good to Be Back," p. 113.

2. Walter B. Lovelace, "You Can't Go Home Again," *Colorado Alumnus* 43 (October 1952): 11.

3. Jean Stafford to Joan Cuyler, July 19, 1952, courtesy Joan Cuyler Stillman.

4. Goodrich Walton to Charlotte Goodman, September 28, 1982.

5. Jean Stafford to Oliver Jensen, July 29, 1952, Norlin.

6. Ibid., August 9, 1952.

7. "An Etiquette for Writers."

8. Jean Stafford to Oliver Jensen, August 9, 1952, Norlin.

9. Ibid.

10. Dick Cavett, "A Dash of Bitters," *Vanity Fair* 46 (September 1983): 127.

11. See Susanna Cuyler, "Jean Stafford Had Humor," *Island Women* (Springfield: Women Writer's Alliance, 1984), pp. 126–135.

12. Oliver Jensen to Mary Lee Frichtel, November 18, 1952, Norlin.

13. Ibid.

14. Jean Stafford to Joan Cuyler, January 3, 1953, courtesy Joan Cuyler Stillman.

15. Ibid.

16. Jean Stafford to Nancy and Robert Gibney, November 30, 1952, courtesy Eleanor Gibney.

17. Jean Stafford to Nancy Gibney, quoted in Flagg, "People to Stay," p. 66.

18. Jean Stafford to Albert Erskine, Albert E. Erskine Papers, Butler Library, Columbia University.

19. Flagg, "People to Stay," p. 70.

20. Jean Stafford to Joan Cuyler, 1953, courtesy Joan Cuyler Stillman.

21. Ibid., January 29, 1953.

22. Ibid., January 3, 1953.

23. Jean Stafford to Eudora Welty and Mary Lou Aswell, undated, Norlin.

24. Jean Stafford to Nancy and Robert Gibney, February 27 [1953], courtesy Eleanor Gibney.

25. Ibid., January 18, 1953.

26. Jean Stafford to Oliver Jensen, February 9, 1953, Norlin.

27. Jean Stafford to Nancy and Robert Gibney, undated, courtesy Eleanor Gibney.

28. Ibid., undated.

29. Ibid., undated.

30. Jean Stafford to Joan Cuyler, July 7, 1953, courtesy Joan Cuyler Stillman.

31. Jean Stafford to Oliver Jensen, undated, Norlin.

32. Jean Stafford to Joan Cuyler, June 29, 1953, courtesy Joan Cuyler Stillman.

33. Jean Stafford to Nancy and Robert Gibney, undated, courtesy Eleanor Gibney.

34. Jean Stafford to Mary Lou Aswell, undated, Norlin.

35. Jean Stafford to Nancy and Robert Gibney, October 27, 1953, courtesy Eleanor Gibney.

36. Ibid., undated.

37. William Peden, *The American Short Story: Continuity and Change, 1940–1945* (Boston: Houghton Mifflin, 1975), p. 1.

38. Ibid., p. 85.

39. *Collected Stories,* p. 110.

40. Jean Stafford, review of Willa Cather's *A Lost Lady, Washington Post Book World,* August 26, 1973, pp. 1–3.

41. Jean Stafford, "The Violet Rock," *New Yorker* 28 (April 26, 1952): 39.

42. "A Reading Problem," *Collected Stories,* p. 335.

43. "In the Zoo," *Collected Stories,* p. 285.

44. *Collected Stories,* p. 317.

45. "The Violet Rock," p. 38.

46. Jean Stafford to Oliver Jensen, July 29, 1952, Norlin.

47. "The Violet Rock," pp. 36–37.

48. *Collected Stories,* p. 309.

49. Ibid., p. 285.

50. Ibid., p. 287.

51. Ibid., p. 288.

52. Ibid., p. 303.

53. Joyce Carol Oates, "*The Interior Castle:* The Art of Jean Stafford's Fiction," *Shenandoah* 30 (Autumn 1979): 61.

54. Jean Stafford, "Divorce: Journey through Crisis," *Harper's Bazaar* 92 (November 1958): 152.

55. Jean Stafford to Nancy and Robert Gibney, October 27, 1953, courtesy Eleanor Gibney.

56. Ibid., February 1954.

57. "Sisterhood."

58. Jean Stafford to Peter Taylor, undated, Norlin.

59. Lillian Hellman, *Three* (Boston: Little Brown, 1979), p. 234.

60. Susanna Cuyler, letter to the editor, *East Hampton Star,* April 23, 1979.

61. Jean Stafford to Nancy and Robert Gibney, Fall 1954, courtesy Eleanor Gibney.

62. Pinkham, "Jean," p. 29.

63. Jean Stafford to Nancy and Robert Gibney, 1955, courtesy Eleanor Gibney.

64. Telephone interview with Joseph Mitchell, January 9, 1985.

65. Jean Stafford to Robert Lowell, undated, Robert Lowell Papers, Houghton Library, Harvard University.

66. Jean Stafford to Nancy and Robert Gibney, February 11, 1956, courtesy Eleanor Gibney.

67. Interview with Joseph Mitchell, September 21, 1984, New York, New York.

68. Jean Stafford to Nancy and Robert Gibney, Summer 1955, courtesy Eleanor Gibney.

69. Katharine White, note about "The Mountain Day," Norlin.

70. Jean Stafford to Nancy Gibney, September 12, 1955, courtesy Eleanor Gibney.

71. Ibid., January, 1956.

72. Ibid.

73. Interview with Patricia McManus, December 11, 1984, New York, New York.

74. *Collected Stories,* p. 451.

75. Ibid., p. 339.

76. Katharine White to Jean Stafford, December 2, 1954, Norlin.

77. Jean Stafford to Katharine White, July 26, 1956, Norlin.

78. Quoted in James Oliver Brown to Jean Stafford, April 18, 1956, James Oliver Brown Papers, Butler Library, Columbia University.

79. Jean Stafford to Albert Erskine, undated, Albert E. Erskine Papers, Butler Library, Columbia University.

11. Life Is No Abyss: Summer 1956–Winter 1963

1. Jean Stafford to Richard Ludwig, undated, courtesy Richard Ludwig.

2. Jean Stafford to James Oliver Brown, undated, James Oliver Brown Papers, Butler Library, Columbia University.

3. Jean Stafford to Ann Honeycutt, June 25, 1956, Norlin.

4. Ibid., undated.

5. Jean Stafford, "My Blithe, Sad Bird," *New Yorker* 33 (April 6, 1957): 38.

6. Katharine White to Jean Stafford, June 19, 1956, Norlin.

7. A. J. Liebling, "Ahab and Nemesis," in *The Penguin Book of Contemporary Essays,* ed. Maureen Howard (New York: Penguin, 1986), pp. 181–197.

8. Raymond Sokolov, *Wayward Reporter: The Life of A. J. Liebling* (New York: Harper & Row, 1980), p. 54.

9. Ibid., pp. 266–268.

10. Ibid., p. 275.

11. Ibid.

12. Jean Stafford, "De Senectute," unpublished manuscript, Norlin.

13. Jean Stafford to Ann Honeycutt, undated, Norlin.

14. Ibid., undated.

15. Katinka De Vries to Jean Stafford, undated, Norlin.

16. Simpson, *Poets in Their Youth,* p. 247.

17. Quoted in Roberts, "Rediscovering Jean Stafford," p. 45.

18. A. J. Liebling to Jean Stafford, undated, A. J. Liebling Papers, Olin Library, Cornell University.

19. Jean Stafford to A. J. Liebling, undated, A. J. Liebling Papers, Olin Library, Cornell University.

20. A. J. Liebling to Jean Stafford, December 8, 1956, A. J. Liebling Papers, Olin Library, Cornell University.

21. Ibid., September 22, 1956.

22. Ibid., October 16, 1956.

23. Ibid., November 13, 1956.

24. *Collected Stories,* p. 29.

25. A. J. Liebling to Jean Stafford, September 13, 1956, A. J. Liebling Papers, Olin Library, Cornell University.

26. *Collected Stories,* p. 24.

27. Ibid., p. 28.

28. Ibid., p. 26.

29. Ibid., p. 33.

30. Jean Stafford to Ann Honeycutt, undated, Norlin.

31. Jean Stafford to James Oliver Brown, undated, James Oliver Brown Papers, Butler Library, Columbia University.

32. Jean Stafford to Mary Lee Frichtel, undated, Norlin.

33. Jean Stafford to James Oliver Brown, October 13, 1956, James Oliver Brown Papers, Butler Library, Columbia University.

34. A. J. Liebling to Jean Stafford, December 13, 1956, A. J. Liebling Papers, Olin Library, Cornell University.

35. Ibid., January 3, 1957.

36. Jean Stafford to Nancy Gibney, December 18, 1956, courtesy Eleanor Gibney.

37. Sokolov, *Wayward Reporter,* p. 283.

38. Jean Stafford to Nancy Gibney, February 1957, courtesy Eleanor Gibney.

39. Ibid.

40. Ibid., May 13, 1957.

41. "New York Is a Daisy," p. 126.

42. Jean Stafford to Emily Hahn, undated, Lilly Library, Indiana University.

43. Jean Stafford to Nancy Gibney, May 13, 1957, courtesy Eleanor Gibney.

44. Ibid.

45. A. J. Liebling to Jean Stafford, March 29, 1957, A. J. Liebling Papers, Olin Library, Cornell University.

46. Ibid., June 7, 1957.

47. Ibid., July 16, 1957.

48. Ibid.

49. Simpson, *Poets in Their Youth,* p. 246.

50. Jean Stafford to Nancy Gibney, June 26, 1957, courtesy Eleanor Gibney.

51. Jean Stafford to Ed Gibney, November 13, 1975, courtesy Eleanor Gibney.

52. Jean Stafford to Nancy Gibney, June 26, 1957, courtesy Eleanor Gibney.

53. Jean Stafford to Oliver Jensen, June 25 [1957], Norlin.

54. A. J. Liebling to Jean Stafford, August 1 [1957], A. J. Liebling Papers, Olin Library, Cornell University.

55. "Truth in Fiction," p. 4560.

56. Walsh, *Jean Stafford,* p. 17.

57. Jean Stafford to James Oliver Brown, September 16, [1957], James Oliver Brown Papers, Butler Library, Columbia University.

58. Ibid., October 5, 1957.

59. Katharine White to Jean Stafford, September 30, 1957, Norlin.

60. Ibid., January 12, 1958, Norlin.

61. See William Leary, "Jean Stafford, Katharine White, and *The New Yorker*."

62. Katharine White to Jean Stafford, January 28, 1958, Norlin.

63. Jean Stafford to Emily Hahn, undated, Lilly Library, Indiana University.

64. Sokolov, *Wayward Reporter,* p. 290.

65. Peter Taylor, "A Commemorative Tribute," *Shenandoah* 30 (Autumn 1979): 58.

66. Sokolov, *Wayward Reporter,* p. 277.

67. See Roberts, "Rediscovering Jean Stafford," p. 45.

68. Quoted in Sokolov, *Wayward Reporter,* p. 290.

69. Jean Stafford to Nancy Gibney, July 1956, courtesy Eleanor Gibney.

70. James Oliver Brown to Jean Stafford, June 8, 1958, James Oliver Brown Papers, Butler Library, Columbia University.

71. Jean Stafford, "Isak Dinesen: Master Teller of Tales," *Horizon* 2 (September 1959): 110–112.

72. Sokolov, *Wayward Reporter,* p. 277.

73. "Truth in Fiction," p. 4564.

74. Interview with Susan Spectorsky, August 20, 1985, New York, New York.

75. Jean Stafford to Ann Honeycutt, September 5, 1959, Norlin.

76. "Samothrace."

77. Jean Stafford to James Oliver Brown, undated, James Oliver Brown Papers, Butler Library, Columbia University.

78. Sokolov, *Wayward Reporter,* p. 299.

79. Jean Stafford to Nancy Gibney, October 10, 1962, courtesy Eleanor Gibney.

80. Ibid., March 27 [1962].

81. Ibid., undated.

82. Jean Stafford, "The Ardent Quintessences," *Harper's Bazaar* 95 (April 1961): 142–143.

83. Jean Stafford to Peter Davison, undated, Atlantic Monthly Press Archives, Boston, Massachusetts.

84. Jean Stafford, "Rara Avis," *Reporter* 23 (December 22, 1960): 40.

85. Ibid., p. 42.

86. Ibid.

87. "Author's Note," *Collected Stories.*

88. Jean Stafford to Nancy Gibney, undated, courtesy Eleanor Gibney.

89. Jean Stafford, *Elephi: The Cat with the High I.Q.* (New York: Dell, 1974), p. 37.

90. James Oliver Brown to Jean Stafford, January 4, 1962, James Oliver Brown Papers, Butler Library, Columbia University.

91. Jean Stafford, *Arabian Nights: The Lion and the Carpenter and Other Tales from the Arabian Nights, Retold* (New York: Macmillan, 1962), p. iii.

92. Jean Stafford to Nancy Gibney, March 23, courtesy Eleanor Gibney.

93. Jean Stafford, "Young Writers," *Analects* I (October 1960): 16.

94. Jean Stafford, "A Statement," *Saturday Review,* October 6, 1962, p. 6.

95. Walker Percy to Jean Stafford, March 19, 1962, Walker Percy Letters, University of Virginia Library.

96. Jean Stafford to the editors of *Harper's* October 10, 1971, Norlin.

97. Jean Stafford to Alfred Kazin, February 9, 1972, Berg Collection, New York Public Library.

98. Jean Stafford to Albert Erskine, May 31 [1962], Butler Library, Columbia University.

99. Albert Erskine to Jean Stafford, June 7, 1962, Norlin.

100. Jean Stafford to Nancy Gibney, undated, courtesy Eleanor Gibney.

101. Jean Stafford, "East Hampton from the Catbird Seat," *New York Times,* December 26, 1971, p. 1.

102. Sokolov, *Wayward Reporter,* p. 319.

103. Jean Stafford to Ed Gibney, November 13, 1973, courtesy Eleanor Gibney.

104. Sokolov, *Wayward Reporter,* p. 319.

105. A. J. Liebling to Jean Stafford, May 15, 1963, A. J. Liebling Papers, Olin Library, Cornell University.

106. Ibid., May 18, 1963.

107. Ibid., May 25, 1963.

108. See Ken Auletta, *The Art of Corporate Success* (New York: G. P. Putnam's Sons, 1984).

109. Quoted in Sokolov, *Wayward Reporter,* p. 319.

110. Jean Stafford to Howard Moss, July 20, 1963, Berg Collection, New York Public Library.

111. William K. Zinsser, "Far Out on Long Island," *Horizon* 5 (May 1963): 27.

112. Sokolov, *Wayward Reporter,* p. 320.

113. Quoted in Cavett, "A Dash of Bitters," p. 127.

114. Joseph Mitchell, quoted in Sokolov, *Wayward Reporter,* p. 323.

115. Jean Stafford to Mary Von Schrader Jarrell, January 12, 1966, Berg Collection, New York Public Library.

12. The End of a Career: January 1964–Spring 1975

1. Jean Stafford to Mary Lee Frichtel, undated, Norlin.

2. The information about Jean Stafford's medical history was supplied by her physician, Thomas N. Roberts.

3. Jean Stafford to Mary Lee Frichtel, January 14, 1964, Norlin.

4. Jean Stafford to Nancy Gibney, February 6, 1964, courtesy Eleanor Gibney.

5. Jean Stafford to Robert Lowell, May 6, 1964, Robert Lowell Papers, Houghton Library, Harvard University.

6. Jean Stafford to Nancy Gibney, undated, courtesy Eleanor Gibney.

7. Ibid.

8. Interview with Paul Horgan, June 18, 1984, Middletown, Connecticut.

9. Jean Stafford to Mary Lee Frichtel, undated, Norlin.

10. John Clendenning, unpublished memoir about Jean Stafford at Wesleyan University, courtesy John Clendenning.

11. Jean Stafford to Nancy Gibney, August 1, 1965, courtesy Eleanor Gibney.

12. John Clendenning to Charlotte Goodman, November 25, 1985.

13. Jean Stafford to Nancy Gibney, undated, courtesy Eleanor Gibney.

14. Taylor, "A Commemorative Tribute," pp. 57–58.

15. Hamilton, *Robert Lowell,* p. 339.

16. "Truth in Fiction," p. 4564.

17. Jean Stafford, "The Strange World of Marguerite Oswald," *McCall's* 93 (October 1965): 194.

18. Jean Stafford to Nancy Gibney, August 1, 1965, courtesy Eleanor Gibney.

19. Clendenning, memoir.

20. Gene Baro, "Breaking out of Isolation," *New York Times Book Review,* October 11, 1964, p. 4.

21. Joyce Carol Oates, "Notions Good and Bad," *Kenyon Review* 27 (Winter 1965): 77–78.

22. Interview with Louis Auchincloss, May 1, 1984, New York, New York.

23. See Auchincloss, *Pioneers and Caretakers,* p. 4.

24. Jean Stafford to Mary Lee Frichtel, undated, Norlin.

25. Jean Stafford to Mary Von Schrader Jarrell, January 12, 1966, Berg Collection, New York Public Library.

26. Jean Stafford to Allen Tate, undated, Firestone Library, Princeton University.

27. Jean Stafford to Nancy Gibney, January 23, 1968, courtesy Eleanor Gibney.

28. Louis Auchincloss to Charlotte Goodman, June 20, 1984.

29. Auchincloss, *Pioneers and Caretakers,* p. 55.

30. Jean Stafford, "Symposium on the Teaching of Creative Writing," *Four Quarters* 2 (January 1961): 16.

31. Jean Stafford to Nancy Gibney, January 4, 1966, courtesy Eleanor Gibney.

32. Telephone interview with Linda Sternberg Katz, November 13, 1986.

33. Anne Freedgood to Nancy Gibney, February 14, 1966, courtesy Eleanor Gibney.

34. Ibid., February 24, 1966.

35. Jean Stafford, "Meet Your Aunty E." *Book Week,* March 6, 1966, pp. 14–15.

36. Peter Davison, memo, March 4, 1966, Atlantic Monthly Press Archives, Boston, Massachusetts.

37. Jean Stafford, "Somebody Out There Hates Me," *Esquire* 82 (August 1974): 109.

38. "Mama Oswald," *Newsweek* 67 (February 28, 1966): 92A–94A.

39. "Mother Knows Best?" *Time* 87 (April 8, 1966): 112.

40. John Gardner, "An Invective against Mere Fiction," *Southern Review* 3 (Spring 1967): 448–449.

41. Walsh, *Jean Stafford,* pp. 83–84.

42. Godfrey Hodgson, "Miss O. and Miss S." *Observer,* 11 (September 1966): 26.

43. Jean Stafford to James Oliver Brown, January [1967], James Oliver Brown Papers, Butler Library, Columbia University.

44. Jean Stafford to Nancy Gibney, January 3, 1967, courtesy Eleanor Gibney.

45. Freda Bluestone to Y.M.H.A.-Y.W.H.A., February 1967, 92nd St. Y Poetry Center Archives, New York, New York.

46. Laurence Lafore to Charlotte Goodman, January 24, 1984.

47. Jean Stafford to Nancy Gibney, August 28, 1967, courtesy Eleanor Gibney.

48. Jean Stafford to James Oliver Brown, September 7, 1967, James Oliver Brown Papers, Butler Library, Columbia University.

49. Interview with Frank McShane, December 13, 1984, New York, New York.

50. Jean Stafford to the President, Consolidated Edison, July 20, 1968, Butler Library, Columbia University.

51. Jean Stafford to Nancy Gibney, October 6, 1968, courtesy Eleanor Gibney.

52. Jean Stafford, "Intimations of Hope," *McCall's* 99 (1971): 77.

53. Draft of letter to Consolidated Edison, Norlin.

54. Thomas Lask, obituary, *New York Times,* March 28, 1979, Sec. B., p. 12.

55. Jean Stafford to Nancy Gibney, October 6, 1968, courtesy Eleanor Gibney.

56. Ibid., March 3, 1969.

57. Jean Stafford to *East Hampton Star,* August 9, 1968.

58. "Why I Don't Get around Much Anymore," p. 8.

59. Jean Stafford to Nancy Gibney, March 3, 1969, courtesy Eleanor Gibney.

60. *Collected Stories,* p. 369.

61. Ibid., p. 364.

62. Photocopied annotations, courtesy Joseph Mitchell.

63. Katharine White to Jean Stafford, February 9, 1969, Norlin.

64. Ibid., March 5, 1970.

65. Thomas Lask, "Points East and West," *New York Times,* February 14, 1969, p. 37.

66. Guy Davenport, *New York Times Book Review,* February 16, 1969, pp. 1 and 40.

67. Jean Stafford to James Oliver Brown, July 8, 1969, James Oliver Brown Papers, Butler Library, Columbia University.

68. Jean Stafford to Nancy Gibney, May 5, 1969, courtesy Eleanor Gibney.

69. Jean Stafford to Allen Tate, undated, Firestone Library, Princeton University.

70. Glenway Westcott to Muriel Ruckeyser, July 18, 1969, Archives of the American Academy and Institute of Arts and Letters, New York, New York.

71. Al Cohn, *Newsday,* May 5, 1970, p. 3A.

72. Citation, National Institute of Arts and Letters, Archives of the American Academy and Institute of Arts and Letters, New York, New York.

73. Jean Stafford to Allen Tate, March 18, Firestone Library, Princeton University.

74. See, for example, "Biographical Sketches of Persons Chosen for 54th Annual Pulitzer Prizes," *New York Times,* May 5, 1970, p. 6.

75. "Why I Don't Get around Much Anymore," p. 132.

76. Charles Mann to Charlotte Goodman, September 23, 1983.

77. Jean Stafford to Ann Honeycutt, undated, Norlin.

78. Jean Stafford to Mr. [Robert] Haugh, March 17, 1970, Archives of the Hopwood Room, University of Michigan.

79. Jean Stafford to Robert Phelps, February 9, 1970, Butler Library, Columbia University.

80. Sheed, "Miss Jean Stafford," p. 98.

81. Jean Stafford, ". . . the Good Life Is Indeed Now," *McCall's* 97 (January 1970): 30.

82. Ibid.

83. Jean Stafford, "My (Ugh!) Sensitivity Training," *Horizon* 12 (Spring 1970): 112.

84. Jean Stafford, "Contagious Imbecility," *New York Times Book Review*, May 5, 1974, pp. 8–12.

85. "Intimations of Hope," p. 71.

86. Jean Stafford, "Topics: Women as Chattels, Men as Chumps," *New York Times*, May 9, 1970.

87. Jean Stafford, "The Utopian Woman," unpublished manuscript, Norlin.

88. "Sisterhood."

89. See "Women as Chattels, Men as Chumps."

90. "Sisterhood."

91. Ibid.

92. Jean Stafford to Nancy Gibney, May 21, 1975, courtesy Eleanor Gibney.

93. "Women as Chattels, Men as Chumps."

94. Jean Stafford, "Don't Use Ms. with Miss Stafford, Unless You Mean ms.," *New York Times*, September 21, 1973, p. 36.

95. Margaret Atwood, "Paradoxes and Dilemmas: The Woman as Writer, in *Woman as Writer*, ed. Jeannette L. Webber and Jan Grumman (Boston: Houghton Mifflin, 1978), pp. 78–79.

96. Peter Taylor to Jean Stafford, undated, Norlin.

97. Jean Stafford to James Oliver Brown, May 13, 1974, James Oliver Brown Papers, Butler Library, Columbia University.

98. Jean Stafford to Shana Alexander, March 1, 1970, courtesy Shana Alexander.

99. Shana Alexander to Charlotte Goodman, March 25, 1980.

100. Jean Stafford to Robert Silvers, September 17, 1971, Norlin.

101. Jean Stafford to Oliver Jensen, undated, Norlin.

102. Jean Stafford to James Oliver Brown, September 29, 1970, James Oliver Brown Papers, Butler Library, Columbia University.

103. Straus, "Jean Stafford," p. 88.

104. Jean Stafford to Mary Lee Frichtel, undated, Norlin.

105. Jean Stafford, "Children's Books for Christmas," *New Yorker* 47 (December 4, 1971): 206.

106. Quoted in *Newsday*, March 28, 1979.

107. Henrietta Stackpole [Jean Stafford] to Dr. Thomas N. Roberts, December 12, 1970, courtesy Thomas Roberts.

108. Elizabeth Janeway, "Women's Literature," *Crossections: From a Decade of Change* (New York: William Morrow, 1982), p. 197.

109. "Barnard Lectures," unpublished manuscript, Norlin.

110. Telephone interview with Martha Peterson, June 8, 1984.

111. Jean Stafford to Mary Lee Frichtel, June 14, 1971, Norlin.

112. Jean Stafford to Thomas Roberts, January 14, 1971, courtesy Thomas Roberts.

113. Maureen Howard, *Facts of Life* (Boston: Little Brown & Co., 1975), p. 152.

114. Jean Stafford to Felicia Geffen, January 13, 1971, Archives of the American Academy and Institute of Arts and Letters, New York, New York.

115. Jean Stafford, "Suffering Summer Houseguests," *Vogue* 158 (August 15, 1971): 112.

116. Jean Stafford to Mary Lee Frichtel, May 1, 1972, Norlin.

117. Ibid., June 30, 1972.

118. Citation, May 24, 1972, Norlin.

119. "Miss McKeehan's Pocketbook," pp. 407–411.

120. Jean Stafford, "Katharine Graham," *Vogue* 162 (December 1973), pp. 202–205, 218–219, 221.

121. Alden Whitman, "Jean Stafford and Her Secretary 'Harvey' Reigning in Hamptons," *New York Times,* August 26, 1973, p. 104.

122. See "Somebody Out There Hates Me," pp. 108–109.

123. Jean Stafford to Nancy Gibney, June 16, 1974, courtesy Eleanor Gibney.

124. Ibid., March 29, 1975.

125. Ibid., January 7, 1976.

126. Ibid., January 20, 1975.

127. Jean Stafford to Robert Lowell, September 23, Harry Ransom Humanities Research Center, University of Texas at Austin.

128. Ibid., October 21.

129. Jean Stafford to Marjorie Pinkham, August 27, Norlin.

130. Ibid., September 18.

131. Jean Stafford to James Oliver Brown, January 16, 1975, James Oliver Brown Papers, Butler Library, Columbia University.

13. In the Snowfall: Summer 1975–Spring 1979

1. Jean Stafford to Dr. Thomas N. Roberts, October 9, 1975, courtesy Thomas Roberts.

2. Jean Stafford to Mary Lee Frichtel, August 14, 1972, Norlin.

3. Interview with Joseph Mitchell, September 27, 1984, New York, New York.

4. Jean Stafford to Nancy Gibney, May 21, 1975, courtesy Eleanor Gibney.

5. Ibid., December 21, 1975.

6. Ibid., undated.

7. Ibid., August 17, 1976.

8. Ibid.

9. Jean Stafford to Marjorie Stafford Pinkham, July 12, 1976, Norlin.

10. John Thompson to Charlotte Goodman, May 13, 1985.

11. Straus, "Jean Stafford," p. 87.

12. Pinkham, "Jean," p. 31.

13. Ibid.

14. Jean Stafford to Nancy Gibney, June 6, 1975, courtesy Eleanor Gibney.

15. Ibid., June 17, 1976.

16. Sheed, "Miss Jean Stafford," p. 98.

17. Moss, "Jean: Some Fragments," p. 81.

18. Sheed, "Miss Jean Stafford," p. 96.

19. Interview with Ann Honeycutt, October 5, 1983, New York, New York.

20. Interview with Eleanor Hempstead, November 30, 1983, New York, New York.

21. Jean Stafford to Nancy Gibney, August 17, 1976, courtesy Eleanor Gibney.

22. Giroux, "Hard Years and 'Scary Days,'" p. 29.

23. Jean Stafford to Marjorie Stafford Pinkham, February 14, 1977, Norlin.

24. Ibid., July 10, 1977.

25. Quoted in Grace Schulman, "Robert Lowell at the 92nd Street Y," record sleeve notes for *Robert Lowell: A Reading,* Caedmon Records, 92nd St. Y Poetry Center Archives, New York, New York.

26. Interview with Joseph Mitchell, September 27, 1984, New York, New York.

27. Craig Claiborne, *Good Life,* November 1984, p. 29.

28. Margaret M. Mills, memo to Committee for Artists and Writers, Archives of the American Academy and Institute of Arts and Letters, New York, New York.

29. Jean Riboud to Jean Stafford, November 9, 1978, Norlin.

30. Interview with Ellsworth Mason, October 17, 1984, Boulder, Colorado.

31. Barbara Hadden to the *East Hampton Star,* May 17, 1979.

32. Jean Stafford to Mary Lee Frichtel, August 14, 1972, Norlin.

33. Interview with Josephine Monsell, June 13, 1984, The Springs, New York.

34. "Suffering Summer Houseguests," p. 112.

35. Cavett, "A Dash of Bitters," p. 128.

36. Straus, "Jean Stafford," p. 89.

37. Giroux, "Hard Times and 'Scary Days,'" p. 29.

38. Katinka Loeser [De Vries], "Taking Care," *New Yorker* 57 (March 24, 1980): 40–48.

39. *Collected Stories,* pp. 363–364.

40. Ibid., p. 369.

41. Interview with John Stonehill, December 12, 1984, New York, New York.

42. Hamilton, *Robert Lowell,* p. 473.

43. Susanna Cuyler, "Jean Stafford: Not Playing the Game," *Soho Weekly News,* May 10, 1979.

44. *The Catherine Wheel,* p. 157.

45. Robert Giroux to Charlotte Goodman, February 23, 1984.

46. Cavett, "A Dash of Bitters," p. 128.

47. Pinkham, "Jean," p. 131.

48. Taylor, "A Commemorative Tribute," p. 59.

Index

Acknowledgments

Grateful acknowledgment is made for permission to quote from unpublished and previously published materials, as follows.

Excerpts from letters, manuscripts, notebooks, grant proposals, and other unpublished materials by Jean Stafford. Reprinted by permission of Russell & Volkening as agents for the author. Copyright Jean Stafford. For permission to use these materials, acknowledgment is also made to the Norlin Library, University of Colorado, Boulder (location of the Stafford Collection); Brendan Gill; Oliver Jensen; Cecile Starr; Archives of the American Academy and Institute of Arts and Letters, New York; Department of Rare Books, Cornell University Library; John Simon Guggenheim Memorial Foundation; Lilly Library, Indiana University; Kenyon College Archives; Hopwood Awards Collection, Department of Rare Books and Special Collections, The University of Michigan Library; Manuscripts Division, University Libraries, University of Minnesota; Henry W. and Albert A. Berg Collection, The New York Public Library, Astor, Lenox and Tilden Foundations; Rockefeller Archive Center; Harry Ransom Humanities Research Center, The University of Texas at Austin; Wesleyan University Archives; and Corporation of Yaddo: Myra Sklarew, President.

Published with the permission of Princeton University Library: excerpts from Story Magazine Archive, Boxes 50 and 172, Letters to and from Jean Stafford, Martha Foley, and Whit Burnett; from Allen Tate Papers, Box 40 and Additional Papers Box 8, Letters to and from Jean Stafford, and Box 36, Letters of Philip Rahv to Allen Tate; from Caroline Gordon Papers, Boxes 37 and 48, Letters to and from Jean Stafford, and Box 27, Dreams of Caroline Gordon.

Published by permission of Marjorie Stafford Pinkham: excerpts from manuscripts "Jean Stafford's Family" and "The McKillop Family."

Published with permission of the writers, except as otherwise indicated: excerpts from letters of Louis Auchincloss; Freda Bluestone (by permission of Archives of the 92nd Street YM-YWHA, New York, N.Y.); James Oliver Brown; Whit Burnett (by permission of Hallie Burnett); Edward, Natalie, and Peter Davison (by permission of Peter Davison); Katinka De Vries; Albert Erskine (by permission of Random House); Ford Madox Ford (by permission of Janice B. Brustlein and Department of Rare Books, Cornell University Library); Anne Freedgood; Nancy and Robert Gibney (by permission of Eleanor Gibney); Caroline Gordon (by permission of Nancy Tate Wood and Special Collections, University of Maryland College Park Libraries); James Robert Hightower; Oliver Jensen; A. J. Liebling (Reprinted by permission of Russell & Volkening as agents for the author; Copyright 1956, 1957, 1963 by A. J. Liebling) (also by permission of Department of Rare Books, Cornell

University Library); Robert Lowell and Charlotte Lowell (by permission of Frank Bidart, Literary Executor for the Estate of Robert Lowell); Walker Percy (by permission of Walker Percy Collection (#10265-c), Manuscripts Division, Special Collections Department, University of Virginia Library); Philip Rahv (by permission of Betty Thomas Rahv); John D. Ramaley; John Crowe Ransom (by permission of Helen Forman); Jean Riboud (by permission of Krishna Riboud); Delmore Schwartz (by permission of Ontario Review Press); Evelyn Scott (by permission of Paula Scott); Mary Jane Sherfey (by permission of William E. Sherfey); John Richard Stafford (by permission of Marjorie Stafford Pinkham); Cecile Starr; Allen Tate (by permission of Nancy Tate Wood); Eleanor Ross Taylor; Peter Taylor; Eudora Welty; Glenway Westcott (by permission of Archives of the American Academy and Institute of Arts and Letters, New York); and Katharine S. White (by permission of Roger Angell, literary executor).

Excerpts from dream journal of Caroline Gordon published by permission of Nancy Tate Wood.

Excerpts from correspondence of A. J. Liebling. Reprinted by permission of Russell & Volkening as agents for the author. Copyright 1956, 1957, 1963 by A. J. Liebling.

Excerpt from "Jean Stafford, a Letter" from *Day by Day* by Robert Lowell. Copyright © 1975, 1976, 1977 by Robert Lowell. Reprinted by permission of Farrar, Straus and Giroux, Inc.

Excerpt from "The Old Flame" from *For the Union Dead* by Robert Lowell. Copyright © 1962 by Robert Lowell. Reprinted by permission of Farrar, Straus and Giroux, Inc.

Excerpt from "1939" from *Collected Stories* by Peter Taylor. Copyright © 1955 by Peter Taylor; Copyright renewed 1983 by Peter Taylor. Originally published in *The New Yorker*. Reprinted by permission of Farrar, Straus and Giroux, Inc.

Excerpt from *Murder in the Cathedral* by T. S. Eliot, copyright 1935 by Harcourt Brace Jovanovich, Inc., and renewed 1963 by T. S. Eliot, reprinted by permission of the publisher and of Faber and Faber Ltd.

Excerpt from *The Mills of the Kavanaughs,* copyright 1951 by Robert Lowell and renewed 1979 by Harriet W. Lowell, reprinted by permission of Harcourt Brace Jovanovich, Inc., and of Frank Bidart, Literary Executor for the Estate of Robert Lowell.

Excerpt from "A Curse against Elegies" from *All My Pretty Ones* by Anne Sexton. Copyright © 1962 by Anne Sexton. Reprinted by permission of Houghton Mifflin Company and of Sterling Lord Agency, Inc.

Excerpt from "An Anatomy of Migraine" from *Archaic Figure* by Amy Clampitt. Copyright © 1987 by Amy Clampitt. Reprinted by permission of Alfred A. Knopf, Inc. Originally appeared in *The New Yorker*.

Excerpt from "The Mad Musician" by Richard Eberhart, in *The Collected Verse Plays of Richard Eberhart.* © 1962 The University of North Carolina Press. Reprinted by permission.